Dedication:
To
Edgar Eugene Robinson

Acknowledgment

I am deeply indebted to my friend and colleague David Potter for the unfailingly helpful criticism he has given my work. The breadth of his knowledge of American history and the generosity with which he has given his time to reading my manuscript have stood me in exceedingly good stead.

Library of Congress Catalog Card No. 76–76304.

Printed in the United States of America.
gional offices of Scott, Foresman and Company are located in Atlanta, Dallas, Glenview, Palo Alto, Oakland, N.J., and London, England.

TOWARD A
PERFECT U

The American Re
1783–1815

JOHN C. MILLE
Stanford University

SCOTT, FORESMAN AND C

PREFACE

TOWARD A MORE PERFECT UNION is addressed to the general reader as well as to the student of American history. The book's central theme is the making of a nation from the disparate sections which composed the republic. Many individuals contributed toward this achievement. Their efforts were inadvertently furthered by the British government which, for many Americans of the postrevolutionary generation, stood as the "eternal enemy" of the republic's territorial and ideological aspirations. It is significant that not until the Second War with Great Britain did Americans truly attain a sense of national identity.

The triumph of nationalism was possible because neither section was able to secure a dominant position in the councils of the republic. The union was established upon the basis of a sectional balance: in 1861 it was almost destroyed when one section felt itself condemned irrevocably to a minority status.

JOHN C. MILLER

CONTENTS

1. **PROSPECTS AND PROBLEMS OF A NEW REPUBLIC** **1**
   The States in Control 6
   Problems of Foreign Trade 10

2. **THE ECONOMIC CONSEQUENCES OF INDEPENDENCE** **19**
   Financing the Government 19
   Relations with Great Britain 23

3. **THE IMPOTENCE OF THE CONFEDERACY** **31**
   State Legislatures and Debtor Relief 31
   The Society of the Cincinnati 36
   Organizing the West 38
   Securing the West 40
   The Necessity of a Stronger Union 44

4. **"A LITTLE REBELLION" AND ITS CONSEQUENCES** **49**
   Shay's Rebellion 49
   The Federalist State of Mind 52

5. **THE CONSTITUTIONAL CONVENTION** **57**
   The Virginia and New Jersey Plans 58
   Results of the Convention 65

6. **THE RATIFICATION OF THE CONSTITUTION** **71**
   The Antifederalists 73
   The Federalists 76
   The Debate over Ratification 78

7. **ORGANIZING THE NEW GOVERNMENT** **87**
   American Navigation Acts 88
   The Bill of Rights 90

8. **THE HAMILTONIAN DISPENSATION** **93**
   Objectives of Hamilton's Fiscal Policy 93
   The Fight over Funding the Debt 96
   The National Bank and the Constitution 98
   The Report on Manufactures 101

9. **JEFFERSON AND HAMILTON** **105**
   Jefferson's Agrarian Philosophy 105
   Controversy Between Jefferson and Hamilton 107

10. CITIZEN GENÊT AND THE FRENCH ALLIANCE 115
Division over Foreign Policy 115
American Neutrality 117

11. JOHN JAY SAVES THE PEACE 123
The Threat of War with England 123
Jay's Treaty 126
The Treaty of San Lorenzo 129

12. THE FAREWELL ADDRESS 133
Washington's Address 134
The Election of 1796 136

13. THE UNDECLARED WAR WITH FRANCE 139
The XYZ Affair 139
The Alien, Naturalization, and Sedition Acts 141
A Navy Versus an Army 144
President Adams and Peace with France 145

14. THE VIRGINIA AND KENTUCKY RESOLUTIONS 149
Opposition to the Alien and Sedition Acts 149
States' Rights and the Virginia and Kentucky Resolutions 151

15. THE ELECTION OF 1800 155
The Election Campaign of 1800 155
The Election in the House of Representatives 160

16. THE JEFFERSONIAN "REVOLUTION" 167
The Republican President 168
Republican Policies 169
Unifying the Nation 172
The Federalist Judiciary 174

17. FOREIGN AFFAIRS: THE BARBARY CORSAIRS AND THE LOUISIANA PURCHASE 179
A Second War in the Mediterranean 179
The Louisiana Purchase 181
Explorations of the Louisiana Territory 185

18. THE ATTACK UPON THE FEDERAL JUDICIARY AND THE BURR CONSPIRACY 189
The Attack upon the Federalist Stronghold 189
Disintegration of the Federalist Party 191
Divisions in the Republican Party 195
The Burr Conspiracy 197

19. THE *CHESAPEAKE* INCIDENT 203
The Impressment Question 204
A British Act of War 206

20. THE EMBARGO 211
The End of Neutral Rights 211
The Attempt to Preserve Neutral Rights 212
Enforcement of the Embargo 213
The Effect of the Embargo 215

21. CONGRESSIONAL DIPLOMACY: THE NONINTERCOURSE ACT 221
Congressional Diplomacy 223
The Battle of Tippecanoe 236

22. THE COMING OF THE WAR 229
War Hawks 229
The Declaration of War 234

23. THE WAR OF 1812: BY LAND AND BY SEA 239
The Attack on Canada 241
Opposition to the War 245
Naval Duels 247

24. A FAMOUS VICTORY 251
The War in the North 251
The Burning of Washington 252
The Battle of New Orleans 255
The Hartford Convention 257

25. THE PEACE OF CHRISTMAS EVE 261
The Treaty of Ghent 261
A National Spirit 263

26. THE UNITED STATES: 1783–1815, THE SOCIAL SCENE 267
Religion in America 267
The American Way of Life 270
American Humanitarianism 277
Science and Invention 279

27. **THE FRANCHISE AND EQUALITY** **287**
The Right to Vote 287
Equality in America 289

28. **AMERICAN NATIONALISM AND THE ARTS** **299**
American Education 299
Republican Literature 304
Painting and Architecture 314

BIBLIOGRAPHY **317**

INDEX **321**

MAPS AND GRAPHS

The United States in 1783 3
Election of 1796 136
The Growth of the Merchant Marine, 1790–1815 157
Election of 1800 161
Federal Government Finances, 1792–1815 170
The Louisiana Purchase 186
Election of 1804 195
American Foreign Trade, 1790–1815 216
Election of 1808 218
Election of 1812 243
The War in the North 244
The War in the South 256
The Sale of Public Land, 1800–1815 273
Western Settlement to 1815 274
Patents Issued, 1790–1815 282
Population in the United States, 1790–1815 294–295

1. PROSPECTS AND PROBLEMS OF A NEW REPUBLIC

The Treaty of Paris, which in 1783 brought an end to the War of Independence, made the United States the largest country fronting upon the Atlantic. Without exaggeration, Americans could call their country an "empire": of the European monarchies, only Russia boasted a greater central landmass. True, the British Empire was larger in extent than the United States, but England itself was comparable in size to Pennsylvania. France, the most populous of the European powers (at this time its population exceeded even that of Russia), comprised a smaller area than did the state of Virginia as its boundaries were then drawn. With three and a half million people, compared to the twenty-seven million inhabitants of France and the eight million people living in the British Isles, the United States enjoyed a rate of population increase markedly higher than that of any European power. Moreover, it possessed in the heartland of the continent an expanse of territory that seemed to promise an amplitude of arable land for many generations of American farmers. No colonial people have begun their career of independence with advantages equal to those bestowed by nature upon Americans.

In addition to these felicities, the British peacemakers of 1782-1783 seemed disposed to give every aid to Americans on their way to empire. By

---

"Washington Entering New York City with the Remains of his Troops, 1783," detail of a painting by Percy Moran, courtesy of The New-York Historical Society, New York City.

One Cent "Constelatio" with Blunt Rays, 1783.

(Editor's note: The coins in this book are courtesy of The American Numismatic Society; they are not always shown in their actual size.)

adopting a policy of conciliation and magnanimity toward the United States, Lord Shelburne, the British Prime Minister, hoped to detach the republic from its connection with France and ultimately to ally the English-speaking peoples against the Bourbon powers. To that end, the British negotiators yielded to the United States the territory lying between the Appalachians and the Mississippi—part of which, it is true, had already been conquered by George Rogers Clark and his Virginians. Surveying the territorial provisions of the treaty of peace, John Adams exclaimed that the United States had attained all its wishes, and George Washington said that he had not talked to a man who did not think that, on the whole, the treaty of peace was more advantageous than could possibly have been expected.

Upon this auspicious prospect, however, lay the ominous shadow of black slavery. Of the three million inhabitants of the United States, almost half a million were in servitude, one of the largest slave populations in the world. Yet in the North, where the slave population was relatively small, the institution had come under attack from the nonslaveholding white majority. Five thousand blacks had served in the armed forces of the republic during the War of Independence and had thereby won their freedom. In Massachusetts, Vermont, and New Hampshire slavery had been abolished during the war by law or by judicial interpretation of the state constitution. Rhode Island, Connecticut, and Pennsylvania adopted schemes of gradual emancipation, but it was not until 1799 and 1804 that New York and New Jersey respectively provided for the gradual manumission of the slaves held in those states.

In the preamble to their manumission acts, Rhode Island and Pennsylvania cited the ideals proclaimed by the Declaration of Independence. In Virginia, likewise, Thomas Jefferson and other slaveowners condemned human bondage as a moral wrong and an economic liability. But revolutionary idealism combined with agricultural distress eventuated only in legislation designed to facilitate manumission by private individuals. In the South, slavery could not be disposed of by appeals to the rights of man. Besides being a system of labor, slavery was a method of disciplining a large and rapidly growing population of blacks. In the eyes of its proponents, slavery had the supreme virtue of keeping the black man "in his place" in white America.

Americans' faith in their high destiny matched the physical grandeur of their country. In their own eyes, they appeared upon the stage of history as the Heaven-appointed custodians of human liberty. "Had it not been for America," said Tom Paine, "there had been no such thing as freedom left throughout the world." In Paris, Benjamin Franklin portrayed the War of Independence as "the Cause of all Mankind": "we are fighting for their Liberty," he said, "in defending our own." Having redeemed their own country from oppression, American patriots urged their countrymen to dedicate themselves to bringing freedom to the rest of the world by making the republic a refuge for "the virtuous part of mankind." If republicanism succeeded in the New World, Americans reasoned, European despots would be compelled to relax their arbitrary systems to prevent the depopulation of their countries.

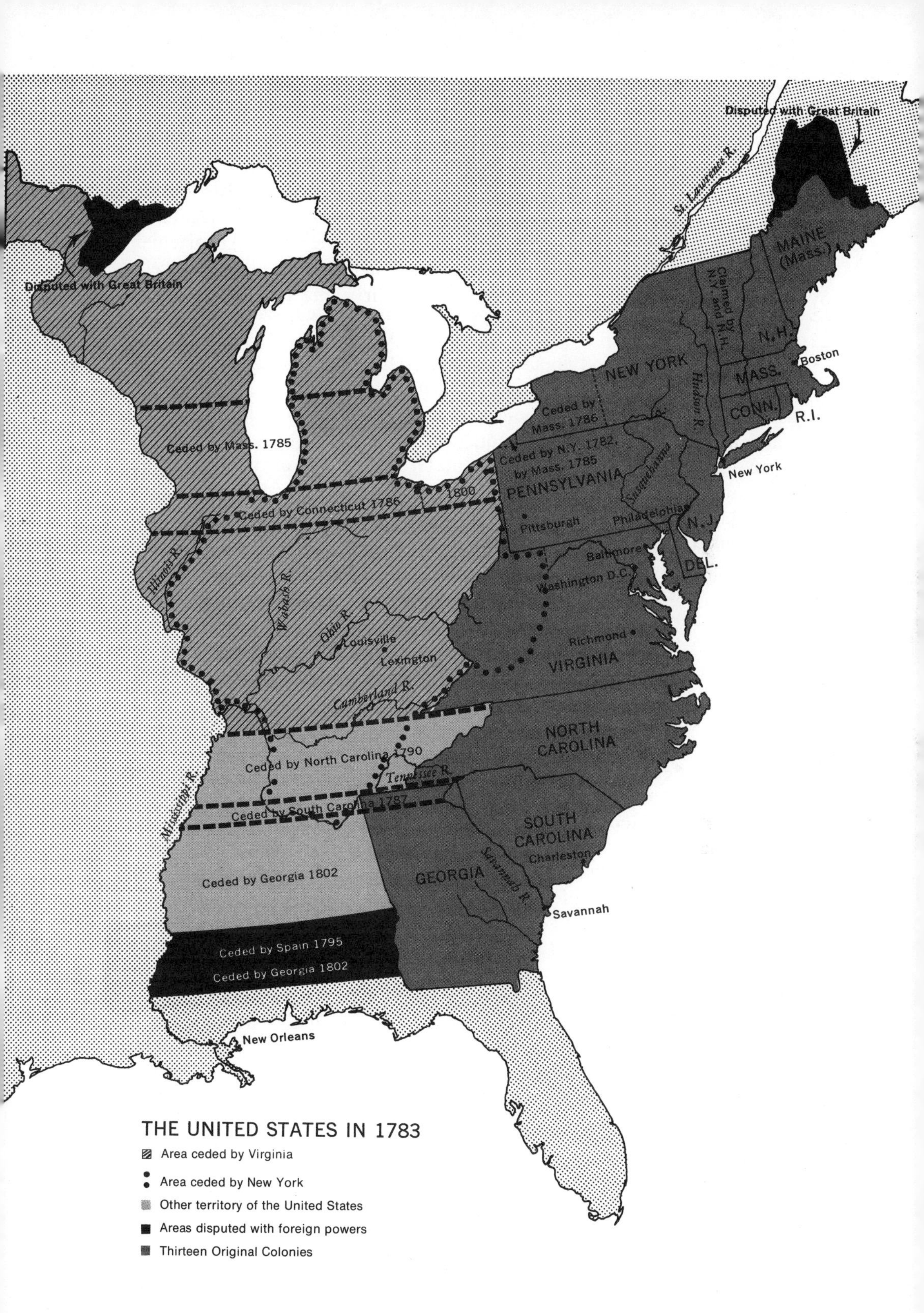

THE UNITED STATES IN 1783

- Area ceded by Virginia
- Area ceded by New York
- Other territory of the United States
- Areas disputed with foreign powers
- Thirteen Original Colonies

Thus, a patriot predicted, "millions will bless the wisdom, fortitude, and perseverance, that have nobly effected the revolution, who will never live in America." The American conquest of the world was to be by the force of its example, not by its arms.

In these stirrings of the spirit that seemed to herald the American Age, Alexander Hamilton predicted that the people of the non-European world would reap the benefit of the struggle for national liberation waged by the thirteen colonies. By means of its superior technology and arms, Europe had extended its dominion over Africa, Asia, and America—with the result, said Hamilton, that Europe had come to regard itself as the mistress of the world and the rest of mankind as created for its own enrichment. "It belongs to us," he asserted, "to vindicate the honor of the human race, and to teach that assuming brother [Europe] moderation."

Some Americans even believed that Great Britain might be redeemed from tyranny—provided that it atoned for the crimes it had committed against liberty and humanity in America and India. But more commonly, Great Britain was accounted lost forever to freedom. Thomas Jefferson declared that the sun of Great Britain's glory was waning rapidly: "her philosophy has crossed the Channel," he said, "her freedom, the Atlantic, and herself seems passing to that awful dissolution, whose issue is not given human foresight to scan." One American who in 1780 tried to penetrate futurity conjured up a vision of two American travelers who, visiting Great Britain in 1980, find London in ruins and the remaining inhabitants starving and in rags. All the best Englishmen had long since emigrated to "the empire of America . . . which now gives laws to so many regions."

Thomas Jefferson was inclined to believe that, as regards eminent men, the New World had already outstripped the Old. America, he pointed out, had brought forth George Washington, Benjamin Franklin, and David Rittenhouse—a triumvirate fit to stand in the company produced by any age or country. Europeans knew Washington and Rittenhouse only by reputation, but they had seen Benjamin Franklin in person. Since 1777, when he had come to France as the representative of the United States, Franklin, the son of a Boston candlemaker, had personified in the courts of kings the liberty and equality for which the new republic stood. With his plain brown coat, unpowdered hair, and fur cap, Franklin played to perfection the part of an American democrat. Acclaimed by the *philosophes* as "the Socrates of modern times," Franklin disported himself at the court of Louis XVI, where beautiful women felt privileged to call him "Papa." At one fete held in his honor, "the most beautiful among 300 women was designated to place upon the silver white hairs of the American philosopher a crown of laurel and two kisses upon his cheeks."

Franklin also embraced every opportunity to practice the new diplomacy by which the republic hoped to usher in the American Age. John Adams declared that the United States was dedicated solely to "promoting reason, justice, truth and the rights of mankind," not to playing power politics. It was in this spirit that in 1784 Thomas Jefferson, then a member of the Continental Congress, drew up a plan of treaties for the guidance of American diplomats abroad, whose company he was shortly to join. In this plan, Jefferson sought to write the Enlightenment into international law. By abolishing privateering, exempting foodstuffs and naval stores from the contraband list, and making the seas safe for neutral shipping, Jefferson's plan of treaties was intended to bring about a new era of free trade and amity between nations. In order "to increase the general happiness and lessen the miseries of mankind," Jefferson proposed to humanize war by placing all private property beyond the reach of belligerents.

To attain full republican stature, Americans were exhorted by the revolutionary leaders to spurn the merchandise as well as the corrupt manners and invidious ideas of monarchical Europe. With the resumption of trade with Great Britain in 1783, the capacity of the American people to endure this kind of self-denial was subjected to a severe test. After seven years of war shortages, the pent-up demand for British manufactures proved stronger than the admonitions of the patriot leaders. Americans had stood up resolutely to British cannon, but they seemed wholly unable to resist British merchandise on easy terms. The scramble to buy British luxury goods dismayed patriots who had expected to see their countrymen behave like Spartans; never had they dreamed they would see "Ladies of *real* virtue, dressing themselves in the same wanton *habits* as Ladies of *easy* virtue." At the risk of his popularity, especially among the ladies, Washington urged his countrymen and countrywomen to stop buying "foreign superfluities and adopting fantastic fashions"—equally injurious, he asserted, to their morals, industry, purses, and the balance of trade. James Madison concluded that so powerful was the "luxurious propensity" of his countrymen that they would spend their last dollar to indulge their whims and go into debt when the money ran out. "Our people," he lamented, "will extend their consumption as far as credit can be obtained."

Some patriots suspected a British plot to debauch Americans and, after they had been thoroughly debilitated by high living, to reconquer them. Washington, John Jay, and John Adams expressed the wish that credit might be totally abolished—then, presumably, finding themselves compelled to pay cash, Americans would practice the frugality recommended by Poor Richard.

By the end of 1785, the buying spree was definitely over—not because Americans had their fill of European merchandise, but because they had temporarily run through their credit. Washington was gratified to see his countrymen settling down to something like the republican austerity he had expected of them; he noted with approval that they were working harder and buying fewer luxury goods. And indeed, chastened by hard times and importunate creditors, Americans did seem ready to devote themselves to plain living and high thinking. But their two-year lapse from republican virtue proved costly: during 1784, the imports of the United States totaled £3,700,000 whereas exports were only £750,000. As a result, many domestic manufactures built up during the war were destroyed by British competition, and much of the country's supply of specie was sent across the Atlantic. In August 1783, the Bank of England held only £590,000 of gold and silver; two years later, the Bank's store of bullion had risen to £5,487,000, part of which came from the United States.

Manifestly, not all this capital and credit had been expended upon luxuries. A considerable part of the goods imported into the United States was essential to the retooling of farms and plantations. It was British credit that enabled Americans to get on their feet economically in the postwar period. Although Great Britain had lost the war, British merchants and manufacturers had no intention of losing Americans as customers, even if it meant advancing credit to unreconstructed rebels.

THE STATES IN CONTROL

Independence had been won, but seven years of war had not created a truly national spirit in which state loyalty was subordinated to an overriding loyalty to the nation. True, the United States had been created by the Revolution; but the emphasis, in the minds of most Americans, was upon "States" rather than upon "United." In general, Americans were prone to think of themselves first as Virginians, New Yorkers, Carolinians, or New Englanders; only secondarily—and sometimes almost as an afterthought—did they admit to being Americans. In fact, "American" was a geographical expression far more than it was the designation of a nationality. Alexander Hamilton said that the affection of the people toward their state governments was "the real rock upon which the happiness of this country is likely to split." For most Americans happiness came in small bundles, preferably no larger than a state.

With the ending of the war and the removal of the presence of the enemy who had initially brought the colonies together, Gouverneur Morris feared that the Continental Congress, "like the traveller's coat in the fable, after having been hugged close through the stormy hour of danger, will be cast aside as a useless burden, in the calm and sunshine of peace and victory." And, indeed, many Americans seemed eager to cast off the threadbare coat and don the flashy raiment of state sovereignty. In 1784, General Nathanael Greene observed that it was not uncommon to hear Americans express the hope that their state would be independent "and that, as soon as our public debts are liquidated, congress should be no more." To this extent, at least, the national debt served as a bond of union: before the confederacy could be dissolved, some equitable division of the debt had to be agreed upon.

Beset by economic and financial difficulties, the new republic lacked a central government capable of acting in the national interest. Under the Articles of Confederation, Americans improved upon the slogan "that government is best which governs least" by achieving a government which governed hardly at all. In the Continental Congress, inaction was the rule: even the minimal functions assigned to government—the maintenance of order, the protection of commerce, and the payment of the public debt—were unfulfilled by the general government. Washington described the Continental Congress as "a half-starved, limping Government, that appears to be always moving upon crutches, and tottering at every step." Such a government could do little to stop the steady drift toward the fragmentation of power that set in after 1783.

Liberty was the touchstone of the revolutionary period. Governor Edmund Randolph of Virginia observed that the framers of the Articles of Confederation were "wise and good men; but human rights was the chief knowledge of the times." The excellence of the Articles was believed to reside in the protection they afforded liberty; at this time Americans were inclined to value government in proportion to its inability to interfere with the inalienable rights of man. Since human rights were often arbitrarily identified with states' rights, it was felt necessary to protect the states against the general government and to safeguard the small states against the ambition of the large states. In effect, the Articles enunciated the doctrine that all states were created equal. Each state was given one vote in the Continental Congress; in that assemblage Delaware and Rhode Island were the equals of Virginia and Pennsylvania.

Because their paramount concern was with liberty, the framers of the Articles of Confederation made no provision for the separation of powers or for checks and balances. All power was concentrated in the legislature; the federal judiciary was almost nonexistent, and the president of Congress was merely a presiding officer. When John Hancock expressed reluctance on grounds of ill health to accept the office of president, he was assured that the president's chair was "the Easiest in the Union for an Invalid." He was also given a house as an official residence, whereas congressmen were obliged to live in boarding houses, "mixing with the landlady, her Aunt's cousins and acquaintances and with all other sorts of company." Congressmen naturally preferred to partake of the president's hospitality, with the result that he became little more than a glorified *maître d'hôtel.*

Elected annually, paid and instructed by the state legislatures, and subject to recall at any time, members of Congress were expected to conduct themselves as ambassadors for thirteen sovereign states. In this confederacy the states were the centers of power, and it was they rather than the people who ordained the general government. Indeed, the name of the people of the United States did not appear in the Articles of Confederation. It was a union of states, not of people. Each state retained its "sovereignty, freedom and independence." As a struggle for local self-government against centralized government, the American Revolution achieved its fullest exemplification in the Articles of Confederation.

Conceived in the idea that centralized government and a powerful executive were by their very nature hostile to liberty, the Articles of Confederation reflected Americans' experience as British colonists rather than their needs as an independent people. Even so, the Articles would have created a viable central government had the states fully performed their obligations under this instrument of government. On paper, the Continental Congress exercised control over a large sphere of the national life: it enjoyed jurisdiction over foreign affairs, (including treaties, alliances, and war); it was authorized to constitute courts for determining appeals in all cases of capture on the high seas; and it could decide, on appeal, all disputes between two or more states concerning boundaries, jurisdiction, etc. It had charge of Indian affairs insofar as the Indians were not subject to the authority of a state; and it could mint and regulate the value and alloy of coins.

Although theoretically supreme within its sphere, the Continental Congress had no means of enforcing its authority. Congress could borrow money, but it could not lay a tax to provide funds for the payment of its debts. It could make treaties of commerce, but it could not establish a customs house anywhere in the United States. Although the states were not permitted to pass laws in contravention of treaties made with foreign powers by the Continental Congress, no courts or judges existed to enforce the terms of congressional treaties. Congress could declare war, commission armies, and direct their operations, but unless it secured the consent of the states it could not provide the means for carrying on war. It had the power to regulate the coinage, but the United States Treasury contained only eighty tons of copper.

The fundamental defect of the Articles of Confederation, however, was that the general government had no power to tax, conscript, regulate, or punish citizens of the United States directly. What authority the Continental Congress possessed bore only upon the states in their corporate capacity, not upon individuals. Above all, control of the purse was left wholly to the states and, as Alexander Hamilton said, "the power which holds the purse strings absolutely, must rule."

By granting power without providing the means of enforcement, the Articles of Confederation deserve to rank as the supreme institutional expression prior to the French Revolution of that faith in the reasoning faculties of man that distinguished the Enlightenment of the eighteenth century. Americans were expected to act from a rational appreciation of their own self-interest; there was no need to compel them to do their duty toward the general government—it was only necessary to tell them plainly where duty lay. As John Jay said, the Articles were based upon the assumption that "the people of America only required to know what ought to be done, to do it."

Under this instrument of government, Congress functioned as an advice-giving rather than as a lawmaking body. It recommended rather than commanded. A large part of the delegates' time and effort was devoted to devising plans that were never adopted. Congress, said John Jay, "may consult, and deliberate, and recommend, and make requisitions, and they who please may regard them." If a state refused to comply, Congress could only supplicate it to do its duty.

It was in the requisition system that the fatal flaw in the Articles of Confederation first manifested itself. The Continental Congress requisitioned money and supplies from the states, but the states acted as though it were entirely within their discretion to pay or not to pay. Thirteen different legislative bodies—about 2500 individuals—sat in judgment upon the requests for funds laid before them by the Continental Congress; and, almost without exception, the legislatures clutched the purse strings so tightly that Congress received hardly more than a pittance. The states were never at a loss for reasons for not honoring Congress's appeals for funds: times were hard, money was scarce, and what money there was could be more profitably used at home. Each state feared that it was doing more than others to support the general government; to guard against overexertion, some states adopted the drastic expedient of doing nothing at all. And, since the Continental Congress appeared to the sovereign states to be a rival for power, it was kept on short rations to prevent it from invading their prerogatives.

Finally, the Continental Congress presented the spectacle of a government almost wholly immobilized by built-in impediments to action. So fearful of majority rule were the framers of the Articles that they left the door open to minority rule. The assent of nine states was required for the passage of all important legislation. This rule meant that if nine states were present, one state could negate the will of eight. But nine states were seldom present because, as James Madison said, "the absent states find almost as much a security in their absence as in their presence against measures which they dislike." As a result, for months at a time, lacking the quorum necessary to transact business, Congress could do no more than meet and adjourn from day to day pending the arrival of delegates from the absent states.

Even the ratification of the definitive treaty of peace with Great Britain was delayed because nine states were not represented in Congress. After a quorum was finally attained and the treaty ratified in January 1784, Congress relapsed into its state of immobility. The French minister reported that one delegate "has been obliged to go home to take care of his sick wife; another to marry; a third had very pressing personal business. I met one who told me that his wife called him back." Congressmen were supposed to take orders from their states, but it would appear that they yielded obedience to a higher power—their wives.

The decline in prestige and authority suffered by the Continental Congress was accompanied by a marked decline in the quality of its membership. Most of the eminent men who had made the name of the Continental Congress illustrious during the War of Independence took posts in the diplomatic service or in the state governments, or retired altogether from public life. Election to Congress was no longer sought by the most distinguished men; too often it was regarded as a tedious, uncomfortable, and unprofitable exile. Some congressmen complained that they were wasting the taxpayers' money by "loitering away their time, to little purpose."

Even Congress's power to erect courts of last resort to decide controversies between states was used sparingly. When South Carolina and Georgia became involved in a boundary dispute, they referred their dispute to a federal court. Congress helped bring peace to the Wyoming Valley, a section of Pennsylvania that became the scene of sporadic fighting between Connecticut and

Pennsylvania settlers, (the so-called Pennamite Yankee War); but New York and Massachusetts settled their differences out of court on the grounds that congressional action was too slow and expensive. Congress's most conspicuous failure, however, lay in its inability to bring peace to Vermont, where the Green Mountain Boys and New Yorkers fought two "wars"—barn burnings and minor skirmishes dignified by the participants into martial exploits—for possession of the region. In 1777, led by the Allen brothers, the Vermonters organized the independent republic of Vermont and, with the support of the New England states, resisted the efforts of the "Yorkers" to take possession of land to which they asserted claim under a charter granted by George III. Rather than surrender to New York, Ethan Allen swore that he would go with his hardy Green Mountain Boys "into the desolate caverns of the mountains, and wage war with human nature at large." When Vermont applied for admission to the Union, the problem was deposited squarely in the lap of the Continental Congress; but Vermonters declared that if Congress's decision went against them they would not abide by it. In preparation for that event, Levi Allen went to England to procure arms and to negotiate for the return of the independent republic to British sovereignty, thereby giving point to Alexander Hamilton's warning that these local conflicts would lead to foreign intervention and plunge the United States into "all the labyrinths of European politics." When Congress ordered the government of Vermont dissolved, the Green Mountain Boys stoutly asserted that they would not permit their country to be divided like Poland. Not until 1790, after the Continental Congress had ceased to exist, was the issue finally settled by the admission of Vermont as a state.

PROBLEMS OF FOREIGN TRADE

Liberated from the restrictions of the Navigation Acts, which had confined most of their trade to Great Britain and its colonial dependencies, Americans expected to make the world their market. Instead, after 1783 the United States found itself in a world dominated by mercantilist empires. Every great colonial power strove to make its empire self-sufficient and to monopolize the commerce of its colonies. In undertaking to destroy the barriers to free trade erected by the colonial powers, the United States exhibited the combination of audacity and optimism which, from the beginning, marked its bearing toward the outside world.

Although the United States sounded the trumpet, the walls of mercantilism did not fall. France, while it permitted American ships to trade with its West Indian possessions, refused to admit American wheat and flour into these colonies or to permit the export of West Indian sugar in American ships. The French West Indies consumed almost half the output of the American fisheries, but in 1785 the French government began to subsidize the importation of fish caught by French fishermen and transported to the Caribbean in

French ships. Efforts to export American tobacco directly to France were frustrated by the monopoly granted the Farmers General over the importation and sale of tobacco in France.

But it was Great Britain that placed the most damaging restrictions upon American commerce. Expecting to enjoy as an independent nation the commercial privileges they had possessed as British subjects, Americans discovered to their dismay that the price of freedom was exclusion from many of their long-established markets. The magnanimity displayed by the British government in the treaty of peace did not carry over into the postwar period. Beginning in 1783, successive Orders in Council deprived Americans of the right to sell American-made ships in Great Britain; Newfoundland, British Honduras, Quebec, and Nova Scotia were closed to American vessels; an alien duty was imposed upon American ships entering British ports; and prohibitive duties were levied upon several important American products.

Of these impediments to trade raised by Great Britain, the most injurious to the United States was the exclusion of American ships from the British West Indies. Before the war, 75 percent of the commerce of the islands had been handled by American vessels. As a result, the rum, fishing, and lumber industries had become dependent upon trade with Britain's Caribbean possessions. After 1783, the importation of salted meat and fish was prohibited, but all other commodities were admitted—provided they were carried in British ships. In consequence, British shipping prospered; most of the British vessels that cleared the port of Philadelphia from 1783 to 1789 were carrying American products to the West Indies or bringing rum, sugar, and molasses to the United States.

In the Mediterranean, American ships encountered the hostility of the Barbary Corsairs. These marauders were subsidized by France and Great Britain to keep that sea free of interlopers. Unprotected by either a naval force or a treaty guaranteeing safe passage through the Mediterranean, American merchant ships fell victim to the sea rovers. More than a score of American seamen were taken prisoner and held as slaves by the Algerians. High insurance rates on American ships forced shippers to make British vessels the carriers of American produce in the Mediterranean.

American shipmasters yearned to make "the swarthy Moor . . . feel the weight of American Metall." In this sentiment Thomas Jefferson heartily concurred. He had come to Europe exuding peace and good will, but the Barbary pirates tried beyond endurance his pacificism and benevolence. To smite the Corsairs hip and thigh became his ruling passion. For that purpose he urged the creation of an international police force that would drive the pirates from the sea and oblige them to take up farming for a livelihood. Jefferson imagined that the outlaws, converted into farmers, would become orderly, law-abiding citizens.

Jefferson believed that the Barbary pirates were "contemptibly weak," but he had to admit that the United States was even weaker. All the state navies built during the War of Independence had been dismantled, and the last ship of the Continental Navy had been sold in 1785. Although few southerners approved of a navy, Jefferson urged that the United States immediately begin constructing a fleet which, he suggested, might be used to coerce financially delinquent American states after it had disposed of the North African sea rovers. As commander of this force, Jefferson nominated John Paul Jones. When Jones's career in the United States Navy had been cut short by its untimely liquidation, he had taken service with the Russians against the Turks in the Black Sea. Jefferson thought that the experience would prove valuable when it came to fighting the Barbary pirates.

Unfortunately for Jefferson's plan, the United States was in no position to make any contribution to the armada upon which the success of the operation depended. For this reason, John Adams advised that the United States pay tribute to the pirates. In 1785, negotiations with Morocco eventuated in a treaty of amity, the terms of which were far more liberal than those usually given European powers. Hopefully, the United States might deal with Algiers, Tunis, and Tripoli in the same way, but even if a high tribute was exacted as a price for peace, it was cheaper, Adams believed, than building a navy and going to war. "We should not call it Bribery," Adams remarked. "We should learn to talk of it, as other nations do, as Gratuity, Generosity, Magnificence, Friendship, Custom."

Jefferson's scheme collapsed when France declined to take part in the proposed league. Unable to wait for Europe to act, the United States was left to shift for itself. So acute was Congress's financial stringency that it could neither fight nor pay tribute. Even American captives held in slavery by the pirates could not be ransomed. In 1788, hopeful that the pirates would release worthless captives, Jefferson let it be known in Algiers that the United States would pay no ransom whatever. But the Algerians refused to believe that a country that claimed to be a great power would allow its citizens to be treated as slaves. As a consequence, the American captives were not released until 1792, by which time many prisoners had died of disease.

Of all the states, Massachusetts was most adversely affected by independence. Shipbuilding came to a standstill, and unemployment was widespread in the cod and whale fisheries. In Marblehead alone, thirty-three vessels remained tied to the wharves. Nantucket, a one-industry island whose whaling fleet had been reduced from three hundred to less than one hundred vessels during the war, experienced a new setback when, after peace had been made, the British and French governments imposed prohibitive duties upon imported American whale oil. Although Massachusetts granted a bounty upon whale oil, the state alone could do nothing to open markets overseas. Despairing of ever regaining these markets, some Nantucket Quakers proposed to declare their island an independent, neutral republic, but emigration to Nova Scotia and France rather than independence was the solution finally adopted by the whalers.

Thus, in 1784, when a representation of the codfish was ordered hung in the Massachusetts House of Representatives as a symbol of the state's prosperity, it seemed more like a memorial to the past than an augury of future affluence. At this time, the Bay State appeared to have gained its independence at the expense of its economic well-being: "she will have the glory," said a disconsolate Yankee in 1784, "of being a sovereign, independent, poor state."[1]

Despite its heavy losses in the war and its exclusion from lucrative foreign markets, the American merchant marine enjoyed important advantages over its foreign rivals. Ships could be built in the United States at two thirds the cost of European shipyards, and American vessels were operated more cheaply than European ships of comparable tonnage. "They navigate with more safety, with more cleanliness, and with more intelligence," said Brissot de Warville of the Americans, "because the spirit of equality, which reigns at home, attends them likewise at sea. Nothing stimulates men to be good sailors like the hope of becoming captains."[2]

Instead of pining over their lost markets in the West Indies and elsewhere in the British Empire, American shipmasters began to seek new worlds of commerce to conquer. The quest took them to the Baltic Sea and the Pacific and Indian Oceans. In 1784, a New England ship carried the American flag for the first time to St. Petersburg; in February of that year, the *Empress of China* set sail from New York for China, returning the next year with a cargo of tea, silk, Nankeens, and silver. In 1788, the voyage of the *Canton* realized a profit to its owners of 125 percent. In 1785, the first ships carrying the stars and stripes arrived in Indian harbors, and Yankee shipmasters quickly opened up markets in India, the East Indies, Mauritius, and the Cape of Good Hope. Before the adoption of the federal Constitution, American ships were supplying European markets as well as those of the United States with spices, teas, and other commodities from the East.

American ships carried to China cargoes of ginseng (which grew wild in the United States and was credited by the Chinese with potency-restoring powers), furs, and sandalwood from Hawaii. The trade in sea-otter skins was especially profitable. In 1787, Captain Robert Gray, master of the *Columbia* out of Boston, took a cargo of sea-otter skins on the Northwest Coast, sailed to China by way of the Hawaiian Islands, picked up a cargo of tea and silk, and returned to Boston in August 1790—the first American shipmaster to circumnavigate the globe. Later that same year, on his second voyage to the Northwest Coast, Gray sailed his ship, the *Columbia,* over the bar into the

---

[1]In *The New Nation,* Merrill Jensen contends that the economic depression was far less severe than that pictured by John Fiske in *The Critical Period of American History.* In Jensen's view, the economic dislocations caused by independence had been essentially overcome before the adoption of the Federal Constitution.

[2]In 1802, Nathaniel Bowditch of Salem, Massachusetts, a self-taught mathematician who had gained much practical experience at sea, contributed to the excellence of American seamanship by publishing *The New Practical American Navigator.* Still in use, it has gone through many reprintings and editions. In this book, Bowditch corrected eight thousand errors in the tables of a standard English work on navigation—a feat which his countrymen did not permit Englishmen to forget.

river that bears its name, thereby establishing United States claims to the Oregon territory. In 1789, forty-four vessels sailed from Boston to the Northwest Coast, India, and China. But by 1825 the fur trade had been ruined by overhunting, and the Hawaiian and Fiji Islands had been stripped of their sandalwood. Whaling, however, continued to attract scores of Yankee ships to the South Seas. As early as 1791, five American ships from Nantucket and New Bedford rounded the Horn and began operations in the whaling grounds off the Peruvian coast.

In actuality, trade with China and the Northwest Coast had only minor bearing upon the American economy during the period of the Articles of Confederation. While shipowners who engaged in this commerce usually made high profits, they failed to open up important markets for American agricultural surpluses. Of much more consequence in this connection was the increase in the trade with Holland which took place after 1785 and the illegal trade carried on by Americans with the British West Indies. Americans put to use their redoubtable skill in smuggling acquired as British colonists to penetrate the markets legally closed to them by the British government.

During the first years of independence, commerce suffered far more than did agriculture from British and European restrictions. The price of tobacco remained high until 1790, and, although wheat and flour could not be exported to Great Britain except in times of scarcity, there was no serious decline in the price of these commodities. In the lower seaboard South, however, the economic consequences of the war and independence brought severe hardship to the planters. Devastated by the civil war that had broken out when the British Army captured Charleston in 1780 and by the heavy loss of slaves that had occurred when the British offered freedom to fugitives, the planters were hampered after the war by the loss of subsidies formerly paid by the British government upon the production of rice, indigo, and naval stores. Not until the lower South turned to the cultivation of cotton did its economy recover.

While exports from the United States increased slightly from 1783 to 1789, the increase was far below the growth of population. On a per capita basis, the national income was lower in 1789 than in 1774. During this period, American cities failed to keep pace with the growth of national population. In 1774, there were twelve towns in the United States with a population over five thousand; by 1790, there were still only twelve. It was a far remove from the burgeoning economy Americans had confidently anticipated as one of the fruits of independence.

Even the tobacco producers of the Chesapeake were not satisfied with the economic consequences of independence. In general, the tobacco trade reverted to its prewar channel: the planters continued to buy and sell almost as though the American Revolution had not occurred. During the colonial period, virtually all American tobacco had gone to Great Britain; from there over 75 percent of the crop was re-exported to the European continent. The planters had flattered themselves that with the opening of direct trade with Europe their tobacco would find a market on that continent. But the credit facilities, the skill in marketing, and the kind and quality of the merchandise they retailed insured British merchants and manufacturers a continuance of their almost monopolistic hold upon American tobacco. By 1789, over two thirds of the tobacco exports of the United States went directly to Great Britain, and Americans were even importing French cambrics from Great Britain.

Chesapeake planters ordinarily sold their tobacco to and bought the manufactures they needed from Scottish or English commercial houses. To cover bad debts, interest charges, and the middleman's profit, these merchants usually advanced the price of goods from 25 to 35 percent over London prices. Toward the repayment of his bills, the planter pledged his next year's crop. In consequence, the Chesapeake tobacco producers were bound to their British creditors until they died or repaid the debt. Since the debts descended from father to son, even death did not secure a final release. Thomas Jefferson said that he never knew of a planter who had escaped from debt once he had gotten fairly into the clutches of a British merchant. Jefferson compared his fellow planters to "a species of property annexed to certain British mercantile houses." Moreover, with few ships or seamen of their own, Virginia and Maryland producers were almost wholly dependent upon British shipping to carry their crops to market. To the planters themselves, the Revolution remained unfinished until they had been emancipated from "economic vassalage," to the capitalists of the former mother country.

If this was servitude, the planters themselves were at least partly responsible for it. The planters owned the means of production. They did not hire labor—they bought it in the person of an able-bodied slave. Accordingly, they raised wheat, rice, and tobacco to buy more black slaves in order to raise more wheat, rice, and tobacco. Under this system of labor, production could not be curtailed in the interest of price stability: the cost of maintaining slaves made it necessary to keep them busy producing raw materials for sale upon the world market regardless of price.

Like many other Tidewater planters, George Washington was in chronic financial trouble. In 1787, although one of the wealthiest landowners in the country, Washington was delinquent in his taxes and unable to pay his current assessment. "I know not where or when," he said, "I shall receive one shilling with which to pay it." For eleven years his estate had not paid its way, and in the past two years his wheat crop had been destroyed by the Hessian fly. He could not sell land, of which he had over 50,000 acres; when he advertised land for sale, no bidders appeared. The only way he could collect from his debtors was to bring them into court. Finally, his expenses were increasing as his income dropped: the slaves had to be clothed and fed, and at Mount Vernon he suffered from a surfeit of visitors, all of whom had to be entertained. He applied to his friend John Carroll of Carrollton—one of the richest men in the United States—for a loan, but Carroll said he had no cash to spare because he could not collect even the interest on the money he had on loan.

In 1789, Washington had to borrow money in Alexandria at 6 per cent interest to make the journey to New York, where he was to take the oath as President of the United States. Eight years later, after completing two terms as president, he was obliged to sell land to help move himself and his family from Philadelphia to Virginia. Apart from his feat of marrying a rich widow, Washington, despite his wealth, could hardly be made to serve as an example of financial success to his countrymen; he was not first in moneymaking. The first President was land poor and slave poor—an infallible way, as Thomas Jefferson, James Monroe, and James Madison learned, of ensuring a lifetime of financial worry.

2. THE ECONOMIC CONSEQUENCES OF INDEPENDENCE

FINANCING THE GOVERNMENT

The economic and financial difficulties confronting individual citizens during the immediate postwar period were compounded by a large public debt incurred during the War of Independence. Although the greater part of that debt had been wiped out by governmental decree—in 1780, the Continental Congress fixed the value of Continental dollars at forty to one specie dollar—and by the depreciation of the paper money issued by the states, the residue of debt constituted a heavy burden for depression-ridden states. The general government, debarred from imposing taxes and wholly dependent upon the charity of the states, was in a particularly disadvantageous position. For, as regards the foreign and domestic debt, the Continental Congress was given full responsibility for payment without the grant of an accompanying power of taxation. In 1783, the United States government owed over $10 million abroad, and citizens of the United States had claims upon it to the amount of almost $40 million. Considering the size of the gross national product and the fact that the Continental Congress had virtually no specie reserves and very little revenue, $50 million dollars could not be lightly brushed aside.

This debt, foreign as well as domestic, was part of the price of inde-

"The Tontine Coffee House, Wall Street Home of the New York Stock Exchange," detail of a painting by Francis Guy, courtesy of the New-York Historical Society, New York City.

Undated Bar Cent, Circa, 1785.

pendence, toward the attainment of which Americans had pledged their lives, their fortunes, and their sacred honor. Their lives were now secure, but their fortunes and honor had not yet been fully tested. As Alexander Hamilton said, Americans had in effect mortgaged all their property for the benefit of their creditors and therefore had no right to regard their estates as free and unencumbered until their debts had been paid. A chilling prospect indeed—but Hamilton always insisted that no government could maintain its credit without paying its debts.

Even meeting the current running expenses of the government taxed the ability and the personal financial resources of Robert Morris, who, in 1781, had been appointed Superintendent of Finance. In July 1783, when Morris asked the Bank of North America for a loan of $100,000 on the security of the United States, the Directors asked if he could not furnish better security. No individual, were he as rich as Croesus (and Morris was reputed to be the richest man in the United States), could have long sustained a government whose expenditures exceeded its revenue as inordinately as did the American government's. Despite the French government's announcement that it would make no further loans to the United States, Morris was compelled to draw drafts upon American ministers abroad. As he expected, when these drafts were presented to the French government for payment, it honored them rather than permit its ally to slide into bankruptcy.

The size of the national debt together with the impotence of the Continental Congress, furnished the most compelling reasons for amending the Articles of Confederation. As early as 1781, Robert Morris and others had proposed that Congress be invested with power to lay and collect an impost—a duty upon imports—in order to pay the interest on the foreign debt. Congress recommended this plan to the states and thereby revived all the passions engendered by the struggle with the Crown and Parliament. By giving Congress power to lay duties upon imports, it was said, the American people would be creating a tyranny far more oppressive than that from which they had recently escaped; the impost was described as a surrender of sovereignty to a "foreign power" which would "absorb the separate sovereignties into one mighty monarchy." Having risked everything to establish free, independent republics, Americans were told that any centralized government, whether exercised by Parliament or the Continental Congress, was incompatible with liberty and the pursuit of happiness.

Since amendments to the Articles of Confederation required the assent of all the states, the possibility of tyranny—and, indeed, of any change in the Articles themselves—seemed remote. It was the rule of unanimity that defeated the impost. Although twelve states signified their approval, Rhode Island categorically rejected it in December 1782. In the fable, a mouse had saved the life of a lion; Rhode Island claimed similar fame on the ground that it had preserved American liberty.

Despite this reverse, Morris demanded that Congress adopt a funding system—the pledging of specific revenue for the payment of the interest and principal of the national debt. Funding the debt would, he predicted, restore public and private confidence, put money in the hands of "the numerous, meritorious and oppressed body of men, who are creditors of the people," promote the flow of capital from Europe, and permit the United States to take its rightful place among the nations—"the last essential work of our glorious Revolution." In January 1783, hoping to force Congress's hand, Morris threatened to resign as Superintendent of Finance unless a complete revenue system was drawn up by May 1, 1783.

Under pressure from the Superintendent of Finance, Congress recommended to the states a second impost together with the grant of supplementary revenue that would have permitted the general government to pay the most pressing of its debts. But by this time Morris had earned the reputation, even among some members of Congress, of being the archenemy of American liberty. He was pictured "wallowing in wealth, rioting in voluptuousness, gorged with honors, profits, patronage and emoluments." Morris himself told a very different story: as the result of neglecting his private affairs for public business, he was growing poorer daily. As for exercising overweening power over the affairs of the republic, he described his office as "a cursed scene of drudgery and vexation." How, he asked, was it possible to save a people who converted everything into grounds for calumny? The final indignity, he said, was that the states demanded that he account for the expenditure of money which they had been asked to pay but had not appropriated.

In 1784, Morris escaped from the purgatory of office by doing what he had frequently threatened—handing in his resignation. The office of Superintendent of Finance was abolished, and a board of three commissioners appointed by Congress was created to manage the fiscal affairs of the government. Morris's enemies breathed easier: American liberty was safe but, unfortunately, the same could not be said for the country's finances.

The Board of Treasury (since the government collected no revenue, it was essentially an accounting and disbursing agency) continued to function until Hamilton took office as Secretary of the Treasury. It addressed itself to the Herculean task of introducing "Order and Economy" in the finances of the United States. Samuel Osgood, one of the Commissioners, predicted that the United States would soon astonish the world by the efficiency of its bookkeeping and by the punctuality and exactitude of the quarterly accounts submitted to Congress. But its quarterly statements regarding the condition of the United States Treasury made such gloomy reading that no one thanked the Board for its pains. As Rufus King said, "so melancholy was the state of the federal treasury, that all men seemed to turn away from it, as an evil which admitted of no remedy."

While awaiting the outcome of its appeal for a grant of additional powers, Congress remained dependent upon the requisition system. The period of waiting lasted four years, during which Congress's financial position went from bad to worse. Revenue from the states shrank to a mere trickle. From October 1781 to September 1785, of the $15,670,000 requisitioned from the states,

Congress actually received only about $2,500,000. In September 1785, Congress requisitioned $3 million from the states; a year later it had received less than $100,000. The total revenue of the general government in 1786 was less than one third of the amount required to pay the interest on the foreign debt alone.

Having large war debts of their own, the states naturally gave priority to liquidating their own obligations. While some states used depreciated paper money for that purpose, other states (such as Massachusetts) imposed heavy taxes, and four states, Pennsylvania among them, funded their debts. Holders of state securities strenuously opposed giving Congress power to lay an impost, for if the states were deprived of revenue it would gravely impair their ability to pay their creditors. So decisively did the balance of fiscal power shift in favor of the states that by 1787 Pennsylvania, New York, and Maryland had begun to assume payment on that part of the Continental debt held by their citizens. By assuming part of the national debt, these states served notice—if more notice was required—upon the public creditors that their best hope of receiving payment lay in supporting the states against the national government. For this reason many of the creditors of the national government began to shift their allegiance to the states.

Among the domestic creditors who were directed to take a place in the long line outside the United States Treasury were the officers and men of the Continental Army. Paid off in interest-bearing certificates and land warrants entitling them to take up land in the public domain, they were treated no differently from civilian creditors who had merely loaned money to the government; military service conferred no special merit and received no special consideration. Those in need of cash—and this included most of the officers and men—sold their certificates and land warrants for a few cents on the dollar.

In its desperation, Congress made heroic efforts at economizing. In 1784-1785, the salaries of American ministers abroad were sharply reduced. (In the debate, it was pointed out that since the principal duty of these representatives consisted in soliciting loans, it would not do to let them appear to be too prosperous.) In 1785, discouraged by its ministers' lack of success in procuring loans, some members of Congress suggested that they all be recalled, leaving only *charges d'affaires* in Paris and London. In March 1787, Congress abolished the offices of comptroller and auditor and cut the salaries of the few remaining officials and clerks. The armed forces were pared to seven hundred officers and men. Despite these retrenchments, Congress fell so far behind in payments to the Army that the troops became mutinous.

In all its declarations of fiscal policy, the Continental Congress gave priority to the payment of the foreign debt. This debt, interest as well as the principal, had to be paid in specie: the foreign creditors were not to be palmed off with paper money or I.O.U.'s. The domestic creditors were told to wait their turn; the best that could be done for them was to pay part of the interest due them in certificates called "indents," which promptly depreciated as did everything else Congress touched.

During the War of Independence, despite its own financial distress, France had generously agreed to postpone the payment of interest on its loans to the United States until 1786. The United States took advantage, and more, of France's liberality. Payment of interest fell into arrears, and French officers who had served in the United States Army remained unpaid until 1790, when, four years late, the United States paid the first installments on its war debt to France.

On the other hand, the Dutch private bankers who had helped finance the War of Independence insisted upon prompt payment of interest and principal. Congress was therefore obliged to borrow additional funds in Holland to service the existing debt to the Amsterdam banking houses. And so the Dutch were paid—but only by advancing more money to the United States. From 1784 to 1789, the Dutch bankers loaned the United States $2,296,000, a sum larger than that contributed by the states during the same period.

This looked like a losing game for the Dutch. They stood a very good chance of becoming receivers in bankruptcy for the United States government. Nevertheless, beginning in 1786, Dutch investors began to purchase Continental and state certificates of indebtedness. Bought at bargain prices—often as low as twenty cents on the dollar—these certificates were certain to rise in price if the United States ever succeeded in putting its financial house in order. By 1788, one Dutch investor had acquired continental and state certificates with a face value of $1,340,000.

RELATIONS WITH GREAT BRITAIN

Because most American trade lay with Great Britain and because the removal of British restrictions on American trade seemed essential to the economic recovery of the United States, in 1784 the Continental Congress sent John Adams to Great Britain to negotiate a commercial treaty. By way of laying the groundwork for discussions, Adams advised British statesmen to rise above their prejudices and recognize that, whether they liked it or not, the United States was "destined, beyond a doubt, to be the greatest Power on earth, and that within the life of man." He coolly told the Queen that the peopling of the United States would prove to be the greatest glory of Great Britain. If it came to another war between the two countries, Adams declared, the United States would undoubtedly suffer distress but Great Britain would just as certainly be utterly ruined. Only by seeking the friendship of the United States, he stoutly asserted, could the island kingdom hope to withstand the numerous and implacable enemies it had created by its aggressions upon the rights of other nations.

Adams had not come to Britain to read a lecture but to make a commercial treaty. He offered such liberal terms that, had the British accepted, an economic union would have been created between the two countries. Adams argued that by freely admitting American ships and products to Great Britain and its possessions, including, above all, the West Indies, His Majesty's government would enable Americans to buy more British goods and to pay their debts promptly to their overseas creditors. By its present policy, he warned, the British government was fostering the growth of manufacturing in the United States and making it impossible for Americans to do justice to their creditors.

In exchange for an unlimited right of access to the American market, the British were called upon to agree, as the Prussian government had already done, that privateering and the capture of neutral ships by belligerents be abolished. This requirement, inserted in Adams' instructions by the Continental Congress despite his protest that Great Britain would "voluntarily burn her Navy and her flag" rather than consent to such a self-denying ordinance, doomed his mission from the outset.

It was soon made plain to Adams that the British government was not interested in making a commercial treaty with the United States on terms of "fair and equal reciprocity" or, indeed, upon any terms whatever. The thinking of British statesmen upon this subject was governed by Lord Sheffield, who in 1783 had published a pamphlet entitled *Observations on the Commerce of the American States.*

Before Englishmen threw themselves into the arms of Americans under the impression that blood was thicker than water, the Earl of Sheffield advised them to remember that the Acts of Trade and Navigation were the palladium of British seapower and that seapower was essential to the survival of the island kingdom. By permitting Americans to share in the trade of the empire, Sheffield predicted that British shipbuilders, shipowners, and merchants would be overreached by rapacious Yankees in the fisheries and carrying trade. On the other hand, if Americans were treated as foreigners—and Sheffield knew them under no other designation—Englishmen would have the empire to themselves, unvexed by American competition. As for American objections to this treatment, Sheffield expected them to protest vehemently—but, he added, they could do little more than vent their indignation in diplomatic notes. It was inconceivable to the noble lord that the disjointed government Americans had established was capable of taking reprisal upon British shipping and merchandise. It was far more probable, he thought, that New Englanders, finding their markets gone, would emigrate to Nova Scotia and Canada in order to regain the privileges they had forfeited. Hopefully, after this disastrous experiment in independence, the chastened rebels would settle down as loyal and orderly subjects of His Britannic Majesty.

Since Americans were already buying more British goods than they could conveniently pay for, British statesmen saw no reason to make a commercial treaty with the United States. Moreover, John Adams was unable to guarantee that, in the event a commercial treaty were made, the Continental Congress could enforce it. The Duke of Dorset sarcastically remarked that this difficulty could be obviated if each of the thirteen states sent a minister to Great Britain.

After a few months of this chilling treatment, Adams said that he would be more profitably employed cultivating cabbages on his farm at Braintree than dancing attendance at the Court of St. James. "I may reason till I die, to no purpose," he cried in anguish of spirit. The refusal of British statesmen to adopt a policy of enlightened self-interest, as Americans conceived it, left Adams with the disquieting conviction that they were bent upon destroying the Americans' merchant marine. Nothing was more likely to put the doughty New Englander into a fighting frame of mind.

In adopting this policy toward the United States, Great Britain was not merely indulging its resentment toward its revolted subjects. Great Britain was experiencing a postwar boom. Far from setting forever, as Jefferson imagined, the sun of Britain's greatness, at least in the economic sphere, seemed verging toward its meridian. Trade with Europe, India, and Asia expanded after the war, while trade with the United States did not fall much below the volume reached in 1775.

Nor, contrary to Americans' allegations, did Great Britain treat the United States as an outlaw nation. In fact, not only was the republic accorded most-favored-nation status, but some of its products were given preferential treatment at the customs.

Whenever Adams talked with British ministers, the conversation usually degenerated into a squabble over the question of which side was guilty of making the first infraction of the treaty of peace. Americans' gratification over the territorial provisions of the treaty was considerably diminished by its stipulations regarding Loyalist estates and the collection of prewar debts. The Continental Congress was committed to "earnestly recommend" to the states the restoration of confiscated Loyalist property, and the states were expressly prohibited from making any further confiscations. Loyalists were to be allowed to return to the United States to recover their property. Nor were the states permitted to place any impediments in the way of British creditors seeking to recover debts owed by American citizens.

Although Congress earnestly recommended to the states that they restore confiscated Loyalist property, none of the states paid any heed. The state governments and individual citizens had profited so substantially from the sale of Loyalist estates—Pennsylvania had seized 21.5 million acres from the Penn family alone—that powerful vested interests had been created opposed to the return of this property. But Congress was able to take refuge in its impotence: it had fulfilled its obligation under the treaty by making recommendations. In this, as in virtually all other matters, Congress proposed but the states disposed.

Indeed, the states continued to confiscate and sell Loyalist property until the ratification of the definitive treaty of peace in March 1784. North Carolina put the last of its Loyalist estates on the market in 1786. To prevent the return of Loyalists and other British subjects, some states enacted laws depriving them of the protection of the laws. In 1783, Governor Patrick Henry of Virginia issued a proclamation, subsequently rescinded by the legislature, ordering British subjects to leave the state forthwith. A Loyalist so hardy as to return to the United States in 1783-1784 stood a better chance of getting a coat of tar and feathers than of regaining possession of his property.

But the most flagrant violation of the treaty of peace on the American side took the form of state laws impeding the collection of prewar debts. These obligations totaled about four million pounds; if interest during the war were added, as British creditors insisted, the amount became much larger. To have compelled debtors, many of whom were southern planters, to repay these debts in a lump sum was certain to bring ruin upon many citizens. Fortunately for them, the treaty did not specify that interest accumulated during the seven years of war be added to the principal. Americans therefore refused to pay the interest demanded by their British creditors; Patrick Henry even went so far as to assert that the entire debt had been extinguished because the British had waged war against Americans with unexampled "barbarity." In this spirit, some states enacted laws permitting American debtors to postpone and in some cases to avoid payment of their debts altogether or to make a token payment in depreciated paper or land in full settlement. Executions against American property by alien creditors were forbidden. Although American citizens were permitted to sue Britons in American courts, state courts refused to take jurisdiction of suits brought by British creditors. By 1785, not a single action for the collection of prewar debts had been prosecuted in Pennsylvania —and few American lawyers were willing to alienate public opinion by serving as counsel for a British creditor.

The British government took the position that these infractions absolved it from the necessity of fulfilling its obligations under the treaty. This decision meant that the United States failed to secure the return of some three thousand black slaves carried away by the British Army when it evacuated New York in 1783 and the delivery of the northwest posts which the British government had promised in the treaty of peace to surrender to the United States "with all convenient speed."

These nine frontier posts, the most important of which were Oswego, Detroit, and Michilmackinac, were an essential link in the chain of communication between Canada and the West; they held the key to the lucrative fur trade of the midcontinent; and they made possible the control of the Indian tribes whose allegiance Great Britain was determined to retain. Americans were thereby denied their share in the profits of the fur trade, estimated at £100,000 annually, to which they were entitled. Despite American efforts to dislodge them by diplomatic means, British troops remained on American soil for twelve years after the signing of the treaty of peace.

Although the British justified their retention of the northwest posts on the ground of prior American violations of the treaty, in actuality they had decided to withhold them even before Americans had been given an opportunity to infringe the treaty. In 1783, when an American general was sent to Canada to make arrangements for the surrender of the posts, he was denied permission to visit them by the British authorities. The ministry of William

Pitt simply chose to disregard what it regarded as the ill-advised generosity of Lord Shelburne and the peacemakers of 1782.

During the confederation period, the diplomatic exchanges between the United States and Great Britain revolved around the question of priority of guilt in violating the peace treaty. Both sides became locked in self-righteous, inflexible positions until 1787, when John Jay, the Secretary of Foreign Affairs, admitted officially, but wrongly, that the United States had cast the first stone. Thereupon the Continental Congress sent a circular letter to the states calling upon them to repeal all laws contrary to the treaty of peace. Most of the states either complied or advised Congress that they had already cleared their statute books of such legislation. But Virginia qualified its repeal of its laws with a proviso that the operation of the repeal should not take effect until Great Britain had surrendered the posts and made provision for restoring the Negro slaves.

Although the British Ministers expected the American confederacy to collapse of its own accord, they had unwittingly adopted the policy most likely to strengthen the Union. At this stage of their national development, Americans needed an external enemy to remind them constantly of the need for cooperative effort. Playing the part of an ogre seemed to come as naturally to British statesmen of the postwar period as it had to their predecessors during the American Revolution. Thanks to their efforts, Americans were provided with an "eternal" enemy—an enemy, moreover, they had learned to love hating.

Thus British policy served the cause of the advocates of a more perfect union. Long before the summoning of the Constitutional Convention, Gouverneur Morris declared that Great Britain was doing more political good than economic damage to the United States, and Washington predicted that the measures adopted in Whitehall would "facilitate the enlargement of Congressional powers in commercial matters, more than half a century would otherwise have effected."

Those powers certainly could stand enlargement. Unable even to reserve the coastal trade to American ships, the Continental Congress was in no position to bargain with Great Britain or, indeed, with any other power. To take reprisals upon British shipping and merchandise, as John Jay, Washington, Jefferson, and John Adams advocated, required a fundamental change in the Articles of Confederation.

Accordingly, in 1784, the Continental Congress appealed to the states for a discretionary authority for fifteen years to prohibit any foreign merchandise from being imported in the vessels of a foreign country which had not made a commercial treaty with the United States. In effect, Congress was asking for power to enact an American navigation act aimed at Great Britain in order to force that country to make a commercial treaty with the United States and fulfill all its obligations under the treaty of peace.

For a nation that had proclaimed the ideal of free trade and offered to negotiate with all nations treaties incorporating this principle, the action of the Continental Congress in 1784 represented a significant retreat from laissez faire to economic nationalism. The harsh realities of international life had compelled the republic to embrace the philosophy of mercantilism. John Adams declared that the United States "must repel monopolies by monopolies and answer prohibitions by prohibitions." Even Thomas Jefferson, the apostle of American economic enlightenment, now demanded retaliatory legislation against Great Britain. As he said in 1786, the British needed "to be kicked into common good manners."

Moreover, American idealism had failed conspicuously to sweep the world. While Jefferson's plan of treaties was presented to most of the maritime powers, only Sweden, Holland, and Prussia actually signed; a treaty negotiated with the Portuguese minister in Paris was not ratified by his government. Austria expressed interest in making a treaty with the United States but, since that monarchy had no overseas commerce, Jefferson rejected its overtures.

Since the proposal to give Congress control of commerce required the unanimous consent of the states, any change in American policy seemed certain to be long delayed. Opposition quickly appeared from two sources: from the states that raised revenue for their own purposes by levying and collecting duties upon commerce, and from the southern states which, having little shipping of their own, were reluctant to consign their commerce to northern shipowners and merchants. James Madison, at this time a staunch nationalist, said that he did not regard it as a mark either of "folly or incivility to give our custom to our brethren, rather than to those (British) who have not yet entitled themselves to the name of friends." But Richard Henry Lee spoke for a large body of opinion in Virginia when he predicted that these northern brethren would use Congress's control over commerce to fix "a most pernicious and destructive Monopoly" upon the freightage of southern staples to overseas markets and the transport of British merchandise to southern planters and farmers.

Impatient with the time-consuming process of amending the Articles of Confederation, ten states took matters into their own hands by levying tonnage duties upon British vessels or tariff duties upon British merchandise. These measures gave satisfaction to patriots who were eager to take reprisals against Great Britain, encouraged the growth of domestic manufactures, and brought sorely needed revenue to the state treasuries. But they also created in the United States a chaos of conflicting state laws and tended to set state against state in commercial wars. States such as New Jersey, Connecticut, and Delaware, which normally had little direct trade with Great Britain, depended for their supplies of imported goods upon commercial states such as Massachusetts, Rhode Island, New York, and Pennsylvania. When these latter states imposed duties upon British merchandise, it was inevitable that the duties should be passed on to the consumer in the noncommercial states. These consumers strenuously objected to being taxed for the benefit of neighboring states. Accordingly, Connecticut, New Jersey, and Delaware, instead of joining the effort to retaliate upon Great Britain, opened their ports to British ships and merchandise and encouraged the overland export of this merchandise to the neighboring states. In 1787, New York struck back by imposing duties upon New Jersey and Connecticut farm products brought into the state. By way of reprisal, New Jersey levied a tax of $1800 a year upon a lighthouse on Sandy Hook recently erected by New York; a group of Connecticut businessmen voted to stop all trading with New Yorkers; and in 1786, the New Jersey Assembly declared that it could not comply with future requisitions by the Continental Congress until New York repealed its tariff or applied the proceeds to the general purposes of the Union.

By taking unilateral action against Great Britain, the states failed to bring that power to the negotiating table. British ships simply avoided the ports of a state that imposed high tonnage duties and unloaded their cargoes in states where they were made welcome. The commercial states learned to their cost that the whole burden of retaliating upon Great Britain and fostering the American merchant marine fell upon them alone. And finally, barriers to interstate trade, already formidably high, seemed certain to become progressively higher as the states became involved in commercial wars with each other. With thirteen competing state economies, each seeking its own advantage rather than the good of the whole, a severe strain was imposed upon the already frayed bonds of union.

Certainly, British shipping did not suffer seriously from the states' uncoordinated attempts at retaliation. In 1787, it was estimated that three quarters of the trade of the southern states was carried on in British vessels. Charleston, South Carolina, rarely saw a ship that did not display the Union Jack. Thus the freight, insurance, and commissions paid by American producers helped to ensure that Britannia ruled the waves.

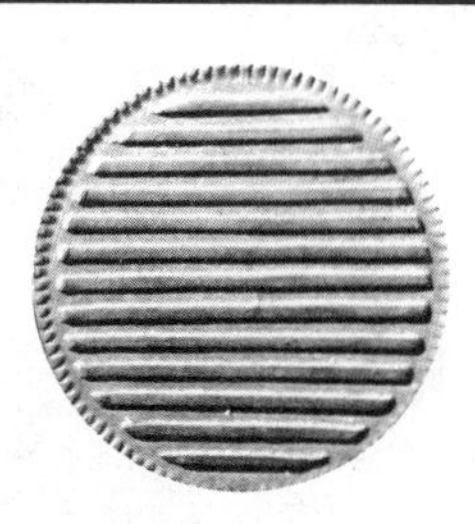

3.
THE IMPOTENCE OF THE CONFEDERACY

STATE LEGISLATURES AND DEBTOR RELIEF

In default of an efficient central government capable of mobilizing the resources of the country, responsibility for combating the depression which struck the United States after the War of Independence devolved upon the states. By retaining power under the Articles of Confederation, the sovereign states in effect assumed the duty of overseeing the welfare of their citizens. They tried to fulfill this responsibility by enacting laws designed to invigorate the economy, provide a dependable circulating medium, and protect debtors from the most oppressive exactions of their creditors.

Unlike the Continental Congress, the state governments could act quickly and intervene effectively in the economy. In most of the states, no institution existed within the government itself capable of thwarting or appreciably delaying the implementation of the popular will. While the state constitutions formally deferred to the theory of the separation of powers, in practice they tended to give all effective power to the legislatures, thereby abandoning the system of checks and balances recommended by James Harrington and Montesquieu. Governors and judges were deliberately made subordinate to the legislatures which, in most cases, had appointed them. Just as the states, under the Articles of Confederation, dominated the general government, so the states themselves, in the practical workings of government, were controlled by their legislatures. As a result, said Alexander Hamilton, most of the state

---

"General Rufus Putnam and his Party of Settlers near Marietta, Ohio," detail from a painting in the Ohio Historical Society, Columbus, Ohio.

Fugio Cent with Pointed Rays, 1787.

governments were hardly more than "the image and echo of the multitude." In his opinion, there was no more unstable form of government.

During the War of Independence, both the Continental Congress and the states had issued hundreds of millions of dollars in paper money, loan office certificates, and other evidences of indebtedness. Wholly lacking in specie support, paper money and certificates had depreciated when the quantity of the emissions and the vicissitudes of war created a crisis of confidence in the solvency of the general and state governments. In the inflation that followed, the worst in American history, "Not worth a Continental" proved to be the epitaph of the dollar issued by the Continental Congress. Even so, the Continental dollar, together with the state paper money, served the country well by helping to finance the War of Independence.

Despite the collapse of paper money during the war, after peace had been restored many Americans demanded that their state governments alleviate the rigors of the depression and the money shortage by printing more paper money. Without enough hard money to pay their taxes or their debts and to carry on ordinary business activities, Americans were in effect trying to make the capitalist system function without the benefit of an adequate circulating medium. Paper money promised to repair this deficiency and, at the same time, to give the economy a bracing fillip of inflation.

The demand for paper money did not come primarily from the backward sections of the Union. Those areas had not entered the money economy; barter was still the prevailing rule. Paper money was a sophisticated medium of exchange which, during the colonial period, Americans had learned to use more successfully than any other people. Without paper money, the economy of the colonies could not have achieved one of the highest growth rates in the world.

Nor was paper money a panacea made to order for "desperate debtors." Many businessmen and substantial farmers expected to reap considerable benefits from paper money. In actuality, there was at this time no "debtor class" in the United States: Even many citizens who passed as wealthy were debtors in varying degrees. Perhaps the experience Americans shared most fully in common was that of being in debt. A nation of debtors, they were capitalists on the make with borrowed money. Citizens were in debt to their state governments; both the state and central governments were in debt to their citizens, and citizens were in debt to each other. Credit was the life blood of the American economy: Beginning with the London and Glasgow counting houses, it extended to American wholesale and retail merchants and finally to the American consumer.

Yet not all debtors welcomed paper money. Merchants who had advanced credit in the form of goods to their customers were generally opposed to paper money because their own debts to British merchants had to be paid in specie. Manifestly, if their debtors were permitted to liquidate their obligations with paper money, these merchants stood to suffer heavy loss. Moreover, since the Revolution, banks had been established in Philadelphia, New York, and

Boston. These banks issued bank notes which helped supply the commercial centers with a stable circulating medium. To this kind of merchant, to affluent mortgagors, and to conservative-minded citizens in general, paper money emitted by the state governments conjured up visions of a runaway inflation. A dose of inflation, a patriot said, "like the pleasures of sin, was but for a season." Experience had proved that overindulgence, wonderful while it lasted, was always followed by debility and remorse.

In 1785-1788, rather than remain on a specie basis and allow deflation to run its course, however ruinous that might prove to individuals, seven states decided to experiment with paper money. To prevent this paper from depreciating as had the fiat money of the revolutionary period, it was secured by land. Paper money was loaned by the state, usually at 6 percent interest, to individuals who put up their land as collateral. Since paper money was usually accepted for taxes, the state regained part of its loan upon the payment of tax bills. Far from emitting the money in order to permit debtors to pay their debts to private creditors with cheap money, the states took every precaution to keep the value of the paper at par.

Paper money, while it facilitated the payment of private debts and taxes, did not provide the immediate relief many individuals required. No state, except Rhode Island, issued large quantities of paper money; in comparison with the amount of private and public debt, the amount of currency was inconsiderable. For this reason, hard-pressed debtors clamored for the enactment of stay laws—suspending the collection of debts—and tender acts—by which debtors were permitted to "tender" land or commodities to their creditors as legal satisfaction of their obligations.

To James Madison, Alexander Hamilton, and many others, these laws represented the triumph of unscrupulous debtors and demagogues over the respectable, honest, and industrious segment of the community. They argued that the states, by taking unilateral action to combat the depression, were threatening to destroy all semblance of centralized government in the United States. Moreover, they were alarmed by the stridency with which the proponents of debtor-relief legislation began to inveigh against men of wealth. The money-making opportunities of the War of Independence had produced a large number of *nouveaux riches* who, commanding disposable capital, had augmented their wealth during the postwar period by buying real estate at bargain prices, speculating in state and Continental securities, and lending money on mortgages at high interest rates. These "nabobs" became the target of such epithets as "merciless usurers," "bloodsuckers," and "harpies." Indeed, so unrestrained became these denunciations of men of wealth that some apprehensive citizens feared that debtors would demand the abolition of all debts and the redistribution of property.

Nevertheless, without these laws, large amounts of property would have passed into the possession of a comparatively few individuals whose titles were derived from the fact that they had loaned money or goods to people who, because of the depression and money shortage, were unable to keep up their payments. The resulting change in land ownership might well have been more revolutionary than the confiscation of Loyalist estates. It would have provided an intolerable anticlimax to the Revolution: the dispossessors of Tories dispossessed themselves by their more affluent fellow patriots.

Paper money, stay laws, and tender acts demonstrated the prevalence of the principle of majority rule in the state governments. Unquestionably, "legislative omnipotence" facilitated the rise to power of numerical majorities. Once they gained control of the lower house of the legislature (several states had no upper house), the entire apparatus of government fell within their grasp. Moreover, rather than abide by the inhibitions placed upon its freedom of action by the state constitution or bill of rights, the legislature often did as it saw fit regardless of "paper restraints" upon its authority.

Americans had fought the Revolution with the slogan "a government of laws, and not of men," by which they meant that the powers of government must be limited to those enumerated in a fundamental law or constitution. During the immediate postwar period, it became apparent that what they had actually achieved in the states was government by numerical majorities in which the fundamental law was made to yield to statute law. Tested strictly by the principles of 1776, the state legislatures were guilty of committing breaches of the fundamental law—as defined by the state constitutions—the very offense with which Americans had charged the British king and Parliament.

Certainly this was the case in Pennsylvania, where the unicameral legislature, to which the executive and judiciary were completely subordinate, rode roughshod over all opposition to its authority. In 1785, when the Bank of North America refused to accept Pennsylvania state bills of credit at par, the legislature revoked the charter granted to the bank by both Congress and the state of Pennsylvania in 1781—an act that Tom Paine denounced as an invasion of the sanctity of contracts. But the legislature deemed it sufficient to point out that the bank was incompatible with the public safety and with "that equality which ought ever to prevail between the individuals of a republic." "All charters granting exclusive rights," the legislators declared, "are a monopoly of the charter of mankind. The happiness of the people is the first law." But the bank's charter was restored in 1787, and it continued to do business until 1929, when the Great Crash swept it into limbo.

On the other hand, some of the most important reforms achieved in the postwar period were the work of state legislatures which refused to conform strictly to the terms of written constitutions. For example, the Virginia legislature abolished primogeniture and entail, prohibited the slave trade, and established religious freedom—constitutional changes for which it did not ask the consent of the people. In Rhode Island and Connecticut, the gradual emancipation of slaves was brought about by legislative enactment. In these instances, legislative bodies were doing things which required constitutional amendments —provided, of course, the constitution was treated as a fundamental law.

In enacting legislation for the relief of debtors, it was assumed that these unfortunates were honest, worthy, and industrious men who, through no fault of their own, found themselves temporarily unable to meet their financial obligations. "Everywhere," remarked a traveler, "the laws are apparently draughted by and for none but upright citizens." Yet laws made in the name of social justice produced a new kind of injustice. Protected by the courts, some debtors extinguished their debts by tendering their creditors depreciated paper money, barren land, spavined horses, and diseased cattle. Creditors, finding themselves pursued by "insolent debtors," raised the cry that the rights of property were being jeopardized by legislatures concerned only with benefiting one economic group in the community.

Of the states that infringed upon the rights of property, Rhode Island was by far the most errant offender. In 1786, with the popular or "debtor" party firmly in control, the state embarked upon a course of unrestricted paper money emission. Soon there was paper money everywhere, but not a hard coin to be found. When the paper depreciated and creditors refused to accept it at face value, the Rhode Island legislature established a special court where recalcitrant creditors and even those who spoke disparagingly of the state's circulating medium were tried without the benefit of a jury. Persons convicted in this court were disfranchised and fined. Partiality to debtors was carried even to the point of permitting them to discharge their debts to creditors who were residents of other states simply by paying Rhode Island currency into the state treasury. Thereupon they received a certificate attesting that the obligation had been paid in full.

Yet, due to paper money, no forced sales of farm or personal property for arrears in taxes took place in Rhode Island, and the state debt was liquidated at about ten cents on the dollar. The grateful taxpayers, no longer burdened with public or, in many cases, private debt and relieved of taxes on real estate, congratulated themselves upon having wrought a financial miracle. Unfortunately, in the process, they had utterly destroyed the state's credit and made Rhode Island a byword throughout the Union for financial dishonesty—an example of knavery, iniquity, and democracy. In 1787, a New York newspaper published an article entitled: *The Quintessence of Villainy, or the proceedings of the legislature of the State of Rhode Island.*

The only serious challenge to the rule of the lower houses of the state legislatures came from the state senates in Massachusetts, Maryland, and Virginia and from the state judiciary in Rhode Island and several other states. In New Jersey, the governor was hanged in effigy for opposing an emission of paper money. Reflecting the creditor-minded electorate from which it drew its authority, the upper house of the Massachusetts General Court successfully withstood pressure for paper money and other "democratic" legislation. In Rhode Island, in the case of *Trevett* v. *Weeden* (John Weeden, a Newport butcher, refused to sell meat to John Trevett for paper money) the judges ruled unconstitutional the state law abolishing jury trials for those who refused to accept paper money. The Rhode Island assembly summoned the judges to appear at its bar to explain their decision, but, in December 1786, the most objectionable features of the law were repealed. Even so, the judges' triumph was short-lived; only one of the five judges who had rendered the decision was reëlected to the Superior Court. Manifestly, while some judges were prepared to act as guardians of the fundamental law, the doctrine of judicial review had not yet taken firm root.

While paper money did not depreciate everywhere—the notes issued by Pennsylvania and New York suffered comparatively little loss—it tended to follow the familiar pattern: lacking public confidence, it lost a third or more of its face value. With such a varied and fluctuating circulating medium, interstate business could not be carried on: The paper money of one state was heavily discounted in a neighboring state or, as in the case of Rhode Island, not accepted at all. New Jersey money had so little value in New York that commerce across the state line was effectually discouraged. In order to convert the currencies of the various states into pounds and shillings, Philip Schuyler of New York found it necessary to compile a small book. By 1788, Luther Martin of Maryland, while defending the intervention of the state legislatures "to prevent the wealthy creditor and the moneyed man from totally destroying the poor though industrious debtor," admitted that paper money and debtor-relief legislation in general had excited the disgust of "all the respectable part of America."

Moreover, the effect of these measures was to destroy confidence in contractual obligations and thereby to discourage loans and investments. When the state governments could, at their discretion, change the terms and conditions of contracts, prudent citizens kept their money at home. By attempting to redress economic and social inequities, the state governments forfeited all claim to be a stabilizing force in the economy. And without stability, propertied conservatives believed, economic recovery was impossible.

THE SOCIETY OF THE CINCINNATI

During the period of the Articles of Confederation, upholders of traditional ways were almost everywhere on the defensive. Although Americans enjoyed the freest society in the world, they were resolved to make it even freer. Except in New York, the feudal system of land tenure was replaced by fee-simple ownership. And in Virginia, primogeniture and entail—vestigial remnants of feudalism—were abolished in 1786 largely through the efforts of James Madison and Thomas Jefferson. In all the states religious freedom prevailed, although officeholders and, in some cases voters, were required to take an oath attesting their belief in Christianity.

The force of this trend toward social equality and freedom was evidenced by the popular reaction to the Society of the Cincinnati. American Army officers, irregularly paid during the war, were denied the half-pay for life they demanded as their due. Instead, they were given full pay for five years—in their eyes, a wholly inadequate commutation. As a result, some officers found themselves, in Washington's words, "reduced to their last shifts by the ungenerous Conduct of their Country." Resentful of this neglect, the officers organized the Society of the Cincinnati, the first American patriotic order, for the purpose of providing for widows and orphans of the members, perpetuating friendships formed during the war, and promoting and cherishing "between the respective States that union and National honor, so essentially necessary to their happiness and the future dignity of the American Empire."

Although the name "Cincinnatus" implied that as citizen-soldiers they would return to their plows, the officers did not let their fellow citizens forget that as the liberators of their country they were entitled to special honors and distinctions. Membership in the society was restricted to American officers and, on an honorary basis, to the foreign officers who had served with American forces during the war. Moreover, membership in the society was hereditary, descending from the father to the first-born son. Finally, the members were privileged to wear as a badge of honor the American gold eagle suspended by a blue-and-white ribbon.

Because it ran counter to the ideal of social equality and accorded special status to the officer class, the Society of the Cincinnati provoked a storm of opposition. Patriots like Sam Adams rang the changes against "an hereditary Military nobility," and Thomas Jefferson declared that the honorary distinctions of the kind created by the Society of the Cincinnati were contrary to the natural equality of man. An agitated clergyman exclaimed that the Cincinnati might prove to be "the Gog and Magog of the Apocalypse." Benjamin Franklin ridiculed the hereditary features of the organization; it would be more appropriate, he observed, to adopt the Chinese custom of having honor ascend to parents rather than descend to offspring. As for using the bald eagle as the insigne of the order, Franklin remarked that L'Enfant's design looked like a turkey. But even a true replica of the bald eagle would not have satisfied Poor Richard: That particular bird, he said, had "a bad moral Character . . . . Like those among Men who live by Sharping and Robbing, he is generally poor, and often very lousy." In Franklin's opinion, this unsavory creature was unfit to serve as the emblem of the United States.

Washington, the first president of the Cincinnati, was so dismayed by this chorus of disapproval that in 1784 he was prepared to recommend to the members that the society be dissolved. But at the general meeting, a compromise was adopted whereby the state branches were asked to eliminate the hereditary feature and the admission of honorary members, to place the charitable funds in the safekeeping of the state legislatures, to ask the members not to engage in political activities, and to consign the gold eagles to bureau drawers. This action served, said Jefferson, to "tranquillize the public mind." But not all the state branches adopted the recommendations of the general meeting, and the Cincinnati survived as an hereditary, but purely honorific, society, with membership passing from father to son to the latest posterity.

ORGANIZING THE WEST

Bereft as was the Continental Congress of cash, it was rich in land. In 1784, Virginia ceded its claims to the region north of the Ohio River to the general government, and most of the other states with western claims followed suit. As a result, the Continental Congress became the custodian of a national domain larger than the settled area of the original thirteen states. With such vast potential wealth at its command and with some of the states themselves holding title to millions of acres of vacant land, the national and state debts did not seem unmanageable. Given time, the Continental Congress and the states could satisfy their creditors by selling land to settlers and speculators.

If this feat were to be accomplished, the region had to be made attractive to settlers. In this respect, the Continental Congress inherited the problem that had confronted the British government during the colonial period. Like king and Parliament before it, Congress tried to stimulate emigration by holding out the prospect of cheap land, religious freedom, and civil liberty. At the same time, the importunities of its creditors obliged Congress to give high priority to the revenue-producing possibilities of its western lands. If the experience of Virginia and North Carolina provided any augury, Congress could ill afford to delay putting its lands on the market. The westward movement accelerated markedly after 1784. Settlers moving into the western parts of Virginia and North Carolina took possession under squatters' right and began to organize separatist governments in Kentucky and Franklin (the latter ultimately became Tennessee). Once the frontiersmen penetrated in large numbers the region north of the Ohio River, Congress might find its best lands preëmpted before they could be sold.

Virginia's cession of her claim to sovereignty over the old Northwest was made on condition that the states carved from this territory be admitted to the Union as the equals of the original thirteen states. In 1784, in compliance with this proviso, the Continental Congress adopted an ordinance drawn up by Thomas Jefferson providing for the eventual self-government of the national domain. According to Jefferson's plan, the region was to be carved into fourteen states; the settlers were to enjoy manhood suffrage and the right to establish a government upon application to Congress of five hundred adult males; and statehood could be attained after the population reached twenty thousand. Jefferson's plan was notable for its repudiation of all suggestion of colonial imperialism: it granted self-government to the inhabitants virtually from the beginning of settlement. Jefferson's original draft excluded slavery from the territory after 1800 but, because of southern opposition, this provision was deleted. In fact, Jefferson's plan, although adopted by Congress, was never put into operation and was superseded by the Ordinance of 1787.

Before its lands could be put upon the market, Congress was obliged to decide between two very different methods of settlement. New Englanders favored the township system of compact settlements with surveys prior to sales and specified areas set aside for schools and churches—the method by which New England's own westward movement had been effected. Southerners, on the other hand, advocated a more open and less orderly method which permitted locations prior to survey. The New England system was adapted to communal settlement (and to land companies), whereas the southern system was better suited to the needs of individual settlers.

In the Ordinance of 1785, Congress effected a compromise between the southern and New England methods, using each alternately when subdividing the territory. But Congress left no doubt that the national domain was to be used as a source of revenue rather than given away to poor but deserving citizens. The smallest amount of land that could be sold was a section of 640 acres, and the minimum price was set at one dollar an acre—a high price even though depreciated securities were accepted at face value in payment for land.

A land office was opened, but few purchasers appeared with cash or securities in hand. Congress turned perforce to the land companies that offered to buy blocs of millions of acres. So acute was its financial distress that Congress was prepared to alienate a large part of the national domain to a comparatively small number of speculators at an average price of about ten cents an acre.

It was primarily to facilitate the transfer of large areas of the region north of the Ohio to land companies that Congress adopted the Ordinance of 1787, the "Northwest Ordinance." Acting upon more exact knowledge of the area than Jefferson had possessed in 1784, Congress directed in the next ordinance that the region should be divided into not less than three nor more than five states. On the other hand it retained Jefferson's principle that the people of the territory were ultimately to enjoy complete equality with citizens of the original thirteen states. Although the initial stage of government was tutelary—federally appointed officials were in charge—the next or territorial stage was more democratic: the Ordinance of 1787 provided for an elected legislature, an appointed governor and council, and the right to appoint a nonvoting delegate to Congress. When a territory acquired a population of sixty thousand it became eligible for admission to the Union as a state—subject to the consent, however, of the existing states through the vote of their representatives in Congress.

In accord with the immediate objective of the Ordinance of 1787—to make the territory north of the Ohio attractive to settlers and thereby to encourage land companies to buy large tracts of land—newcomers were assured of the right to acquire land in fee simple and were guaranteed trial by jury and the right of habeas corpus—the first instance of a bill of rights promulgated by the general government. Equally important, slavery was excluded from the entire region—a provision which met with the approval of many southern congressmen who by 1787 had concluded that, if slavery were permitted, Virginia, Maryland, and North Carolina would be obliged to compete with a new tobacco-producing area.

As the Continental Congress had hoped, the Ordinance of 1787 resulted in the sale of large tracts to land companies. The Ohio Company, the Scioto Associates, and the Symmes Associates contracted to buy millions of acres of the national domain. In 1787-1788 Marietta and Cincinnati were founded, the first permanent settlements north of the Ohio. It was a promising beginning, and, because the land companies bought depreciated government securities in order to make their installment payments to the land office (this arrangement enabled them to buy some of the choicest real estate in the Northwest at about ten cents an acre), the price of government securities began to rise for the first time since the treaty of peace was signed.

And yet even disposing of the national domain at bargain prices did not bring the Continental Congress surcease from its financial difficulties. The land companies failed to meet the installments as they fell due: the Symmes Company paid nothing, and the Ohio Company made only an initial payment of $500,000 in depreciated certificates. In 1792, without having secured title to any land, the Scioto Associates failed; its only accomplishment consisted in having induced seven hundred French *émigres* to settle at Gallipolis, Ohio.

As the event proved, the Continental Congress was land poor. The states as well as the general government had millions of surplus acres on their hands at the same time that the Continental Congress and the land companies were trying to raise money by selling land. Pennsylvania alone put five million acres upon the market. And, equally shattering to the hope of making land pay the public debt, the region north of the Ohio, although nominally United States territory, was outside the effective control of the republic.

SECURING THE WEST

Having "organized" the West, the Continental Congress was confronted with the problem of securing the territorial boundaries claimed by the United States under the treaty of peace of 1783. On both the northern and southern frontiers, Americans were denied access by foreign governments and their Indian allies to territory over which the United States asserted sovereignty. In the North, the British and Indians barred the way to the advance of the American agricultural frontier. In the South and West, Spaniards and the tribes tributary to them contested the right of Americans to take up land in the territory lying between the Appalachians and the Mississippi and to use the rivers flowing into the Gulf of Mexico.

In addition to controlling the fur trade and the line of communication to the West afforded by the Great Lakes, the northwest posts gave the British a vantage point from which to influence the Indians and to intrigue, when occasion offered, with disaffected Americans. Even though the Indians were not abetted officially by the British government, agents of the Crown—many of whom were exiled Loyalists—attended Indian council fires and urged the tribesmen never to yield their land to the United States. Unauthorized but nonetheless effective pledges of British armed support were given the Indians; and the credulous tribesmen were supplied with guns, ammunition, and scalping knives by the Crown and by British traders operating in the Northwest.

Promises of aid and comfort were likewise extended to Vermonters and Kentuckians to induce them to secede from the Union. Every disaffected American was given to understand that he had a friend in the British government.

As long as the British retained possession of the northwest posts and the allegiance of the Indian tribes, American settlers ventured into the region north of the Ohio at their peril. The hostility of the Indians helped to aggravate the financial problems of the republic: after a party of settlers passing down the Ohio was massacred by the tribesmen, a noticeable drop in sales was observed at the land office. With an army of less than a thousand men and no money to spare for presents to the tribesmen, the United States appeared to be anything but a conquering power in the West.

On its southern frontier, the United States asserted title to the territory north of the 31st parallel lying between the Mississippi and the Atlantic. But Spain, resolved to keep Americans away from the Mississippi and Spanish Louisiana, tried to convert the region into an Indian buffer state. In consequence, the Creeks, Choctaws, and Cherokees, encouraged by Spanish officials and armed by British traders, succeeded in turning a large part of present-day Georgia, Kentucky, and Tennessee and virtually all of Mississippi and Alabama into a dark and bloody ground.

When the Continental Congress ratified the treaty of peace, it assumed that the United States had secured the right to navigate the Mississippi to its mouth. But the lower part of the river between Natchez and New Orleans ran through Spanish territory on both banks, and the Spanish government had never agreed to open the waterway to American traffic. In 1784, the Spaniards officially closed the river and seized American boats at Natchez. By a stroke of His Majesty's pen, Americans were excluded from the great artery of commerce upon which the growth of the American West depended.

The ordinary methods of diplomacy afforded the United States little hope of establishing its boundaries and opening the Mississippi to American flatboats. Few European governments recognized this loose aggregate of sovereign states as a great power. An American diplomat abroad usually found himself ranked with the minister from Sardinia. Nevertheless, despite its minuscule Army and total lack of a navy the American republic was a force to be reckoned with by European monarchs whose territories adjoined those of the United States. American frontiersmen, always prone to take the law into their own hands, constituted a serious and growing threat to the Spanish and, to a lesser degree, to the British position in North America. In 1785, aware of this danger, His Catholic Majesty instructed Don Diego de Gardoqui, the Spanish minister to the United States, to offer a commercial treaty admitting American fish, naval stores, and ship timbers on terms more favorable than those given any other nation, in exchange for a relinquishment for thirty years of the republic's claims to the use of the Mississippi. An ancillary clause required each signatory to guarantee the possessions of the other in the Western Hemisphere.

Secretary of Foreign Affairs John Jay, a New Yorker, welcomed Gardoqui's overtures for a commercial treaty certain to benefit the American fisheries and shipping interests. Moreover, Jay believed he saw in the Spanish monarch's action the first long-awaited crack in the walls of mercantilism: a commercial treaty with Spain might lead to the admission of American ships and products into the Spanish Empire.

To Jay's way of thinking, the proposed thirty years' abstention by Americans from the navigation of the Mississippi where it flowed through Spanish territory was almost as desirable as the commercial advantages he expected from the treaty. He believed that uncontrolled migration was filling the West with "white savages" who, he predicted, would prove "more formidable to us than the tawny ones which now inhabit it" and whose avidity for land would involve the United States in endless border wars. Jay advocated settlement by orderly, compact communities or, better still, by keeping Americans at home where they belonged.

Much of Jay's dread of "white savages" sprang from the fear, widespread among easterners, that the westward movement would deprive their section of its most valuable asset—people. The exodus that would presumably follow the opening of the Mississippi would deprive the eastern states of potential taxpayers, artisans, and farmers, depreciate the value of vacant lands, and make it impossible to carry on manufactures. For these reasons Rufus King of Massachusetts declared that "every Citizen of the Atlantic States, who emigrated to the westward of the Allegheny is a total loss to our confederacy."

Equally important, it was apparent to northerners that the growth of the West was strengthening the position of the South in the confederacy. For the most part, Jay's "white savages" were southerners. Of the thousands of men and women seeking homes west of the Appalachians and south of the Ohio, the great majority came from the South; Virginia and North Carolina were the principal colonizing states of the Union. Northern migration was still moving slowly across New York or, as in the case of Connecticut, directed toward establishing an enclave in Pennsylvania. Not until the beginning of the nineteenth century did the human wave reach the Old Northwest.

Unlike most Virginians, George Washington did not regard the westward movement as an unmixed blessing. Washington fully shared Jay's fears of weakening the ligaments of union: cut off from communication by the Appalachian mountain barrier, the settlers, said Washington, would "become a distinct people from us, have different views, different interests and, instead of adding strength to the Union, may in case of a rupture with either of those powers (Spain and Great Britain), be a formidable and dangerous enemy."

To prevent the dismemberment of the Union, Washington helped organize the Potomac Company, chartered in 1785 by the states of Virginia and Maryland. This company raised £50,000 by selling its stock to private investors and to the states of Virginia and Maryland (Washington himself was given one hundred shares by vote of the Virginia lesiglature) for the purpose of linking the eastern seaboard with the West by improving the navigation of the rivers, especially the Potomac, and by constructing canals. With the Potomac

Company ready to begin operations, Washington favored a temporary renunciation by the United States of its claim to the navigation of the Mississippi. During this interval he expected to see the connection between the East and West solidified by commerce. "There is nothing which binds one country or one state to another but interest," he declared.

So high were his hopes that Washington told his friends in 1787 that the Potomac Company's stock would produce "the greatest returns of any speculation I know of in the world." Unhappily for those who took Washington's advice, the stock never paid a dividend. The engineering techniques of the times proved inadequate to the task. Although the canal itself was completed in 1802, the Potomac Company did not succeed in clearing the river channel. In the end, it proved easier to open the Mississippi to American traffic than to build an east-west all-water route over the Appalachians.

In 1785, unwilling to let negotiations for a treaty with Spain escape from its control, Congress instructed Jay to submit to its scrutiny every proposal made by Gardoqui. In the summer of 1786, the Secretary of Foreign Affairs asked Congress to repeal these instructions and to give him a free hand in negotiating with the Spanish minister. The conflict that ensued in Congress revealed how fragile was the sectional alliance by which the United States was constituted. Requiring immediate decision was the question whether a change in Jay's instructions required the approval of nine or seven states. Virginia and other states opposed to surrendering the navigation of the Mississippi insisted that the vote of nine states was required; Massachusetts and other "commercial" states took the position that seven states could free Jay's hands.

Voting as a unit, the five southern states opposed changing Jay's instructions, but seven northern states voted to authorize Jay to try to arrange a treaty with Gardoqui. The impasse produced talk of disunion: some northern congressmen despaired of ever making a commercial treaty against southern opposition, whereas southerners declared that their vital interests would never be safe under the rule of a northern majority. James Monroe urged his fellow Virginians to make sure that if a southern confederacy were created Pennsylvania would be included even at the risk of fighting to keep it out of northerners' hands. "It were as well to use force to prevent it," he said, "as to defend ourselves afterward."

Even James Madison, who had hitherto advised southerners to sacrifice their agricultural interests to the imperative commercial needs of the Union, denounced the proposed Jay-Gardoqui negotiations as "a voluntary barter of the rights of one part of the empire to the interests of another part." Madison argued that nature had clearly ordained that Americans should navigate the Mississippi and stay out of the "labyrinth of European politics." Patrick Henry took the position that "the South" and "the southern people" must unite against the North. Once an advocate of a stronger central government, Henry now became an ardent southern nationalist: He would, he said, "rather part with the Confederation than relinquish the navigation of the Mississippi and thereby check the growth of the West," the region which, he said, "must principally support the Glory of America in future Times."

Despite its minority status, the South succeeded in preventing John Jay from entering into formal negotiations with Gardoqui. The Spanish government thereupon tried a new tack: in 1787 American flatboats were permitted to descend the Mississippi below Natchez upon payment of a duty. In the following year, His Catholic Majesty offered Americans a large land grant as a reward for settling in Spanish Louisiana or Florida. As an American remarked, the Goths were being invited within the gates.

THE NECESSITY OF A STRONGER UNION

The abortive Jay-Gardoqui negotiations, by revealing the depth of sectional animosity in the United States, served notice upon the advocates of a stronger central government that time was running out. And, indeed, the trend of events in 1786-1787 conspired to reinforce this conviction.

Although the Articles of Confederation professed to establish "a perpetual union," the American confederacy seemed in 1786 to be going the way of the Amphictyonic and other leagues of antiquity upon which James Madison, a scholar in politics, was doing research in the hope of discovering the causes of the decline and fall of confederacies. In 1784, Alexander Hamilton's brother-in-law wrote from England to inquire what had become of the Continental Congress, so completely had it disappeared from view. And, indeed, some states seemed to have forgotten the existence of the general government: Georgia sent no delegates for over a year and paid so little heed to congressional recommendations that it was proposed the errant state be expelled from the Union. Despite important business that demanded attention—western lands, treaties, payment of the debt, and settlement of the public accounts—Congress was unable to produce a quorum for months at a time. During the winter of 1786-1787 only four to six states were represented. Among the absent states was New York, despite the fact that the Continental Congress was meeting in New York City.

Although contemporaries had no way of knowing it, the worst of the economic crisis was over by 1786. The demand for paper money—a reliable indicator of the economic state of the nation—reached its peak in most states in 1785-1786. Except in Rhode Island, commerce began to revive and the export of staples remained constant. But improvement was far from spectacular, and even those who were aware of it could not be sure that the upturn would continue.

In any event, the economic recovery was not reflected by any betterment in the condition of the general government. The Continental Congress suffered from a debility seemingly beyond cure by improvement in the national economy; indeed, the political crisis intensified as the country slowly struggled out of the trough of depression. While the resources of the country were more than sufficient for its needs, neither the states nor the Continental Congress could call them forth. The nation needed leadership, but it was far from clear how this vital element of government could find expression within the framework of the Articles of Confederation.

The financial crisis reached its climax in the spring of 1787, when interest payments on the Dutch loan fell due. The Dutch bankers warned Adams and Jefferson that, unless payment was forthcoming, the United States government would be declared bankrupt and all prospect of future loans would be foreclosed. Early in 1787, both ministers hurried to Holland, where Adams, without waiting for authorization from Congress, floated a last-minute loan from the Dutch that permitted the United States to meet the interest charges on its existing debts.

Although Jefferson and Adams thus staved off bankruptcy for two more years, they knew that spoon-feeding by Dutch bankers was no way to sustain a government. Borrowing to pay interest due, while providing temporary relief, inevitably increased the principal of the debt. The day of reckoning was fast approaching: payments on the principal of the debt to France were scheduled to begin in 1788, and the Dutch bankers refused to extend their period of grace beyond 1793. Clearly, something more than improvisations was required of American statesmen.

By 1786, although some states had imposed qualifications, every state but one had ratified the impost. The sole holdout was New York, even Rhode Island having reluctantly agreed to give Congress permission to impose custom duties. One of the first to approve in 1781-1782, New York had subsequently turned its back upon its earlier nationalism. New Yorkers found that their own tariff duties took the burden of taxation off land and placed it upon commerce. Governor George Clinton, the champion of the plain people of the state, held the impost to be an unconstitutional encroachment upon the rights of the states. In 1786, at his instigation, the New York legislature effectively killed the impost by imposing conditions which it knew were unacceptable to Congress.

As for the amendment giving the Continental Congress control over commerce, it was languishing in the state legislatures, the graveyard of every effort to reform the Articles of Confederation. By 1786, eleven states had approved the proposal, but the outlook in the two remaining states was bleak. Thus, after five years of effort, not a single change recommended by Congress in the Articles of Confederation had gone into effect. It was a triumph of minority rule. Americans were living under a frame of government that could not reform itself no matter how imperative the need for change. On the other hand, the dimensions of liberty—conceived of in terms of states' rights—were steadily being enlarged at the expense of the general government.

In 1786, recognizing its own impotence, Congress considered issuing an appeal to the states in which the Union was declared to be on the verge of dissolution, the commerce of the United States ruined almost beyond repair, and the finances of the country in hopeless disarray. Heart-rending as was this report on the state of the Union, Congress reluctantly decided to lay it aside. After all, the states had heard it before and had not been visibly affected —at least not to the extent of coming to the aid of the general government. Besides, it was certain to be greeted at the Court of St. James as the last shriek of the expiring Continental Congress.

In this crisis, counsels of despair did not prevail. In 1786, James Madison proposed to the Virginia House of Burgesses through his friend John Tyler that the states be invited to appoint delegates to a convention for the purpose of devising a uniform system of commercial regulations for the Union. As a meeting place, Madison suggested Annapolis, Maryland, the principal merit of which was its remoteness from "the marts of trade" and the residence of the Continental Congress. By making the convention appear to be the work of the Virginia and Maryland planters, sympathetic toward the plight of northern merchants, Madison hoped to ease the sectional crisis that had reached such alarming proportions as a result of Spain's overtures for a commercial treaty.

Although Virginia and five other states sent delegates to the Annapolis Convention, none of the New England states—the region which stood to benefit most from strengthening Congress's control over commerce—was in attendance. Only twelve delegates appeared at Annapolis in September 1786—too few to do anything about commerce or, indeed, any other matter of national concern.

The delegates might have announced their failure and have gone home to let events take their course. But the bolder spirits, led by Alexander Hamilton, audaciously tried to snatch victory from defeat by converting the Annapolis Convention into a stepping stone to a constitutional convention. The delegates responded to this challenge by calling for another convention empowered to consider commerce and to propose such changes "as shall appear . . . necessary to render the Constitution of the Federal Government adequate to the exigencies of the Union." Ostensibly, the agenda of the proposed meeting was to be confined to revising the Articles of Confederation along the lines already recommended to the states. But Hamilton and Madison were already maturing plans that envisaged the subversion, not the reform, of the Articles of Confederation and the existing government of the United States.

4. "A LITTLE REBELLION" AND ITS CONSEQUENCES

SHAYS' REBELLION

John Adams' success in securing a loan in Holland was the more remarkable because in the winter of 1786-1787 the United States exhibited to the world the spectacle of a country in the throes of civil war. At the very time that Adams was negotiating with the Dutch bankers, George Washington was lamenting "the humiliating and contemptible figure we are about to make in the annals of mankind."

As a result of its exertions in the War of Independence, Massachusetts had incurred the largest debt (about $15 million) of any state in the Union. Instead of taking the easy way of inflating the currency, the Massachusetts legislature decided to pay this debt in full, including interest, in specie. Moreover, in 1786 the state took upon itself the burden of paying the interest on the continental certificates owned by its citizens.

The tax system adopted by the state meant that the weight of taxation fell upon those least able to bear it. About 40 percent of the state's revenue came from a poll tax which, by its very nature, discriminated against the poor with large families. While the poll tax, like other taxes, was made payable in specie, the state ignored the fact that most people received very little income in specie. Taxpayers were simply told to pay or suffer the consequences —which meant that they were haled into court, where the machinery of law, with rare efficiency, separated them from their property.

Defaulting debtors might put their property up for public auction, the

---

"Farmers Attacking Officials at the Springfield Arsenal under Daniel Shays' Leadership in 1786," detail from a drawing in Scribner's Popular History of the U.S., 1897, photo from The New York Public Library.

Massachusetts Half Cent, 1787.

proceeds going to their creditors. If, however, the sum realized from this forced sale was insufficient to cover their debts, they were liable, at the discretion of their creditor, to be sentenced to serve a term in jail, there to reflect upon their financial sins. Thus was the punishment made to fit the crime.

Massachusetts, which had furnished more men for the armed forces during the War of Independence than any other state, also produced a particularly militant breed of debtor-farmers, many of whom were veterans of the Continental Line or the state militia. Officers and men, having sold at a fraction of their face value the certificates they had received in lieu of pay, now discovered that they were heavily taxed in order that the state might pay off at face value with accrued interest these same certificates, now held by speculators and investors, among them Harvard College.

For many marginal farmers in western Massachusetts, staying out of the courts—and out of jail—presented a major problem. The interest rate on mortgages ran at 25-40 percent, and the tax bill alone of some farmers exceeded the family's cash income. In 1786, a tax bill of $1,500,000 was presented to the people of Massachusetts, a sum estimated to be one-third the value of all the real estate in the state. Under such circumstances, even vaunted New England thrift could not make both ends meet.

Since the law seemed wholly on the side of creditors, western farmers began to take matters into their own hands. As early as 1782 a flurry of rebellion swept Worcester county, at that time regarded as "the West." Samuel Ely, a Yale graduate, unfrocked clergyman, and revolutionary war veteran, at the head of a large number of irate farmers, forcibly closed the Northampton court that was hearing cases involving debt and, more often than not, rendering judgment in favor of creditors. Ely denounced the Massachusetts Constitution as a fraud perpetrated by the rich upon the poor; he had in his pocket, he declared, a constitution so perfect in every particular that the Angel Gabriel himself could not find fault with it. Ely was promptly arrested for sedition. His followers forcibly released him from jail and he escaped to Vermont, the refuge of malcontents and debtors.

But these forceful methods of repressing demonstrations against authority did not allay discontent. Conventions summoned upon the authority of "the people" demanded the transfer of the seat of government from Boston to Springfield, the abolition of the Massachusetts Senate, tender acts, the suspension of legal proceedings against debtors, and the printing of paper money. With the exception of a tender act adopted in 1786, none of these demands was met by the government, largely because the Senate was solidly arrayed against all forms of debtor-relief legislation.

In the meantime, the transfer of property from debtors to creditors proceeded at an accelerated pace: in 1785-1786, over 4000 suits involving debt were instituted in the courts of Worcester county alone. In desperation, armed farmers closed the courts of justice; during the last five months of 1786, civil courts ceased to function in the three western counties of the Bay State.

Daniel Shays, a former Army officer, helped to convert civil disobedience into a full-scale insurrection. In January 1787, over a thousand farmers took down their muskets and prepared to attack the United States Armory at Springfield. Congress was helpless: in November 1786, it had requisitioned 2000 troops from the states, ostensibly for protection against the Indians, but the states were so slow in responding that the armory was left defenseless. Compelled to rely upon its own resources, the state of Massachusetts, aided by contributions from well-to-do citizens, drafted enough men from the militia to put the rebels to rout. After a brief cannonade in which four insurgents were killed, the rebel army melted away. Shays and his lieutenants did not stop until they had reached sanctuary in New York.

Even though, as Fisher Ames of Massachusetts said, the western farmers were "turning against their teachers the doctrines which were inculcated in order to effect the late revolution," the leaders of that Revolution wholly dissociated themselves from the movement. Unlike the American Revolution, Shays' Rebellion had no support from the aristocracy. Sam Adams, the implacable enemy of British tyranny, declared in 1786-1787 that "there is a Decency and respect due to Constitutional Authority, and those Men who under any Pretence or by any Means whatsoever, would lessen the Weight of Government lawfully exercised, must be Enemies to our happy Revolution and the Common Liberty."

Despite its tame ending, Shays' Rebellion had an important bearing upon the course of political events and upon the thinking of the men who were soon to guide those events. For Shays and his men were not alone: by 1786, in several other states where conservatives had succeeded in frustrating attempts to enact debtor-relief legislation, popular discontent had assumed menacing shape. In Maryland, for example, where the Senate had prevented the issuance of paper money, armed attacks upon creditors and tax collectors had occurred. In New Hampshire, a band of armed men descended upon the legislature and threatened to force it to remain in session until it had passed a paper money law. Although the legislature had been rescued by a force of militia and armed citizens, the incident demonstrated that Americans were becoming increasingly prone to use force to redress their grievances when constitutional methods failed. James Wilson, a member of the Constitutional Convention, said that in 1787 "the flames of internal insurrection were ready to burst out in every quarter. . . . From one end to the other of the continent, we walked on ashes, concealing fire beneath our feet."

Alarmed conservatives began to fear that American villages harbored more aspiring Caesars and Cromwells than unknown and unsung Miltons and Shakespeares. True, as Alexander Hamilton said, Shays was no Caesar, but it was a melancholy commentary upon the state of the union that it had been saved by the incompetence of the leader of the rebellion.

To John Marshall and other upholders of law and order, the most disconcerting thing about Shays' Rebellion was that it had occurred in a state "inferior in wisdom and virtue to none in the union." Massachusetts' constitution, thanks to John Adams, its principal architect, incorporated the principles of the division of powers and checks and balances. Moreover, it had been ratified by a popular plebiscite—the only state whose constitution had been submitted to the people for their approval. Most surprising of all, after their defeat in the field, the Shaysites succeeded in achieving most of their demands at the ballot box. In the spring of 1787, Governor Bowdoin, the hero of the conservatives, lost his office to John Hancock, a popular leader who, in the opinion of his opponents, owed his political influence to his willingness to cater to popular follies.

THE FEDERALIST STATE OF MIND

Early in 1787, spurred by the events in Massachusetts, the Continental Congress approved the convention summoned by the abortive meeting held at Annapolis. But by this time, piecemeal reform of the Articles of Confederation was no longer acceptable to American leaders. Having engaged in fruitless efforts to enlarge the powers of the Continental Congress, they now raised their sights to a higher objective—the creation of a wholly new government. Such a radical change of purpose implied a revolution in the thinking of influential Americans. In fact, the Federalist state of mind antedated the drafting of the Federal Constitution and the organization of the Federalist party.

The shots heard at Springfield were still reverberating in the ears of the American statesmen who assembled in Philadelphia in May 1787 to write a new constitution for the United States. No event of the Confederation period had revealed more glaringly the impotence of the Continental Congress and the imperfection of human nature even among these new men, the Americans. Washington, who ever since he resigned his post as commander-in-chief in 1783, had been urging his fellow countrymen to concentrate more power in general government, now declared that such a government was urgently needed to "chastize vice and reward virtue." "Let the reins of government be braced and held with a steady hand," he said; "we are far gone in every thing ignoble and bad."

A government empowered to chastise vice would, Washington was now persuaded, find numerous objects for its attention in the United States. Taking a second look at "the boasted virtue of America," Washington was inclined to believe that the framers "probably had too good an opinion of human nature as we find it: perfection falls not to the lot of mortals." It would not do, he said, to base a government upon the idea that Americans were the most moral, law-abiding, and rational people on earth; the new reading of the American character indicated that they were self-seeking, actuated by "a rage for property," sadly deficient in public spirit, prone to work injustice, and apt to become so engrossed in the pursuit of individual happiness as to totally neglect public happiness and national honor.

Human nature being what it was, Washington believed that its shortcomings must be compensated for by a centralized, efficient, and coercive government. It could no longer be supposed that a republican government automatically produced virtuous citizens; rather, human nature itself stood revealed as a constant to which all governments, including those of a republican cast, must conform. Nothing could be more fatal than to erect a government upon platitudes and wishful thinking.

The men who were called upon to save the country from the consequences of what they now regarded as a misplaced faith in human nature and decentralized government realized that the winning of freedom was no more than the prelude to the wise use of it. As they visualized it, the Constitutional Convention was a last effort to save the country by the exercise of reason from "ungoverned passion," "popular tyranny," and "the turbulence and follies of democracy." These men were inclined to regard the revolutionary period as an Age of Innocence when solutions to every problem had seemed deceptively simple and when men had supposed that the paramount purpose of government was to guarantee every individual the maximum of freedom. From the perspective afforded by the events of 1783-1787, it seemed that there had been altogether too much emphasis upon the word "liberty." The framers of the Articles of Confederation, observed John Jay, loved to talk about the rights of man but said hardly a word about their duties.

In the minds of these spokesmen of the conservatism of 1787, direct democracy was identified with fraud, repudiation of debts, and armed attempts at social revolution. Theodore Sedgwick, later one of the leading New England Federalists, defined this kind of democracy as "a war against virtue, talents and property carried on by the dregs and the scum of mankind." Government by majority, as exemplified in the state legislatures, seemed to place all rights, especially property rights, at the mercy of popular caprice. The real danger was seen to be not that the people would be oppressed but that the people themselves would become oppressors; there was more to fear, it was said, "from the licentiousness of the people than from the bad government of rulers." Had the Declaration of Independence been rewritten in 1787, the phrase "life, liberty, and the pursuit of happiness" would undoubtedly have included the word "property"—if only to remove any doubts that its protection was one of the cardinal duties of government.

But it did not follow that human nature was wholly evil or that liberty would inevitably degenerate into licentiousness. One of the basic defects in the existing system, as these men saw it, was that the Articles of Confederation, by stifling nationalism and fostering state loyalty, put a premium upon narrow, illiberal, and selfish conduct. Because they exalted the principle of state sovereignty, the Articles of Confederation had created, it was supposed, an insuperable obstacle to the development of a national spirit, the security of property, and the success of the republican experiment itself. As General Henry Knox said: "The vile state governments are sources of pollution which will contaminate the American name for ages. . . . Smite them, in the name of God and the people." It followed that the first step toward the rehabilitation of the American character must be the establishment of a central government capable of enlisting the loyalty, affection, and self-interest of the majority of the people.

In addition to love of country that transcended state boundaries, the nationalism that actuated Washington, Madison, and many others was compounded of a sense of frustration produced by the failure of a supine and palsied general government to achieve the goals set during the Revolution, the inability of the republic to throw off the commercial and financial trammels of colonialism, and a deep-seated resentment against Great Britain. Of the forces working for the creation of a more efficient central government, the conviction that all the troubles experienced by the republic could be traced to British machinations against the United States was, to the people at large, one of the most compelling. By 1787, a "conspiracy theory" had gained wide currency. Great Britain was held responsible for Indian forays against the American frontier, for the depredations of the Barbary corsairs, for the high prices paid by Americans for manufactured goods, for the unfavorable balance of trade, and for the low esteem in which the United States was held abroad. When the United States failed to negotiate treaties with Portugal and Denmark, cries of indignation against "British influence" were raised. Everything, in short, was made to point to a British plot to destroy the rising glory of the United States and to bring Americans under the rule of King and Parliament. Thus George III, the "tyrant" whose crimes against liberty had driven his subjects to rebellion, served the cause of Americans who sought to give cohesion to the American Union.

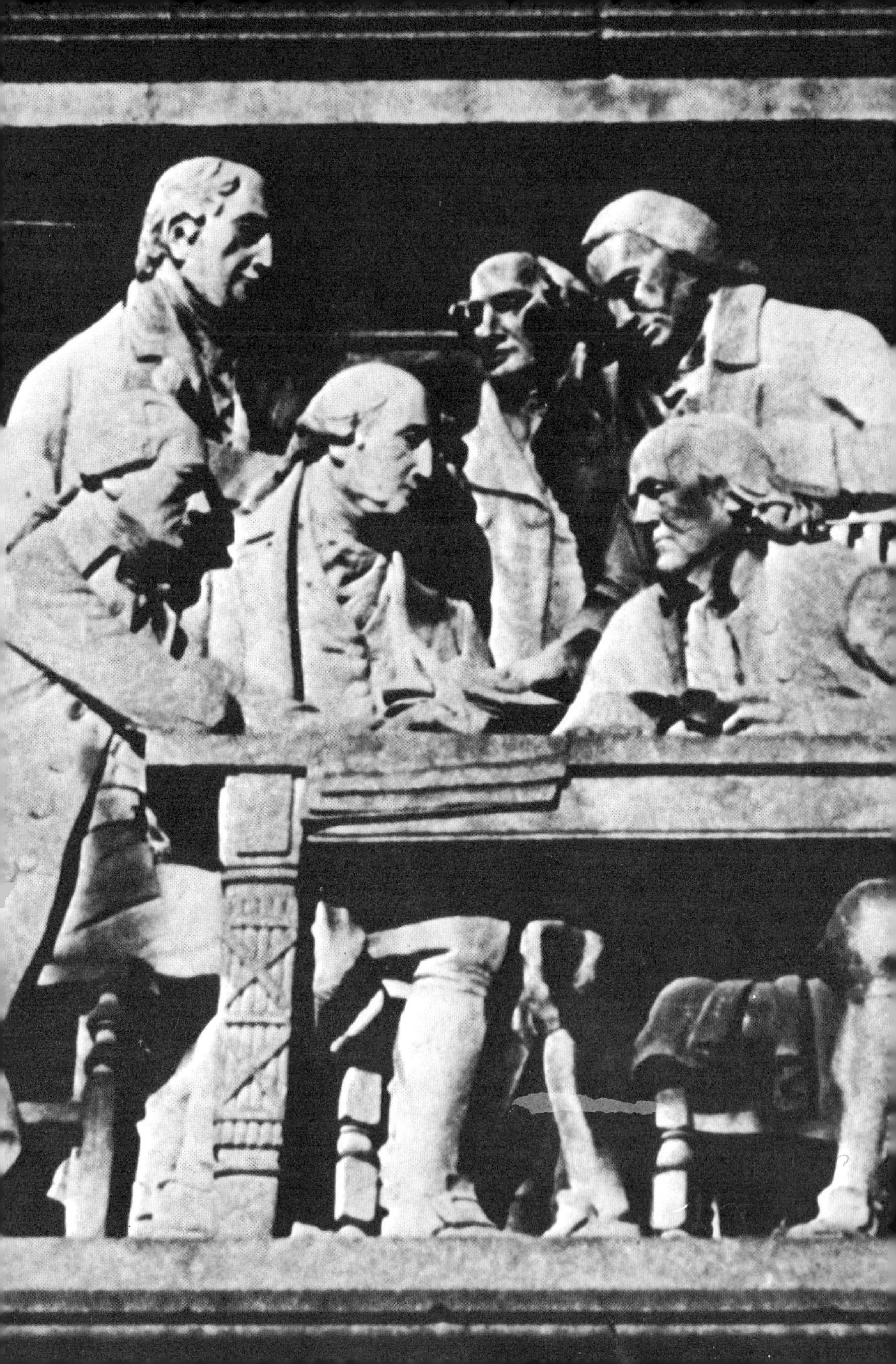

5.
THE CONSTITUTIONAL CONVENTION

John Adams called the members of the Constitutional Convention "heroes, sages and demigods." More prosaically, Washington described them as "the leading characters of the Continent." Each state sent its first citizens to Philadelphia in 1787: the Virginia delegation, for example, consisted of the governor of the state, the chancellor, James Madison, and George Washington. Benjamin Franklin compared the Constitutional Convention to the French Assembly of Notables which met in Paris in May 1787, but the American "Notables" were far more experienced in public affairs than were their French counterparts: the roster included signers of the Declaration of Independence, state governors, judges, lawyers, merchants, army officers, planters, and past or present members of the Continental Congress. It was not a cross section of the American people, for no delegate could be described as a yeoman farmer. Richard Henry Lee of Virginia later deplored "how disproportionately the democratic and aristocratic parts of the community were represented."

Nor did the sections enjoy equal representation. The cities and plantations were overrepresented at the expense of the West; not a single spokesman of the western back-country sat in the Convention. It was said that Charleston and the surrounding lowland parishes were represented at Philadelphia but that South Carolina was not.

Although the Continental Congress and several of the states had limited the agenda of the Constitutional Convention to the amending of the Articles, Patrick Henry alleged he "smelled a rat" and refused to serve as a delegate. Rhode Island, too, declined to participate, but its absence was not regretted

---

"Drafting the Constitution," detail from a frieze by Lee Laurie at the Nebraska State Capitol Building, photo courtesy of the Nebraska Game Commission.

Nova Eborac, 1787.

by Madison and others who regarded that state as a sink of "wickedness and folly." In actuality, not more than eleven states were represented in Philadelphia at any one time. The New Hampshire delegates were late in arriving, and when they finally did appear two of the New York delegates had already left, leaving that state without a vote.

The presence of George Washington as president of the Convention did much to allay apprehensions of the kind expressed by Patrick Henry. Many Americans felt that as long as Washington was there nothing could go really wrong. But Washington had accepted election to the Convention with deep misgivings: "having happily assisted in bringing the Ship into Port, and having been fairly discharged," he said, "it is not my business to embark again on a sea of troubles." He much preferred to take a long shore leave at Mount Vernon while others took over the helm. But Madison and Hamilton persuaded Washington that his presence in Philadelphia was indispensable. Apparently, saving the republic was a full-time occupation for an American Hero.

Since most of the delegates came from the stratum of American society most adversely affected by the absence of a central government capable of disciplining the states and upholding American rights abroad, they were almost unanimous in believing that a strong central government was essential. Yet as political realists aware of the limited possibilities open to them, they did not seek a short cut to Utopia. They aimed at creating "a more perfect union," not a perfect union. Had they been perfectionists, they might have produced an ideal frame of government, but the states probably would have rejected it. As John Dickinson, the delegate from Pennsylvania, told the Convention: "Experience must be our only guide. Reason may mislead us."

Distrustful of pure reason, the delegates were equally averse to making the American people privy to the deliberations in Philadelphia. The Convention worked in absolute secrecy: sentries were stationed at the door of the Pennsylvania State House, the Convention's meeting place, and the members were forbidden to divulge its proceedings to their friends or constituents. Clearly, the Constitution was not intended to be a covenant openly arrived at.

THE VIRGINIA AND NEW JERSEY PLANS

From the opening day of the Convention, the ultra nationalists, although they controlled only two state delegations, took charge of the proceedings. On May 30, 1787, Edmund Randolph of Virginia formally submitted the "Virginia Plan." This sketch of a frame of government embodied the thinking of James Madison upon the problems of government and of union.

Randolph and Madison made no pretense of staying within the boundaries of permissible change laid down by the Continental Congress: they dismissed the Articles of Confederation as wholly inadequate to the exigencies confronting the country. Randolph made clear that he came to bury the Articles, not to praise them. In their place he proposed a national government invested with sweeping powers directly bearing upon the people. This government was divided into three branches—a system already followed in the state governments—but its innovative features lay in the fact that the legislative branch was constituted according to the numbers of people rather than upon the principle of state equality, and that the national government was to exercise plenary powers in taxation and other functions and was to have a negative upon all state laws. Virtually no restraints were placed upon the powers of the national government. Like the British Parliament, it could bind the lesser jurisdictions in all cases whatsoever.

After Randolph sat down, a delegate inquired if he intended to abolish the states altogether. Randolph assured the Convention that the states would be preserved, but he indicated that he preferred "a strong, consolidated Union in which the Idea of States should be nearly annihilated." Madison thought that they might be useful if reduced to the status of the existing counties within the states. In a long, brilliantly argued speech, Alexander Hamilton went beyond even the Virginia Plan in calling for a concentration of power and the reduction of the states to the status of administrative districts of the central government. He dismissed the Virginia Plan as a cut from the same slice of pork from which the Articles of Confederation had been manufactured; the fact that there was "a little change of the sauce" did not make the Virginia Plan any more palatable. He made clear that his dish was the British Constitution, with a president and senate elected for life. It was observed by a delegate that, while everyone acclaimed Hamilton's bold and vigorous exposition, none believed that his plan could be put into effect. On his first appearance upon the national political stage, Hamilton, the great "realist" of American history, appeared to be an impractical theorist.

Yet few delegates disapproved of Hamilton's strictures upon democracy. Hamilton himself observed that "the members most tenacious of republicanism . . . were as loud as any in declaiming against the vices of democracy." But it was not the ultra nationalists who gave fullest voice to their distrust of the people. This was reserved for men who, like John Sherman of Connecticut, Elbridge Gerry of Massachusetts, and Charles Pinckney of South Carolina, advocated the election of members of the House of Representatives by the state legislatures. Pinckney even wished to apportion representation in Congress according to wealth. With few exceptions, the champions of a highly centralized government were prepared to admit a larger measure of democracy into the system than those who felt that sovereignty must be retained by the states.

By far the most vehement opposition to the Virginia Plan came, however, from the small states. Because it provided for proportional representation in both Senate and House of Representatives, the Virginia Plan insured that the most populous states would dominate the national government. Under this method of apportioning representation, Virginia, Massachusetts, and Pennsylvania would control half the votes of the Senate. And, since the president was to be chosen by the national legislature, the chief executive would be in fact the nominee of the large states. With good reason, the Randolph-Madison plan was called the Large State Plan.

Upon one point the delegates from the small states were adamant—they would not surrender the principle of one state, one vote. Speaking for the small states, William Paterson of New Jersey rejected the Large State Plan *in toto* and introduced in its stead the Small State or New Jersey Plan as the basis of discussion. Essentially, the New Jersey Plan was an amendment of the Articles of Confederation—and therefore conformed more closely than did the Virginia Plan to the expectations of the American people. While state equality in the Continental Congress was to be preserved, the general government was to be permitted to levy an import tax, regulate commerce, and establish a system of federal courts.

The introduction of the New Jersey Plan signalized the end of the harmony that had hitherto prevailed in the Convention. For two weeks in June 1787, the meeting was "on the verge of dissolution, scarce held together by the strength of a hair" at the very time that the newspapers were reporting that unanimity prevailed. Rather than accept proportional representation, the delegate from Delaware declared that the small states would cast their lot with a foreign power. On the other hand, the representatives of the large states asserted that if forced to accept state equality they would walk out of the meeting. Benjamin Franklin reminded his fellow delegates that they were sent to consult, not to contest, with each other. He recommended calling in a clergyman for prayers, but Alexander Hamilton objected that if a minister were seen entering the Philadelphia State House it would give rise to rumors that the delegates were so hopelessly at odds that they were obliged to call in outside—or, as one delegate reported it—"foreign" aid.

At this point, Washington lamented that he had ever exchanged the peace and quiet of Mount Vernon for "the dark and thorny paths of politics." And yet, bitter as the dispute was, it did not mean that the delegates had forsaken the objective of creating a strong, coercive national government. Both the New Jersey and Virginia Plans recognized the necessity of a stronger central government; the New Jersey Plan disagreed mainly as to whether this strength should be exercised by the states equally or by population, and it was put forward largely for bargaining purposes. From the outset, Paterson and other delegates from the small states were prepared to compromise with the large states upon terms that left the powers of the national government intact. All that the small states really demanded was equality in the Senate; once this was conceded, the large states could have proportional representation in the other house. The impasse that developed in the Convention in June-July 1787 resulted primarily from the refusal of James Madison and other delegates from the large states to compromise.

Admittedly, the cause of democracy would have been better served by proportional representation than by state equality. But democracy was not at issue in this dispute: Madison's objective was to redress the "wrong" of 1777 whereby the small states had extorted equality in the Continental Congress from the large states. Furthermore, the Jay-Gardoqui *contretemps* had demonstrated that state equality worked in favor of the North. Finally, the New Jersey Plan was unacceptable to Madison and other nationalists because it gave the states a foothold within the citadel of the central government where, presumably, they would work unremittingly to undermine its authority.

But the intransigence of the small states compelled the large states to agree to the appointment of a committee consisting of one member from each state to break the deadlock. On July 5, 1787, the report of the committee was presented to Congress. It recommended the adoption of an arrangement originally proposed early in June by the Connecticut delegation and actively supported by Benjamin Franklin. The "Great Compromise," sometimes called the "Connecticut Compromise," established the principle of state equality in the Senate and proportional representation in the House of Representatives. By a vote of five states to four, this settlement was adopted on July 16. Only because the Massachusetts delegation was evenly divided and therefore unable to vote did the compromise carry. Three states were absent and not voting.

The narrow margin by which the Great Compromise was adopted meant that it might be nullified by a later vote. Madison worked toward that end: in his opinion, if the compromise stood, much of the good he expected from the Constitution would be destroyed. And yet, in the course of its labors, the Convention made it easier for the large states to accept the settlement of July 16. Senators were permitted to vote individually rather than as ambassadors commissioned to register the will of sovereign states, as had been the case in the Continental Congress. Their six-year term made them less dependent upon the states than when they were elected annually and subject to instant recall. Finally, as a concession to the large states, it was provided that revenue bills must originate in the House of Representatives.

By virtue of the Great Compromise, the states were made an essential part of the system of government devised by the Philadelphia Convention. As John Marshall said, the states could put an end to the federal government simply by refusing to act: "They have only not to elect senators, and it expires without a struggle." Moreover, state equality in the Senate was written into the Constitution so indelibly that it could not be removed even by an amendment approved by three-fourths of the states. The Constitution requires that any amendment depriving a state, without its consent, of its equal vote in the Senate must receive the unanimous approval of the states.

Equality in the Senate proved far less important in divisions between large and small states than in divisions between the sections. As James Madison predicted during the debate over the New Jersey Plan, the course of American history would be determined by the rivalry of the sections rather than by a struggle for power between the small and large states. And, in truth, while the large states never tried to reduce the small states to vassalage, equality in the Senate became a vital factor in the preservation of the sectional balance of power. In this sense, the benefits of the Great Compromise to the South were inestimable. In 1860, for example, the state of New York, with a population of four million, sent two senators to Congress, whereas the fifteen southern states, with a population of eight million, had thirty senators in Washington.

While the Great Compromise saved the Convention from imminent dissolution, it did not resolve all the problems confronting the delegates. On the contrary, wisdom, forbearance, and what Washington called "accommodation and mutual concession" remained as imperative as before. The framing of the Constitution required many adjustments of jarring views.

One such adjustment resulted when it became evident that the opponents of the extreme centralization of power proposed by the Virginia Plan were in a majority in the Convention. The opposition focused upon the Virginia Plan's proposal for a veto by the national legislature upon all laws passed by the states. Despite Madison's assertion that, unless this power were given the national legislature, the government would be deprived of its gravitational pull and "the planets will fly from their orbits," on July 17 it was stricken from the plan of government. Responsibility for keeping the states in their place in the firmament was entrusted at least by implication to the federal judiciary.

Nor did the idea of a central government of unlimited powers withstand the pulling and hauling to which the Virginia Plan was subjected in the Convention. Late in the session, it was decided to create a government of enumerated powers, thereby making the general as well as the state governments subordinate to a written constitution that restricted the lawful exercise of authority.

But nothing after the adoption of the Great Compromise gave the delegates more trouble than the office of president—how he was to be elected, the duration of his term of office, and powers with which he was to be vested. These questions sorely taxed the skill, patience, and resourcefulness of the framers.

The Virginia Plan directed that the president be elected by the national legislature and should not be eligible for a second term. It was immediately objected that the president would be a "creature" of the legislature and therefore unable to play an independent part in the government. On no less than twenty different occasions, the method of electing the president was put to the vote, but the delegates always came back to election by the legislature as the least objectionable.

Nor did the Convention find it easier to fix the term of office and the powers of the president. At various times during the summer of 1787, his tenure of office was set at periods ranging from four to fifteen years. As long as it was agreed that the president should be appointed by the national legislature, a term of at least seven years was favored in order to lessen his dependence upon the legislature. In order to defend his authority against the encroachments of the legislative branch and to prevent the enactment of unwise legislation, he was given a veto upon its proceedings. But whether this veto should be absolute or qualified was left undecided. Hamilton and James Wilson advocated an absolute veto, but the majority of delegates favored a suspensive veto that could be overridden by Congress.

Unable to reconcile these divergent views, the Convention appointed a committee consisting of one member from each state—the same kind of committee that had worked out the Great Compromise—to rescue it from its dilemma. Again this method produced results: the committee's report, submitted on September 6, 1787, ten days before the Convention was to conclude its labors, was accepted by a majority of the states represented in the Convention. The regal powers assigned the president revealed that the committee had drawn explicitly upon the example afforded by the constitutional monarchy of Great Britain. Although the indirect method of electing the president and vice-president by means of an electoral college found a precedent in the constitution of Maryland, it appealed to the members because it avoided both direct election by the people and the even more objectionable alternative of entrusting the choice to the legislature. Hamilton went so far as to say that the electoral college system afforded "a moral certainty that the office of President will never fall to the lot of any man who is not in an eminent degree endowed with the requisite qualifications."

Despite Hamilton's panegyric, of which he was one of the first to repent, few of the framers believed that the electoral college system would really work. In the ordinary course of events, because each state could be expected to support a favorite son, it seemed improbable that any one individual would receive a majority of votes in the electoral college. Accordingly, the completed Constitution provided that, in case of failure in the electoral college, the election was to be transferred to the House of Representatives, where, at the insistence of the small states, each state was to have one vote.

Thus the small states seemed to have scored another victory. The electoral college, dominated by the large states, seemed likely to afford only a process for nominating candidates for the highest office in the land: the actual election would be made in the House of Representatives under the principle of state equality.

Efforts to create a more perfect union were certain to bring up the slavery question. Northern antislavery sentiment heightened differences in economics, labor, and social attitudes existing between the two sections. Though slavery was not yet the "peculiar institution" of the South, it tended to make that section conscious of its separate identity. At the Constitutional Convention, every member from the slave states insisted that slaves must be counted in the census and thereby be represented in any national government that might be established. During the period of the Articles of Confederation, three-fifths of the slaves had been included in determining the amount of revenue requisitioned from the states. Accordingly, the southern delegates in the Convention refused to settle for anything less: over weak northern opposition, the southern states wrote into the Constitution a provision requiring that three-fifths of the slaves be counted in apportioning representatives in Congress and votes in the electoral college. This stipulation was not the result of a compromise: the South simply stated its terms, and the North capitulated. Gouverneur Morris, who did not believe that black slaves were entitled to be counted in the census returns, said that because of southern intransigence on this issue he was "reduced to the dilemma of doing justice to the Southern States or to human nature, and must therefore do it to the former."

The three-fifths rule proved to be the greatest concession made by either section to secure the adoption of the Constitution. As a result of giving partial representation to the slaves, five free persons in a southern state were potentially equal to seven free persons in a nonslaveholding state. Without benefit of the three-fifths rule, Thomas Jefferson would not have been elected president of the United States in 1800. Finally, by inserting this clause in the Constitution, the framers gave slavery a vested interest in the government and thereby insured that it would become a potent source of political as well as moral discord between the two sections.

Negro slaves won no rights under the Constitution. Neither the word "slave" nor "bondservant" is used in the document; instead, the slaves are covered by the phrase "persons held to Service or Labor," which in 1787 included white indentured servants as well as black slaves. In order to placate southern slaveowners, the Constitution provided that escapees should be "delivered up on Claim of the Party to whom such Service or Labour may be due." As for free Negroes, they were left to take their chances with the several state governments; there was no mention of "race, color or condition of servitude" in the original Constitution.

Likewise, the South imposed its will upon the treaty-making process. Many northerners wished to permit treaties to be ratified by a majority of the Senate, but southerners insisted that a two-thirds majority be required. When James Wilson protested that in all governments the majority should govern, "it was replyed that the Navigation of the Mississippi after what had already happened in Congress was not to be risqued in the Hands of a meer Majority." Wilson withdrew his objection and said no more.

In their efforts to protect their position as the staple-producing and exporting region of the United States against the commercial interests of the northern states, southerners were at first equally successful. The northern states wished to write into the Constitution provisions permitting Congress to lay a tax upon exports and to enact a navigation system by mere majority vote. By acting as a unit, the southern states, with the aid of some northern votes, were able to insert an outright prohibition upon taxes on exports and to require a two-thirds majority of Congress for the enactment of navigation laws.

But at this point the South broke the united front to which it owed its success. When the Convention came to consider the slave trade, Virginia, which had a surplus of slaves, was willing to grant Congress power to stop the slave trade despite the contention of Georgia and South Carolina that they needed an unlimited supply of prime field hands. Charles Pinckney of South Carolina delivered an encomium upon slavery and the slave trade—he was almost the only speaker who spoke in their defense—in which he served notice that his state would not accept any plan of government that prohibited the slave trade. The South Carolinians and the Georgians threatened to go home, whereupon the Convention, as was now its settled practice, appointed a committee to find a way out of the impasse.

Having precipitated the crisis, it was fitting that South Carolina and Georgia should resolve it. These two states, resentful of Virginia's "treachery" (which Charles Pinckney attributed to the Tidewater planters' hope of selling their slaves at high prices to purchasers in the lower South), decided to pay back the Old Dominion in its own coin. A deal was arranged in the committee whereby South Carolina and Georgia agreed to vote in favor of empowering Congress to enact navigation laws by a mere majority in exchange for northern endorsement of a clause permitting the slave trade to remain open until 1808. It was the Virginians' turn to cry "treachery," but the bargain was consummated in spite of the Old Dominion. As a result, between 1789 and 1808, at least fifty thousand black Africans suffered the ordeal of the Middle Passage and a lifetime of slavery in order to make possible the more perfect union.[1]

RESULTS OF THE CONVENTION

Despite the conflict between sections and between the large and small states, the basic agreement that prevailed among the delegates was not seriously impaired. Vital as was the willingness of the members to adjust, moderate, and compromise differences of opinion, the drafting of the Constitution was made possible only because they resolutely pursued the all-absorbing objective of establishing an efficient central government capable of upholding the credit, dignity, and rights of the United States.

No one supposed that this transformation could be wrought without cost to the taxpayers. The finished Constitution left no doubt on that score: in place of a government with no powers of taxation whatever, the proposed Constitution authorized the federal government to levy, at its discretion, every kind of tax except the income tax. Even the poll tax was included, although the federal government has never seen fit to tap this particular source of revenue.

One cardinal objective the framers never lost sight of—to clip the wings of the sovereign states and thereby prevent them from playing fast and loose with the rights of property. Accordingly, the states were forbidden by the Constitution to make paper money legal tender, to impair the validity of contracts (including mortgages), and to pass *ex post facto* laws. Here the founding fathers were concerned not only with erecting safeguards around personalty—public securities, mortgages, ships, etc.—but with protecting property in general. Although the state legislatures had not confiscated landed property, except in the case of the Loyalists, they had convinced apprehensive property owners that with popular majorities nothing was sacred. In this sense, the

---

[1]The slave trade was illegal by state law in all states except Georgia and South Carolina. South Carolina closed the trade but reopened it in 1804.

Constitution represented a reaffirmation of one of the cardinal principles of the American Revolution. As in 1776, the rights of property were not distinguished from the other rights of man. The framers of the Constitution assumed that, if a government possessed arbitrary power over the property of an individual, that individual had no freedom worthy of the name.

Since most of the members of the Convention attributed the insecurity of property to the ascendancy gained by "furious democrats" in the state legislatures, they took every precaution to insure that democrats could not gain control of the national government. From the framers' viewpoint, they would have labored to little purpose if the central government were merely the government of Rhode Island writ large. While everyone acknowledged that some admixture of democracy was necessary in the system, no one wished to make democracy the only or, indeed, the dominant ingredient. Instead, a judicious mixture of monarchy, aristocracy, and democracy was thought to be the form of government best calculated to guarantee stability, order, and liberty. Thus the Federal Constitution contained, along with democracy, a saving portion of aristocracy and monarchy—these three elements being represented by the House of Representatives, the Senate, and the presidency. Besides, the principle of the separation of powers was applied far more efficaciously than in the state constitutions. And, lastly, by a system of checks and balances, each of the three departments was provided with constitutional means of defending its own powers against the encroachments of coordinate departments.

Even more important, checks and balances were intended to safeguard liberty from attack by any group or interest, including the rich. But the immediate purpose, as Madison remarked, was "to secure the permanent interests of the country against innovation—especially innovation by unprincipled majorities that threatened the property interests of the "opulent minority." Since these inroads were the work of popularly elected legislatures, the framers provided for the indirect choice of the president, senators, and federal judges and equipped the Senate and the president with powers designed to hold the lower house of Congress in check. So intricate was this system of "power as a rival of power" that Hamilton declared that it would be "next to impossible that an impolitic or wicked measure should pass the great scrutiny." Here the delegates acted under the conviction that liberty could not long endure in a government based upon the right of the majority to govern arbitrarily. While the majority must govern, it can act constitutionally only if the laws are equal in operation. In this sense, checks and balances, like the Bill of Rights, have tended to function as guarantees of individual freedom. Washington said that if the frame of government drawn up at Philadelphia, with its elaborate built-in checks upon arbitrary rule, degenerated into oppression, it would simply prove that human wisdom was incapable of devising a system capable of withstanding the all-too-human "lust for power."

The framers clearly intended that the Constitution be regarded as a fundamental law expressive of the laws of nature, which placed certain inalienable rights beyond the reach of governmental authority—in short, implementation of the principle of a government of laws, not of men. Although the people are declared to be sovereign, there are certain things that even a majority cannot do. The Constitution itself, for example, cannot be amended except with the concurrence of three-fourths of the states. By thus exalting a written constitution into the supreme law of the land, the framers acted in accord with the revolutionary tradition.

The Federal Constitution did not envision a government in which the people govern. The peoples' role is much more restricted: they merely decide who shall govern and, broadly speaking, to what ends. Washington defined government of the people as "a government in which all power is derived from, and at stated periods reverts to them [the people]." The people exercise power only on election days; after the votes are counted, power passes into the hands of the officials who have won office. The people do not determine day-to-day policy-making, but those who do fashion policies are responsible to the will of the people. Within these limits, it is government by the consent of the governed. In the American system, the people reign but they do not govern.

Instead of erecting a unitary government along the lines laid down by the Virginia Plan, in which the states were hardly more than administrative agents of the central authority, the Constitution established a division of the exercise of sovereignty between the states and the general government. Each entity, the states and the national government, exercised sovereignty within its sphere. Neither was subordinate to the other; instead, they were made coordinate powers. Some functions—especially those regarded as common to the entire country—were assigned wholly to the general government; other functions were placed exclusively in the hands of the states; and a third area was shared by the two jurisdictions concurrently. Since the states and the general government coexist within the same territory, the United States was given diverse systems of law, state and federal; a multitude of taxing powers; and distinct police and armed forces. Both the state and federal governments operate directly upon the people; each citizen is subject to two governments.

Within the definition accepted in 1787, this frame of government was not "federal." Madison admitted that while it was federal in some respects it was of a "consolidated nature" in other respects—a compromise between a confederation and a centralized government. Yet Madison, like other proponents of the Constitution, took the name "Federalist" rather than "Nationalist." The word "nationalism," with its frightening connotations to parochial-minded citizens, was dropped early in the debates in the Constitutional Convention and it nowhere appears in the Constitution itself. On the other hand, "federalism" (although it, too, is not mentioned in the so-called Federal Constitution) conveyed comforting assurances that the states were still sovereign. For that reason, Madison deliberately emphasized in public statements the similarities between the Articles of Confederation and the Constitution, and Gouverneur Morris, the principal draftsman of the Constitution, borrowed wherever possible the phraseology of the Articles. As a result, by appropriating the name of "Federalists," thereby leaving to their opponents the invidious name of

"Antifederalists," the advocates of the Constitution won the first battle in the campaign for ratification: they routed their opponents upon the field of semantics.

In framing the Constitution, the Convention was especially mindful of what the Articles had failed to do. From the point of view of the nationalists, one of the most serious deficiencies of the Articles was their failure to create an integrated national market. This defect the Constitution remedied by making possible a single, all-embracing monetary system; by prohibiting the states from laying tariff and tonnage duties without the consent of Congress; by directing that all federal duties, imposts, and excises were to be uniform throughout the United States; by requiring that "the citizens of each state shall be entitled to all the privileges and immunities of Citizens in the several states"; and by giving the federal government exclusive power to regulate interstate trade and to prescribe a common standard of weights and measures.

Although the Constitution did not establish the "high-toned" central government envisaged by Hamilton, it contained several clauses which admitted of a constructive expansion of federal power: the clauses which give Congress power "to promote the general welfare," "to regulate commerce with foreign nations and among the several states," and "to make all laws which shall be necessary and proper for carrying into execution the foregoing powers, and all other powers vested by the Constitution in the Government of the United States." Despite the fact that some of these phrases were lifted from the Articles of Confederation, in the frame of government devised in 1787 they assumed new and far-reaching implications. In brief, unlike the Articles of Confederation, the Constitution created a government capable of adjusting to changing circumstances through the interpretation as well as the amendment of the original document.

Once the necessity of a more efficient central government had been accepted, the people recognized that they were the beneficiaries of the work of the Constitutional Convention. They gained a general government over which they exercised a far larger measure of control than they had over the Continental Congress. They were now privileged to elect directly their representatives to the lower house of Congress, and in some states, and ultimately in all, they gained the right to elect presidential electors. Samuel Langdon pointed out that the general and state governments were different institutions for promoting the good of the American people. "In transferring power from one to the other," he said, "I only take out of my left hand what it cannot so well use, and put it into my right hand where it can be better used."

If the American people were the gainers by the adoption of the Constitution, the states were certainly the losers. From a position of humiliating impotence, the general government became dominant in fact as well as in name. Although unable under the Articles of Confederation to impose its authority directly upon citizens, the general government now dealt directly with persons; no longer did the states enjoy the position of middlemen between the general government and the American people. Finally, the state governments were effectively isolated from each other by the provision that "no state shall, without the consent of Congress . . . enter into any general agreement or compact with another state." The tables were turned completely: the federal government became the guarantor of a republican form of government in the states.

All this was done without impairing the democratic gains of the American Revolution. Unlike the state constitutions, the Federal Constitution required no property qualifications of officeholders, and it advanced the principle of religious freedom by dispensing altogether with religious tests. A Jew, Roman Catholic, or even a nonbeliever was not debarred from serving in the Congress of the United States or in any other federal office. In this spirit, Washington, as President, later declared that the United States government was "not in any sense founded upon the Christian religion."

In the Federal Procession held in Philadelphia on July 4, 1788, seventeen clergymen marched arm in arm. In order to show how free government aided in promoting good will among men, ministers of the most dissimilar religions joined together. "The Rabbi of the Jews locked in the arms of two ministers of the gospel was a most delightful sight," said Dr. Benjamin Rush, a Philadelphia physician. "There could not have been a more happy emblem contrived of that section of the new Constitution which opens all its power and offices alike not only to every sect of Christians but to worthy men of *every* religion."

HAMILTON
HAMIL

6.

THE RATIFICATION OF THE CONSTITUTION

Because no single individual, group, or section had succeeded in writing into the Constitution everything it thought desirable, few delegates were prepared to acclaim it as the best of all possible constitutions. More often, it was regarded by the framers as an experiment, the success of which depended largely upon the good sense, moderation, and "virtue" of the people. James Madison expressed the prevailing attitude when he said that the Constitution was "the best that could be obtained from the jarring interests of the States, and the miscellaneous opinions of Politicians."

Despite Benjamin Franklin's plea for unanimity, three of the 42 delegates present on September 17, when the Constitution was ready for signing, refused to put their signatures to the document. These were Elbridge Gerry, George Mason, and Edmund Randolph—a New Englander and two Virginians. Mason, the most uncompromising of the three, declared that he would sooner cut off his right hand than sign. All of the nonsigners predicted that the proposed Constitution would end in a consolidated despotism and urged that another convention be called to try its hand at framing a more acceptable instrument of government.

Nevertheless, it was deemed so important to convey to the public the impression that complete unity had prevailed in the Convention that the Constitution was declared to be ratified "unanimously" by eleven states and Alexander Hamilton of New York. (As the only member of his delegation present on September 17, Hamilton had no authority to sign for his state.) The claim

---

"The *Hamilton* Offers a Thirteen-Gun Salute in Honor of the Ratification of the Constitution, July 1788," detail of an engraving from Brown Brothers.

Connecticut Cent, Mailed Bust Facing Right, 1788.

of unanimity was deceptive inasmuch as it applied only to the states, not to individual delegates. But, said Washington, "this apparent unanimity will have its effect. As the multitude are often deceived by externals, the appearance of unanimity in that body on that occasion will be of great importance." Once Mason, Randolph, and Gerry returned to their states, however, the illusion of a consensus in the Convention was certain to be shattered.

Yet, the Constitution did bear the signatures of thirty-nine members. At one time or another, fifty-five men attended the Convention, but of this number sixteen left Philadelphia before the Convention finished its labors. Of these sixteen, four were known to disapprove of the Constitution.

Even though the Constitution did come recommended with an impressive array of signatures, Washington's among them, the delegates would have found that they had wasted a long hot summer in Philadelphia if the rules laid down by the Articles of Confederation had been scrupulously observed. One of those rules required that any changes in the fundamental law be approved by all thirteen state legislatures. Every effort to amend the Articles had been wrecked upon the rule of unanimity; and it was a foregone conclusion that the state legislatures, whose authority was certain to be diminished by the adoption of the Constitution, would not give it a dispassionate examination. Rhode Island, although not represented in the Convention, was very much in the minds of the delegates: that "paultry state" was known to be waiting for an opportunity to play its favorite role of spoiler. The signs from New York were almost equally unpropitious: Governor Clinton considered the Constitution to be a mortal blow to state sovereignty. There were simply too many "erring sisters" in the Confederacy for the Convention to follow rules which had been drawn up on the assumption that all the sisters were chaste. The delegates therefore had the option between letting these delinquents undo its work or permitting the majority, as in 1776, to change the form of government without regard to regulations prescribed by constituted authority.

The Convention chose the revolutionary alternative. It declared that the Constitution was to be submitted for ratification not to the state legislatures but to popularly elected conventions, and that the new instrument of government should go into effect after nine states, not thirteen, had signified their assent.

Although the Constitutional Convention had no authority to order these changes in the fundamental law, they were more democratic than the procedures stipulated by the Articles of Confederation. By appealing directly to the people to sanction its handiwork, the Constitutional Convention applied the doctrine of the sovereignty of the people to the process of constitution-making. A specially qualified convention, elected for the specific purpose of drafting a constitution, submitted a frame of government to the people in each of the states. Consequently, the Constitution, if adopted, could be regarded as the creation of "We, the people of the United States," though acting severally by states and not collectively as one people. Hamilton later justified the Convention's action on the ground that "the fabric of American empire ought to rest on the solid basis of *the consent of the people*. The streams of national power ought to flow immediately from that pure, original fountain of all legislative authority."

THE ANTIFEDERALISTS

In presenting the Constitution to the American people, the framers were asking them to make a revolutionary change in their thinking about government and its functions. The colonial period and the American Revolution had taught Americans to fear centralized government and cherish local government; in 1787-1788, they were told to look upon a central government as the protector of their property and of republican government itself. In short, before they could embrace the Constitution they had to discard many ideas they had regarded as eternal truths.

In essence, Antifederalism was a state of mind that perpetuated attitudes deriving from the colonial period and the American Revolution. Antifederalism made distrust of centralized government the supreme concern of the citizen; eternal vigilance against their own government, not merely against the King and Parliament, was the price of the people's liberty. Antifederalism drew its support mainly from those Americans who equated freedom with local autonomy and who viewed any energetic central government as a potential despotism. Few businessmen or any other group of Americans who thought continentally and internationally were Antifederalists. The special appeal of Antifederalism was to farmers, particularly the less prosperous ones, who lived outside the intellectual and economic radius of the seaport towns, to politicians whose personal fortunes were bound up with the preservation of state rights, and to the thousands of plain citizens who could not divest themselves of the conventional wisdom of the day.

But even more decisive in determining attitudes toward the proposed Constitution was how it affected the interests of individuals and those of their localities and states. This is why the same economic groups in different states sometimes took antithetical positions toward the Constitution. Governor Clinton and his partisans were Antifederalists primarily because the new frame of government threatened to deprive the state of tariff duties, its main source of revenue. In Pennsylvania, a vote for the Federal Constitution was accounted a vote against the Pennsylvania Constitution of 1776. In some of these local struggles for power, the intrinsic merits of the Constitution were of secondary importance. Similarly, Maine (at this time a district of Massachusetts) feared that the adoption of the Constitution would prejudice its chances for separate statehood; and Kentuckians and other westerners were apt to see in the Constitution the spectre of Spanish control of the navigation of the Mississippi. The Virginia Baptist Association and the Baptists of Western Massachusetts opposed the proposed Constitution, while the Baptists in the Carolinas were staunchly Federalist.

For many westerners, the fact that the East favored the adoption of the Constitution was enough to damn it. The long-established antagonism between the settled areas of the seaboard and the newer communities of the interior contributed to fixing attitudes toward the proposed frame of government. In South Carolina and Massachusetts, the scenes of a struggle for power between East and West, the back country decisively rejected the Philadelphia plan. Nevertheless, resentments born of sectional rivalry within the states did not prevail everywhere. The inhabitants of western Georgia, having stirred up the Indians by encroaching upon their lands, looked to a strong central government to save them from the vengeance of the tribesmen. Some western Pennsylvanians and Kentuckians saw in the adoption of the Constitution a means of dislodging the British from the western posts and of "pacifying" the Indians who barred the way to the Ohio Valley.

In the capacity of propagandists, the Antifederalists felt free to give full rein to their imaginations in depicting the horrors that would follow upon the adoption of the Constitution. The rich, it was said, would establish a despotism and enslave the poor. Patrick Henry warned that the president, at the head of his legions, would make a "bold push" for the American throne; others thought that the president would make himself a king simply by taking advantage of the failure of the Constitution to set a limit upon the number of terms he might serve. Russia was sometimes cited as an example of what lay in store for the United States if the Constitution were ratified: once started upon the course of centralized government, the United States, like Muscovy, would end as a despotism ruled by a rod of iron.

Whereas Federalists tried to overcome provincialism by emphasizing the essential unity of Americans, Antifederalists deliberately exacerbated sectional animosities. They warned that a powerful national government, by attempting to create uniformity out of diversity, would enable a section to dominate the Union and to impose its will upon rival sections. Governor Clinton of New York, for example, pictured southerners as indolent, spendthrift slave drivers consumed with jealousy of the prosperity of the commercial cities of the North. James Winthrop, a Massachusetts Antifederalist, feared that New Englanders' natural superiority in morals and manners (except, of course, Rhode Islanders') would be contaminated by a too-intimate association with raffish New Yorkers, Pennsylvanians, and Virginians.

While conceding that the American people had a sufficient store of virtue to conduct their affairs without calling upon the government for aid, the Antifederalists' faith emphatically did not include politicians. Put a man in political office, particularly one which gave him power over national affairs, they averred, and all the worst qualities of human nature—ambition, avarice, self-love, and lust for power—were almost certain to gain ascendancy. Original sin (although it was hard to see how a politician could sin originally in a profession so filled with reprobates) seemed to await only the vivifying touch of political office—the people might elect the best man to office but the exercise of power would almost certainly bring out his evil qualities. Although Antifederalists thought that the doctrine of total depravity applied only to federal officeholders, Hamilton pointed out that the representatives of the people in a single state were not less susceptible to the "lust for power or other sinister motives, than the representatives of the people of the United States."

As for national glory and prestige, the Antifederalists were not prepared to pay the price that these commodities cost upon the international exchange. Liberty and happiness, not empire and splendor, they declared, were the main concerns of Americans. George Mason said that to be powerful and respected abroad, Americans must first secure their liberty and happiness at home. Patrick Henry deprecated the danger of European aggression as a reason for adopting the Constitution: "from that quarter," he said, "there is no cause of fear: you may sleep in safety forever from them." But even if Europeans descended by the thousands upon these shores, Americans would be in no peril because, Henry asserted, "the superiority of our cause would give us an advantage over them." From the Antifederalists came the first trenchant exposition of the isolationist philosophy.

Although some of the Antifederalist leaders were themselves aristocrats, they incited class feeling in the struggle against the Constitution. In the role of spokesmen of the plain people against the elite, they pictured the Constitution as a plot of the rich and wellborn; and in resisting unification they claimed to be upholding the natural equality of man and the right of the individual to the pursuit of happiness. Nevertheless, they did not rise to the defense of debtor-relief legislation. They seemed far more inclined to draw a veil over the "horrid ravages" committed upon property by the state legislatures than to justify or even to condone them.

Nor were they willing to forego the right of the white man to own black slaves. Although Patrick Henry and George Mason deplored slavery, their opposition to the adoption of the Constitution derived in part from their fear that a strong central government would invoke the general welfare clause to interfere with the labor system of the South. Slavery might be a wrong, but it was sacred and inviolable insofar as any adverse action by the federal government was concerned. Recognizing that slaves were to the South as population and wealth were to the North, Patrick Henry warned his fellow-southerners that a northern commander at the head of a northern army might decree the forcible abolition of slavery. "May Congress not say," he asked rhetorically, "that every black man must fight?"

If slavery were insecure under the Constitution, other economic and political interests of the South seemed to the Antifederalists to be in much more immediate danger. Federal courts were certain to be used by British creditors to recover their debts and, presumably, federal judges would afford them every facility in plucking southern debtors clean. George Mason declared that the commerce clause, in the hands of a northern majority, would be converted into a weapon to aid northern merchants and shipowners to monopolize the staples of the southern states and reduce the price of those commodities by 50 percent, at the same time that they doubled freight rates and middlemen's commissions. Compared with rapacious and unconscionable Yankees, British merchants were made to seem almost generous and considerate toward their customers.

THE FEDERALISTS

Without exaggeration, the Federalists could claim that the weight of talents, property, education, and wealth was on the side of the Constitution. In general, the Federalist spokesmen came from the highest echelons of American society; the aristocracy of the country was far more united in support of the Federal Constitution than it had been of the Declaration of Independence. In the Federalist ranks were arrayed an impressive number of lawyers, large landowners, slaveholders, manufacturers, shipowners and shipbuilders, merchants, and ex-army officers. Members of the Society of the Cincinnati were welcomed as auxilaries by the very men who a few years before had castigated them as a menace to republicanism, and the organization they had established for fraternal and patriotic purposes was pressed into service to further the adoption of the Constitution. One of the Antifederalists' objections to the Constitution was that it was "the wicked and traitorous fabrication of the Cincinnati."

As Madison said, the seacoast seemed everywhere in favor of the Constitution. There was no class conflict over the Constitution in the maritime towns. The antifederalists' tirades against "the rich and wellborn" were not echoed by the laborers and artisans who, like the merchants and professional men, had suffered from the postwar depression and the money stringency. From hearing the Boston crowds cheering the news of the ratification of the Constitution, John Quincy Adams said that "one would have thought that every man from the adoption of the Constitution had acquired a sure expectancy of an independent fortune."

But the towns alone could not have carried the Constitution to victory. Over 90 percent of the population lived on farms and plantations, and the great majority were small farmers. Had the Federalists not been able to win the support of rural areas, the Constitution would have gone down to defeat. After the Constitution had been adopted, the Federalists acclaimed "the solid good sense of American farmers and mechanics." Of the two, the vote of the farmers was numerically the most important.

Nor was support of the proposed frame of government confined to any one section. An alliance of sections made possible the adoption of the Constitution, and the principal parties to this coalition were northern merchants and southern planters. True, the parties expected different things from the change in government, but it was only later that these anticipated benefits were seen to be wholly incompatible.

As between these allies, it was the northerners who owned the bulk of the outstanding government securities. Having little disposable cash, southern planters failed to accumulate large quantities of these certificates even after the price level made them attractive for speculation or investment. Northern businessmen and well-to-do farmers, on the other hand, often had the cash as well as the inclination to buy at the low and hope for a rise.

The Constitution pledged the new government to pay the debts (not necessarily in full, however) contracted by the Continental Congress. As a result, Continental securities were certain to appreciate in value if the Constitution were ratified—indeed, they could hardly go any other way than up. Since a large number of Federalists who sat in the Constitutional Convention and the state ratifying conventions owned these securities, they had a direct pecuniary interest in the outcome. Consequently the Antifederalists (and later historians) were able to allege that the Constitution was the work of mercenary speculators who voted themselves a financial windfall.

While it is true that the northern Federalists generally belonged to the economic group that had bought government certificates of indebtedness at low prices, in few cases was their political attitude shaped exclusively by these specific holdings. While they no doubt hoped to be the beneficiaries of an increase in security prices, this was incidental to the other economic and political advantages to which they looked forward—a government capable of regulating, protecting, and expanding the commerce of the United States; providing an adequate circulating medium; safeguarding property against the depredations of the state legislatures and "domestic violence"; and securing the fulfillment of the terms of the treaty of peace and making a commercial treaty with Great Britain. Compared with these achievements, a rise in the value of government securities was usually relegated to a secondary place. Finally, many of the financial advantages that accrued to security holders from the adoption of the Constitution actually resulted from Hamilton's fiscal program of 1790-1792, which, far from being foreseen in 1787-1788, took the country by surprise and astonished even many of those who had expected to gain from an increase in the price of securities.

Even supposing that security ownership may have determined individuals' attitude toward the proposed Constitution, it cannot be said, as did Charles Beard, that the owners of state and continental certificates constituted a true "consolidated economic interest." For security holders, like other individuals, were caught in the economic and financial crosscurrents generated by the Philadelphia plan. In the three or four states that had assumed payments to their citizens of interest upon the continental as well as upon their own debts, many security owners feared that any change in the existing relationship between the states and the central government might cost them their income from these certificates. On the other hand, Pennsylvania had assumed so much of the federal debt that it was widely questioned if the state alone could carry the financial burden. But nothing was said in the Constitution about the assumption of state debts by the general government, nor did the proponents of the Constitution hold out such a prospect as bait. Precisely because the Constitution offered nothing to state creditors, it tended to divide rather than to unite holders of state and Continental securities.

Economic considerations often pulled individuals in opposite directions; self-interest was not always an unambiguous guide. Large land speculators in particular acutely experienced the ambivalence of the Constitution. On the one hand, they wished to keep the price of securities low because securities could be exchanged for public land and cheap securities meant cheap land; on the other hand, they needed the protection against the Indians and the removal of the British from the northwest posts that only a strong central government could accomplish. Patrick Henry, a heavy speculator in Yazoo lands who was committed to pay large sums in depreciated certificates, opposed the Constitution. Yet the rise in the price of those certificates that resulted from the adoption of Hamilton's funding-assumption plan made Henry a far richer man than he could have hoped to become from his land speculations.

THE DEBATE OVER RATIFICATION

Although the Constitution was written without benefit of public scrutiny, there was no lack of popular discussion after the finished document had been laid before the people. Every word and phrase of the Constitution was subjected to rigorous inspection by the Antifederalists, and their criticisms were answered by Federalist pamphleteers. A free and open debate preceded the adoption of the Constitution; in no instance were restraints imposed upon the press; and the dissemination of opinion was facilitated by the large number of newspapers that served the reading public in the towns.

On the Federalist side, the most cogent exposition of the merits of the Constitution came from the pens of Hamilton, Madison, and Jay who, late in 1787, began bringing out the *Federalist* in weekly installments in a New York newspaper. Originally addressed primarily to the voters in New York, its scope was broadened until it became a philosophical commentary upon the Constitution. For Federalists throughout the United States it served as a storehouse of arguments in behalf of the Constitution.

The central theme of the *Federalist* is that a republican form of government, equipped with proper checks and balances and with power judiciously distributed between the central authority and the states, is entirely compatible with the stability and order essential to the well-being of society. Madison tried to allay Antifederalist fears of a "consolidated government" by explaining that the proposed Constitution created neither a truly national nor a federal form of government but "a composition of both." Without denying that power is predisposed to encroach upon liberty, the authors of the *Federalist* argued that the Constitution contained so many devices designed to safeguard freedom from the abuse of power that danger was reduced to a minimum.

Madison contended that the vast territorial expanse and the diversity of interests produced by differences in occupation, manners, and geography offered a further guarantee of the success of republican government in the United States. In this country, he believed, no local demagogues or factions would ever succeed in gaining control of the federal government. Instead, men of enlarged views and national outlook would be elected to national office. "Society itself will be broken into so many parts, interests and classes of citizens," he predicted, "that the rights of individuals, or of the minority, will be in little danger from interested combinations of the majority." He was not equally optimistic about the future of the state governments: experience had taught conservatives that in these jurisdictions the legislatures were seminaries of faction, local prejudice, and low, pimping politics.

The authors of the *Federalist* indulged in some extraordinarily plain talking to the American people. They disdained flattery as a means of winning public favor for the proposed frame of government. The *Federalist* abounds in pungent observations regarding "the folly and wickedness of mankind," "the ordinary depravity of human nature," and the "impulses of rage, resentment, jealousy, avarice and of other irregular and violent propensities" to which mankind were unhappily prone. Yet Hamilton, Jay, and Madison acknowledged that there was "a portion of virtue and honor among mankind" and that the American people usually intended, although they often went wide of the mark, to promote the public good.

In passing these strictures upon the people, the authors of the *Federalist* did not intend to portray themselves as antidemocratic elitists. If the people were given proper institutions in which their good qualities could find outlet and which restrained their disposition to act upon impulse, the *Federalist* did not despair of the republic. Indeed, the frame of government which the *Federalist* so eloquently elucidated was based upon the principle of the sovereignty of the people.

Nor did the *Federalist* share the Antifederalists' obsessive fear of a central government and of the men elected to administer it. Jay, Hamilton, and Madison took the position that a government must have power commensurate with its responsibilities. While admitting that elected officials were peculiarly susceptible to the impulses of power, the *Federalist* insisted that they were worthy of trust until proved otherwise. As the *Federalist* saw it, high office had a regenerative, sometimes even an ennobling effect, upon its possessors. Ambition was directed toward serving the people and leaving an honorable name to posterity. The *Federalist* held out the prospect that, if the Constitution were adopted, all economic groups would benefit from the security given property rights, the advancement of the general welfare by an "energetic" national government, the relative immunity from foreign wars and domestic convulsions, and the enhancement of national power, dignity, and prestige. Even so, the *Federalist* did not promise Utopia: Hamilton cautioned his readers against expecting "to see realized in America the halcyon scenes of the poetic or fabulous age."

Since the primary purpose of the *Federalist* was to secure the adoption of the Constitution rather than to produce an enduring work of political literature—had the Constitution failed of ratification, the *Federalist* might have been relegated to the obscurity that has overtaken the Antifederalist tracts. Therefore, the authors occasionally felt compelled to resort to outright propaganda. If the *Federalist* could be believed, under the Articles of Confederation the country was "almost at the last stage of national humiliation. There is scarcely anything that can wound the pride or degrade the character of an independent nation which we do not experience." National engagements had been broken; the United States was excluded from the western posts and from the full use of the Mississippi River, yet because it had "no troops, nor treasury, nor government" it could not even remonstrate with force or dignity. Commerce was said to be "at the lowest point of declension," property was everywhere threatened by state legislatures under the control of debtors bent upon defrauding their creditors; the wheels of government had been brought to "an awful stand," and "the frail and tottering edifice seems ready to fall upon our heads, and to crush us beneath its ruins." The Antifederalists were on solid ground in pointing out that *The Federalist* exaggerated the extent and degree of the postwar economic decline in order to win votes for the Constitution.

The writing that was most influential in bringing about the adoption of the Constitution was George Washington's signature. Washington put his fame and prestige upon that single line. In listing the factors working in favor of the adoption of the Constitution, Alexander Hamilton awarded first place to the "very great weight of influence of the persons who framed it, particularly in the universal popularity of General Washington." The Antifederalists were naturally less disposed to celebrate Washington's popularity; they compared the veneration felt by Americans for Washington and Franklin to the adulation paid by "European slaves" to their kings.

Even though the *Federalist* predicted that the rejection of the Constitution "would in all probability put a final period to the Union," and Washington warned that the choice was between the Constitution and chaos, the people seemed strangely apathetic. Only a small proportion of the qualified voters went to the polls to elect the members of the state ratifying conventions. In Boston, where 2700 were entitled to vote, only 700 actually cast a ballot; 6000 of 25,000 voters in Maryland registered an opinion, as did 13,000 of the 70,000 freeholders of Pennsylvania. Obviously, something more than the property qualifications imposed by the state constitutions kept the voters away from the polls.

This seeming indifference stemmed in part from the indecision and even bewilderment felt by a large number of citizens when they were presented with the Constitution. In general, the debate was carried upon such a high level of rationality that the electorate was not stirred by any sense of emotional involvement. Despite the adjurations of the Federalists and Antifederalists, the mass of the people was not convinced that what they did in 1787-1788 would determine the entire course of American history. Many were not even sure whether the adoption of the Constitution would be a good or bad thing—and so they retreated into a kind of wait-and-see neutralism. By thus abnegating the voting function, they permitted a minority to determine the future of the American political system.

Other circumstances that militated against large voter participation were the absence of organized political parties and the difficulty, particularly in rural areas, of getting to the polls. Effective popular control of government awaited the emergence of political parties capable of informing, exciting, and mobilizing the electorate, and an improvement in the means of transportation. Since the seaports and inland towns were strongholds of Federalism, the comparative ease of access to the voting places in those population centers worked in favor of ratification.

Finally, voting was not yet an established habit among Americans. Rarely did more than 5 percent—often it dropped as low as 2 percent—of the adult males take the trouble to participate in an election. The paucity of the turnout of voters in 1787-1788 did not surprise contemporaries: this was the pattern of voting behavior to which they were accustomed. Only in Pennsylvania did the Antifederalists complain that they were cheated of a victory by the failure of voters to go to the polls.

As the framers feared, a determined effort to amend the proposed Constitution was made in the Continental Congress by Richard Henry Lee, a Virginia Antifederalist. While the Federalists succeeded in keeping the Convention's handiwork intact, they failed to induce Congress to stamp its approval upon the Constitution. In adopting a resolution to transmit the Constitution to the state legislatures, Congress neither approved nor disapproved of the frame of government drawn up in Philadelphia. Nevertheless, the procedure recommended by the Constitutional Convention—the submission of the Constitution to state conventions and the abandonment of the rule of unanimity—had received at least the tacit sanction of Congress.

In later months, the Federalists professed gratitude to Providence for the order in which it had disposed the state conventions. Certainly it is true that the first five conventions to consider the Constitution gave it their enthusiastic endorsement. From December 1787 to February 1788, the Constitution was ratified in quick succession by Delaware (the first state to act), Pennsylvania, New Jersey, Georgia, and Connecticut. Three of these states—Delaware, New Jersey, and Georgia—ratified unanimously.

By February 1788, a clear-cut pattern had emerged. The small agricultural states, reconciled by the adoption of the Great Compromise, eagerly embraced the Constitution. Since only one large population center (Philadelphia) existed in any of the first five states to ratify, it was clear that farmers, when they took the trouble to vote, favored adoption.

The Constitution did not run into trouble until it reached Massachusetts. In that state, the auspices were far from favorable. The Shaysites, defeated in the field, had come back to win the state elections of 1788. John Hancock had defeated Governor James Bowdoin, who had endeared himself to the conservatives by his part in suppressing Shays' Rebellion. The former insurgents voted as they shot—against the domination of the eastern conservatives who were the chief proponents of the Constitution in the Bay State. As a result, when the Massachusetts convention assembled in February 1788, a "black cloud" of enemies of the proposed Constitution descended upon Boston from the three western counties.

The Federalists explained the presence of this Antifederalist majority in the convention on the ground that "every Blockhead and Bankrupt in the State has as good a Vote as a better Man." As for the Antifederalists, they complained that lawyers, judges, clergymen, and educated men in general were in favor of the Constitution, "and for that reason they appear able to make the worse appear the better cause." Only the people, the Antifederalists said, were on their side. But they also had the support of Elbridge Gerry and Sam Adams, while Governor Hancock was prepared to trim his sails to the prevailing breeze.

Although elected president of the Massachusetts convention, Hancock remained in seclusion, alleging ill health. Yet he was not too ill to enter into negotiations with the Federalists behind the scenes. An ambitious man, he found that the Federalists could offer far more in the way of political jobs than could the Antifederalists. A bargain was consummated whereby in exchange for his endorsement of the Constitution—an event certain to stagger the Antifederalists—he received the Federalists' promise of support for the presidency of the United States, provided Virginia did not accede to the Constitution or, if Virginia ratified, the consolation prize of the vice-presidency. This prospect wonderfully restored Hancock's health. During the War of Independence, he had aspired to be commander in chief, only to see Washington carry off the prize. Surely Fate would not play the same trick upon him a second time!

Even with Hancock's aid, the Federalists were obliged to agree to nine recommendatory amendments to the Constitution demanded by the Antifederalists before the Constitution could be squeezed through by a vote of 187-168. Still, the Constitution was ratified unconditionally in a state where, at the beginning of the Convention, Antifederalism had appeared invincible.

But the Federalists' season of rejoicing was cut short by the bad news from New Hampshire. That state had been expected to return a Federalist majority; instead, when the convention assembled in February 1788, it was so loaded with Antifederalists that had the Constitution been put to the vote it would have been rejected. The badly shaken Federalists deemed themselves fortunate to secure an adjournment until June 1788.

After the close call in Massachusetts and the reverse in New Hampshire, the Constitution had a comparatively easy time in Maryland and South Carolina. But in June 1788, it was required to run the most strenuous part of the gauntlet: the states of New Hampshire, North Carolina, New York, and Virginia. In each of these states the ratification of the Constitution was in doubt; the best that the Federalists could hope for was a narrow margin of victory.

Already firmly in control of the governorship and the legislature and sensing that public opinion was averse to the Constitution, the New York Antifederalists removed all property qualifications upon voting for delegates to the state ratifying convention. No other state adopted this procedure, but it is also true that in no other state was the party in power so sure of increasing its majority by enlarging the electorate. The Antifederalists cherished democracy because it seemed likely to produce a vote against the Constitution.

Governor Clinton's faith in the people was fully vindicated. The election returned to the convention nineteen Federalists and forty-five Antifederalists. Wealth and ability may have been on the side of the proponents of the Constitution, but they were compelled to admit that they were overpowered by numbers. Hamilton had hoped that the *Federalist* would turn the tide, but he admitted that while his arguments confounded they did not convince the opposition.

Although the Federalists found nothing in the convention to raise their spirits, they were cheered by New Hampshire's ratification of the Constitution in June 1788. Nine states having ratified, the Constitution officially went into effect. But the New York Antifederalists acted as though they still held the trump cards. Single-handed, New York had defeated the impost in 1787, and the Antifederalists appeared to think that they could mete out the same treatment to the Constitution.

Despite their numbers, the Antifederalists were divided over the question whether the Constitution should be rejected outright or accepted with amendments. They even failed to agree whether amendments should be mandatory or recommendatory. Yet, in spite of this division of opinion within the Antifederalist ranks, the Federalists in New York were obliged to pay a higher price than in any other state to secure the unconditional ratification of the Constitution. Rather than accept ratification on the condition that amendments be adopted—certain to reopen the question of ratification even in the states that had already acted—the New York Federalists promised to work toward the convening of a second convention where, presumably, the Constitution would be rewritten to satisfy the Antifederalists' objections.

Whenever a state ratified, the Federalists all over the Union celebrated by firing cannon, waving flags, displaying fireworks, and drinking patriotic toasts. In February 1788, for example, the day after New Yorkers learned that the Constitution had safely cleared the Massachusetts convention, General Samuel Webb wrote that he was "much afflicted with Headache this day (owing to drinking and rioting in a good cause)." But when New York ratified in July 1788, the Federalists really had something to drink and riot about. "The whole night was spent in loud acclamations of Joy," remarked a participant, "and continued until past 8 o'clock this morning." In the parade that followed, a federal ship with a figure on the bowsprit of Hamilton holding the Constitution in his right hand, with flowing sails and canvas waves dashing against her sides, was wheeled triumphantly down Broadway. It was a glorious day and the exulting Federalists topped it off by wrecking the press of an Antifederalist printer.

The Virginia ratifying convention, scheduled to meet in February 1788, had been postponed in order that the Old Dominion might exert a decisive influence upon the course of events. In the event that many states rejected the Constitution, Virginia, said James Monroe, "might mediate between contending parties and lead the way to a union more palatable to all."

Until the Virginia convention assembled in July 1788, the Federalists had enjoyed the advantage in all the state ratifying conventions of better leadership, the support of more men of wealth, education, and prestige, and more newspaper coverage for their arguments. In Virginia, however, the situation was reversed. George Mason and Edmund Randolph, together with Patrick Henry, the former governor and the most powerful individual in the state, led the Antifederalist forces in the state convention. And, since the majority of delegates was opposed to adoption, the Antifederalist leaders enjoyed a commanding position.

But Virginia aspired to lead the Union, not to isolate itself from the rest of the country in the unlikely company of Rhode Island. And, as in other states, the numerical strength of the Antifederalists did not tell the whole story: they had neither the solidarity nor the unity of purpose of the Federalists, nor did they have the important advantage which the Federalists enjoyed, of being able to hold out promises of political office. Edmund Randolph, a moderate Antifederalist, was persuaded to switch sides partly by the promise of the office of attorney general in the new government. Nevertheless, the issue remained in doubt almost to the last moment, and the ratification was by the thin margin of 89 to 79. Yet it was without conditions—the amendments proposed were recommendatory—and nothing was said about a second constitutional convention.

Although the North Carolina convention rejected the Constitution, and Rhode Island refused to take any action whatever, by the autumn of 1788 eleven states had gathered under the "New Roof" erected by the framers in Philadelphia. Washington hailed this achievement as "a new phenomenon in the political and moral world; and an astonishing victory gained by enlightened reason over brute force." By assembling wise men rather than armies, Americans had demonstrated that a free people, acting with moderation, can abolish and institute governments. Although it was a peaceful, voluntary, and deliberate transition from one government to another, it was rightly regarded as a revolution. From the points of view of Rhode Island and North Carolina, the revolutionary nature of the event was plain enough: they had remained loyal to a government from which the other states had seceded. They were the "Loyalists" of the Second American Revolution.

7. ORGANIZING THE NEW GOVERNMENT

The accession of New York and Virginia removed the last obstacles to making the Federal Constitution the law of the land. In general, the Antifederalists took their defeat without rancor: after all, the contest had been over a form of republican government, not over republicanism itself. The promise of amendments and, possibly, a second constitutional convention took much of the sting from their failure to prevent the adoption of the Constitution. Nevertheless, while professing their willingness to abide by the result of the elections, they made it clear that they would work against the centralizing tendencies they detected in the new frame of government. As a result, the Antifederalists ceased to be mere obstructionists and attained the respectability of a states' rights party.

Yet, as the elections of 1788 demonstrated, the Antifederalists had not succeeded in conveying their apprehensions regarding centralized government to the people as a whole. Except in Virginia, where two Antifederalist senators were returned, few of the former opponents of the Constitution were elected to Congress. The large Federalist majority in both the House and Senate insured that the new government would be administered by its friends. Moreover, the sectional alliance between North and South remained intact. Washington, a Virginian, was unanimously chosen president (the only President to be so honored by the electoral college), and John Adams of Massachusetts was elected vice-president.

The conservative mood of the American people that had made possible the adoption of the Constitution was reflected in some of the state constitu-

---

"The Inauguration of Washington," engraving from a painting by Alonzo Chappel, courtesy of The New York Public Library.

New Jersey Cent, Horse's Head Facing Right, 1788.

tions that were revised in 1789-1792. In Pennsylvania, for example, the Constitution of 1790 abolished the unicameral legislature and the plural executive that had permitted unchecked majority rule. In South Carolina, the reaction against "popular licentiousness" was evidenced in the Constitution of 1790, by which the rule of the low country (where only one-fifth of the free population lived) was strengthened and the property qualifications for officeholding were raised. The Kentucky Constitution of 1792 directed that the governor and senate should be chosen by electors rather than by the people directly.

Before the Federalists could administer the new government, they had to create it. The Constitution, a relatively short document (it can be read in about twenty minutes), merely laid down a blueprint: the framers were the architects of the more perfect union, but the work of actually constructing the government and of making it function efficiently devolved upon the first Congress and upon the Executive Department. Because of the magnitude of the task and the skill with which it was executed, the first Congress won the distinction of being the most productive of all Congresses in the history of the United States. The year 1789-1790 spent by Congress in New York ranks second in importance only to the summer of 1787 spent by the Constitutional Convention in Philadelphia.

The first Congress of the United States even met in an unfinished building. For the reception of the new government, the city of New York was engaged in applying the finishing touches to a splendid new edifice in Wall Street called the Federal Building. "In short," a New Yorker exulted, "there is nothing equal to it in any part of the world." It was apparent what New Yorkers were up to: they hoped to fix the capital of the United States permanently in their city by making it so comfortable that congressmen could not bear to leave.

AMERICAN NAVIGATION ACTS

Because of the slowness of transportation—the delegates came by horseback, stage, and ship, and it required a month of hard riding to travel overland from South Carolina to New York—neither house had a quorum until April, and President Washington was not inaugurated until April 30. The country could ill afford this delay, for many matters urgently required Congress' attention. Chief among them was revenue: as yet, the federal Treasury was quite as bare as it had been under the Articles of Confederation. Congress acted quickly to remedy this situation: in May 1789, a comprehensive schedule of tariff duties was imposed upon foreign merchandise, mainly manufactured goods, imported into the United States. While this tariff of 1789 afforded some protection to domestic manufacturers, its primary purpose was to raise revenue.

To the tariff law, Congress added legislation designed to encourage the growth of the American merchant marine—the reward claimed by northern merchants, shipowners, and shipbuilders for their support of the Constitution. By the Tonnage Act of 1789, the United States government granted a discount of 10 percent of the duties on goods imported in United States ships. At the same time, the tonnage duties on foreign vessels entering American ports were set at a rate more than eight times as high as upon ships built and owned in the United States, and the fisheries and the coastwise trade were virtually reserved for American vessels. After spending more than six years vainly trying to destroy mercantilism, the United States ended by adopting one of mercantilism's most essential features—a system of navigation acts.

The debate over the tariff and tonnage bills revealed the first evidence of dissension within the Federalist party. Some southern Federalists complained that the tariff of 1789 would make the agricultural South the "Milch cow out of whom the substance would be extracted"; northern manufacturers, on the other hand, criticized the tariff on the ground that it afforded insufficient protection to "infant industries." Clearly, the creation of a central government capable of controlling the domestic economy of the country had intensified the struggle for power between the sections.

It also sharpened the conflict over foreign policy. Indeed, it was a difference of opinion over foreign affairs that created the widest rift among the "friends of the Constitution." The dissension began in 1789, when James Madison attempted to insert in the tariff and tonnage bills a provision imposing discriminatory duties upon the ships and merchandise of Great Britain and other foreign nations that had not made commercial treaties with the United States.

In 1787-1788, it had been generally supposed that one of the first acts of the new government would be to retaliate against Great Britain. This expectation had been one of the most compelling reasons for summoning the Constitutional Convention and adopting the Constitution; and almost all leading Americans had gone on record in favor of using the economic force of a strengthened union to bring the former mother country to terms. Madison did not doubt that, without firing a shot, the United States could compel Great Britain to surrender the northwest posts and open the West Indies to American ships. By thus demonstrating at the outset that the government was resolved to use its power to redress "National wrongs," Madison hoped to attach the people firmly to the federal government. Madison admitted that discrimination against British ships and merchandise would operate as a tax upon southern producers, who were their principal users, but he nevertheless argued that it was a tax they must pay for national security and their own release from economic vassalage to Great Britain. To achieve these ends, he told his fellow southerners, they ought to be willing to pay for increasing the size of the United States merchant marine and rebuilding the United States Navy. That his policy would redound to the advantage of France enhanced Madison's satisfaction: he believed that there was owing a debt of gratitude to France that could only be repaid by diverting American trade to that country at the expense of Great Britain.

Although Madison predictably failed to unite the South in support of discrimination against Great Britain—one of the most vehement opponents of the plan was William L. Smith, a South Carolina Federalist—he unexpectedly encountered the most strenuous opposition from the New England merchants and shipowners, the very people upon whom he proposed to confer a near-monopoly of the southern market. Beginning to taste the sweets of returning prosperity, these businessmen were unwilling to jeopardize their economic well-being by engaging in a commercial struggle with Great Britain, which would be certain to result, among other things, in a cutting off of British credit. Alexander Hamilton protested that to curtail imports from Britain, the duties on which constituted the major potential source of federal revenue, would paralyze the government before it was fairly on its feet. Finally, Hamilton and other northern Federalists deplored Madison's efforts to force American trade into channels beneficial to France; gratitude, they said, ought to play no part in the republic's foreign policy particularly when, as in the present instance, it promised to injure the United States.

Madison's plan passed the House of Representatives only to be defeated in the Senate. A committee of both houses decided to eliminate discrimination from the tariff and tonnage bills. Accordingly, Great Britain was given the same privileges in United States ports that France, the most favored nation, enjoyed. In effect, by rejecting discrimination, Congress turned over to the Executive Department the task of securing redress of grievances by diplomatic rather than by legislative means.

THE BILL OF RIGHTS

Even though the Constitution was adopted without requiring that it be amended, the threat of a second constitutional convention hung over the first Congress. To ward off this menace, to conciliate the "honest opponents" of the Constitution, to facilitate the entry of Rhode Island and North Carolina into the Union, and to honor the commitment he had made to his constituents in Virginia, James Madison put the drafting of a Bill of Rights high on the order of priorities. While Madison did not share the Antifederalists' fear that the federal government would infringe upon civil liberties, he saw no harm and even some good in a Bill of Rights. Political truths enunciated in a solemn manner, he said, might acquire by degrees "the character of fundamental maxims of free Government" and thereby "counteract the impulses of interest and passion" and strengthen the defenses of liberty.

This half-grudging admission had been forced from Madison by the Antifederalists' insistence upon a Bill of Rights. In the Constitutional Convention, Madison had joined the majority of delegates in rejecting the suggestion that a Bill of Rights be incorporated in the Constitution; not a single state voted in favor. At that time, it was pointed out that since the federal government possessed only enumerated powers and that since jurisdiction over civil liberties was not among them, a Bill of Rights was wholly redundant. Moreover, "parchment barriers" that could be broken through with impunity by majorities were held in low esteem by the framers; Madison said that the Virginia Bill of Rights had been violated "in every instance where it has been opposed to the popular current."

Yet six states, including five of the largest, had accompanied their ratification of the Constitution with the recommendation that amendments be adopted.

These proposed amendments, 210 in all (Virginia alone had submitted 40 amendments), were directed toward the same end: to limit the powers granted to the federal government by means of restrictions or prohibitions. Manifestly, the intent of many of these changes was not to protect civil liberties but to weaken and, if possible, to paralyze the federal government.

While admitting the necessity of tranquilizing the public mind with a Bill of Rights, Madison was resolved to confine "the passion for amendments" to the comparatively limited subject-matter of civil liberties. Under no circumstances, he said, must there be any abridgment of "the sum of power transferred from the states to the general government." As he conceived it, amending the Constitution was like performing a delicate surgical operation; the knife could not be permitted to touch any of the vital organs.

From the amendments recommended by the states Madison therefore selected for action by Congress those dealing with what Americans held to be "the great rights of mankind." During the summer of 1789, twelve amendments were adopted by Congress and submitted to the states. Two of the proposed amendments were rejected. Of the ten adopted, the first eight properly constitute the Bill of Rights; the ninth and tenth amendments were intended to make sure that the enumerated powers granted the federal government should not be construed to diminish the reserved rights of the people or of the states. One of the amendments introduced by Madison prohibited the states from infringing upon the rights of conscience, free speech, a free press, and trial by jury. Although he considered this to be the most important of all the changes he recommended, it was rejected by the Senate and therefore never presented to the states. As a result, the Bill of Rights operated only upon the federal government; it gave citizens no rights whatever against action by the states.

Because Madison was careful to leave the structure and powers of the federal government intact, those Antifederalists who had hoped to use amendments as a weapon to cripple the federal government denied all responsibility for the Bill of Rights. Patrick Henry, still anticipating "all the terrors of paramount federal authority," declared that the Bill of Rights would injure rather than serve the cause of liberty. By thus deprecating the importance of the first eight amendments, Henry and other Antifederalists enabled the Federalists to undo the damage they had inflicted upon themselves by their earlier resistance to a Bill of Rights and to adopt the role of champions of the "inalienable rights" of man.

8.
THE HAMILTONIAN DISPENSATION

OBJECTIVES OF HAMILTON'S FISCAL POLICY

The drafting of the Bill of Rights compelled Congress to divert its attention from the pressing task of organizing the federal government. In consequence, it was not until the late summer of 1789 that the Judicial and Executive Departments were ready to take up their duties.

By far the weakest branch of the government was the judiciary. The Judiciary Act of 1789 which created the District, Circuit, and Supreme Courts of the United States withheld from these tribunals much of the jurisdiction which Congress might legitimately have bestowed upon them under the authority granted by the Constitution. Reflecting the framers' confidence in the state courts—in sharp contrast to their distrust of the state legislatures—and their eagerness to conciliate the Antifederalists, the Judiciary Act awarded original jurisdiction in many cases to the state courts. Even so, it did provide for appeals from state courts to the Supreme Court whenever a state court upheld a state law alleged to be in violation of the Federal Constitution. The act thereby established the principle of judicial review of state legislation by the highest federal tribunal.

The branch of the government generally regarded as the most powerful and most likely to encroach upon the authority of other departments was the legislative. Madison expected that in this regard, Congress, especially the House of Representatives, would prove to be the chief troublemaker in the new government. Usually considered to be the prime victim of the legislature's

"Portrait of Alexander Hamilton," painting by John Trumbull, courtesy of the White House Collection.

Connecticut Cent, Mailed Bust Facing Left, 1788.

will to power, the Executive Department received in 1789 a notable accession of strength in the persons of Alexander Hamilton and Thomas Jefferson, whom President Washington appointed Secretary of the Treasury and Secretary of State, respectively.

It was Hamilton who, early in 1790, seized the leadership of the government in the field of domestic policy from James Madison and the House of Representatives and vested it in the Executive Department—or, more precisely, in the Treasury. Hamilton's paramount objective was to carry forward the process of national unification begun by the Revolution and advanced by the adoption of the Constitution. Himself an ultra-nationalist, Hamilton acted upon the assumption that the United States could not attain the place among nations which Nature had marked out for it unless it adopted the kind of fiscal and economic policies that had enabled Great Britain to become the greatest commercial, manufacturing, and maritime power in the world.

As Hamilton saw it, one of the principal obstacles to the realization of his private version of the American Dream—a rich, powerful, and highly centralized nation—was the seemingly inveterate loyalty the American people bore their states. As a West Indian by birth and a New Yorker by adoption, Hamilton felt himself to be an alien in the "American World" partly because he was such a complete and thorough-going nationalist. Because of Americans' misplaced affection, as he conceived it, for their states, he had no hope that a close-knit union could be built upon the sentiment of nationalism alone. To his way of thinking, only self-interest could solidify the Union, for self-interest, particularly "pecuniary interest," was the most powerful of the human passions. Greater even than state-love, in his philosophy, was self-love.

Not everyone, Hamilton acknowledged, knew wherein his self-interest consisted; therefore it fell to the political leaders of the country to give proper direction to this fumbling, often misdirected desire for material self-betterment. In the Report on Public Credit which he presented to Congress in January 1790, Hamilton made a powerful case for the proposition that the affluent citizens of the United States could best foster their own interests by supporting the federal government to the hilt. He proposed, in brief, to convert the national debt into "cement of union" by doing justice, and more, to the public creditors. He recommended that the foreign debt be paid in full, including accrued interest; that the domestic debt be paid virtually at par, also including accrued interest; that the federal government assume the debts contracted by the states in prosecuting the War of Independence; and that all these debts be "funded," i.e. that a portion of the government's revenue be allocated to the payment of interest and principal.

Hamilton's motives in advising Congress to honor its own obligations to the full at the same time that it assumed the state debts were a mixture of political, economic, and fiscal considerations. He knew that the only way to restore the government's credit—i.e. its ability to borrow—was to win the confidence of capitalists by paying its existing debts. By congressional assumption of state debts, he hoped to concentrate the financial power of the country in the federal government—for the responsibility of paying the debt required the exercise of the authority to tax—and to compel the state creditors to look to the federal authority for redemption of their certificates. In short, Hamilton hoped that the states, stripped of their functions by an all-powerful central government, would simply wither away into mere administrative districts of the federal government. The irresistible force of self-interest, by enlisting public creditors and men of property in general on the side of the central government, would, he hoped, remake the whole political character of the nation. And, finally, by giving the public creditors more than even the most sanguine had expected, Hamilton intended to concentrate large quantities of negotiable securities, which served the purpose of capital, in the hands of those best able to employ that capital for the economic advancement of the country.

In the arguments for funding the national debt put forward by Hamilton in his report, there was nothing to stamp him as an innovator in either fiscal or economic theory. Many other men had recognized that the national debt might be converted into a cement of the Union and a vivifying force in the national economy. Bishop Berkeley had called the English national debt "a mine of gold to England," and Sir James Steuart—an eighteenth-century economist with whose work Hamilton was familiar—declared that "the effect of public borrowing, or national debt, is to augment the permanent income of the country out of stagnant money and balances of trade." During the War of Independence, Tom Paine had urged that the debt be used to strengthen the "American Empire." Moreover, funding had already proved its worth in the United States. The government of Pennsylvania had pledged part of its revenue to the amortization of its debt—with the result that the state's securities had risen so sharply in value that they yielded an interest rate of almost 30 percent to those who had bought when the price was low.

Therefore, in proposing to fund the national debt, Hamilton disclaimed any pretensions to originality. He said that he had "heard no lisp from any description of men in the national legislature of an objection to this idea" and that he was pursuing not only "the true principles of credit and the true policy of the case, but the uniform general sense of the Union." To those acquainted with the workings of the British economy, Hamilton's report had a familiar ring. Great Britain bore witness to how a funded national debt, with the aid of a central bank, could be converted into a national blessing by attaching men of wealth to the government, stimulating capitalistic enterprise, and stabilizing the pound sterling. The ability of the British government to pay its debts had become, Hamilton marveled, "in the British mind, an article of faith, and is no longer an article of reason." He was prepared to believe that the credit of the British government was immortal. Hamilton's task was to confer a similar immortality upon the credit of the United States government without, he lamented, the benefit of the British Constitution, British capital resources, or the British national character.

THE FIGHT OVER FUNDING THE DEBT

Although James Madison had said that one of the cardinal purposes of the Constitution was to afford protection to the "opulent minority" he had never supposed that it was a duty of the government to enrich that minority in order to secure its allegiance. Madison envisaged a union of the whole people, not merely the affluent part thereof. As a southerner, he had no desire to reward, as Hamilton's plan would have done, northern speculators and investors who held the bulk of the outstanding federal and state certificates of indebtedness. Nor, as a southerner, could he overlook the fact that, with the exception of South Carolina, the southern states, Virginia among them, had already liquidated most of their war debts and that, in consequence, the northern states would be the chief gainers by the assumption of state debts.

For these reasons, to Hamilton's consternation, Madison took the lead in Congress in opposing the adoption of the Report on Public Credit. Rather than see speculators, some of whom had bought government securities at ten cents on the dollar, appropriate the entire increment resulting from the funding of the debt, Madison demanded an equitable division of the profit between the original holders and later speculative-minded purchasers. He thereby injected a humanitarian note into American politics, for most of those who had sold their certificates for what they would bring were soldiers and plain farmers who had fought or labored for American independence. At the same time, Madison pleaded for justice to the states that had liquidated the greater part of their debts and therefore stood to gain little from Hamilton's plan. If these two points were conceded, Madison was willing to accept Hamilton's Report. But the Secretary of the Treasury opposed all compromise: foreign investors, he pointed out, had bought American securities upon the assurance of the Continental Congress that no discrimination would be made between original holders and later speculators. If Congress violated this promise, the credit of the United States government would be destroyed beyond redemption.

For six months, as a result of the conflict between the Madisonians and the partisans of the Treasury, virtually all business in Congress was brought to a halt. Because of its patently sectional bias, Hamilton's Report on Public Credit seemed to have disrupted the already shaky coalition of northern businessmen and southern planters which had made possible the adoption of the Constitution and upon which the perpetuation of the union depended. Except for South Carolina, whose large debt gave it a vested interest in the adoption of Hamilton's report, most of Madison's following came from the southern states. The public creditors, it was observed, were in the North; the taxpayers (i.e., those who paid the duties on imports) were in the South. Northerners, it appeared, would not be content until they had extracted the last drop from the southern "Milch-cow."

Uncertainty and delay tended to increase the incidence of speculation in the public debt—the very "evil" Madison sought to curb. Early in 1790, in the expectation that the assumption of state debts would be carried, northern speculators dispatched fast-sailing ships to South Carolina to buy that state's certificates of indebtedness before the news of Hamilton's report arrived.

But by July 1790 the speculators realized, if they did not know it before, that they were not betting on a sure thing. The Secretary was accused of wanton recklessness, and some of his erstwhile admirers began to unload their holdings, particularly of state securities, convinced that Hamilton's report would never pass Congress. But even more alarming than the credit situation was the injection into the dispute of sectional rancor that seemed to put the Union itself in jeopardy.

Yet a basis for compromise existed, and there were men ready to act upon it. Throughout the debate over Hamilton's report, the question of the permanent site of the federal government had never been lost sight of. Hamilton himself tried to strike a bargain with the Pennsylvania representatives and senators whereby in exchange for enough votes to insure the adoption of his report the national capital would be located in Philadelphia or on the Susquehanna. When the Pennsylvanians failed to produce the necessary votes, Hamilton turned perforce to the Virginians, who, despite the vehemence of their opposition to the funding-assumption plan, were eager to move the capital to the Potomac.

No one felt more strongly the importance of transferring the capital to the Potomac than did Thomas Jefferson. Hitherto, although his sympathies were entirely with Madison, the Secretary of State had taken no direct part in the controversy. He was known, however, to be a moderate and to fear for the continuance of the Union. When Hamilton made an overture to Jefferson, the Virginian agreed to arrange a meeting of the leaders of the contending factions. Over a bottle of wine—the Secretary of State served only the finest French vintages—the two cabinet officers and James Madison agreed to a compromise: the debt was to be funded much as Hamilton had proposed; the present holders of government certificates were to be paid in full; the assumption of state debts was to be "sweetened" for Virginia and other states with small war debts by an outright gift from the federal government; and the national capital, after a period of ten years during which Philadelphia served as the government's residence, was to be relocated on the Potomac.

Although it ran against the grain of Virginia congressmen to vote for the settlement worked out by Jefferson, Madison, and Hamilton, the Virginians mustered enough votes to carry it through Congress. Still, it was a sectional victory: far more northerners than southerners voted to adopt Hamilton's report. Nor was there any question as to who reaped the financial windfall: in 1795, citizens of Massachusetts were paid over $300,000 in interest on United States government securities, whereas Virginians received only $62,000. The speculators, upon whom descended a golden harvest in the form of unearned increment, sang hosannas to the sagacious Secretary of the Treasury.

And with good reason: the funding of the debt incurred by the Continental Congress and the assumption of state debts gave security holders about $70 million for their depreciated paper. Backed by the financial resources of the federal government, these securities had a cash surrender value which permitted them to be used as money in business transactions, including the payment of private debts to foreign creditors. Moreover, the credit of the United States was so firmly established that by 1792 the federal government enjoyed a better credit rating than any Continental European country.

Hamilton was well satisfied with the bargain he had struck with Jefferson: to secure the passage of the funding-assumption bills, he would gladly have moved the national capital to an even hotter spot than the Potomac in August. At first, too, Jefferson was content; among other advantages he foresaw from this arrangement was an opportunity to participate personally in the planning of the federal city and in designing its public buildings. Captivated by this prospect, Jefferson momentarily forgot his aversion to cities: he expressed the hope that the federal capital would attract "foreigners, manufacturers and settlers" to the Potomac, thereby shifting southward the balance of population, political power, and wealth. But after 1791, when the Virginia legislature condemned the assumption of state debts, Jefferson changed his mind about the transaction: he now said that he had been made to "hold the candle" while Hamilton looted the United States Treasury for the benefit of his "corrupt squadron."

THE NATIONAL BANK AND THE CONSTITUTION

Having brought the state creditors into the national fold, unlimbered the taxing powers of the federal government (the assumption of state debts required the imposition of an excise), and floated loans in Holland at a low rate of interest upon the credit of the United States, Hamilton was ready to embark upon the second stage of his program for centralizing political, fiscal, and economic power in the federal government and stimulating, by means of governmental aid, the development of the country's resources. Accordingly, in December 1790, Hamilton submitted to Congress a Report on a National Bank in which he urged that a quasi-public bank called the Bank of the United States be authorized by the federal government with a charter to run for twenty years. Ownership and control of the bank were to be shared by the government and private stockholders: the government would contribute part of the bank's capital of $10 million and appoint five members of a twenty-five-man Board of Directors; the larger share of the capital and the actual management of the bank would be vested in the twenty directors appointed by the private stockholders. Yet the government was not wholly a silent partner in the Bank of the United States: the Secretary of the Treasury was privileged to examine its books periodically and, as Hamilton later demonstrated, a forceful Secretary of the Treasury could make the bank an instrument for effecting the government's overall fiscal objectives. Finally, according to Hamilton's plan, the bank was authorized to make loans to private borrowers as well as to the government and to issue bank notes which, hopefully, would circulate throughout the country and thereby provide a national currency.

Central banks had been established in Great Britain and in most of the important continental countries including Russia. Although France did not have a central bank until Napoleon created the Bank of France in 1800, the experience of other nations demonstrated to Hamilton's satisfaction that a central bank was necessary to the proper functioning of the government and to the commercial and industrial development of the nation. In the United States, the lack of a circulating medium made such an institution imperative. The three banks operating in 1790 in New York, Philadelphia, and Boston issued paper notes that circulated as money, but not even the mercantile needs of those cities were fully met. Outside these commercial centers, virtually the only hard money in circulation was Spanish coins. In 1789, the provisional state of Franklin (later Tennessee) proposed to pay the governor a salary of one thousand deer skins; legislators were to receive three racoon skins *per diem;* and justices of the peace were authorized to charge one muskrat skin for every warrant they signed. As late as 1806, a British traveler observed that, in the West, the words *buy* and *sell* were almost unknown; in business transactions, everything was conducted as *trade.*

The bill chartering the Bank of the United States passed Congress but not before the constitutionality of the institution had been questioned by James Madison. President Washington, who attached great weight to Madison's view of the Constitution, was deeply troubled. Before signing the bill, therefore, he asked the members of his cabinet to submit in writing an opinion regarding the constitutionality of the proposed bank.

Like Madison, Jefferson's view of the Constitution was colored by his fear of Alexander Hamilton and the rule of a northern majority of speculators, bankers, and merchants. In the opinion of the Virginians, the Bank of the United States was another milestone on the road to monarchism, centralization, and the Leviathan State. Naturally, therefore, they found no sanction in the Constitution for such an institution. Indeed, from their reading, it appeared that the federal government had no power to create corporations of any kind, that the general welfare clause was merely a general statement of purpose and therefore conferred no substantive power, independent of the enumerated powers, upon the federal government, and that the necessary and proper clause intended that only means absolutely essential, not merely convenient or even appropriate, to carry out an enumerated power, were authorized.

This was strict construction of the Constitution at its most rigid and uncompromising. Jefferson and Madison revealed themselves to be legal fundamentalists; if their views had prevailed, the federal government would have been bound at every turn by the literal interpretation of a definitive text. Although Jefferson did not admit it, the rule of the majority, which he regarded as the very essence of republicanism, would have been largely nullified by the application of his formula. For the amending process—the only way in which he believed that the Bank of the United States could be legalized—required the consent of three-fourths of the states.

If the application of this doctrine had rendered the federal government powerless to promote the national welfare in the economic sphere, Jefferson would not have regarded it at this time as a deprivation. In his opinion, the most important clause in the preamble to the Constitution was that which pledged the government "to secure the blessings of Liberty to ourselves and our Posterity." To him, liberty was not a mere abstraction: it meant such a complete absence of governmental control that a citizen was hardly aware that government existed. "This," he said, "is the perfection of human society." He always preferred the inconveniences attending too much liberty to those resulting from too little. An energetic government he held to be the eternal enemy of liberty.

Like most opposition leaders in American history, Jefferson and Madison exalted the rights of the states at the same time that they depreciated the powers of the federal government. While denying power to the federal government to charter corporations, they conceded this power to the states. Jefferson insisted that his only purpose was to preserve the "beautiful balance" established by the Constitution between the states and the federal government, but his constitutional theory would have given the states exclusive control of a vital sector of the national economy.

The brief presented by Hamilton to the President justifying the constitutionality of the Bank of the United States took a more permissive view of the powers of the federal government under the Constitution. Applying to that document what later came to be designated a broad interpretation, the Secretary of the Treasury argued that the necessary and proper and the general welfare clauses gave Congress the power to charter corporations when they were necessary to the execution of an enumerated power. Since the Bank of the United States, at least in Hamilton's opinion, was a necessary auxiliary to the power to levy taxes, collect revenue, pay government obligations, and take care of the banking business of the government, its constitutionality seemed to him clear and unquestioned. When a power was delegated to attain specified objectives, he reasoned, all the known and usual means of effecting them must be considered as incidental to it. Finally, Hamilton found in the general welfare clause a grant of power to Congress to appropriate money to any purpose that served the general, as distinct from the local, welfare. In short, the federal government, like all other viable governments, was authorized by the Constitution to do whatever was needed to fulfill the ends for which it had been instituted.

While his doubts and misgivings were not wholly removed by Hamilton's arguments, President Washington signed the bill incorporating the Bank of the United States. The bank opened its doors in April 1791. For the duration of its existence, its headquarters remained in Philadelphia but, as a result of the directors' decision to establish branch banks in the important commercial centers of the United States, its operations became national in scope.

THE REPORT ON MANUFACTURES

Hamilton never supposed that a viable union could be erected solely upon the "pecuniary interest" of the rich. Vital as were their capital, energy, and talents to the building of a nation, he was always sensible of the necessity of broadening the base of the Union. By 1792, he had learned, not wholly to his satisfaction, that his policies tended to concentrate wealth and financial control in the hands of northerners; he expressed concern, for example, that so little stock of the Bank of the United States was bought by southerners. The planters and farmers of the South, he admitted, had to be given a stake in the new economic and fiscal dispensation which, so far, had tended to lavish its bounties upon northern businessmen.

As Hamilton projected it, the capstone of his grand design was to be the solidification of the Union by integrating the economies of the North and South. If sectionalism could not be eradicated, Hamilton believed that by wise political management it could be made to serve the cause of nationalism. Since he discounted patriotism as a foundation of an enduring union, Hamilton addressed himself to the task of harnessing the acquisitive instincts to his purpose; the sections were to be welded together by bonds of material interest.

He began with the premise that the United States could not become rich or powerful or truly united as long as it remained an agricultural country living by exporting its surpluses. In 1790, nine-tenths of gainfully employed Americans were engaged in the production of food or raw materials, and virtually all the country's shipping was occupied in the fisheries and in carrying agricultural produce to overseas markets. As Americans continued to bring new land under cultivation, they increased the quantity of the products they put upon the world market. Since, according to Hamilton's analysis, supply tended to outrun demand, Americans were working to depress the price level and to keep their country poor and at the mercy of all the political and economic vicissitudes that befell the Old World.

Hamilton was keenly aware that an industrial revolution was in progress and that the United States could not afford to trust to the traditional handicrafts when newer and more efficient methods were being utilized by its rivals. For the American economy as then constituted, Hamilton drew a gloomy prognosis: the European market for the produce of American farms and plantations would steadily contract as Great Britain and the continental countries moved toward self-sufficiency. To prepare for the impending loss of their foreign markets and to solidify the Union, Hamilton believed that Americans must cultivate the vast domestic market opened up by the American Revolution and the Federal Constitution. Instead of being tied economically to Europe, the sections must be tied to each other. Only then, Hamilton thought, would the Union be secure and the American people set upon the highroad that led to national wealth and power.

Instructed by Congress in December 1790 to prepare a report upon methods of increasing manufactures, Hamilton, with the aid of Tench Coxe, the Assistant Secretary of the Treasury and an ardent proponent of manufacturing, made a survey of manufacturing as it then existed in the United States. His inventory of American resources revealed that almost all manufacturing was confined to the first stage in the treatment of raw materials—flour was milled from wheat, hops were converted into beer, rum from molasses, etc. Of all American industries, shipbuilding required the most advanced technology. Several textile mills, incorporating the newest type of machinery, had been established in Rhode Island and Massachusetts. (Although the British government prohibited the export of machinery, Samuel Slater, an English mechanic, emigrated to the United States carrying the complete design, of a textile factory including the machinery, in his head.) Manufactures, Hamilton admitted, were still in an embryonic stage, but, if this "precious embryo" were assiduously nurtured, it promised to grow into something very big indeed.

Hamilton's Report on Manufactures, submitted to Congress in January 1792, was the third step in his plan for remaking the American economy and the most revolutionary, in its implications, of all Hamilton's reports. The Secretary of the Treasury proposed that, under the sanction of the general welfare clause, the federal government force the pace of the incipient industrial development of the United States and stimulate the growth of selected manufactures by means of premiums, bounties, and tariffs. The industries designated to receive government aid were those essential to a self-sufficient economy. Special emphasis was laid upon the production of cotton and woolen cloth, the textiles for which the United States was largely dependent upon Great Britain. But Hamilton was careful not to invoke anti-British feeling as an argument for promoting domestic manufactures. Rather, he pictured manufacturing as a potential "cement of the union." Northern factories would consume southern raw products, and southerners in turn would buy northern manufactured goods, thereby demonstrating that "mutual wants constitute one of the strongest bonds of political connection." In 1794 he told Talleyrand that "great markets, such as formerly existed in the old world, will be established in America"; "we only need two markets, but they are indispensable to us: one for the Northern and one for the Southern states." Hamilton's vision was of one nation, economically indivisible.

Clearly, Hamilton did not believe that checks and balances and the separation of powers debarred an energetic federal government from molding the national economy. All that was needed, by his reckoning, was wise planning and purposeful leadership. Given these, Hamilton did not doubt that every difficulty could be surmounted. He was persuaded that even the shortages of capital and labor, the principal impediments to manufacturing in the United States, would yield to the domestic sources of capital made available by the funding system, the Bank of the United States, and the inflow of foreign capital. As for overcoming the labor shortage, the Secretary rested his hopes upon utilizing the labor of women and children in factories and upon the introduction of labor-saving machinery.

Jefferson considered the proposals made in the Report on Manufactures to be patently unconstitutional. If the federal government could do everything

Hamilton asserted it was competent to do under the general welfare clause, Jefferson said that there was nothing the federal government could not do. In Jefferson's opinion, the constitutional implications contained in Hamilton's Report on Manufactures went far beyond his Report on the Bank of the United States. The bank, after all, was considered as incidental to an enumerated power of Congress: in the Report on Manufactures, on the other hand, Hamilton was relying mainly upon the general welfare clause. Visibly agitated by his fears and forebodings, the Secretary of State told the President that the way Congress acted upon Hamilton's Report on Manufactures would determine "whether we live under a limited or an unlimited government."

Jefferson's constitutional objections had little effect upon President Washington, who was one of the most fervent advocates of domestic manufactures in the United States. It was a source of regret to Washington that as President he was debarred from investing in a woolen factory a group of Virginians planned to establish at Alexandria. The President delighted in appearing publicly in clothing woven in American textile mills (when he was inaugurated in 1789 he proudly wore a suit of clothes manufactured in Connecticut), and when he toured the New England states in 1790 he did not fail to inspect every factory that lay along his route.

Yet, judged by its immediate results, the Report on Manufactures was the least productive of Hamilton's reports. Even though Washington strongly recommended a program of government aid to manufactures and the establishment of government-owned and operated factories for the production of military supplies, Congress did little more than erect a bounty system for encouraging the fisheries. What rendered Hamilton's Report on Manufactures abortive—at least until Henry Clay breathed life into it and christened it the American System—was not the constitutional objections raised by Jefferson but the outbreak of the wars of the French Revolution. Contrary to Hamilton's prediction that the European market for American exports would suffer steady constriction, European countries with their manpower engaged in war needed agricultural produce from America as never before. In exchange for foodstuffs and raw products, Americans imported British manufactures in unparalleled quantities. As a result, Americans continued to direct their efforts toward agriculture and commerce and felt little incentive to engage in manufacturing. Not until the embargo of 1808-1809 did manufacturing begin to assume the proportions Hamilton had envisioned two decades previously.

9.
JEFFERSON AND HAMILTON

JEFFERSON'S AGRARIAN PHILOSOPHY

Behind the constitutional objections raised by Jefferson and Madison against Hamilton's Report on Manufactures was their deep concern for republicanism, the South, and the agrarian way of life. Viewed from this perspective, Hamilton's report appeared to be a transparent effort to enrich the North at the expense of the South and to provide Hamilton with additional means for corrupting Congress and subverting republicanism. If, as Hamilton seemed to intend, the South should become a supplier of raw materials for northern factories, Jefferson and Madison believed that their section would be consigned to the position of a colonial dependency and that the taxes imposed upon southerners by the federal government would be used for the purpose of fostering the industrial development of the rival section.

Rather than put the southern staple states in thrall to northern commercial and manufacturing states, Jefferson and Madison took the position that the government ought to stay out of the economy, leaving, in Madison's words, "to the sagacity of individuals, and to the impulse of private interest, the application of industry and capital." Yet in 1789, both men had advocated governmental intervention in the economy in order to divert American trade from Great Britain to France and other Continental countries. Nor did they renounce this policy out of respect for mere consistency.

Before 1790, Madison would have argued that it was better for southerners to do business with northern merchants and manufacturers than with their

---

"Portrait of Thomas Jefferson," painting by Caleb Boyle, from the Allen P. Kirby Collection of Historical Paintings, Lafayette College, Easton, Pa.

Connecticut Cent, Mailed Bust Facing Right, Small Head, 1788.

British counterparts, but Alexander Hamilton had given the Virginian a new and sobering insight into the consequences of integrating the American economy. For the same reason, Jefferson's devotion to the agricultural way of life and his aversion to cities and large-scale manufacturing became more pronounced after 1790. In his mind, farming became ever more closely identified with republicanism; manufacturing and cities he associated with monarchism. Although as late as 1790 he had advocated erecting a great commercial and manufacturing center on the Potomac, he now reverted to his earlier position that industrialism was a curse that brought wretchedness and degradation upon the working class, a conviction that had been firmly impressed upon his mind even before he went to Europe in 1784. In Hamilton's Report on Manufactures, Jefferson beheld not the beginning of a creative partnership between American agriculture and manufacturing but a conspiracy against republicanism that would lead to the enrichment of the privileged few and the creation of large cities where free Americans would be ground into a degraded, vicious, Europeanized proletariat. Jefferson's advice to his countrymen was: keep the factories in Europe if they hoped to preserve their republican institutions, engage in the pursuit of happiness, and realize the American dream.

Yet Jefferson's repugnance to cities was at variance with his passion for city planning: while he deplored the conditions of life in cities, he believed that they could be made tolerable by wise planning. If every house fronted upon an open square, he remarked, the atmosphere of a town would be hardly different from that of the country. Nor did he condemn town dwellers indiscriminately: in 1793, when a large part of the population of Philadelphia demonstrated its support of the French Revolution, he called them the "yeomanry" of the city. Nevertheless, he would have been the first to assert that city people suffered from their lack of direct contact with the good American earth.

As Jefferson saw it, the distinctive qualities that set Americans apart from the rest of mankind were derived from their unique environment. By providing them with a seemingly inexhaustible expanse of arable land, a benevolent Providence, as he interpreted its designs, had set aside the United States for agriculture. By so doing, Providence had made it possible for Americans to engage in what Jefferson regarded as the most wholesome, morally uplifting, and productive occupation man could know upon earth—farming.

Faith in the people—the first article of Jefferson's political creed—was inseparable from his conception of the nature of the universe. His political philosophy presupposed the existence of a universe ruled by law and a benevolent Creator, who had endowed mankind with reason and social instincts, including altruism and a passion for justice. He believed that the rights of man were an essential part of the infrastructure of this divine order. Being self-evident truths, they could be apprehended by the human mind. When he spoke of the necessity of showing a decent respect to the opinion of mankind, he assumed that this opinion was an expression of the moral element inherent in the nature of the universe.

Jefferson's social criterion was always: What kind of people would a given society be likely to produce? The quality of its citizens, not their number or even their degree of wealth, determined for him a nation's claim to greatness. Since every society rested upon an ethical foundation, that society ought to be accounted best which gave the widest latitude to the growth of the moral instincts with which men were endowed by nature. In a society which conformed to the designs of nature, as did the United States, Jefferson assumed that there would be little need of compulsion or even of government: men's behavior would be governed by their innate moral sense, now brought into full flower by a moderate government which, after providing a basic education, left them free to follow their instinctive sense of right and wrong. This sense, he believed, was far more reliable than prescriptions regarding thought or conduct laid down by any government.

To Jefferson, the United States was always "this heavenly country," destined, if it remained true to the principles upon which it had been founded, to achieve the closest approximation which mankind would ever attain to heaven upon earth. Naturally, therefore, he envisaged progress in terms of a forward movement along the lines upon which Americans had already embarked: more farms, more household manufactures, a wider diffusion of the ownership of land, more education, more equality, more moral improvement, and more solid happiness.

Jefferson loved not only his own land but all the land comprised by the American republic. While Monticello always occupied a special place in his affections, he took almost as much satisfaction and pride in a neighbor's well-ordered prosperous farm. Yet comparatively few Americans shared Jefferson's reverence for the land and his gratitude for the blessings with which nature had so lavishly endowed the United States. For most of Jefferson's contemporaries and their posterity, the land was something to be exploited, the forests to be ruthlessly despoiled, the mineral wealth to be extracted with little regard to the needs of future generations. By its very bounty, nature seemed to insure that Jefferson's message would be ignored—at least until the "inexhaustible" resources of the country began to show signs of serious depletion.

CONTROVERSY BETWEEN JEFFERSON AND HAMILTON

To Jefferson, the struggle for control of the federal government that began in 1789 was nothing less than a confrontation between monarchism and republicanism. On every hand, especially within the federal government itself, he saw evidences of the rising power of monarchism: in the effort in the Senate to give the President a title such as "His Highness the President of the United States and Protector of their Liberties"; in John Adams' alleged defection from republicanism to the monarchal camp; in the levees and other evidences of "monarchal pomp" affected by President Washington; and in the dinner-table conversation in New York and Philadelphia where the British system of government was openly praised. At the head of this "monarchal conspiracy" he placed Alexander Hamilton: in Jefferson's book (he set down his opinions, together with the rumors and gossip he picked up from his friends, in a book he called the "Anas"), Hamilton figured not merely as the advocate of consolidated government but as a monarchist bent upon subverting the Constitution and establishing in the United States a government of kings, lords, and commons.

In consequence, the controversy between Hamilton and Jefferson could not be conducted wholly under the decorous guise of constitutional interpretation. As Jefferson and Madison saw it, so long as the dispute was kept upon this lofty intellectual plane, the American people were not likely to realize the full danger in which they and their free institutions stood from Hamilton and his partisans. Persuaded that nothing less than the fate of republicanism was at issue, Jefferson and Madison keenly felt the need of a national newspaper capable of alerting the people to Hamilton's real designs. Such a newspaper seemed all the more essential in view of the fact that since 1789 the *Gazette of the United States,* edited by John Fenno and subsidized by Hamilton and his friends, had been engaged in fabricating an image of the Secretary of the Treasury as a patriot and statesman beyond reproach.

To counteract the adulation dispensed by Fenno's *Gazette of the United States,* Jefferson and Madison persuaded Philip Freneau, the "Poet of the Revolution" turned newspaper editor, to establish in Philadelphia a newspaper called the *National Gazette.* The main financial inducement held out by Jefferson to bring Freneau to Philadelphia was the offer of a clerkship in the State Department.

As editor of the *National Gazette,* Philip Freneau made the Federalists regret that he had not confined his talents to writing poetry. He specialized in heaping coals upon Hamilton: every measure conceived by the Secretary of the Treasury, Freneau declared, had as its ulterior objective the creation of a king, lords, and commons in the United States. On July 4, 1792, for example, the *National Gazette* printed an article entitled "Rules for changing a limited republican government into an unlimited hereditary one." The first rule was to increase the national debt and to establish a central bank.

What Freneau was saying about Hamilton in the *National Gazette,* Jefferson was saying directly to President Washington. Early in 1792, the Secretary of State told the President that Hamilton was interfering in the conduct of foreign affairs, ruling Congress by means of a "corrupt squadron," and working to make the United States a monarchy. In May 1792, he asserted that the crisis of republicanism was at hand: Congress must either be purged of all holders of government securities and bank stock or the monarchists would take over the country. Monarchists, according to Jefferson's definition, sought to aggrandize the power of the Executive; true republicans, on the other hand, exalted the legislature as the direct representative of the people. He wished to see Congress wholly free of direction from the Executive Branch; only then, he said, could separation of powers ordained by the Constitution be preserved.

Despite his deep respect for Jefferson, President Washington refused to be alarmed by the bogey of monarchism. He did not know of ten reputable men in the United States, he told Jefferson, who seriously contemplated erecting a monarchy, and, he added, he would give the last drop of his blood to insure that the republican experiment was given a fair trial. As for Hamilton's work, the President took the position that, lacking some infallible rule of reason, it must be judged pragmatically. When he contrasted the state of the country as he had known it under the Articles of Confederation with its present prosperity and financial stability, he was prepared to give Hamilton the benefit of every constitutional doubt.

Hamilton, too, registered his complaints of his colleague with the President. He told Washington that Jefferson intrigued with members of Congress to defeat administration measures and to discredit Hamilton himself and that the Virginian's ambition was so inordinate that he aspired to the presidency itself. But neither man succeeded in shaking the President's confidence in the other; instead of taking sides, Washington urged them to compose their differences. Both men replied that they could never sacrifice their principles. As Jefferson said, republicanism and monarchism could never lie down together in peace.

In August 1792, Hamilton learned that, while remaining discreetly in the background, Jefferson had been instrumental in bringing Freneau to Philadelphia. He immediately assumed that Jefferson was responsible for everything that appeared in the *National Gazette* and that he supplied the libels and gossip with which Freneau regaled his readers. Writing in the newspapers under a pseudonym, Hamilton accused the Secretary of State of having hired with government money a character-assassin to destroy the peoples' confidence in the Secretary of the Treasury. Although Jefferson himself did not respond publicly, his friends, including James Monroe, filled the newspapers with attacks upon Hamilton. Among other things, he was called an apostate from the principles of 1776, who wished to introduce into republican America that "class of human lions, tygers and mammoths called kings."

By singling out Jefferson as his prime enemy, Hamilton succeeded in making the Secretary of State appear to be the leader of the anti-Hamiltonian opposition. Hitherto, James Madison had been regarded as its chief spokesman —that opposition had been known as the "Madisonian" party; henceforth, it was called the "Jeffersonian" or Republican party. Madison continued to supply ideas and to devise political strategy, but he took care to subordinate himself to his older friend. It was the author of the Declaration of Independence to whom the adversaries of the Hamiltonian system looked for leadership.

The conflict which began at the center of the government—in Congress and within the administration itself—spread quickly to the people as a whole.

From this confrontation of interests, ideals, and slogans there began to emerge two political parties, each national in scope, that sought to gain control of the government and to enact legislation and shape the Constitution according to its views of the national welfare. This struggle of political parties had a unifying effect inasmuch as it tended to concentrate the peoples' attention upon the actions of the federal government. Jefferson and Madison, no less than Hamilton, were telling the people that it mattered very much to them what laws were enacted in Congress and what party prevailed in the councils of the nation.

In this contest, antimonarchism provided Hamilton's adversaries with a rallying cry far more effective in agitating the public mind than did such things as centralization of power, governmental favoritism to bankers, speculators, and businessmen, and disregard of the "farming interest." Moreover, antimonarchism suffered from no sectional taint: true republicans in all parts of the country could respond with fervor when they were told that republicanism was in danger. By taking the name of "Republicans," Jefferson and his adherents intended to distinguish themselves from the "monarchists," otherwise known as Federalists.

Jefferson always denied the charge that he was the spokesman of a section. In his own eyes, he appeared as nothing less than the champion of the majority of the people of the United States; it was in their name and in their behalf that he entered the lists against Hamilton. He aimed at the creation of a national party that would unite the plain people of the country—solidly republican to the core—against a minority composed of financiers, speculators, and pro-British merchants—all of whom he supposed to be monarchists—which had gained temporary control of the federal government. Waging battle against these "monocrats," Jefferson saw no need to distinguish between the interests of the South and those of the majority of the people in every section.

While monarchism and republicanism did excellent service as political slogans, they did not adequately express the differences between Hamilton and Jefferson. What Jefferson regarded as evidences of monarchism in Hamilton's work was actually an effort on the part of the Secretary of the Treasury to centralize the administration, to diversify the economy, and to strengthen the capitalistic system—all with a view to making the United States a world power. To Hamilton, a monarchy in the United States was strictly a last resort; only after republicanism had fully demonstrated its inadequacy, he said, should hereditary office be established. In actuality, Hamilton found fault with the Constitution not because it had failed to establish a monarchy but because he feared that it gave too much power to the states. The charge that Jefferson might justly have leveled against Hamilton was that he did not really believe in federalism. Yet Hamilton was certain in his own mind that his policies offered the only hope of counteracting the strong centrifugal tendencies at work in the United States which threatened to make the Federal Constitution almost as ineffective as the Articles of Confederation. In 1793, however, when the tide seemed to be running strongly in his favor, Hamilton, by Jefferson's own account, expressed fulsome praise of the Constitution. It all depended upon who was administering the government and interpreting the sacred text. If Hamilton despaired of the republic, it was mainly because he feared that Thomas Jefferson and his partisans would gain possession of the federal government.

Unlike Jefferson, Hamilton did not invest farmers with special sanctity: to him, farming was merely a way of making a living which was no more approved by heaven than any other productive employment. Farmers, far from being the most virtuous of mankind, seemed to him to be prone to violence and unsound finance. While he acknowledged that agriculture ought to enjoy primacy in the United States, he thought that more Americans ought to be working in factories which turned out goods that would make the United States less dependent upon European sources of supply and which consumed the surplus raw products produced on American farms and plantations.

Ambitious as Hamilton was for the growth and prosperity of his adopted country, he always doubted that the American people were quite up to the destiny Nature seemed to have marked out for them. On one occasion he exclaimed that this "American world" was not for him. He had caught a vision of a powerful, centralized, affluent republic, and yet, he complained, the majority of Americans could not break themselves of the habit of thinking small: state rights, a weak central government, and *laissez faire*. For this reason, among others, Hamilton had little confidence in the American people. Jefferson always felt that he had the majority of the people on his side, but this heartwarming certainty was never granted Hamilton. If the United States were ever to achieve the status of a world power, Hamilton thought that it might have to be accomplished in spite of the American people. Their reluctance to grasp the greatness within their reach afforded little hope that his private version of the American Dream would be realized through their efforts.

Hamilton saw no danger to liberty in centralized government, but, then, liberty was not his primary concern. Without being an enemy of liberty, he thought that the American people were altogether too much inclined to make free with it. With such confirmed opponents of governmental authority, he had no fear that liberty would be overborne; rather, the danger came from the other side—that government would be weakened to the point of debility by passionate but irresponsible lovers of freedom. Hamilton viewed every problem from the point of view of a nationalist: in his opinion, that government was best which most effectively promoted the power, prosperity, and glory of the United States.

With his cabinet in disarray and he himself charged with having fallen under the sway of his insidious Secretary of the Treasury, Washington repented that he had allowed himself to be persuaded to leave private life. He lamented his "extreme wretchedness" in office and yet, when he expressed a desire to relinquish the presidency after the expiration of his first term, both Jefferson and Hamilton declared that they, too, would quit public office. Reluctantly, therefore, Washington laid aside a farewell address upon which he and Madison were working and agreed to stand for a second term. Again he had the gratification of receiving the unanimous vote of the electoral college, but even his surpassing fame was beginning to bear the tarnish inseparable from long continuance in political office.

Even though both cabinet officers agreed to remain at their posts, the struggle for power went on without remission. In 1792-1793, having failed to turn the President against Hamilton, Jefferson tried to procure his colleague's dismissal by means of congressional vote of censure. William Giles, a member of Congress from Virginia, presented to the House a series of resolutions condemning Hamilton's conduct of the Treasury and requesting the President to remove him from office. These resolutions, particularly the most virulent, were the work of Thomas Jefferson. Their rejection by the House did not in the slightest weaken Jefferson's conviction that Hamilton was guilty of malfeasance in office and of plotting to overthrow the republican institutions of the United States.

10. CITIZEN GENÊT AND THE FRENCH ALLIANCE

DIVISION OVER FOREIGN POLICY

During the years 1790-1792, while the struggle between Jefferson and Hamilton revolved upon issues relating to domestic policies, foreign affairs thrust themselves increasingly to the fore. Jefferson and Hamilton, like the American people themselves, were no more agreed upon questions of foreign policy than upon the domestic issues raised by Hamilton's reports. Caught up in the rush of events occurring on the other side of the Atlantic, Americans were agitated by passions they had not known since the Revolution. Politics did not stop at the water's edge; for over two decades they were focused upon foreign affairs.

Under both the Federal Constitution and the Articles of Confederation the cardinal objectives of American foreign policy were to secure the cession of the northwest posts, to make a commercial treaty with Great Britain, and to establish the right of American citizens to navigate the Mississippi River to the sea. The adoption of the Constitution did not immediately move the attainment of these objectives appreciably closer. At first, the British government treated the new federal government with no more deference than it had displayed toward the moribund Continental Congress: no British minister attended the inauguration of President Washington. However, unofficial relations were kept up on the British side through Major George Beckwith, and President Washington sent Gouverneur Morris to London as his personal envoy to hold informal talks with British ministers.

"Citizen Genêt Formally Presented to Washington," illustration by Howard Pyle from The Bettmann Archive.

Kentucky Token, 1792.

From the beginning of his administration, President Washington made a practice of asking all four members of the cabinet for written opinions upon important questions of foreign as well as domestic policy without regard to their special areas of expertise. He consulted the Secretary of the Treasury upon subjects relating to foreign affairs, and he attached much importance to the opinions expressed by the Secretary of State upon fiscal matters. As a result, each head of a department was encouraged to regard the entire government as his province.

This method was followed by the President when, in the summer of 1790, war seemed imminent between Spain and Great Britain as a result of the Spanish seizure of British ships at Nootka Sound on Vancouver Island. The President and cabinet agreed that, while remaining neutral, the United States ought to try to improve the occasion by securing the navigation of the Mississippi and the cession of East and West Florida. Hamilton hoped to gain these ends by making concessions to Great Britain, whereas Jefferson preferred to ask France to use its good offices with Spain to grant American demands. Before the United States could take advantage of this promising situation, Spain surrendered Nootka Sound to Great Britain and the threat of war passed. But the Secretary of State was not disheartened: sooner or later, he predicted, Europeans would resume their occupation of cutting each others' throats, thereby giving the United States an opportunity of acquiring by diplomatic pressure everything upon the North American continent that belonged to it by the laws of nature.

Pending this event, the cession of the northwest posts and the formation of a commercial treaty with Great Britain occupied the attention of the Washington administration. When Gouverneur Morris failed to make any progress in his talks with British ministers in London, Jefferson became even more firmly convinced that economic reprisals offered the only hope of bringing Great Britain to terms. In preparation for the commercial war he had come to regard as almost inevitable, the Secretary of State began in 1791 to compile a statistical survey of American trade with Great Britain and France with a view to showing that the former mother country was doing everything in its power to hamper the commercial growth of the republic. Yet, in order to give a fair trial to the administration's efforts to secure the surrender of the northwest posts and make a commercial treaty with Great Britain, Jefferson withheld his report from Congress. Hamilton, on his own initiative and without the approval of President Washington, broached to Major Beckwith the idea of an alliance between the two countries and warned the Major against Jefferson, whom he described as a moon-struck lover of all things French. Beckwith hardly needed the warning: in official circles in London, the Secretary of State was regarded as an incurable anglophobe.

Even though the British government failed to respond to Hamilton's overtures, it did accredit a minister to the United States in 1791, largely because it feared that Congress would adopt the discriminatory legislation favored by Jefferson and Madison. But Jefferson quickly ascertained that George

Hammond, the British representative, had no power to negotiate a commercial treaty or to arrange for the transfer of the northwest posts. Conversations between the Secretary of State and the British minister bogged down in a controversy over responsibility for infractions of the treaty of peace. Naturally, Hammond preferred to do business with the Secretary of the Treasury; even Ternant, the French minister, found Hamilton's company more congenial than that of Jefferson.

AMERICAN NEUTRALITY

The outbreak of the French Revolution gave fresh impetus to Jefferson's and Madison's efforts to divert American trade and commerce toward France. The two countries' common dedication to liberty reinforced the gratitude which Jefferson had always deemed sufficient in itself to warrant giving special consideration to France. After 1789, Hamilton and other advocates of rapprochement with Great Britain labored under the disadvantage that France had espoused the cause of Liberty, Equality, and Fraternity. But as the revolution ran its course, taking a bloody toll of its friends as well as its enemies, conservative Americans recoiled from its "excesses." Hamilton and John Adams were among the first of many Americans to dissociate the American Revolution from the "crimes" taking place in France in the name of liberty.

In September 1792, France became a republic, an event which to Jefferson's way of thinking consummated the ideological alliance between France and the United States. But in February 1793, the French Republic declared war upon Great Britain, and for the next twenty-two years, except for a brief truce in 1801-1803, Europe did not know peace. Here, assuredly, was the opportunity for which Americans had waited. In order fully to exploit the situation, however, the United States itself had to stay outside the European conflict. It remained to be seen whether the European belligerents would permit the United States to remain neutral, to enjoy all the rights and immunities it claimed under that status, and to expand its boundaries at the expense of the warring European powers.

The prospect of maintaining neutrality was compromised by the fact that the United States, as an ally of France, was committed to the defense of the French West Indies against hostile attack if France requested such aid—an eventuality that seemed certain to occur in a naval war between France and Great Britain. Moreover, under the terms of the Treaty of Commerce of 1778, the United States was obliged to open its ports to French warships and privateers and their prizes, while denying similar privileges to British warships and privateers. If the Franco-American treaties were strictly observed, therefore, the neutrality of the United States was certain to work in favor of France and to the disadvantage of Great Britain.

The dilemma confronting the Washington administration was aggravated by the arrival at Charleston, South Carolina, in April 1793 of Edmond Genêt, the new French minister to the United States. Genêt demanded that he be received as the accredited representative of the French Republic. President Washington sought the advice of the heads of departments by summoning for the first time regular cabinet meetings, where, as Jefferson later said, the Secretary of State and the Secretary of the Treasury were pitted against each other in gladiatorial combat. The Secretary of the Treasury took the position that the United States could stay out of the war only if it suspended the alliance with France and refused to receive Genêt until the new French government had demonstrated its stability. Jefferson gave the President very different advice: arguing that the Franco-American alliance was a compact between the French and American peoples rather than their governments, he urged that it be honored, even including the guarantee of the French West Indies. As for Genêt, the Secretary of State favored receiving him officially despite the fact that no other government had as yet recognized the French Republic.

Upon the most crucial question of all—American neutrality in the European war—Washington, Hamilton, Jefferson, and Secretary of War Knox were in agreement. Despite his ardor for the cause of the French Republic, Jefferson was prepared to believe that the United States could be of more use to France as a neutral than as a belligerent. But the accord between Jefferson and Hamilton did not extend to the manner in which neutrality should be declared. Because Congress was not in session in April 1793, the crisis seemed to require prompt action by the Executive. Hamilton thought that the President ought to issue forthwith a proclamation of neutrality, but Jefferson demurred; in his opinion, the President could not constitutionally commit the country to peace any more than he could commit it to war. Since these powers fell within the competence of Congress, Jefferson favored a mere announcement by the President warning American citizens against committing unneutral acts but at the same time making clear that the United States had no thought of abandoning its republican ally.

Upon the questions concerning domestic policy that had arisen from 1790 to 1793, Hamilton had scored an impressive series of victories over Jefferson. In 1793 the center of the struggle having shifted to foreign policy, each man was prepared to engage with all his forces upon this new battlefield, and each felt that the adoption of his policy was essential to the preservation of American neutrality. Everything depended, of course, upon the attitude of President Washington. Hamilton's success in the domestic field was owing in large measure to the tacit support of the President; had Washington in any way indicated that he disapproved of Hamilton's plans, the Secretary of the Treasury's influence would have come to an abrupt end. Jefferson ascribed Hamilton's triumphs to the fact that he operated behind the smoke-screen of Washington's prestige; no wonder, Jefferson exclaimed, that the Secretary of the Treasury burned incense at the presidential shrine! The unanswered question was: in charting the Republic's course in foreign affairs would President Washington give Hamilton the same almost unvarying support that he had accorded the Secretary's fiscal and economic plans?

While Washington made a practice of consulting at length with the members of his cabinet and of withholding his decision until he had exhaustively canvassed every question, he was not, as he himself said, a "believer in the infallibility of the politics or measures of any *man living*." If he appeared to take Hamilton's as opposed to Jefferson's advice, it was because his own views accorded more closely with those of the Secretary of the Treasury than with those advanced by the Secretary of State. Neither Jefferson nor Hamilton could bend the President to his will. Nor did they make the attempt: even a slight acquaintance with Washington's character would have effectively discouraged such a thought.

President Washington's handling of the crisis of 1793 effectively disposed of the idea that Hamilton was the spoiled darling of the administration. Upon the fundamental points of difference between Hamilton and Jefferson, President Washington supported the views of the latter. Like Jefferson, Washington believed that the French alliance was the sheet-anchor of American security and that it ought to be preserved at all costs. Yet, while he did not share Hamilton's partiality for Great Britain in its war with revolutionary France, he did not, on the other hand, thrill with Jefferson at the news of French military victories.

Moreover, despite the fact that he concurred with Jefferson's view that the French alliance was still binding and that Genêt ought to be received officially, Washington refused to defer to the Secretary of State's constitutional scruples. Without claiming a right to bind Congress, President Washington issued on his own authority a proclamation designed to keep the United States out of the European conflict. In deference to Jefferson, the word "neutrality" was omitted from the declaration. Even so, the Secretary of State expressed displeasure over what he called "a sneaking neutrality" which pointedly omitted any references to the community of interests and ideals that linked the United States with France. By making neutrality a bargaining point, he said, the United States could have exacted from Great Britain a guarantee to respect American neutral maritime rights. But, he lamented, the opportunity had been lost because Hamilton, as usual, was "panic-struck, if we refuse our breech to every kick which Great Britain may choose to give it."

For the moment, however, most of the kicks were administered by Citizen Edmond Genêt. While the President and cabinet were deliberating in Philadelphia, the French minister in Charleston, South Carolina, was engaged in converting the United States into a naval and military base of operations against Great Britain and Spain. He commissioned French privateers in American ports, signed on American crews, directed French consuls to condemn and order sold British ships captured by French warships and privateers operating in American territorial waters, and dispatched emissaries to the West to recruit an American legion for the invasion of Canada and Spanish Louisiana.

So ardently did most Americans support revolutionary France that Genêt's overland journey from Charleston to Philadelphia resembled a triumphal progress. In every village and town and almost at every crossroads, he was acclaimed as an apostle of liberty. In these demonstrations there appeared quite as much anti-British feeling as enthusiasm for France: when Genêt reached Philadelphia, some revolutionary patriots thought that they were reliving the days of '76. In this spirit, many Americans celebrated French victories quite as though their own armies had triumphed in the field. In 1795, Jefferson said that he would be willing to leave Monticello, fond as he was of it, to go to London to drink tea with victorious French generals. The French army did not succeed in "liberating" the people of England, but Jefferson never ceased to believe that the world would not be safe for republicanism until Great Britain itself became a republic.

Although President Washington received Genêt with cold formality, Jefferson more than made up for the President's reserve. The Secretary of State regarded Genêt as an ally against the "monarchists" in the United States. The view from the State Department was that the fate of American republicanism might well be decided upon the battlefields of Europe; if republican France fell before the onslaught of Great Britain and the European monarchies, Jefferson feared that the American "monocrats" would succeed in their efforts to destroy republicanism at home. On the other hand, if the French won in Europe, Jefferson believed that the "monocrats" at home would suffer a crushing reverse. From his perspective, Genêt was performing an invaluable service to the cause of republicanism by awakening the American people to the danger of monarchism, European as well as American, and reinvigorating American democracy with salutary injections of Liberty, Equality, and Fraternity.

Intoxicated by the acclaim he received in the United States, Genêt began to assume the imperious bearing of a proconsul. Having picked up the idea from the Republicans that the proclamation of neutrality was not valid until approved by Congress, Genêt threatened to appeal to Congress from the judgments of "old man Washington." Despite Jefferson's pleas, the French minister converted the captured British merchantman *Little Sarah* into a privateer, renamed it *Le Petit Democrat*, and ordered it to put to sea from Philadelphia. Although the United States declared in 1793 that its jurisdiction extended three miles beyond its shore (the span of a cannon ball), French privateers disregarded all limitations upon their freedom of action. In Boston, the French consul, at the head of an armed body of French sailors, even seized a ship from the custody of a United States marshal.

This flagrant disregard of American neutrality compelled Jefferson to take a second look at this irrepressible young Frenchman. He concluded that Genêt—"hot-headed, all imagination, no judgment, passionate and even indecent toward the President"—would bring ruin upon the "republican interest." Yet Genêt's antics did not abate Jefferson's love of France and his devotion to the principles of the French Revolution. He attributed that minister's erratic behavior to a quirk of personality rather than to any design on the part of the French government to embroil the United States in war with Great Britain. The Secretary of State continued to refer to France as "the friendly nation" and to Great Britain as "the hostile one."

Nevertheless, Genêt's "friendship" threatened to involve the United States in war with Great Britain. With its shipping being scooped up by Genêt's American-based privateers, the British government demanded that the United States government enforce its neutrality. Hamilton was happy to oblige the British, and orders were sent to the Treasury agents and district attorneys, upon whom the enforcement of the neutrality proclamation depended, to stop the departure of all French-commissioned privateers. At Hamilton's insistence, the government asked the French Directory to recall Genêt. But Jefferson succeeded in averting what he feared might prove to be the signal for a French declaration of war upon the United States—the dismissal of Genêt by the United States government without waiting for an official disavowal of its agent by the French government. The event proved that there was no danger that the French would go to war over Genêt; Genêt, a Girondist, was *persona non grata* to the Jacobin leader, Robespierre, who denounced him as a traitor before the National Assembly. Late in 1793, a new minister was sent to the United States with orders to return Genêt to France for trial. Genêt saved himself from the guillotine by marrying the daughter of Governor Clinton of New York and taking political asylum in the United States.

This happy ending did not obscure the fact that Genêt had helped to widen the gulf between Federalists and Republicans over foreign policy. As a result of the events of 1792-1793, opposition to revolutionary France became the hallmark of the Federalist party. American conservatives saw in French Jacobinism an exportable social and political doctrine that menaced the established order everywhere, including the United States. The Jacobin or "Democratic" clubs that sprang up in the United States in 1793-1794 seemed to confirm the link between French revolutionaries and American subversives; like their French counterparts, these "Democratic Societies," "the impure offspring of Genêt," appeared to be bent upon bringing the good, the wise, and the rich, as the Federalists described themselves, to the same kind of violent end that had overtaken thousands of French aristocrats.

JAY

11.
JOHN JAY SAVES THE PEACE

THE THREAT OF WAR WITH ENGLAND

If Genêt's breaches of American neutrality threatened to involve the United States in war with Great Britain, the British themselves brought the prospect of hostilities appreciably closer by their own violations on the high seas of what Americans considered to be their neutral rights. In the war between France and Great Britain, the United States asserted the full complement of neutral rights it had written into the commercial treaties made by the Continental Congress. These treaties enunciated the doctrines that the flag covered the cargo, that neither foodstuffs nor naval stores were contraband, and that blockades to be binding must be effective. These were not yet accepted tenets of international law; Great Britain, above all, had not recognized them as rules governing its conduct in time of war.

Engaged in a struggle for national survival, Great Britain and France were not inclined to respect the rights of neutrals, particularly when the exercise of those rights seemed to benefit the enemy. In May 1793, France began to seize American ships carrying provisions to Great Britain, and in June of that same year, the British issued an Order in Council—the so-called Provision Order—designed to starve France into submission by cutting off food supplies carried by neutral vessels. To compound this offense, seamen, presumed to be British nationals, were impressed from American ships by British boarding parties. And in November 1793 another Order in Council directed British naval officers to seize all neutral ships carrying supplies to or from the French West Indies. Since this order was sprung without warning, several hundred

---

"John Jay Hung in Effigy," engraving from the New York State Historical Association, Cooperstown, N.Y.

Washington Eagle Half Dollar, 1792.

American ships were seized upon the high seas. Captain Horatio Nelson, in particular, distinguished himself by the exemplary zeal with which he enforced His Majesty's edict. Since officers and crews of the Royal Navy received a share of the proceeds derived from the confiscation of neutral vessels condemned by British Admiralty Courts, Nelson combined duty with personal profit.

Jefferson declared that the British, in their arrogance of power, must not be permitted to make the United States merchant marine an instrument for subjugating the French Republic. Yet, strong as was the United States in moral fervor, righteousness, and idealism, it had no navy with which to protect its ships from belligerent privateers and men of war. Unless the government took reprisals upon British ships and merchandise entering American ports, the Secretary of State could do little more than give vent to his indignation in diplomatic notes.

In December 1793, just before his retirement from office, Jefferson submitted to Congress his long-deferred Report on Commerce. His conclusion—that the restrictions imposed upon American commerce by Great Britain were far more oppressive than were those imposed by France—was calculated to revive the demand for discrimination against British merchandise and shipping. Events conspired to give peculiar timeliness to the Secretary's report. Early in 1794, believing that war between the United States and Great Britain was inevitable, Lord Dorchester, the Governor-General of Canada, tried to enlist the Indians on the British side. In preparation for the impending rupture, the British built a new fort on the Maumee River in American territory.

The result was the worst crisis in Anglo-American relations since the establishment of the republic. Led by James Madison, the Republican members of Congress demanded that severe economic punishment be meted out to Great Britain. Sequestration of the debts owing by Americans to British subjects—even though certain to destroy American credit—was on the verge of passing Congress when news arrived that the British government had repealed the Order in Council of November 1793. But this concession did not prevent the House of Representatives from adopting in April 1794 Madison's proposal of discriminatory duties upon British ships and merchandise. Economic war with Great Britain—long advocated by Jefferson and Madison—seemed at last to be put to the test.

At this juncture, President Washington, Hamilton, and a group of Federalist senators intervened to prevent the adoption of measures they feared would foreclose the possibility of a peaceful settlement with Great Britain. Chief Justice John Jay of the United States Supreme Court was named by President Washington, with the Senate's approval, minister plenipotentiary to the Court of St. James's. In May 1794, Jay set sail for England carrying instructions written by Hamilton for concluding a treaty of commerce and settling the outstanding causes of dispute with Great Britain. Jay was directed not to threaten economic reprisals nor to align the United States with the League of Armed Neutrality then in the process of being formed by Denmark and

Sweden at the instigation of France. Contrary to the view held by Jeffersonian Republicans that Englishmen were indifferent to everything except their material interest, Jay was told to appeal to the reason of British ministers without a hint even of economic coercion.

While John Jay was preparing to test the capacity of British ministers to act "rationally" toward the United States, an American army under the command of General "Mad Anthony" Wayne was demonstrating that the federal government could dispose of the Indians upon whom British depended as allies in the event of war with the United States. Up to this time, things had gone no better for the United States in the West than on the diplomatic front. Certain in his own mind that the British government, despite its disavowals, was arming and inciting the Indians against the United States, President Washington was determined to reach a military decision in the Northwest. But the Indians badly mauled a small force under General Harmar and in 1791 massacred an American army under General Arthur St. Clair. When it came to walking into Indian ambushes, General Braddock, the British commander who suffered a disastrous rout in 1754 at the Monongahela, had no monopoly upon that particular form of ineptitude: General St. Clair bears the unhappy distinction of having experienced the most bloody defeat ever inflicted by Indians upon a British or American army. Better things were expected of Anthony Wayne, who commanded a force of 5000 men called the Legion of the United States and made up of German redemptioners, Irish indentured servants, Kentuckian and Tennessean riflemen, artillerymen, and a small corps of cavalry. In August 1794, after devastating the Indian villages that lay in his path, Wayne caught up with the main body of the enemy at Fallen Timbers near the site of what is now Toledo, Ohio. Here his care in training his men to fight Indian-fashion was rewarded: the tribesmen involved were so soundly defeated that they did not again offer serious organized resistance to the white advance.

Instead of following the time-honored custom of putting captives to the sword, Wayne treated them humanely and even complimented them upon their valor. Several of the chiefs were sent back to their tribes with offers of peace. Wayne's magnanimity bore fruit in August 1795 in the Treaty of Greenville, by the terms of which the signatory Indian nations relinquished title to a large part of the Midwest north of the Ohio River, including the site of Chicago, and put themselves under the exclusive protection of the United States. As a result, most of the present state of Ohio was thrown open to settlement—and so rapidly did Americans move into the region that in 1802 Ohio was ready to apply for statehood.

At the same time that Wayne was chastising the Indians, the federal government was confronted by a rebellion of western farmers. Trouble had been brewing in the West since 1791, when a high excise duty on whiskey had been imposed by the federal government to pay part of the costs of assuming the state debts. In the interior parts of the country where little or no cash or bank notes circulated, whiskey provided a medium of exchange as well as a source of refreshment. As long as the lower Mississippi remained closed to American flatboats, distilled whiskey was the only form in which grain was economically portable. For these reasons, many western farmers reckoned their fluid wealth in Monongahela rye and regarded collectors of the excise as enemies of the people.

In the summer of 1794, these discontents erupted into violence. In the four western counties of Pennsylvania, excise officers were terrorized; the Pittsburgh mail was robbed; federal judicial proceedings were stopped; and a small body of regular troops guarding the house of the excise inspector for western Pennsylvania was forced to surrender.

These events seemed to portend the disruption of the American Union, long predicted by British statesmen. Had the insurrection succeeded, John Jay might have returned from London empty-handed. But the federal government demonstrated that it could deal with Indians and rebellious western farmers at the same time. At the head of almost 10,000 troops, Washington moved upon the stronghold of the rebels. The troops encountered nothing more menacing than liberty poles bearing placards inscribed with such rousing slogans as "Liberty and No Excise, O, Whiskey." As for rebels in arms, not one was sighted even though the army marched across the Alleghenies. The ringleaders fled across the Ohio to the comparative safety of the Indian country. Only two of the twenty prisoners captured by the army were found guilty of treason, but President Washington pardoned them both. One, he said, was a simpleton, the other clearly insane.

Aspiring to the rights and dignities of a world power, the United States discovered that the problems inseparable from that status were also worldwide. Menaced on the high seas by the British and French navies and on the North American continent by Indians and their British allies, the United States was also compelled to deal with its old adversaries, the Barbary corsairs. Seizure of American ships and crews, accompanied by demands for ransom and tribute, put the issue of war or peace (peace with the pirates always bore a price tag) squarely before the Washington administration. In 1794, despite the aversion of southern Republicans to a navy, Congress authorized the construction of six frigates (subsequently reduced to four) to protect American shipping in the Mediterranean and to give the "presumptuous Moor" a long-overdue taste of American metal. But the crisis was eased in 1796 by a treaty between the United States and Algiers by which the Americans bought the release of prisoners and the immunity of American shipping in the Mediterranean by agreeing to pay tribute to the Bey of Algiers.

JAY'S TREATY

Despite the government's victories over Indians and western farmers, John Jay found the going rough in London. His difficulties owed something to James Monroe who, as minister to France, demonstrated the solidarity of the Franco-

American alliance by publicly embracing the leaders of the French Convention. While Monroe's open partisanship endeared him to the French, it quickened the British Ministry's suspicions that the United States was wholly committed to the support of France. Moreover, the British still hoped for a quick military victory on the Continent; not until November 1794, after suffering defeat in the Netherlands, did the London government fully appreciate the importance of cultivating the friendship of the United States. On the other hand, reconciliation between the two countries was made easier by the fact that Jay carefully avoided any speeches or acts likely to nip the tender shoots of Anglo-American goodwill.

In November 1794, after five months of desultory negotiations, Jay and Lord Grenville, the British Foreign Secretary, agreed upon a treaty of commerce. Both sides retreated from their original positions: the British gave up their demand for a large slice of territory along the Canadian border, and the United States abandoned its claim to compensation for the black slaves carried off by the British Army in 1783. Jay also accepted the British contention that the United States government should assume responsibility for the still unpaid prewar debts owing by Americans (most of whom were Virginians) to British subjects. Instead of securing immediate reparation for British depredations upon American shipping in 1793-1794, the question of damages, together with British claims upon the United States for losses suffered by British merchants and shipowners from Genêt's privateers, was referred to a mixed commission—Britons and Americans—a method of arbitration pioneered by Jay's treaty. Jay won the right for American ships of fifty tons burden or less to enter the British West Indies, but he was compelled to promise that the United States would not export cotton in American ships for ten years, the period of the treaty's duration. Nothing was said about impressment, and the United States in effect renounced the principle of freedom of the seas by consenting to the seizure of American ships carrying contraband, as defined by Great Britain, and enemy-owned cargoes. But the effect of this concession by Jay was mitigated by the fact that since early in 1794, under the doctrine of the "broken voyage," the British had permitted American ships to carry to Europe cargoes originating in the French West Indies provided that those cargoes were first brought to the United States, where, presumably, they became American property. The British government also promised in Jay's treaty to pay promptly for all American ships and cargoes condemned by the Admiralty Courts.

By far the most significant provisions of Jay's treaty were those giving the United States possession of the northwest posts and extending the boundary between the United States and Canada along the line of the 49th parallel. By this last article, the United States gained title to an area that included, although it was not known until the 1890's, the fabulous riches of the Mesabi iron range of northern Minnesota.

Jay had purchased these concessions by violating his instructions. If the United States had any neutral rights, they did not appear in the text of the treaty. The permission given to small American ships to trade with the British West Indies and the prohibition upon the export of cotton were immediately pronounced unacceptable by the United States Senate. Even Hamilton and President Washington were at first inclined to think that Jay had been too conciliatory. Yet the salient fact was that Jay had averted war with Great Britain, and the consequence of rejecting his handiwork—the reopening of the dispute with Great Britain—really left the Federalists no alternative but acceptance. After some hesitation, the business community rallied to the treaty's support. The Senate ratified it by a narrow and purely partisan majority, and President Washington, suppressing his misgivings, signed it.

The President and Senate acted in the face of bitter opposition from the Republican party. Jay was accused of having sold his country for "British gold," and he was burned in effigy by people all over the country. The crux of the Republicans' objections to Jay's treaty was that it put the resources of the United States at the disposal of Great Britain and precluded the government from sequestering British debts or imposing discriminatory duties upon British ships and merchandise. Jefferson thought that Jay's treaty ought to be given a place in the annals of treason rather than of diplomacy because, he said, the "monocrats" had "entered into a conspiracy with the enemies of their country to chain down the Legislature at the feet of both."

From his mountaintop at Monticello, Thomas Jefferson resumed his active collaboration with James Madison in devising Republican strategy. The Republican leaders decided to make their fight in the House of Representatives, their last remaining line of defense. Departing from their usual method of strictly construing the Constitution, they claimed for the House of Representatives concurrent power with the Senate in the ratification of treaties; without the explicit consent of the House, they insisted, no treaty could become the law of the land. Even if this interpretation was open to question, there was no doubt that Jay's treaty, because it required an appropriation of $90,000 by the House of Representatives, could be effectively nullified by a bare majority of the members. And, since the Republicans did possess a small majority in the House, merely by withholding the necessary funds the party seemed to be in position to annul the ratification of the treaty by the President and Senate.

The ensuing debate in Congress was marked by an acrimonious exchange between President Washington and the House: when the members insisted upon examining documents relevant to Jay's treaty, the President refused on the ground that the Executive alone could decide whether such disclosures were in the national interest. While accepting the President's decision, the House asserted its right to demand such papers without assigning a reason for its action. In this struggle, for the first time, the Republicans acted like a disciplined corps, and the party caucus made its initial appearance in American politics. But the majority voice, impatient with what was becoming a struggle for power between the Executive and Legislative branches rather than a debate on the merits and demerits of the treaty, turned against the Republicans. In July 1796, by a vote of 51 to 48, the House appropriated the funds necessary to effect Jay's treaty.

As Jefferson and Madison feared, Jay's treaty marked the beginning of a rapprochement between the United States and Great Britain. Trade between the two countries brought prosperity to American merchants, and an ever-increasing share of the carrying trade of Europe continued to pass into American hands. If Jay's treaty was, as Jefferson insisted, "a triumph over the cause of republicanism," American shipowners and merchants might have been excused for praying for more such triumphs.

Yet these commercial and territorial gains were achieved at a cost to internal harmony. The cleavage between the two parties was deepened by the protracted struggle in the House of Representatives. The Federalists, by their adamant defense of Jay's treaty, laid themselves open to the charge of being a "pro-British faction," while the Republicans, in the eyes of their adversaries, had never appeared more truly a "Jacobin" faction, wholly devoted to France and spoiling for war with Great Britain. Even President Washington, hitherto almost an Olympian figure in American politics, began to take on mortal status. Each party had learned to look to him as an arbiter of their disputes; except for Republican insinuations that he deferred too much to Hamilton, he had almost attained the position of a president who can do no wrong. But after 1795, the Republican newspapers no longer pretended to spare the President's sensibilities, and even Thomas Jefferson, in an indiscreet letter to his Italian friend Mazzei, pictured Washington as a Samson whose head had been shorn by "the harlot, England." When the letter was printed in French newspapers without Jefferson's consent, he denied that the "Samson" to whom he had referred was President Washington. It was the Society of the Cincinnati, Jefferson explained, that was engaged in tearing down the pillars of the temple of American republicanism.

THE TREATY OF SAN LORENZO

If, as the vote in Congress plainly indicated, Jay's treaty represented a victory for the northern "commercial interest," the treaty negotiated by William Pinckney with the Spanish government and ratified by the Senate in 1795 could be accounted as a victory for the South and West. It also bore out Jefferson's theory that European wars—provided the United States stayed out of them—could be made to yield territorial gains to the United States.

Spanish ministers had long been haunted by the vision of thousands of armed American frontiersmen invading Spanish Louisiana and the Floridas to make good their claim of a natural right to navigate the rivers flowing into the Gulf of Mexico. Against such an incursion, the Spaniards could offer little resistance. Not only were the defenses of the empire weak but Spain was deeply involved in the European war. Even though the Spanish government had corrupted General James Wilkinson, the American commander in Kentucky and Tennessee, George Rogers Clark, the Revolutionary war hero, and Alexander McGillivray, the Creek leader—all of whom were simultaneously on the payrolls of the United States and Spain—it still did not feel secure. In 1794, the Spanish minister, Manuel Godoy, Prince of the Peace, offered to redraw the southern boundary of the United States and to concede the privilege of navigating the Mississippi in exchange for a defensive alliance and territorial guarantee with the United States. But in 1795, after Spain had abandoned Great Britain and joined France as an ally, Godoy was ready to go to almost any lengths to conciliate the United States which, he believed, was about to ally itself with Great Britain. Pride and obstinacy gave way to panic, and the chastened Spaniard offered to close with the United States upon terms that a few years previously would have been considered humiliating.

In consequence, the American minister, Pinckney, found himself in the happy position of receiving the Spanish capitulation under the guise of a treaty. In 1795, at San Lorenzo he agreed to a treaty that pushed the boundary southward toward Florida in accord with American claims, gave American citizens the privilege of navigating the Mississippi together with the use of an entrepôt at New Orleans for three years, without mention of a guarantee of Spanish territory in the New World, and awarded the United States jurisdiction over the Indian tribes that had long brought terror and devastation to the southern frontier.

Although Spain postponed until 1798 the exercise by the United States of the privilege (it was not conceded to be a right) of deposit at New Orleans and the evacuation of the border posts, the Treaty of San Lorenzo marked the beginning of the disintegration of the Spanish Empire. Dreading the American frontiersmen's insatiable appetite for territory, Spain found in France, its terrible ally, an even more deadly enemy to the territorial integrity of its empire. As Jefferson had foreseen, the end of Spain's dominion over the New World was accelerated by its involvement in the European war. When the collapse came, the United States was prepared to pick up the choicest pieces of the Spanish Empire.

12. THE FAREWELL ADDRESS

For France, the ratification of Jay's treaty represented a defeat as intolerable as that suffered by the Republican party. The French government regarded Jay's treaty as an alliance in everything but name between the United States and Great Britain—precisely the point Republicans made against it. Whether or not it constituted an alliance, it certainly put an end to France's hope of sowing discord between the United States and Great Britain, and it placed the American merchant marine at the disposal of Great Britain. For these reasons, Pierre Adet, the French minister, aligned himself with the Republican opposition and lobbied against the treaty in both the Senate and the House of Representatives—the kind of interference in the affairs of independent nations that in Europe usually preceded "emancipation" by the French Army.

Of all the American statesmen of the day, President Washington was the most impartial toward the European belligerents. Mindful of the part played by France in the winning of American independence and of the importance to the United States of having at least one friendly power upon the European continent, Washington always avowed that he was a friend of France and the French Revolution. Nor did his anger against Genêt and French seizures of American merchant ships make him a British partisan. In 1796, resentful as he was of France's efforts to prevent the ratification of Jay's treaty, Washington was almost equally aroused by British seizures of American ships carrying foodstuffs to France. Nevertheless, he rejected the Republican charge that Great Britain exerted decisive influence in the councils of the United States

"A New England Town Meeting," engraving in John Trumbull's *M'Fingal,* 1795, from the Library of Congress.

Washington Piece, Ship Halfpenny, 1793.

government. The only nation interfering in American domestic affairs, he said, was the French Republic. He believed that this interference extended even to his cabinet: when letters were found in the intercepted correspondence of the French minister which seemed to implicate Secretary of State Edmund Randolph in an intrigue with the French minister at the time of the Whiskey Rebellion, Randolph was charged with corruption by Washington and the cabinet. Protesting his innocence, Randolph resigned. His later attempts to vindicate his reputation met only with incredulity from Washington and the Federalist party.

WASHINGTON'S ADDRESS

These considerations were uppermost in the President's mind when, in the spring of 1796, having resolved not to stand for a third term, Washington gave his attention for the second time to the composition of a Farewell Address. For aid in writing this valedictory to the American people, he turned to Alexander Hamilton, now a private attorney in New York City, the last of the triumvirate of Jefferson, Madison, and Hamilton to retain the confidence of the President. Although Hamilton was far more hostile to France than was Washington, the two men agreed in deploring French interference in American domestic affairs. Their collaborative effort was unmarred by any difference of opinion on the important issues of the day.

Like most of the framers of the Constitution, Washington had not anticipated the rise of political parties. The Constitution made no provision for their existence: political power, it was supposed, would be exercised by men chosen because of their talent rather than because of party affiliation. Traditionally, political parties or "factions" were believed to have a divisive effect upon a nation and to be the vehicles by which foreign influence could undermine a nation's independence. The course of events in Europe, where France was exploiting political divisions to subvert neighboring countries, seemed to Washington to offer a salutary lesson to the United States, where the two political parties, Federalist and Republican, were sharply divided upon foreign policy. Although the President gave the Federalists a clean bill of health as regards the introduction of British influence into the domestic affairs of the republic, he could not absolve the Republican party of the charge of abetting French influence and subordinating the interests of the United States to those of France. If Pierre Adet was a power in American politics it was because Republicans had made him so.

The root of the trouble, as the President saw it, was that the American people, in consequence of their preoccupation with events in Europe and the inordinate partisanship they felt for one or the other of the belligerents, had ceased to think and act like Americans. In his opinion, they were behaving much more like transplanted Europeans, imbued with all the nationalistic passions of the Old World, than as trueborn Americans. Even though the United States was officially neutral, the people had permitted themselves to be drawn emotionally into the vortex of the European war.

Thus, to the President's way of thinking, there existed an intimate connection between political parties, foreign influence, and partisanship toward the European belligerents. Accordingly, in his Farewell Address of September 1796 (it was not delivered in person; the American people read it in the newspapers), Washington called upon his countrymen to turn away from Europe, to cultivate a sense of American nationalism, to avoid the pitfall of sectionalism, and to give primacy to the interests of the United States. When Americans thought and acted like true indigenous men of the western world, the President was persuaded that political parties would disappear; for how could they exist if they were deprived of foreign attachments, their principal source of sustenance?

In Washington's opinion, the American people would never be truly happy until they had done away altogether with political parties. Parties, or factions, as he preferred to call them, seemed to him to be opposed not only to the policies of his administration but to the government itself. Whatever the case in foreign countries, in the United States Washington believed that the system of checks and balances made party politics unnecessary for the preservation of ordered liberty. Like other statesmen of the early republic, Washington failed to see that men will differ on public issues and express their convictions in concerted political action.

For the guidance of Americans, Washington laid down in the Farewell Address what he thought to be the basic principles of a sound foreign policy. In 1795, he had succinctly expressed the ideas which he elaborated in his valedictory: "to be upon friendly terms with, but independent of all, the nations of the earth. To share in the broils of none. To fulfill our own engagements. To supply the wants, and be the carriers for them all." By following these precepts, Washington believed that the United States could be sure of extracting the maximum profit from the distresses Europeans brought upon themselves by their rivalries and wars and of enjoying the kind of internal harmony that was essential to the preservation of the Union.

The Farewell Address, the so-called charter of American isolationism, was not as isolationist as it appeared to succeeding generations. Washington did not say that it was of no concern to Americans which side won in Europe or that the United States had no vital interest in the maintenance of a balance of power in Europe. Moreover, in warning his countrymen against foreign alliances, the President did not exclude the possibility that future events might make such alliances imperative. He hoped that the United States would be able to pursue a policy of neutrality and that the wars of Europe would pass the republic by, but he never made hope alone the basis of American foreign policy.

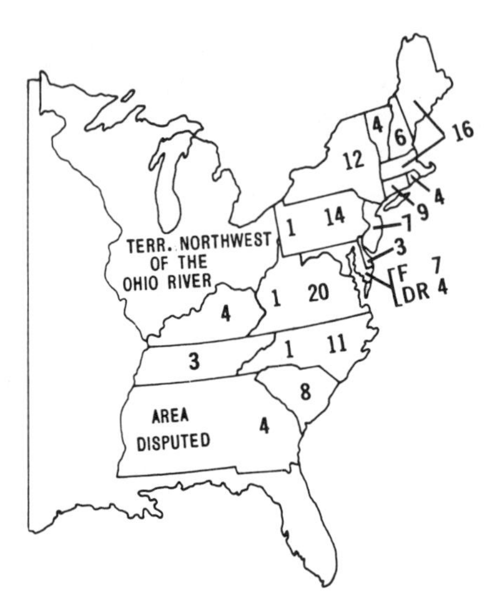

THE ELECTION OF 1796

	ELECTORAL VOTE BY STATE
FEDERALIST John Adams	71
REPUBLICAN Thomas Jefferson	68
	139

THE ELECTION OF 1796

The election of 1796, the first truly contested presidential election, revolved around questions of foreign policy and, contrary to Washington's solemn injunctions, Americans permitted their sympathies with the individual European belligerents to affect their judgment of the merits of the candidates for the presidency. Differences in the attitudes of John Adams and Thomas Jefferson toward the war in Europe were made to appear to be the cardinal differences between them. By the Republicans, John Adams was arraigned as a pro-British monarchist, while the Federalists pictured Jefferson as a Jacobin, a disorganizer, and a French "philosopher" who, if elected, would try to uproot the Christian religion and make the United States a fighting ally of the French Republic.

Moreover, the message of the Farewell Address had not visibly affected Adet. Instead of confining himself to his diplomatic duties, the French minister redoubled his efforts to turn the United States into a French satellite. In the presidential election he openly supported Jefferson, even going so far as to threaten French reprisals if John Adams were elected president. Adet left no doubt that France was resolved to make itself a power in American politics and that its principal objective was to reverse the foreign policy adopted by the Washington administration.

Even though the chill that had fallen upon Franco-American relations tended to diminish Jefferson's popularity, John Adams' margin of victory was dangerously thin. In the electoral college, Adams received seventy-one votes compared with sixty-eight for Jefferson. As the Constitution directed, Jefferson, by virtue of standing second in the vote of the electoral college, became vice-president despite the fact he and the President belonged to different political parties. Moreover, the sectional distribution of the vote indicated that the Federalist party was being compressed into its northern enclave: from the states south of the Mason and Dixon line, Adams received only two votes, whereas Jefferson, a more national figure, garnered eighteen votes from Pennsylvania.

13. THE UNDECLARED WAR WITH FRANCE

THE XYZ AFFAIR

Foreign affairs dominated the presidency of John Adams; even the important domestic issues of his administration sprang directly from events transpiring in Europe. Although Jay's treaty had not settled all the issues between the United States and Great Britain, it did afford a respite in a quarrel that had brought the two countries to the verge of war. After 1796, France took Great Britain's place as the chief disturber of domestic tranquillity. Even had Americans been disposed to follow Washington's advice and insulate themselves from partisan involvement in European affairs, France would not have permitted them to enjoy this felicity.

The ratification of Jay's treaty and the outcome of the presidential election in 1796 set in motion a chain of events that brought France and the United States to a shooting, albeit undeclared, war. Relying upon the Republican party to prevent effective retaliation by the United States government, the French began to seize American ships carrying British merchandise. When the Adams administration recalled James Monroe as minister to France, the Directory signalized its disapproval by refusing to accept his successor, Charles C. Pinckney. The United States was given to understand that it must obey the edicts issued in Paris or suffer the consequences of France's displeasure. Since the United States had agreed in Jay's treaty to obey edicts issued in London, it was impossible for the republic to comply with French demands without running the risk of war with Great Britain.

"Engagement Between the *United States* and the *Macedonian,* 1812," detail from a painting by Thomas Birch, courtesy of the New-York Historical Society, New York City.

Large Cent, Flowing Hair, Chain Type Reverse, 1793.

But to the French it was no answer for the United States to cite its commitments to Great Britain: the whole purpose of the Directory was to compel the United States to abandon Jay's treaty. To that end, within the space of a few months, over three hundred American merchantmen were bagged by French privateers and condemned in French admiralty courts. Even the territorial waters of the United States afforded no security against these marauders. So many bankruptcies occurred in Philadelphia as a result of these seizures that Jefferson reported that the local prison was crowded with "the most respectable merchants in town." France was still nominally the friend and ally of the United States, but its conduct occasioned some Americans to wonder what the enmity of the Grand Republic would be like.

From the Federalists' point of view, the Directory's policy had a highly satisfactory effect: it tended to destroy French influence in the United States and to unite Americans against that nation. It was now the Republicans' turn to call for the exercise of patience and restraint toward a power that violated American neutral rights. There was high talk of war in Congress, but President Adams was determined to exhaust every resource of diplomacy before resorting to arms. Accordingly, while the army was strengthened and the frigates that had remained on the stocks since the crisis with Algiers in 1794 were ordered completed, the President's main reliance was upon diplomacy. In 1797, a commission consisting of Elbridge Gerry, Charles C. Pinckney, and John Marshall was appointed to demand a cessation of French depredations and compensation for losses already suffered by the actions of French privateers.

The American peace commissioners could hardly have arrived in France at a less opportune time. In 1797, the First Coalition collapsed leaving only Great Britain, weakened by a financial crisis and disaffection in the Navy, to contest the power of revolutionary France. French-inspired revolutions occurred in Switzerland and Rome; Ireland seemed ripe for "liberation"; and a French army, the so-called Army of England, was being assembled for the invasion of the British Isles. Getting somewhat ahead of events, Jefferson hailed the French as "the conquerors of the Universe."

Imperious in victory, France was in no mood to appease the United States. Instead of being received officially by Talleyrand, the French foreign minister, the envoys were approached by Talleyrand's agents, designated by the letters X, Y, and Z in the correspondence later submitted by President Adams to Congress. These agents demanded £50,000 as a bribe, the promise of a large loan, and a disavowal of certain passages in President Adams' message to Congress regarded as offensive by France. Although the envoys were prepared to pay a reasonable *douceur* to get negotiations underway, they rejected X, Y, and Z's demands as extortionate. Marshall and Pinckney indignantly left France, but Gerry remained behind under the persuasion that only his continued presence in Paris could avert war.

When President Adams received the news from Paris, he informed Congress that negotiations had been broken off, and he requested a large appropriation to strengthen the military and naval defenses of the United States. Both parties demanded to see the letters sent by the envoys that had so deeply disturbed the President. The Republicans supposed that this correspondence would prove that the administration had deliberately sought to widen the breach with France and that the Directory was innocent of any blame. President Adams promptly laid the correspondence before Congress, and the Republicans were struck with consternation. The French government stood revealed as having treated the United States with the contempt it usually displayed toward a third-rate power it was about to revolutionize.

Borne upon the wings of a slogan that an inventive journalist put into the mouths of the American envoys—"Millions for Defense but not one cent for Tribute"—war fever swept the United States. Diplomatic relations with France were severed, and the Franco-American treaties suspended. Fifty thousand additional men were ordered raised for the Army; and in the summer of 1798, three frigates—the *Constitution,* the *United States,* and the *Constellation*—carried the flag of the United States Navy into the Atlantic for the first time since the War of Independence. President Adams tasted the heady wine of popularity: he was acclaimed as the "second Founder of the Republic" who had "laid the axe to the root of Jacobinism." When, in May 1798, the President proclaimed a day of fasting and prayer, 10,000 people paraded the streets of Philadelphia to demonstrate their support of the President's policies. Patriots furnished Adams with "piping hot addresses every morning for breakfast" praising his noble firmness and intrepidity in facing down the Jacobin "monster." The President was kept so busy answering these complimentary addresses that his wife Abigail feared that his health would be undermined. His answers seemed to rule out the possibility of a peaceful settlement with France: he declared that there was no alternative to war and that further efforts at negotiations could only be "disgraceful and ruinous."

THE ALIEN, NATURALIZATION, AND SEDITION ACTS

Everything pointed to a speedy declaration of war against France. But so impatient were congressional Federalists to proscribe their political opponents that they did not wait for a formal declaration. Instead, even though the country was officially at peace, they proceeded to curtail freedom of the press and of speech and to take action against the "alien menace." By means of the Alien, Naturalization, and Sedition Acts of July 1798, foreigners and citizens alike were brought under the control of the national government. The Alien Act authorized the President, even in time of peace, to order the deportation of any alien he suspected of seeking to subvert the government. The Naturalization Act extended from five to fourteen years the period of residence required of aliens before qualifying for citizenship. The Sedition Act declared it to be a high misdemeanor for citizens or aliens to enter into combinations opposing the execution of the laws of the United States, to prevent any federal officer from performing his duties, and to aid or take part in "any insurrection, riot, unlawful assembly, or combination." Its most important provision dealt with freedom of the press and of speech. A fine of not more than $2000 and imprisonment not to exceed two years were provided for those convicted in federal courts of uttering or publishing "false, scandalous and malicious writing" bringing into contempt or disrepute the federal government, the president, or Congress.

Despite President Adams' willingness to use the Alien Act against certain aliens he regarded as incorrigble disturbers of the peace, the act was never put in force, largely because some French aliens prudently left the United States and the British journalists who believed themselves marked for deportation took out naturalization papers before they could be apprehended. The effect of the Naturalization Act was counterbalanced by the practice of the state governments of granting citizenship to aliens. The storm center of these Federalist laws was the Sedition Act; around it raged the debate between Federalists and Republicans regarding the powers of Congress to set metes and bounds to some of the basic liberties of Americans.

Certainly journalism as practiced by both parties had become scurrilous and defamatory beyond all bearing except by the most thick-skinned politicians. Political feeling derived much of its virulence from the press: Americans were inflamed by newspaper accounts of treachery in high places. Nothing, it appeared, was too calumnious to be printed in the newspapers. When George Washington left the presidency, Benjamin Bache (the grandson of Benjamin Franklin and known as "Lightning-Rod Jr." because of his penchant for delivering high-voltage shocks to Federalists in his newspaper, the Philadelphia *General Advertiser*), urged that the event be celebrated as a day of jubilee because it marked the retirement of the man who had been "the source of all the misfortunes of our country." As for President Adams, he was ridiculed by Bache as "old, querulous, bald, blind, crippled, Toothless Adams." Abigail Adams declared this to be an intolerable libel, but the President admitted that his age and baldness were matters of common knowledge.

Although the Sedition Act represented an intrusion of federal power into an area hitherto left wholly to the states, it also incorporated the most liberal ideas of the day concerning libel. According to common law, in cases involving libel, truth was not a defense, and the judge was authorized to decide matters of fact as well as of law. The Sedition Act, on the other hand, made truth a defense and gave the jury the privilege of deciding matters of fact, including the all-important fact whether or not the publication was actually libelous. In theory, at least, the Sedition Act was far in advance of the contemporary British law. In the nineteenth century, the states adopted in their own statutes regarding libel the innovations made by the Sedition Act.[1]

[1]In *New York Times v.* Sullivan, the United States Supreme Court declared in 1964 that "debate on public issues should be uninhibited, robust and wide-open." It ruled that a public official cannot collect libel damages even for false criticism of his official acts unless he can prove "actual malice."

In actuality, the Alien and Sedition Acts were symptomatic of fear and vindictiveness rather than of any desire to ameliorate the usages of the common law. At this time, New England was swept by fear of the machinations of the Bavarian Illuminati. Founded in Bavaria by Adam Weishaupt in 1776 as a league of intellectuals dedicated to waging war against the Jesuits and other enemies of free thought, the Order of the Illuminati had been suppressed in 1785 by the King of Bavaria. But fear of the Order and its designs was revived by the advent of the French Revolution; in almost every country conservatives saw the dread hand of this organization undermining the established order. In Massachusetts, where the established church had come under severe attack and "Jacobinism" had demonstrated its power in 1796 when the aging Sam Adams, a Republican, was elected governor of the state, pious "Friends of Order and Government" trembled lest the Illuminati succeed in stamping out all order, decency, and religion. "Shall our sons become the dragoons of Marat," asked the Reverend Timothy Dwight, the President of Yale, "and our daughters the Concubines of the Illuminati?"

But the Sedition Act laid its hand not upon the elusive Illuminati but upon Republican journalists and one Republican Congressman. Acting upon the maxim that "Government should be a terror to evil doers," the Adams administration brought fifteen indictments for seditious libel under the Sedition Act. Of these, ten resulted in conviction and punishment. Three of the most prominent Republican newspaper editors were convicted of violating the law and sentenced to pay a fine and serve a prison term. The most prominent of those convicted were James Callender, a radical British journalist who had taken refuge in the United States (fined $200 and sentenced to nine months in jail); Matthew Lyon, a Republican member of Congress from Vermont who was reelected while in jail (fined $1000 and imprisoned in a jail with common malefactors); and Dr. Thomas Cooper, the English scientist and freethinker (imprisoned for six months).

The moving spirit behind most of these prosecutions was Secretary of State Timothy Pickering, vigorously abetted by Justice Samuel Chase of the United States Supreme Court. Justice Chase's grossly partisan conduct on the bench nullified the liberalization of the law of seditious libel made by the Sedition Act. However, few Republicans could employ truth as a defense: their allegations were too flagrantly false to admit of that line of argument.

Yet a declaration of war—the measure which the Alien and Sedition Acts had anticipated—was not forthcoming from Congress. Having rushed to the brink of war, the Federalists could not bring themselves to take the plunge. The party elders looked to President Adams to give the lead, but the President chose to leave the decision wholly to Congress. Rather than attempt to force a declaration of war through Congress, where it was certain to encounter strenuous resistance from the Republicans, the Federalists took the easier course of waiting for France to declare war. In view of the French government's habit of bullying weaker countries that defied its edicts, it seemed improbable that the Directory would disappoint the Federalists.

In the meantime, the undeclared war was being fought at sea by armed American merchantmen and the ships of the American Navy. French privateers, outgunned and outmanned by the spanking new frigates commissioned in 1798, were quickly driven from the coastal waters of the United States, and in 1799 the fight was carried to the West Indies, where four squadrons, one of which was commanded by Captain Thomas Truxton, forced the privateers to take cover in French harbors. Early in 1799, Truxton met in battle the French frigate *L'Insurgente,* and the Frenchman struck his colors.

A NAVY VERSUS AN ARMY

As this was a quasi-war, however, both the United States Navy and American privateers fought under wraps: neither the ships of the Navy nor armed merchantmen were permitted to capture unarmed French ships; only armed cruisers, privateers, and ships of war were considered lawful prey. As a result, the Navy's bag of French ships was disappointingly small: only about eighty ships, most of them of modest size, were taken by American warships. The proceeds realized from the sale of these prizes were divided between the officers of the captor ship and the government. No one grew rich from these operations: the undeclared war with France yielded little plunder and no territory, and the Navy devoured far more revenue than even the Republicans had predicted.

But the frustrations experienced by the Navy were nothing compared to the vexations suffered by the Army. Whatever glory the war afforded was preempted by the Navy; the Army sat out the war waiting for an enemy that never came. Indeed, the Army became a far greater source of discord within the administration and the country itself than an object of terror to the enemy.

George Washington was called from retirement to head the Army, authorized by Congress in 1798 to be augmented by 10,000 recruits and 50,000 provisional troops. Despite Adams' anguished protests he was compelled by Washington to appoint Alexander Hamilton second in command. This event marked the beginning of President Adams' metamorphosis from a hawk to a dove.

Although the Army remained inactive, it required a large amount of money for its maintenance. In 1798-1800 American taxpayers learned how much even an undeclared war can cost. In 1798, the government attempted to float a loan of $5 million at 8 percent interest—a higher rate than that at which John Adams and Thomas Jefferson had borrowed money in Holland in 1788. President Adams said that his hobbyhorse was a Navy, but he never regarded the Army as his proper steed, particularly after it became apparent that Alexander Hamilton intended to ride it to power, perhaps even to the presidency itself. Like many other citizens, President Adams blamed the Army for unbalancing the budget: "This damned army," he exclaimed, "will be the ruin of this country." By 1799, he was predicting national bankruptcy within a year—all in order, complained the distraught President, "to support an army already called ragamuffins and cannibals, in total idleness and inaction, unless they spent their time in pillage and plunder, in debauching wives and seducing daughters."

Alexander Hamilton had not pulled all the wires in order to become second in command of an army that would rest on its muskets. The adventurous West Indian proposed to lead the Army into Louisiana and the Floridas and, after those provinces had been subjugated, "to squint at South America." Having survived the European crisis of 1797-1798, the British government was already directing its attention in that direction. Francisco Miranda, a Venezuelan patriot, tried to persuade both Great Britain and the United States to give armed support to his plan of emancipating Venezuela. Miranda had been received by William Pitt, and the British government seemed strongly inclined to make common cause with the Spanish-American revolutionaries.

In this turn of events, Hamilton believed that he saw an opportunity for the American Army to distinguish itself in action. The vast Spanish empire, closed by mercantilist laws to the commerce of other nations, offered unlimited possibilities of trade to the merchants and manufacturers of Great Britain and the United States. Hamilton therefore conceived of the projected intervention in Spanish America as a joint Anglo-American enterprise in which the British would furnish the fleet while the Americans would supply the army, of which Hamilton himself would provide the generalship. But this grandiose scheme came to nothing, partly because President Adams was unwilling to embark upon an adventure that promised to involve the United States more deeply in European affairs, to produce a British alliance, and to expend American lives and money in behalf of a people who, in his opinion, were not prepared to receive the blessings of liberty.

PRESIDENT ADAMS AND PEACE WITH FRANCE

In fact, President Adams was far more disposed to put an end to the war with France than to expand it into Latin America. As he saw it, by its victories at sea, the United States had achieved the cardinal objective of the quasi-war: making the seas safe from the depredations of French privateers and men-of-war. Moreover, the Directory, instead of declaring war upon the United States, as the Federalists hoped and expected, seemed strongly inclined to call off the unprofitable contest with the American republic as a miscalculation on the part of Talleyrand. No one had been more taken aback by the result of his effort to shake down the American commissioners than had Talleyrand himself: these unaccountable Americans had turned a simple request for money into a *casus belli.*

Particularly ominous, from the French point of view, was the fact that the quasi-war was accelerating the rapprochement between the United States and Great Britain that had begun with Jay's treaty. American merchants and shippers were beginning to discover that renouncing the freedom of the seas could be good for business. For the British did not deny Americans a chance to make a profit: all they asked was that Americans conform to British regulations. The course of wisdom, therefore, for American businessmen seemed to consist in cooperating with the mistress of the seas rather than risking disaster while shrieking slogans about neutral rights.

Late in 1798, the President began to receive unmistakable peace feelers from the Directory. Among the bearers of these good tidings was George Logan a Pennsylvania Quaker, who, as a private citizen, had gone to France to explore the possibilities of peace. His action resulted in 1799 in the passage of the Logan Act, which makes such unauthorized acts by private citizens punishable by fine and imprisonment.[2] Elbridge Gerry and William Vans Murray, the United States minister in the Netherlands, confirmed Logan's report of the Directory's pacific disposition.

As a man of peace, President Adams was isolated from his own cabinet. When he assumed the presidency he had retained intact his predecessor's cabinet, the members of which looked to Alexander Hamilton as their leader. Adams invited his own supersession by long absences from the seat of government. President Washington had set an example by retiring to Mount Vernon for intervals that lasted up to two months, but President Adams remained away from Philadelphia for periods as long as nine months. Thanks to the excellent mail service, Adams said, all the business of the government could be satisfactorily conducted at his home in Braintree, Massachusetts. While this protracted absenteeism afforded opportunity for reflection upon the problems of government, it tended to enable Alexander Hamilton to take over the direction of affairs.

In later life, Adams spoke of the heads of departments as his "masters" who took their orders from Hamilton. Particularly reprehensible, in this regard, was Secretary of State Pickering, of whom Adams said: "I wanted to whip the rogue, and I had it in my power, if it had been in my will to do it, till the blood came." Fortunately for the dignity of the presidential office and for Pickering's hide, the President contented himself with dismissing Pickering in 1800—but not until the executive branch had been torn apart by a struggle for power between Adams and Hamilton.

Not surprisingly, therefore, when Adams decided to respond to the Directory's peace overtures, he acted without consulting his cabinet: he knew in advance how the heads of department would respond. Without warning, the President proposed to the Senate that William Vans Murray be commissioned to enter into peace talks with the French government. The Federalist-controlled Senate was aghast, but the utmost it could do was to add two additional members to the peace commission and to hope that it would never leave the country. Secretary of State Pickering bent every effort to prevent the commissioners from sailing, but the President prevailed, and in November

---

[2]The Logan Act, which remains in force today, was the work of the congressional Federalists opposed to peace with France.

1799 the peace envoys embarked for France. The Hamilton Federalists wished them an unsuccessful mission and a speedy and empty-handed return; a humiliating rebuff on the order of the XYZ affair would have admirably suited the purposes of the war party.

President Adams' determination to end the war as quickly as possible was strengthened by the internal state of the country. To pay for the war, Congress had imposed a direct tax upon land, houses, and slaves. The experiment was not successful: many citizens refused to pay the tax, and, because the federal government lacked the means of enforcement, they were able to avoid payment. In Pennsylvania, Peter Fries, a German Federalist, led a march of irate citizens on Bethlehem, Pennsylvania, and released tax-evaders held in prison by the federal government. Although no one had taken up arms, President Adams ordered the militia and, later, part of the federal Army to put down the "insurrection." Fries and some of his associates were captured, tried in a federal court, and convicted of having "levied war, insurrection, and rebellion against the United States." The justices took the position that forcibly releasing federal prisoners was an act of treason.

At most, Fries was guilty of riot or incitement to riot; nothing he had done constituted a threat to the national security. But the Federalists, prone to magnify every sign of discontent, including criticism of the administration, into treason and sedition, applauded the conviction of Fries. To their dismay, President Adams pardoned Fries and his associates. But the damage had been done: the Republicans had been given a martyr, and the Army had vastly increased its unpopularity by serving as an instrument of repression.

Royal Sport

14. THE VIRGINIA AND KENTUCKY RESOLUTIONS

OPPOSITION TO THE ALIEN AND SEDITION ACTS

The quasi-war served notice upon France and, indeed, upon all Europe, that the United States was not, as Talleyrand had supposed, to be treated like Geneva or Savoy. But the war notably failed to produce domestic union; instead, it accentuated political differences not only over foreign policy but also over the fundamental question of civil liberty. By accusing the Republicans of being abettors of French imperialism, the Federalists forfeited all opportunity to unite the country against foreign aggression. The situation was a far remove from the kind of single-minded devotion to the national interest and united front toward Europe that Washington had called for in his Farewell Address.

Upon the Federalist party, the effects of the war could only be accounted disastrous. President Adams later declared that the sending of peace envoys to Europe "was one of the most glorious deeds he ever did and that he would order it to be ingraved on his Coffin." It was indeed the act of a statesman, but it disrupted the Federalist party on the eve of the presidential election of 1800. With few exceptions, the party leaders deplored the President's initiative in foreign policy and demanded that the war continue. As a result, the Federalist party was divided on the all-important question of peace or war.

In Republican annals, the period 1798-1800 figures as "The Reign of

"Physical Violence, for the First Time on the Floor of Congress, 1798, a Federalist and a Republican Clash," courtesy of the New-York Historical Society, New York City.

Half Cent, Liberty Cap, Head Facing Left, 1793.

Terror"—a reference to the "White" or Thermidorian Terror that occurred in France after the downfall of Robespierre in 1794. Yet, even though the federal government appeared in the full panoply of power, few Republicans were terror-struck. Indeed, the number of anti-administration newspapers actually increased, and the virulence of their attacks upon prominent Federalist officeholders showed no sign of abating. As a means of disciplining the press, the Sedition Act could hardly be accounted a success even by its warmest advocates.

As a means of exciting open hostility to the federal government, however, the Sedition Act proved eminently successful. In Virginia, armed resistance was advocated: hotheads urged that an armory under construction at Richmond be used to oppose the enforcement of an "unconstitutional edict." Alexander Hamilton was prepared to march the United States Army to the Virginia line. In 1798-1799, the Federalists seemed more likely to have a civil rather than a foreign war on their hands.

Thomas Jefferson considered the Sedition Act to be as unconstitutional as if, he said, Congress had ordered Americans to bow down and worship a golden image. Compared with this iniquitous law, the Bank of the United States, the Report on Manufactures, and Jay's treaty seemed to him to be "unconsequential, timid things." Even more than the Sedition Act itself, Jefferson feared the theory upon which it was based. According to the Federalist interpretation of the Constitution, the common law conferred upon Congress full power to legislate upon all subjects not specifically excluded by the Constitution itself and gave the federal courts authority to take cognizance of all cases, including seditious libel, arising under the common law. In this doctrine, Jefferson saw the destruction of the state courts, the extinguishment of state sovereignty, and the triumph of Hamiltonian consolidationism and monarchism—in which event he believed that the American people would find themselves at the mercy of a government that regulated their lives from cradle to grave, taxed them unmercifully, and even told them what to think.

To prevent the execution of the Sedition Act, Jefferson said that every citizen ought to be ready to suffer martyrdom. Jefferson himself could have attained martyrdom simply by speaking his mind about the Sedition Act. The Vice-President already stood suspect by Federalists of being the moving spirit if not the actual author of the libels against Washington, Adams, and Hamilton that filled the Republican newspapers and of plotting "some diabolical Plan against the Federal Government." But, to the chagrin of his enemies, Jefferson did not take this opportunity of going to jail for his opinions. Instead, he moved with his customary circumspection to alert the American people to the threat to civil liberty posed by the Sedition Act and to propose a constitutional method of resistance.

The emphasis, in Jefferson's mind, was upon *constitutional methods*. He could not condone the kind of overt resistance contemplated by some Virginians. To John Taylor of Caroline, one of the advocates of force, Jefferson counseled prudence: "the reign of witches," he said, would soon be over. In his opinion, there was nothing quite as effective in restoring sanity as high taxes imposed to prosecute an unpopular war.

Impressed with the necessity of organizing peaceful resistance to the Alien and Sedition Acts, Jefferson and Madison drew up a series of resolutions which their friends submitted to the Kentucky and Virginia legislatures in 1798-1799. Denying any common law jurisdiction in the federal government, Jefferson and Madison argued that its powers were confined to those delegated in the Constitution, that the Sedition Act went beyond the enumerated powers granted Congress and violated the First Amendment prohibiting any laws "abridging the freedom of speech or of the press." Jefferson and Madison argued that the Constitution was a compact between the people of thirteen distinct sovereign states, not the people of a single, unitary, consolidated nation.

STATES' RIGHTS AND THE VIRGINIA AND KENTUCKY RESOLUTIONS

To prevent what they considered to be a palpable violation of the compact, Jefferson and Madison called upon the states to assert their right to act as the final interpreters of the Constitution. Only concerning the method of exerting that power was there disagreement between the two Republican leaders. Jefferson thought that a single state had the right to nullify unilaterally an act of Congress it judged unconstitutional. Madison, on the other hand, believed that the collective action of the states was required in such instances. The Vice-President yielded to advice of Madison and John Breckinridge of Kentucky at least to the extent of agreeing to omit the word "nullification." Even so, the Kentucky Resolutions were more forthright than were those drawn up by Madison and adopted by the Virginia legislature. The Kentucky Resolutions asserted that, when the federal government exercised powers not specifically delegated to it, each state "has an equal right to judge for itself, as well of infractions as of the mode and measure of redress." The Virginians contented themselves with stating that the states "have the right and are in duty bound to interpose for arresting the progress of the evil." In this form, both sets of resolutions were sent to the legislatures of all the states, even to those controlled by Federalists. Both Jefferson and Madison took extreme care that their part in the drafting of the resolutions was not made public.

In a second set of resolutions drawn up for the consideration of the Kentucky legislature in 1799, Jefferson was prepared to argue that secession might be the final constitutional resort. Again Madison dissuaded him from broaching a doctrine which the younger man feared would recoil upon its sponsors. As a result, the second Kentucky Resolutions did not mention secession. But these resolutions did contain the word "nullification," the method which Jefferson, at least in theory, clearly favored.

It is significant that the Virginia and Kentucky Resolutions took the form of instructions to the states' senators. Among the amendments to the Constitution proposed in 1789, one asserting the right of state legislatures to instruct senators had been rejected by the House of Representatives. While the people were expected to control the national government, Congress indicated that this control should not be exercised through the agency of the state governments. Yet this decision was contested by Jefferson and Madison: to the end, they insisted upon the right of instructing senators. Had the theory of the Virginia and Kentucky Resolutions prevailed, senators would have represented not the people of the states but the state legislatures, which at this period elected them to office.

Even more important, the federal government would have had no power to punish seditious libels in federal courts, no matter how egregiously its officials were vilified. But the Virginians had no intention of removing all restraints upon freedom of the press and of speech. To do so, in their opinion, would produce licentiousness rather than freedom. Accordingly, while denying cognizance over seditious libel to the federal courts, Jefferson and Madison were careful not to deprive the state courts of jurisdiction over the rights of individuals to seek legal redress and to punish seditious speech or writings. Every citizen, including the President of the United States, could take his complaints into a state court and there, Jefferson and Madison believed, find complete justice.

While it is true that Jefferson and Madison were upholding state rights rather than an absolute right to speak and write without restraint, they did believe that the states would be more friendly to these basic freedoms than would the federal government. The answer given by Madison to the argument that a republican form of government could not be extended over a country the size of the United States—that a federal system would prevent any party or faction hostile to the liberties of the people from coming into power—was applied by Madison and Jefferson to the freedom of the press. By leaving the power of punishing libel to the states, Americans would be insuring themselves against a nation-wide assault mounted by the federal government upon the freedoms guaranteed by the Bill of Rights.

In the minds of their framers, the cardinal purpose of the Virginia and Kentucky Resolutions was not to safeguard the freedoms guaranteed by the First Amendment but to overthrow a theory of the relationship between the states and the general government that would have decisively shifted the balance of power in favor of the general government. As Jefferson and Madison saw it, freedom of speech and of the press were merely the first rights to be subverted by a government bent upon destroying the "beautiful equilibrium" established by the Constitution and arrogating to itself all power.

Regarded in this light, the Virginia and Kentucky Resolutions furnished an answer not only to the Alien and Sedition Acts but to the reports of Alexander Hamilton. Against the permissive or loose interpretation of the Constitution favored by Hamilton, the Virginians supported the strict, states' rights interpretation together with a theory of the origin and nature of the Constitution that would have forever precluded the exercise by the federal government of many powers it employs today as a matter of course.

Even after they had been toned down by Madison and other moderates, the Virginia and Kentucky Resolutions struck most of the members of the state legislatures to whom they were addressed as too radical. Indeed, in the Virginia legislature itself, about 40 percent of the delegates, led by John Marshall, registered their disapproval of the resolutions. Not a single state approved them: many states simply ignored them altogether. Massachusetts reminded the Virginians and Kentuckians that it was the province of the United States Supreme Court, not of the states, to determine the constitutionality of acts of Congress.

Nevertheless, the Virginia and Kentucky Resolutions and the debate which they stimulated, helped to draw public attention to the Alien and Sedition Acts. Already on the defensive in explaining the continuation of an expensive war that seemed to have accomplished its main objectives, the Federalists found themselves, on the eve of a presidential election, arraigned as enemies of American freedom.

Even so, time proved itself to be on the side of the Federalists. The preservation of the nation has always taken precedence over constitutional restraints. Likewise, the theory of the constitutional relationship of the states and the federal government advanced in the Virginia and Kentucky Resolutions was itself nullified by the Civil War. Yet from 1798 to 1860, the opponents of centralized government were able to cite the Virginia and Kentucky Resolutions in defense of states' rights. Whatever Jefferson may have intended, nullification as a sovereign defense against unconstitutional laws was not confined to laws that infringed the civil liberties of citizens.

15. THE ELECTION OF 1800

THE ELECTION CAMPAIGN OF 1800

Since at the beginning of the nineteenth century, presidential electors were chosen by the legislatures rather than by the voters in ten of the states, the campaign of 1800 largely took the form of local contests between Federalists and Republicans for control of the state legislatures. In the states where the people chose electors, the dominant party tried to have the electors chosen either on a state-wide or on a district basis, whichever seemed most likely to serve its purposes. In several states, including Virginia, the basis of choice was changed on the eve of the election for partisan purposes.

As a result of the congressional elections of 1798-1799, the Federalists augmented their majority in the House of Representatives. Even Virginia, with nineteen seats, returned eight Federalists. Manifestly, if this trend continued, the Federalists were certain to retain control of the presidency and Congress in 1800. Even so, as party strategists well knew, the Federalists' margin of victory in 1796 had been so razor-thin that they could not afford to lose a single one of the states they had carried at that time.

Of the two parties, the Republicans had by far the better organization in such key states as Pennsylvania and New York, where, for the first time, such innovations as party "tickets," placards, and get-out-the-vote drives were introduced. Moreover, because Jefferson, Madison, and other Republican leaders had taken definite positions upon such issues as the necessity of re-

---

"The Verdict of the People," detail from a painting by George Caleb Bingham, collection of the Boatmen's National Bank of St. Louis.

Talbot Allum & Lee Cent, 1794.

ducing the national debt, cutting the defense budget, guaranteeing freedom of speech and the press, and pursuing a policy of "free commerce with all nations but political connections with none," the Republicans had a platform ready-made for the campaign of 1800.

Above all, the Republicans held the allegiance of the western states. The electoral vote of either Kentucky or Tennessee would have given the election to John Adams, but the Federalists were weaker in the West than in the South. Despite their dedication to nationalism, many Federalists opposed the movement of population and the transfer of political power to the West, the most nationalistic section of the Union. In his abortive negotiations with Gardoqui, John Jay had adopted an attitude toward the West that set the pattern for the Federalist party. Alexander Hamilton had reinforced this attitude by contending in his Report on the Bank of the United States that the settlement of the West tended to diminish "the active wealth of the country" and hampered the development of manufactures. More importantly, it promised to upset the political balance between the North and South. For this reason, the Federalists had opposed the admission of Kentucky to the Union unless Vermont were simultaneously brought in as a state. The Federalists' carried their point: Vermont was admitted in 1791 and Kentucky came in the following year. But in 1796, over the northern Federalists' objections, Tennessee became a state without the concurrent admission of a northern territory.

On the other hand, the Federalists had the advantage of the unprecedented prosperity produced in the United States by the European war. The stability provided by the Federal Constitution and the business expansion fostered by Hamilton's innovations enabled the United States fully to exploit the opportunities presented by the wars of the French Revolution. American exports to Europe and the American merchant marine more than doubled during the decade of Federalist rule. This burgeoning prosperity led to the construction by private enterprise of a network of roads and canals, a large increase in the number of corporation charters granted by the state legislatures, and to land speculation on a colossal scale—Robert Morris and his associates, for example, owned most of the western part of the state of New York.

But the land-boom collapsed in the late 1790's, and Robert Morris, once the wealthiest man in the United States, went to jail as a debtor. Moreover the "economic miracle" by which the United States had been raised from depression to affluence did not confer its benefits uniformly over the economy. Merchants, shipowners, shipbuilders, lawyers and other professional men, wheat farmers, and cotton growers were the chief beneficiaries of the war-induced boom. The tobacco-producers of the Chesapeake, on the other hand, profited not at all: having reached its high in 1790, the price of tobacco went into a steady decline. Nor, until 1823, did the quantity of tobacco exported from the United States equal the figure attained in 1790. In consequence, the Tidewater planters tended to regard themselves as disadvantaged members of the community, neglected if not wholly forgotten by the Federalist administration.

THE GROWTH OF THE MERCHANT MARINE, 1790-1815

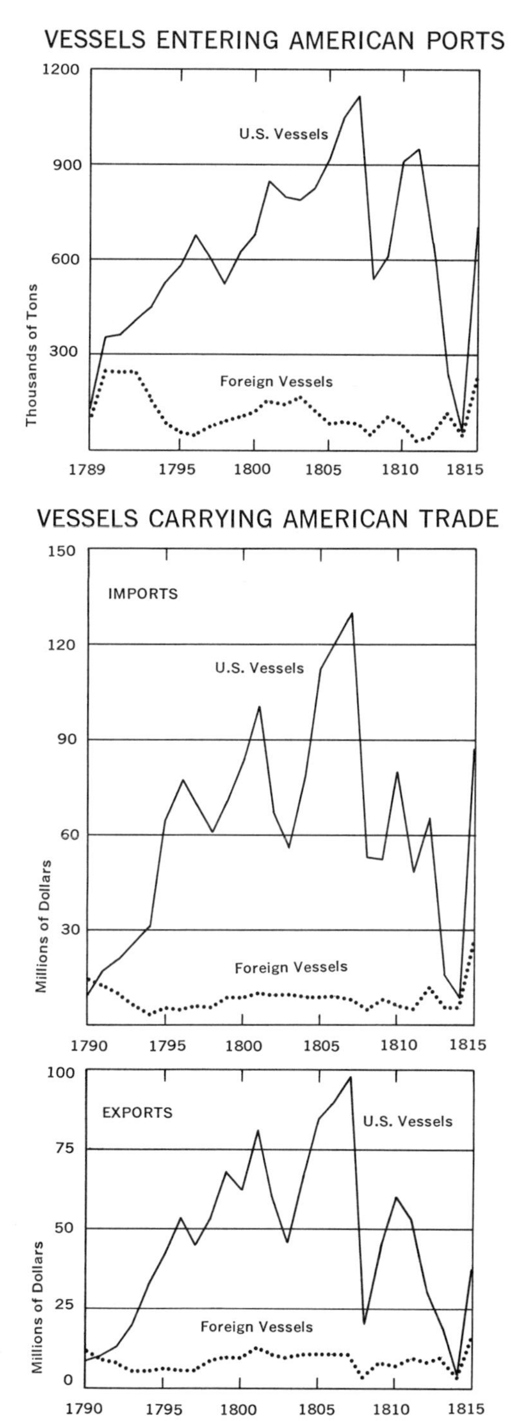

To help the American shipping industry, the First Congress passed discriminating import duties, which imposed higher duties on merchandise imported in foreign vessels and charged higher tonnage taxes for foreign vessels. These advantages and the European war, which increased the demand for American goods and gave American shipping a large carrying trade, caused a rapid growth in the shipping industry. Consequently, the merchants disliked the embargo and the war, which may have defended their maritime rights, but also ruined their booming business. *Source: Historical Statistics of the United States.*

By 1800, even the most warlike Federalists were compelled to admit that protracting the war with France for undefined and unlimited objectives was likely to cost them dearly in the election. Accordingly, early in 1800 they ordered a reduction in the size of the Army and later began to economize at the expense of the Navy. But nothing would induce them to sacrifice the Sedition Act; to the end, they clung to that law as their testament to the American people and the shield of national security. In January 1801, when an attempt was made to reenact the Sedition Act before it expired automatically, it received more votes in the House of Representatives than had the original act of July 1798.

The first sign that the Federalists would not have an easy sweep in the forthcoming presidential election came in October 1799, when Thomas McKean, a Republican, was elected governor of Pennsylvania, and the Republicans gained control of the state House of Representatives. Only in the state Senate did the Federalists retain a small majority. This political upset had an important bearing upon the outcome of the presidential election of 1800, but, more immediately, it marked the beginning of the spoils system. Governor McKean purged Federalist officeholders and, a Federalist lamented, "brought forward every scoundrel who can read and write into office, or expectations of one."

Even worse was in store for the Federalists. In May 1800, they suffered a defeat in New York that put the Republicans in a position to determine the electoral vote of that state. The Republican victory in New York City was largely owing to Aaron Burr's novel methods of electioneering: among other things, he helped organize the patriotic Order of Saint Tammany—the privates' and non-commissioned officers' equivalent of the Order of the Cincinnati—into a political arm of the Republican party. The Republican congressional caucus demonstrated its gratitude to Burr by pledging that the party would give him the same measure of support that it gave to Thomas Jefferson. This meant that Republican electors would cast one vote for Jefferson and one vote for Burr without designating which was to be president and which to be vice-president. Such an arrangement was in accord with the provision of the original Constitution which prescribed that electors should vote for two candidates, the presidency going to the individual who stood highest in the poll.

With Jefferson and Burr as the party's nominees, it was apparent that the Republicans had succeeded in forging an alliance between Virginia and New York, the dream of party strategists. If Pennsylvania could be held, victory seemed assured. "With Pennsylvania on our side," said Jefferson, "we can defy the universe."

In the face of these ominous signs of rising Republican strength, the Federalist party split asunder. Whereas the Republicans scrupulously observed all the rules for winning the election, the Federalists displayed an equally impressive genius for doing the wrong thing at the wrong time.

John Adams was the Federalist candidate to succeed himself in the presidency. As his running mate, the Federalist congressional caucus chose Charles

C. Pinckney of South Carolina, a state whose electoral vote seemed likely to determine the outcome of the election. Like the Republican caucus, the Federalists pledged the party to equal support of the two candidates. Contrary to this pledge and contrary to the implicit understanding that John Adams stood first on the ticket, Alexander Hamilton tried surreptitiously to swing enough votes to Pinckney to give him the presidency. Hamilton was never successful as an intriguer and his efforts in the state legislatures on Pinckney's behalf soon came to the attention of President Adams and his supporters. The peppery New Englander denounced Hamilton's breach of faith, whereupon Hamilton answered in a pamphlet entitled "Letter from Alexander Hamilton Concerning the Public Conduct and Character of John Adams." Here the American people read that their President was guilty of "disgusting egotism," "distempered jealousy," and "ungovernable indiscretion," and that his policies were conceived not in wisdom and rectitude but in passion, spite, envy, and malice. The President did not lack for good advice—the cabinet was always ready to set him straight—but, Hamilton lamented, Adams was an obstinate as well as a short-sighted man. Nevertheless, after laying bare the President's deficiencies, Hamilton conceded that Adams did possess integrity, that he was a patriot, however misguided, and that he even was endowed with "talents of a certain kind"—unfortunately, however, not of the kind required by the presidency. Even so, he concluded lamely that Adams ought to be supported equally with Pinckney in accord with the agreement reached by the Federalist caucus. Few could fail to see, however, that Hamilton's purpose was not to reinforce the pledge of equal support but to relegate Adams to second place on the ticket.

Despite Hamilton's character-study of Adams, the rank and file, together with many of the party leaders, remained loyal to the President. After the untoward events in New York, most Federalists redoubled their efforts to elect Adams. Indeed, the President's friends attempted to create a third party, called the Constitutionalists, but they found that the two-party system, even in its infancy, could not be successfully challenged.

As custom prescribed, neither Adams nor Jefferson mounted the hustings or otherwise indicated any interest in public office. At this time, candidates "stood" for office, they never ran. For aspirants to the presidency, a state of statuesque immobility was the approved stance; the office was expected to seek the man. Jefferson tried to keep in touch with his lieutenants through the post office, but even this avenue of communication was closed to him when it became apparent that the Federalists were reading his mail. Only when letters were carried by his friends did Jefferson feel safe in committing his views to writing. No one was indicted for libeling Thomas Jefferson, although the fact that a man conceived himself to be qualified for the highest office in the land made him, Jefferson said, "a target for every man's dirt." Jefferson was called an atheist, a voluptuary, a "French philosopher," and a believer in the perfectibility of man. When not engaged in devising schemes for subverting the Christian religion and orderly government, he was said to be frolicking with his "Congo Harem" and adding to the labor force at Monticello by an annual increment of mulattoes.

Nor did President Adams fare much better in this ordeal by slander. In some ways, despite the Sedition Act, President Adams was more vulnerable than Jefferson, for Adams was reviled by members of his own party as well as by the opposition. To the harried President, the shafts of Hamilton sunk deeper and seemed more venomous than the familiar charges leveled by the Republicans.

Despite dissension within the Federalist party and the unpopularity of the war and the taxes and repressions it had spawned, the Federalists could not be counted out. The electoral vote of Pennsylvania seemed vital to a Republican victory, but the deadlock between the Federalist Senate and the Republican House threatened to nullify the state's vote in the electoral college. Governor McKean, fearing that Jefferson would lose the presidency unless Pennsylvania voted, consented to a compromise by which Jefferson received eight and Adams seven of the state's electoral vote. The Federalists fared well in this division: public opinion in the state was far more preponderantly Republican than the vote in the electoral college indicated.

The election went right down to the wire—the wire, in this case, being South Carolina, whose legislature met in December 1800 to cast the state's electoral vote. Although the Federalist candidate, Charles C. Pinckney, enjoyed the status of a favorite son, his cousin, Charles Pinckney, a Republican, outmaneuvered the Federalist delegates and delivered the state's electoral vote to Jefferson and Burr.

THE ELECTION IN THE HOUSE OF REPRESENTATIVES

The news of the Republican triumph in South Carolina reached Washington on December 12, 1800. Everyone, including Burr and Jefferson himself, assumed that Jefferson would be the next president of the United States. But it soon became apparent that something had gone wrong; Burr and Jefferson were tied in the electoral college with 73 votes apiece.

In the election of 1800, it has been seen, both parties had pledged equal support to their candidates for president and vice-president. This arrangement was particularly important in the case of the Republicans because Burr felt that he had been badly let down in the election of 1796 when, as candidate for vice-president, he had not received the full electoral vote of Virginia. But both parties intended to scratch the name of the vice-presidential candidate in one or more states to obviate the embarrassment of a tie in the electoral college. The Federalists executed this strategy without a hitch: one of the Rhode Island electors voted for John Jay instead of Pinckney, thereby giving Adams 65 and Pinckney 64 electoral votes. Jefferson trusted his lieutenants to do the same for him: South Carolina, Tennessee, and Georgia were expected to drop votes for Burr, thereby assuring Jefferson of first place. Fearful of

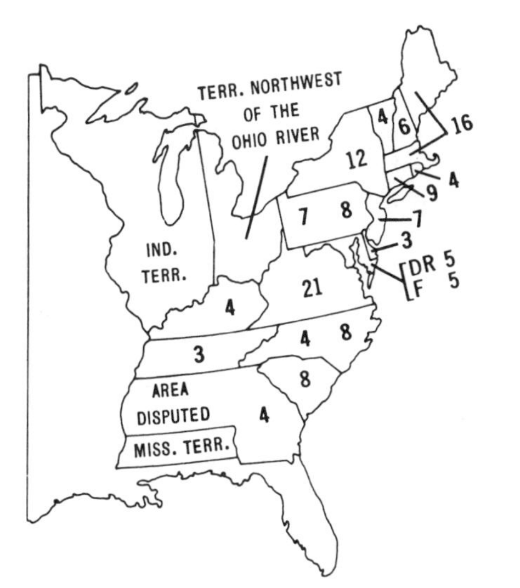

THE ELECTION OF 1800

	ELECTORAL VOTE BY STATE
REPUBLICAN Thomas Jefferson	73
FEDERALIST John Adams	65
	138

wounding Burr's well-known susceptibilities and aware that the vote would be close, no one was eager to take the step that would relegate him to the vice-presidency. As a result, no state broke the pledge of equal support, and Jefferson and Burr were tied in the electoral college.

Since, in case of a tie in the electoral college, the choice of president and vice-president devolved upon the House of Representatives, Aaron Burr was presented with the intriguing possibility of attaining the presidency. Although he profusely protested his loyalty to Jefferson and his disdain of intrigue, Burr could not get the idea of the highest office out of his mind. His hopes were whetted by Federalist members of the House, who decided unanimously to support Burr over Jefferson. It made no difference to the Federalists that during the election no one had voted for Burr as president and that Burr himself had not sought the office.[1]

It was, of course, within Burr's power to have settled the question forthwith: all he had to do was to say that he would not serve as president if elected. But Burr refused to eliminate himself from consideration; when he was asked to renounce his pretensions in favor of Jefferson, he dismissed such suggestions as "unreasonable, unnecessary and impertinent."

The Federalists' sudden affection for Burr was mainly compounded of fear and hatred of Jefferson. Few sincerely esteemed the enigmatic New Yorker, but even taking him at his worst—his ambition, deviousness, and "Machiavel-

[1]The confusion created by the tie in the electoral college (actually there are electoral colleges which meet in each state on the same day, not a national electoral college) gave rise to the Twelfth Amendment to the Constitution, adopted in 1803, which obliged electors to distinguish in their ballots between president and vice-president.

lianism"—he seemed infinitely safer than did Jefferson. For Burr, it was alleged, was no zealot; he held no "pernicious theories"; and his principles were sufficiently elastic to permit him to serve in any party. The Federalists persuaded themselves that, as president, Burr would uphold Federalist policies if only because he would have forfeited all support from the southern Republicans by snatching the first office from Jefferson. Thus the Republican party would be rent by schism and the menace of the Virginia-New York axis dispelled.

Even though this was an event ardently desired by Alexander Hamilton, he did not trust Burr to save the country and the Federalist party from "the fangs of Jefferson." Burr, he observed, was unscrupulous, ambitious, and corrupt, a devotee of French revolutionary doctrines who would plunge the country into war with Great Britain and "employ the rogues of all parties to overrule the good men of all parties." "Adieu to the Federal Troy," Hamilton exclaimed, "if they once introduced this Grecian horse into their citadel."

It would be far better for the Federalists, Hamilton thought, to settle the terms of surrender with Agamemnon himself. Admitting that everything the Federalists were saying about Jefferson was true—that his politics were "tinctured with fanaticism"; that he was much too earnest in his views of democracy; that he was "crafty and persevering in his objects"; that he was capable of using every means at his disposal to attain his ends; that he was a liar and "a contemptible hypocrite"—still, Hamilton was willing to concede that Jefferson was not an enemy to the power of the Executive—that would be proved, he felt, once Jefferson became president—and that as a popularity-seeker he would be the first to abandon France if it seemed politically expedient. Therefore, Hamilton recommended that the Federalists in Congress vote for Jefferson, provided that the Virginian would promise to preserve the Hamiltonian fiscal system, adhere to a policy of neutrality, maintain the Navy, and retain Federalists in office except at the cabinet level.

Hamilton's appeals made little impression upon the Federalist congressmen: their fear of Jefferson was not in the slightest allayed. Moreover, they believed it to be within their power to prevent Jefferson's election. The Constitution directed that in the election of a president and vice-president, each state should have one vote. A majority of the states was required to elect. Although the Republicans had won control of the House of Representatives in the election of 1800—65 Republicans as against 41 Federalists were returned—in the House as it was constituted until March 4, 1801, the Federalists would still be in the majority. Thus it fell to a Congress composed of a large number of lame ducks to choose between Burr and Jefferson. From these vindictive birds Jefferson expected no quarter: "after the most energetic efforts, crowned with success," he lamented, "we remain in the hands of our enemies by want of foresight in the original arrangement."

Yet he could take comfort in the fact that, owing to the heavy geographical concentration of their strength, the Federalists did not control the delegations of enough states to make Burr president. Alone, the Federalists could not elect a president, but they could prevent a Chief Executive from being chosen.

In February 1801, when the first ballot was taken, Jefferson had eight states, Burr had six and two were divided. Whereas Jefferson had to gain the vote of only one additional state, Burr had to pick up three. In terms of individual members of Congress, Jefferson could win by securing the vote of one Federalist—James Bayard of Delaware, the sole representative of his state—whereas, Burr needed to change the votes of four Republican members of Congress. Three of these key Republican congressmen, Burr was told by his Federalist supporters, were open to offers—one of them was a blockhead and the other two willing to be corrupted. Yet Burr remained in Albany, preparing for the marriage of his daughter Theodosia, and, much to the Federalists' chagrin, refused to exert himself to win the presidency. In this crisis of his fortunes, Burr did not bear out Hamilton's description of him as a man "sanguine enough to hope everything, daring enough to attempt every thing, wicked enough to scruple nothing." Being a circumspect man who carefully calculated his every move, Burr did not join the Federalists openly—a move that would be certain to cost him his position as heir apparent to Jefferson. Instead, he left the intrigue and the corruption, if it came to that, to his Federalist managers. On the other hand, Jefferson's lieutenants, without their principal's knowledge, freely promised political appointments in exchange for votes—and Jefferson duly honored these pledges after the election.

If they could not have Burr as president, many Federalists swore that they would have no president at all. During the presidential interregnum, executive power would presumably be exercised by the president *pro tem,* of the Senate (a Federalist). Coming from the self-styled "friends of government," this was a truly remarkable proposal: to subvert the Constitution unless they were permitted to negate the will of the majority of the people of the United States.

While Congress balloted day after day without changing the lineup of states, angry crowds gathered on Capitol Hill; Governor McKean of Pennsylvania was reported ready to call up the Pennsylvania militia; and, as Jefferson said, Virginia was "bristling up." Nevertheless, the majority of Federalists stood firm for Burr or chaos.

In the meantime, disgusted by Burr's failure to take an active part in his own behalf, James Bayard of Delaware, who had made himself Burr's unofficial floor manager, let Jefferson know through an intermediary that he could have the presidency the moment he gave the guarantees stipulated by Hamilton. But Jefferson seemed quite as adamant as the Federalists themselves: "I will not come into the government by capitulation," he declared, "I will not enter on it, but in perfect freedom to follow the dictates of my own judgment." In actuality, however, the case was not as desperate as it appeared: Jefferson's own attitude toward these matters did not greatly differ from that of the Federalists. When Jefferson, in a private conversation with General Samuel Smith, indicated the policies he would pursue as president, Bayard accepted it as a full compliance with his demands. It was not that, but Bayard was looking desperately for a way to break the impasse. On February 16, 1801, he told the Federalist caucus that he would vote for Jefferson.

Bayard's threat to break the Federalist "phalanx" served notice upon the party that the game was up. Yet, rather than vote for Jefferson, the Federalist members of the evenly divided Vermont and Maryland delegations simply abstained from voting on the 36th ballot, thereby delivering the vote of those states to Jefferson. Not a single Federalist congressman—not even Bayard—voted for Jefferson; the party went down to defeat with all its prejudices proudly nailed to the masthead. Ten states voted for Jefferson, the New England states remained loyal to Burr, and two states declined to vote.

FOUNDED A.D. MDCCXCV.

16.
THE JEFFERSONIAN "REVOLUTION"

Jefferson believed that the election of 1800 was as real a revolution, even though effected by the peaceful instrument of popular suffrage, as the revolution of 1776. In arriving at this conclusion, he assumed that the Federalists had been trying to warp the government into a monarchy and to make the United States an ally of Great Britain. Now, as a result of the election of 1800, as Jefferson conceived it, the United States had a government dedicated to fostering republicanism and nonalignment in the European war. In Jefferson's opinion, the revolution consisted in the change that had occurred in the spirit by which the government was animated: for the first time, the United States had a government that did not fear the people, that chose "to let the good sense of the nation have fair play, believing it will best take care of itself," that recognized the popular will as a standard that made every citizen feel that he was a participant in public affairs, that did not go out of its way to reward the undeserving rich, and did not rejoice in the cuffs and kicks administered by John Bull.

Jefferson's first inaugural speech contained a major exposition of his political philosophy. In the spirit of Washington's Farewell Address, Jefferson called upon Americans to cool their political passions and to display the "harmony and affection" without which, the President asserted, "liberty and even life are but dreary things." He assured his audience (few could hear him because he spoke in such a low tone of voice) that every difference of opinion was not a difference of principle and that Americans enjoyed the inestimable felicity, if they would but see it, of being in agreement upon fundamentals—an

"Bank of the United States, Philadelphia, Pa.," detail of an engraving by W. Birch from The Granger Collection.

Washington Grate Cent, 1795.

agreement that made republican government possible in the United States. "We are all Federalists, we are all Republicans," the President declared. He called upon the minority to accept the outcome of the election with good grace, and he pledged in turn that the victorious majority would not oppress the defeated party. Only by accepting the principle of majority rule and minority rights, he held, could the American people realize the ideals of equal justice, peace, and good will among men. Recognizing the intimate connection between partisan politics and foreign affairs, President Jefferson promised to preserve strict neutrality: "peace, commerce and honest friendship with all nations, entangling alliances with none" became the guiding principle of his administration. Finally, he promised the payment of the national debt, the "sacred preservation of the public faith"—obviously intended to reassure the Federalists—and to conduct a "wise and frugal government, which shall restrain men from injuring one another, which shall leave them otherwise free to regulate their own pursuits of industry and improvement, and shall not take from the mouth of labor the bread it has earned. This is the sum of good government, and this is all that is necessary to close the circle of our felicities."

THE REPUBLICAN PRESIDENT

To signify the triumph of republicanism, Jefferson abolished all the monarchical pomp and parade introduced by the Federalists. In place of personal appearances before Congress, reminiscent of the speech from the throne, Jefferson sent written messages to the legislature; he proscribed the wearing of wigs in the English fashion by justices of the Supreme Court (Jefferson wore his hair straight, but John Adams said that he thought that curled hair was as republican as straight); to the intense mortification of the ladies, he refused to hold levees and, since he was a widower, the capital was spared what Republicans called "the burlesque of a female levee"; and he used his chariot drawn by four horses only when his daughters were visiting him. The rest of the time he rode horseback, often unattended, into the wildest and most remote parts of the District of Columbia.

As the president of a republic of plain farmers, Jefferson dressed like a farmer. Although when he entertained at dinner he appeared in a decent black suit with white hose, clean linen, and powdered hair, he often received visitors in a state of *deshabille:* A Federalist congressman found the President in a blue coat, red vest, ragged slippers with his toes out and his hair disheveled. When Anthony Merry, the British minister, made his first official call, he found the President sitting on a sofa, throwing up his slipper and catching it on his toe. John Augustus Foster, Merry's successor in Washington, reported that the President "had still so much respect for European opinion as to take occasion to tell me how often he washed his feet, no doubt lest I should suppose from his dress that he was really an unclean animal."

As for protocol, it vanished with the rest of the monarchical "lumber." At a dinner party at the President's, Merry was left to escort Mrs. Merry to the dinner table while Jefferson, Madison, and assorted congressmen took in the more attractive women. The fuming British minister and his indignant consort went home resolved that they never again would set foot in the President's house. Merry believed that all the discourtesies he received at Jefferson's hands were not ignorant but deliberate. After all, the man had spent five years in the politest society in Europe.

Despite this carefully contrived air of rusticity, the President's table contained choice viands prepared by a Parisian cook and was loaded with as many as eight different wines. He added wine cellars to the President's house and kept them stocked with the products of the finest French vineyards. No President of the United States surpassed Jefferson as a gourmet.

REPUBLICAN POLICIES

After what he regarded as a saturnalia of governmental extravagance under the Federalists (he estimated that the national debt had increased by $24 million since 1791; in actuality the increase was a little over $3 million), Jefferson felt that drastic economizing was long overdue. Although the academy at West Point was established in 1802, the Army was subjected to the pruning knife: its numbers were reduced to 3000 men and officers. Nor did the diplomatic service escape attention: the ministers to Holland, Portugal, and Prussia were recalled and no successors were appointed.

In actuality, even though he did not admit it, Jefferson had inherited a good estate from the Federalists. Whether animated by a republican or a monarchical spirit, the United States was very much a going concern. The government's revenues amounted to $10,600,000 annually, and the Treasury contained a surplus of over $3 million. True, the national debt stood at $83 million, but the growth of the economy and the steady increase in governmental revenue, together with the inflation produced by the war in Europe, gave every assurance that the debt was susceptible of management.

Even peace with France was included in the Federalist legacy. In September 1800, the United States emissaries to France signed a convention that brought an end to the quasi-war. In effect, the United States Senate purchased the annulment of the Franco-American alliance by agreeing to hold in abeyance claims for spoliations upon American ships committed by French privateers and warships during the undeclared war of 1798-1801. These claims were not finally settled until 1915 when $7 million was paid by France to the United States.

Jefferson's task of curing the American people of their European attachments and antipathies was made easier by events in Europe itself. In 1800, Madison admitted that North America was "the only Theatre on which true liberty can have a fair trial." Jefferson himself had been weaned of his strong

FEDERAL GOVERNMENT FINANCES, 1792-1815

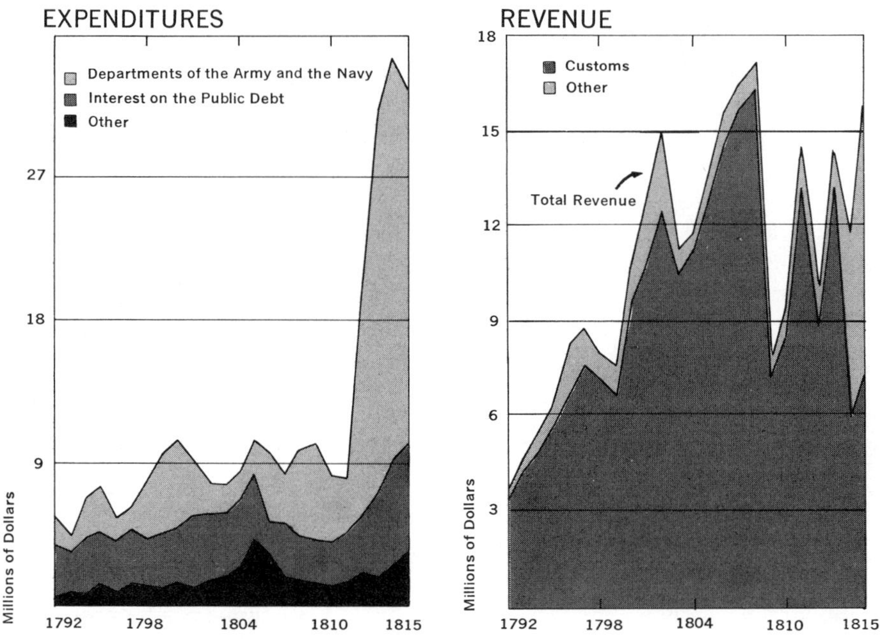

Source: Historical Statistics of the United States.

predilection for France—Napoleon provided a powerful antidote for that particular kind of "love-sickness." He no longer expected the downfall of Great Britain, and, had that event occurred, he was no longer in the mood to drink tea in London with the victorious French generals. The President now took pains to emphasize his cordial feeling for Great Britain. Nor did he contemplate reviving the French alliance: "we have a perfect horror," he said, "at anything like connecting ourselves with the politics of Europe." Except for buying and selling, he made clear, the disengagement of the United States from Europe was to be complete. Treaties were permitted to expire without renewal. Even the assertion of neutral rights was held in abeyance: "if we can delay but for a few years the necessity of vindicating the laws of nature on the ocean," he declared, "we shall be the more sure of doing it with effect."

Toward civil liberties and the naturalization of foreigners, Jefferson's attitude was consistent with the principles he had enunciated in the Kentucky Resolutions. The Federalist-inspired Naturalization Act, which required fourteen years of residence prior to naturalization, was replaced by a law reducing the probationary period to five years. Although the Sedition Act expired before he took office, he pardoned and ordered released from prison the victims of that law. Restraints upon the freedom of the press were, he made clear, to be applied exclusively by the state courts. In 1804, without doing violence to his principles, Jefferson advised his supporters to institute libel suits in the state courts in order to discipline Federalist journalists.

As a counter-revolution against "monarchism," the election of 1800 might have been expected to purge the government of the last vestiges of Hamiltonian finance—the principal instrument, by Jefferson's reckoning, of effectuating the monarchical conspiracy. He had pronounced the Bank of the United States to be deadly hostile to republican institutions and had repeatedly declared that this "powerful enemy" must be eliminated root and branch. Yet after taking office, Jefferson found himself inextricably caught in the toils of the Hamiltonian fiscal system. Without irreparably injuring the government's credit, Jefferson could not interfere with the Bank of the United States. His Secretary of the Treasury, Albert Gallatin, declared that the Bank facilitated the extinguishment of the national debt, a fiscal objective to which Jefferson always gave priority. The rapid growth of the economy was reflected in the steady increase of government revenues; simply by cutting expenditures and letting the money roll into the Treasury, Gallatin predicted that the national debt would be paid off in twenty years.

And so, the President accepted the benefits conferred by the Hamiltonian system at the same time that he lamented the hard fate that prevented him from undoing his great rival's work. "It mortified me to be strengthening principles which I deem radically vicious," he said, "but this vice is entailed on us by the first error." To this extent, the sins of the original Secretary of the Treasury descended upon posterity and, to Jefferson's way of thinking, vitiated the revolution of 1800.

Nevertheless, Jefferson did mount an indirect attack upon the Bank of the United States by selling the government's shares in the institution and by encouraging the chartering by the state governments of banks organized by Republicans. Jefferson made clear that he found banks objectionable only when they were controlled by Federalists; he not only gave his blessing to Republican banks but made them the depository of federal funds. Banks became appurtenances of political parties: in the northern states, successful politicians often had their own banks whose resources were used to win the support of influential citizens.

In thus extending governmental favor to Republican-controlled, state-chartered banks, President Jefferson was not thinking primarily of the needs of farmers. Uncompromising as was Jefferson's devotion to agrarianism in theory, it was tempered in practice by his awareness that commerce and, to some extent, manufacturing were vital segments of the national economy. Moreover, he could be confident that he had the farmers' vote, particularly in the West and the South. Like the astute politician he was, he strove to strengthen his political position where it was weakest—in the business community. Despite the strong Federalist bias of most northern businessmen, Jefferson believed that they belonged within the Republican fold: "a merchant," he said, "is naturally a Republican."

Even so, the farmers were not forgotten in the Jeffersonian dispensation.

In 1802, to the delight of whiskey drinkers everywhere and of the western farmers in particular, the excise tax was repealed by Congress. Years later, the President ruefully admitted he had made a mistake: the consumption of whiskey and the incidence of drunkenness, he discovered, were geared to the price of that intoxicant. He hoped to wean his countrymen from distilled liquor to wine—"no nation is drunken," he said, "where wine is cheap"—but reducing the price of whiskey was not the way to effect this refinement of taste. At the moment, however, it seemed to be a shrewd political move: westerners acclaimed the statesmanship of the man who had freed them from the hated tax.

Having reinforced the ligaments which united the West with the Republican party, President Jefferson undertook to bind the West economically to the eastern section of the Union. Like Washington, he believed that Virginia ought to serve as the connecting link between the two sections. In 1802, Congress authorized the construction of the National or Cumberland Road, the first stage of which was to run from the upper Potomac to Wheeling in what was then the state of Virginia. Despite his constitutional scruples, Jefferson signed the bill. His conscience, however, was not wholly at rest: after all, even Hamilton admitted that an amendment of the Constitution would be necessary to permit the general government to open canals through the territory of two or more states. In 1807, the President called Congress' attention to the necessity of a constitutional amendment authorizing the federal government to construct internal improvements (roads, canals, and other public works) between two or more states, but Congress took no action. Nor did the President see fit to exert his usually effective influence in behalf of the amendment: a few dinner parties at the President's house and the thing might have been done. A similar fatality attended almost all the other constitutional amendments deemed necessary by the President: only one—the Twelfth Amendment—was presented by Congress to the states.

UNIFYING THE NATION

President Jefferson said the first object of his heart was to restore "harmony and social love" and to make Americans "one people, acting as one nation." To achieve this objective, he declared that he would gladly sacrifice everything but principle. He did not believe that any sacrifice of principle would be exacted of him. In adversity as well as in success, he was buoyed up by the conviction that his principles were held by at least 90 percent of the American people. While the Federalists had obscured, they had not destroyed the consensus based upon devotion to the principles of the revolution. Let the Federalists rage, he told his friends, the American people would never be swept from their republican moorings. Yet, paradoxically, he made the fear of "monarchism" one of the most effective articles, from a vote-getting standpoint, of his political creed.

Nevertheless, Jefferson never asserted that all Federalists were monarchists. Particularly after he became president and the necessity of articulating a unifying ideology took precedence over all other political concerns, he drew a sharp distinction between the Federalist leaders and the rank and file of that party. The leaders, he concluded, were monarchists to a man, whereas their followers were at heart all good republicans. For the leaders, the prime movers of the "monarchical conspiracy" he had no charity and no hope: politically, he said, they were madmen who deserved to be locked up.

In his inaugural address, President Jefferson had invited Federalists to become Republicans; he never meant to suggest that Republicans should become Federalists. Privately, he said that he aimed "to sink Federalism into an abyss from which there will be no resurrection." Certainly he never permitted the dictum "We are all Federalists, we are all Republicans" to govern his appointments to office. For him, only one party existed with respect to this vital sphere of government. In making appointments, he consulted only party allegiance and geographical balance. He named two New Englanders to his cabinet, and his Postmaster General was Gideon Granger of Connecticut.

When Jefferson took over the presidency, he found all branches of the government staffed with Federalists. Presidents Washington and Adams had appointed only "friends of government" to important offices; in the distribution of patronage their concern was to maintain a geographical, not a party, equilibrium. In consequence, of the six hundred offices at the disposal of the Chief Executive, Jefferson found only eight occupied by Republicans and even they, the President lamented, were mostly "half-breeds." "I found the country entirely in the enemy's hands," was the way he put it.

Jefferson's problem, therefore, was how to dispossess the enemy of this strategic terrain and at the same time to achieve his objective of mitigating party zeal and intolerance. Wholesale removals of Federalist incumbents from office, he feared, would revive the drooping spirit of party. On the other hand, his own partisans were clamoring for a distribution of the loaves and fishes. And, much as he recoiled from the "horrid drudgery" of effecting removals from office—he much preferred to hunt out and abolish useless offices rather than dispossess incumbents—he admitted that some sort of balance had to be effected in the civil service.

Here neither nature nor the Federalists themselves proved cooperative: few officeholders died and none resigned. The President therefore adopted the policy of selective removals in cases of incompetence, "monarchism," and political zeal carried to the length of thwarting administration measures. Yet he did not make the expression of political opinion a cause for dismissal. At the end of his second administration, he claimed that he had never deprived a man of office simply because he was a Federalist or because he voted the Federalist ticket. It is true, however, that in some states, notably Connecticut, where the Federalist regime had rooted out all Republicans from the state civil service, Jefferson retaliated by purging Federalists.

To a large degree, Jefferson's difficulties stemmed from the fact that the Federalist civil service he had inherited was of generally high quality; there were really not enough rogues, scoundrels, and malefactors whose removal would provide room for deserving Republicans. As a result, every removal ordered by President Jefferson evoked anguished cries from the Federalists: "the whole herd have squealed out," Jefferson observed, "as if all their throats were cut." Yet, in spite of this uproar, the Federalist rank and file appeared strangely unperturbed by the spectacle of their leaders being led to the abattoir: "they (the people) seem to pant so much for repose," remarked a Federalist, "that they are ready to submit to any state of things short of Parisian Massacres." Since many Federalist leaders expected that Jefferson would inflict this ultimate horror upon the country, they consoled themselves with the reflection that sooner or later the people, or at least the sober, God-fearing part of them, would see through the plans of the great "Jacobin."

THE FEDERALIST JUDICIARY

Having lost control of the Executive and Legislative branches of the government as a result of the election of 1800 the Federalists found themselves down to their last branch—the federal judiciary. So far, the judiciary had proved a disappointment to its friends. From 1790 to 1800, the Supreme Court had decided only six cases involving important questions of constitutional law. The first United States attorney general worked only part time for the government because there simply was not enough work to keep one lawyer busy. And when the Supreme Court put itself in direct conflict with a sovereign state, the judges came off the field with their robes trailing in the dust. In 1793, in the case of *Chisholm* v. *Georgia,* the Court upheld the right of a citizen to institute an original suit for breach of contract in the Supreme Court against a state of which he was not a resident. The Georgia legislature took steps to prevent the execution of the Court's decision, and the issue was not resolved until 1798, when the Eleventh Amendment to the Constitution was adopted by the requisite number of states. The Eleventh Amendment represented a victory for the states over the Court. It provides that "the Judicial power of the United States shall not be construed to extend to any suit in law or equity, commenced or prosecuted against one of the United States by a citizen of another State, or by Citizens or Subjects of any foreign State." The justices of the Supreme Court thereupon beat a strategic retreat from the high ground to which they had laid claim in 1793; in the case of *Calder* v. *Bull* (1798), the Court ruled that it had no power to declare a state law unconstitutional on the ground that it conflicted with the state constitution.

On the other hand, in 1796 the Supreme Court asserted the supremacy of national treaties over state laws and upheld the constitutionality of a tax imposed upon carriages by the federal government. Yet the shortcomings of the federal judicial system were so forcibly impressed upon Chief Justice John Jay that in 1795 he resigned to become governor of New York, and he did not think that he lost by the exchange. In 1800 he declined reappointment to the bench on the ground that the Supreme Court was wholly lacking in "energy, weight and dignity." In 1799, Chief Justice Ellsworth followed Jay's example by resigning from the Court to serve as special envoy to France.

In 1801, just before surrendering power to the new administration, the Federalist-controlled Congress had enlarged the jurisdiction of the federal courts, increased the number of district courts and judges, and relieved the Supreme Court justices of the necessity of presiding over circuit courts in all parts of the Union. Ostensibly, this legislation was intended to correct the deficiencies of the Judiciary Act of 1789, which, among other things, had required the six justices of the Supreme Court to make a tour of the United States twice a year in order to preside over trials arising in the district courts of each circuit. As Gouverneur Morris said, members of the bench were expected to combine the agility of jockeys with the erudition of savants. Since such paragons were not readily found, the administration of justice in federal courts was slow and tedious; prisoners sometimes were confined in jail for months awaiting trial.

But, patently, there was more to the Judiciary Act of 1801 than the expediting of litigation in the federal courts. Gouverneur Morris put it this way: "they [the Federalists] were about to experience a heavy gale of adverse wind: can they be blamed for casting many anchors to hold the ship through the storm?" The approaching storm was Jeffersonian Democracy; the enlarged federal judiciary was intended to "quell the fierce passions of a victorious faction" and to provide shelter for the wise, the good, and the rich. To that end, they inserted a provision in the Judiciary Act of 1801 preventing the incoming president from filling an impending vacancy in the Supreme Court.

Jefferson was resolved not to permit the Federalists to convert the federal judiciary into a fortress from which judges, armored in life tenure, could defy the popular will. At one time a defender of the doctrine of judicial review, the President had become sharply critical of the practice of justices of the Supreme Court in declaring acts of the state legislatures unconstitutional and the evident enthusiasm with which they enforced the Sedition Act. By 1801, he regarded the federal courts as the prime instrument for effecting a consolidation of all power in the federal government.

In his message to Congress of December 1801, President Jefferson gave the signal to his party in Congress to press for the repeal of the Judiciary Act of 1801. The Republicans rested their case upon the argument that the Judiciary Act created more judges than the business conducted in the federal courts warranted. In March 1802, the repeal was carried in the Senate by a vote of

16 to 15 (Vice-President Burr's casting vote was decisive) and in the House by a vote of 59 to 32. The Jeffersonian Judiciary Act of 1802 cut back the number of judges to the pre-1801 figure, the Supreme Court justices were again required to ride circuit, and the jurisdiction of the federal courts was confined within the limits imposed by the Judiciary Act of 1789. Not until 1875 did the courts regain the powers they had briefly enjoyed in 1801.

President Jefferson congratulated his followers upon having lopped off the "parasitical plant" grafted upon the government by the Federalists. In the opinion of the Federalists, however, the Jeffersonians had inflicted a fatal wound upon the Constitution. One distraught congressman was moved to write an epitaph: the Constitution, he lamented, "expired, after suffering extreme convulsions, on the 3rd of March, 1802, in the evening, aged just 13 years."

Many Federalists and Republicans expected the Supreme Court to declare the repeal of the Judiciary Act of 1801 unconstitutional and thereby bring the Supreme Court and Congress into direct confrontation. To prevent such an occurrence, the Jeffersonians suspended all meetings of the Supreme Court during the calendar year 1802. The precaution proved unnecessary: John Marshall, the greatest statesman ever to occupy the office of Chief Justice, refused to be drawn into what he feared would prove to be, for the Court, a disastrous encounter. In 1803, to the astonishment of the Republicans and the mortification of the Federalists, the Supreme Court upheld the constitutionality of the Judiciary Act of 1802.

But Marshall was merely biding his time; the Chief Justice, an incomparable strategist, fought only on ground of his own choosing. His opportunity to assert the authority of the Supreme Court over both Congress and President came in 1803 in the case of *Marbury* v. *Madison*. Marbury, one of President Adams' "midnight" appointees to the office of justice of the peace in the District of Columbia, brought suit when Secretary of State Madison withheld the commission to which Marbury deemed himself entitled.[1] The case was carried to the Supreme Court, where Marshall handed down a decision holding that, because the section of the Judiciary Act of 1801 under which Marbury brought suit was unconstitutional, the Supreme Court had no jurisdiction. But at the same time he delivered an *obiter dicta* to the effect that Secretary of State Madison (which really meant President Jefferson) had no right to withhold the commission and that Marbury could secure redress by bringing his case before another court.

Thus, at one stroke, Marshall managed to assert the right of the Supreme Court to declare acts of Congress unconstitutional, rebuked the President for violating the law, and vindicated Marbury. Although President Jefferson

---

[1]To fill the offices created by the Judiciary Act of 1801, President Adams labored until nine o'clock of the night of March 3, 1801. Despite his industry, not all the commissions could be delivered before he vacated the presidency. When Jefferson took office, he refused to deliver the commissions to these so-called "midnight judges."

deeply resented the strictures upon his conduct passed by Marshall, he did not immediately make a major issue of the Supreme Court's claim of right to declare acts of Congress unconstitutional. After all, the law in question was a piece of Federalist legislation which the Republicans were not sorry to see expunged from the statute book. Marshall had asserted the power of judicial review in a case where the Republicans were least likely to challenge it.

17. FOREIGN AFFAIRS: THE BARBARY CORSAIRS AND THE LOUISIANA PURCHASE

A SECOND WAR IN THE MEDITERRANEAN

By giving primacy to the national interest as distinguished from the interests of Europe, Jefferson hoped to avoid involvement in war. Peace, he said, was his passion, and he made clear in his Inaugural Address that the United States threatened no one and asked only to be left alone in the enjoyment of its geographical isolation from the wars of the Old World. But it proved insufficient to proclaim the pacific intentions of the United States. Aggressors were neither disarmed nor mollified by the desire of the American government to avoid combat. Within a month of taking office, President Jefferson found himself with a war on his hands.

While the United States had agreed to pay tribute to Algiers and Tunis, it had no largesse to spare for the Dey of Tripoli. In April 1801, deeply offended by what he regarded as unfair discrimination, the Dey declared war upon the United States. In default of tribute, American ships and seamen were seized

---

"U.S. Negotiators Signing the Treaty of Transfer with Napoleon's Ministers," detail of a lithograph from a painting by Victor Adam from The Bettmann Archive.

Large Cent, Liberty Cap Type, 1795.

in the Mediterranean. A full-blown crisis similar to that of 1794 greeted the incoming President.

Jefferson responded by dispatching a naval force to the Mediterranean. But, as he later told Congress, he deliberately chose to send "the least possible competent force." Even in war, the President did not forget the necessity of observing frugality and economy and deferring to the will of Congress. But half-measures did not incline the Dey of Tripoli to make peace. By 1803, so little had been accomplished by the small squadron operating in the Mediterranean that Secretary of State Madison offered to pay tribute to Tripoli, but the Dey, convinced that he was winning, raised the price for ending hostilities. In October 1803, the United States suffered its worst reverse of the war: the U.S.S. *Philadelphia,* Captain Bainbridge commanding, ran aground chasing a Tripolitan vessel, and the American ship and its crew of 307 men were captured. But the Tripolitans were not permitted to use the *Philadelphia* against the United States; in 1804, Captain Decatur entered the harbor of Tripoli and burned the *Philadelphia.* Nevertheless, with his prisons overflowing with American captives, the Dey raised the price of peace and ransom to three million dollars.

The war produced naval heroes who became household names in the United States: Bainbridge, Preble, Decatur, and others. Improbably enough, it also brought fame to a landlubber. William Eaton, at the head of a ragtail army with a claimant to the throne of Tripoli in its train, marched from Cairo across a thousand miles of desert to Derna, where, for the first time, the United States flag was raised in Africa. Although Eaton's exploit made him a popular hero in the United States, in actuality he and his men were saved from massacre only by the timely arrival of United States ships and marines. The administration took little notice of him: he entered a claim of $46,000 against the government for his services in Africa, but he finally agreed to take $10,000 in full payment.

Not until 1804 when Congress imposed new taxes to build additional ships and to carry on large-scale operations in the Mediterranean did the Corsairs begin to feel the weight of American naval power. By 1805, two thirds of the ocean-going craft of the United States Navy was engaged in blockading Tripoli. Sensing that the game was up, the Dey indicated his willingness to make peace—at a price. In 1806, a treaty was ratified by the Senate which, while it committed the United States to pay tribute to Tripoli, gave the Americans more favorable terms than any western nation had yet received. Not until 1815, after another war with the Barbary pirates, were these payments discontinued.

Of the four-year struggle with Tripoli, President Jefferson said that though it was a small war it was "big in principle. It has shown that when necessary we can be respectable at sea, and has taught to Europe a lesson of honor and of justice to the Barbarians." But it did not persuade him of the necessity of building a larger navy or even of keeping at fighting strength the force already at sea.

THE LOUISIANA PURCHASE

Ironically, with regard to Europe, President Jefferson's immediate problems arose from peace rather than from war. In 1802, the Peace of Amiens put a temporary halt to the hostilities that had racked Europe for a decade and, incidentally, had enriched the United States. Peace fell upon American business, said a New Yorker, "almost like the hand of death." The price of wheat, corn, flour, and the southern staples dropped; ships were sold at bargain prices. Because France and Spain regained their colonial trade, the United States lost its reexport trade in colonial produce, the most lucrative branch of its commerce.

Of much greater significance in its long-range effects was the opportunity the truce afforded Napoleon to shift his attention from Europe toward the realization of his Grand Design in the western hemisphere. Napoleon planned to create a new French colonial empire based upon the twin pillars of Louisiana and Santo Domingo. Santo Domingo was a French possession, but since 1763 Louisiana had been Spanish territory. In his usual forthright way, Napoleon settled the problem of title by compelling the King of Spain in the secret convention of San Ildefonso (October 1800) to retrocede Louisiana to France in exchange for territory in the Italian peninsula.

The "secret" of San Ildefonso was soon making the rounds of the whispering galleries of Europe. Reports reached the United States early in 1802 that the French would soon arrive in force in Louisiana. Napoleon did not disguise his intentions: two expeditions were prepared for duty in the western hemisphere; a fleet and army were sent to Santo Domingo and a second expeditionary force, destined for Louisiana, was held in readiness in Holland.

Americans' worst fears of French intentions were confirmed when, in October 1802, the Spanish Intendant at New Orleans suspended the right of deposit guaranteed to United States citizens by the treaty of 1796. Unable to transship their farm products to Europe by way of New Orleans, westerners vowed to force a passage with the aid of their rifles. But President Jefferson was unwilling to appeal to arms until all the resources of diplomacy had been exhausted. Accordingly, James Monroe was sent as minister plenipotentiary to back up Edward Livingston, the resident minister in Paris. The outcome of this mission, the President said, would decide "whether we are to be a people consigned to peace with all nations, unmeddling in the affairs of Europe, or are to take part in their broils and become an unhappy nation."

But Jefferson did not rely wholly upon diplomacy to prevent a French occupation of Louisiana. From April 1802 through May 1803, he made preparations for war. The army was increased in size, troops were concentrated in western military posts, and attempts were made to pacify the Indians. The Lewis and Clark expedition projected by Jefferson in January 1803 was originally intended as a military reconnaissance of French Louisiana. Through his friend Du Pont de Nemours, Jefferson tried to impress upon Napoleon that the presence of French troops in Louisiana would prove to be "the embryo of a tornado which will burst on the countries on both sides of the Atlantic." If all else failed, President Jefferson was prepared, contrary to his own injunctions against entangling alliances, to marry the United States to the British fleet and nation. Of course, on the President's part, it would have been strictly a marriage of convenience designed not only to save Louisiana from the French but also to prevent the British from establishing themselves at the mouth of the Mississippi. Spain was the only foreign power whose presence in Louisiana the United States would tolerate, and this because Spain was a declining power whose course of empire seemed almost run.

Monroe and Livingston were instructed to offer France $2 million for New Orleans and the east bank of the Mississippi. The President expected that the United States might have to pay as much as $10 million for this small but highly strategic area. The administration's attention was riveted upon the mouth of the Mississippi—the French could have kept the rest of Louisiana without risk of war with the United States.

But by the time Monroe arrived in France, Napoleon's own dream of empire was rapidly running its course. The Santo Domingo expedition ended in disaster: having come to restore slavery to the island, the French encountered desperate resistance from the Negroes led by Touissant l'Ouverture. "In this insurrection," reported General Leclerc, the French commander, ". . . the men die with unbelievable fanaticism; they laugh at death. It is the same with the women." Leclerc demanded that Napoleon send more troops to the island: "We must destroy all the Negroes in the mountains, men and women, retaining only children under twelve years old," he told Napoleon; "destroy half of those in the plains; and not leave in the colony a single colored man who has worn an epaulet." By dint of massacres and the wholesale killing of prisoners, Leclerc made a promising start toward this objective. But the blacks took to the mountains and waged guerrilla warfare marked by bloody counter-massacres. Although Touissant was captured by a ruse and sent to die in a Swiss prison, the blacks continued the fight under Christophe and Dessalines. They were aided by an epidemic of yellow fever which killed thousands of French troops. In November 1803, the remnants of the French Army surrendered to the British fleet in order to escape massacre by the blacks.

The bad news from Santo Domingo and the impending resumption of the war with England—in March 1803 Napoleon gave the British government a choice between surrendering Malta or renewing hostilities—compelled the First Consul to change his plans radically toward the western hemisphere. He had no intention of creating an empire that would fall to the British Navy when the first shot was fired in Europe. And so the Louisiana expedition was called off and the French troops were told that there had been a slight change of destination—they were bound for the British Isles instead of New Orleans.

For these reasons, Napoleon decided to cut his losses by liquidating the still embryonic French empire upon the North American continent. Talleyrand told Livingston that the First Consul was not interested in selling a part of Louisiana: the entire territory was up for sale. Monroe arrived just in time to take part in the negotiations over the price of this imperial domain. But even here the American emissaires found Napoleon disposed to be reasonable: for $15 million, less than three cents an acre, all of Louisiana was sold to the United States. Livingston and Monroe joyfully signed the treaty on April 13, 1803, still hardly able to believe their good fortune but already competing between themselves for the honor of having carried it off. They of course gave no credit whatever to the British Navy which, in actuality, had been the major factor in Napoleon's decision to sell Louisiana.

The news reached Washington on the night of July 3, just in time for President Jefferson to announce the event on July 4, 1803. It was the most momentous Fourth of July the American people had celebrated since 1776.

When President Jefferson's first flush of elation subsided, he began to be troubled by doubts as to the constitutionality of the Louisiana Purchase. Unless the Constitution were interpreted in the Hamiltonian manner, he found no sanction for purchasing foreign territory and incorporating it in the Union. Moreover, Napoleon had complicated Jefferson's problem by insisting upon inserting in the Louisiana Treaty a clause requiring that the white inhabitants of the territory be given all the rights and privileges of United States citizens. If the United States honored this agreement, the area would ultimately be divided into states and admitted into the Union as the equals of the original thirteen states. Thus, in selling Louisiana, Napoleon dictated how the United States should treat its new acquisition.

Had Jefferson been bound by the literal text of the Constitution, he would have rejected the Louisiana Treaty. He had said repeatedly that the doctrine of implied powers would make the Constitution a blank paper and permit the federal government to use power without stint to effect all manner of purposes never contemplated by the Founding Fathers. The last thing he wanted to do was to make a breach in the Constitution that would let in the floodwaters of Hamiltonian consolidationism and monarchism.

And so Jefferson concluded that only a constitutional amendment could legitimize the Louisiana Treaty. Yet here again Napoleon called the tune to which the President was obliged to dance. By specifying in the treaty that ratifications had to be exchanged within a period of six months, the First Consul deprived Jefferson of an opportunity of indulging his constitutional scruples. Time was of the essence of the contract. Moreover, the President's sense of urgency was reinforced by letters from James Monroe warning that Napoleon might call off the bargain unless the United States acted before the deadline.

For these reasons, the President urged the House of Representatives to approve the issuance of $11,250,000 in government bonds ($750,000 of the purchase price was to be paid by the United States to American claimants who had suffered losses as a result of French action during the quasi-war). "The less that is said about any constitutional difficulty, the better," he told his floor managers in Congress. " . . . It will be desirable for Congress to do what is necessary *in silence*." He wanted to hear no "metaphysical subtleties" such as he himself had raised against Hamilton's reports. True, after the treaty had been ratified and the title cleared, Jefferson intended to ask for a constitutional amendment. But his friends advised against it, and the Louisiana Purchase took its place as a conspicuous example of Hamiltonian constructionism.

Not the least of Jefferson's achievements was his triumph over his own constitutional theories. A doctrinaire would have let the opportunity slip, but Jefferson acted upon the principle that "what is practicable must often control what is pure theory." The feeling among Republicans, fully shared by the President himself, was that the Constitution was perfectly safe as long as they administered the government. Even though they did occasionally take liberties with the sacred document, it was always done for the people's own good—hence no harm could come of it.

Certainly it was true that, if in this instance Jefferson adopted Hamilton's permissive attitude toward the Constitution, he acted for Jeffersonian ends. By doubling the size of the country, Jefferson seemed to have insured that the agrarian way of life would be in a position to resist for generations the inroads of commerce and manufacturing. The yeoman farmer was given renewed encouragement; in the great heartland of America he would reap and multiply until Hamilton's vision of an industrialized nation faded away altogether. Moreover, Jefferson believed that, by adding these millions of acres to the national domain, he had averted all danger of monarchism, for no more resolute enemies of hereditary honors and distinctions were to be found than among the tillers of the earth.

It was the Federalists, not the Republicans, who raised "metaphysical subtleties" to the Louisiana Purchase. Many of these onetime advocates of centralized government and broad construction now demanded that all of Louisiana be handed back to Napoleon because the government of the United States did not have the constitutional power to purchase and administer it under the conditions laid down by the treaty. The Republicans, in their most doctrinaire period, had never gone to quite *that* length. It was characteristic of the Federalists that when they adopted an idea formerly held by their opponents they displayed an extremism that astonished even the Republicans themselves.

And yet the Federalists, in opposing the Louisiana Purchase, were remaining true to the principle that had always governed their conduct—that the growth of the West redounded to the political and economic advantage of the South and was therefore to be resisted. In the case of Louisiana, the New England Federalists regarded its acquisition under the terms of the Louisiana Treaty as a finishing stroke to their section. On the other hand, they did not deny that the federal government had the constitutional power to conquer Louisiana and to govern it as a province. As they said, "Louisiana is of itself a world" which promised wholly to destroy the sectional balance upon which the continued existence of the Union depended. All they asked, in short, was that the West be kept in permanent subordination to the East, thereby precluding any sectional advantage to the South.

By taking their stand against the Louisiana Purchase, the Federalists succeeded only in demonstrating that they were an impotent minority, hostile to the West, and disposed to put the narrow interests of a section above those of the Union as a whole. The popular will, as distinguished from the will of the Federalist party, was clearly manifest in the vote in Congress: the Senate ratified by 24 to 7 votes, and the House of Representatives, with 89 votes in favor and 23 opposed, appropriated the funds necessary to implement the treaty.

EXPLORATIONS OF THE LOUISIANA TERRITORY

In addition to the constitutional issue, the Federalists raised the equally sensitive question of whether Napoleon had any right to sell Louisiana. If their suspicions proved correct, Napoleon had bilked the gullible President out of $15 million. And, indeed, the Spanish government did cry fraud (the Treaty of San Ildefonso debarred Napoleon from alienating Louisiana to a third party), but both Napoleon and President Jefferson declared that a clear title had passed. In case there was any question on this score, the President ordered the army to take forcible possession of New Orleans if the Spaniards balked. But the Spaniards yielded, and on November 30, 1803, the Spanish governor formally turned over control of Louisiana to a French official who in turn promptly surrendered it to the United States.

Splendid as was the bargain struck by Livingston and Monroe, by far the greater part of the Louisiana Purchase was bought sight unseen. Jefferson himself was inclined to believe that the United States had purchased a great wasteland: in December 1803, he told Congress that the few settlements beyond the Mississippi were separated from each other by "immense and trackless deserts." It was to establish the nature of the topography of the Louisiana Purchase, trace to their source the rivers that drained it, and to cross the continent to the Pacific Ocean, that the Lewis and Clark expedition left St. Louis early in 1804.

Thomas Jefferson, since 1796 president of the American Philosophical Society, was a man of wide-ranging scientific interests, all of which were evidenced in the instruction he gave Meriwether Lewis and Captain William Clark. The two leaders of the expedition were told to study the mineral resources, climate, soil conditions, flora and fauna, and the languages, customs, and history of the Indian tribes living in the regions which they traversed.

After ascending the Missouri River and surmounting the Rockies, the expedition, consisting of thirty-one men, the Indian woman guide Sacajawea, and Captain Lewis' big Newfoundland dog, followed the Snake and Columbia Rivers to the Pacific. This was not the first overland crossing of the continent —in 1793 Mackenzie, a Scotchman, had reached the Pacific at 52 degrees north—but Lewis and Clark were the first to make the journey by means of the waterways that flowed east and west from the Rockies. On December 28, 1806, twenty-seven months after leaving St. Louis and after traveling 8000

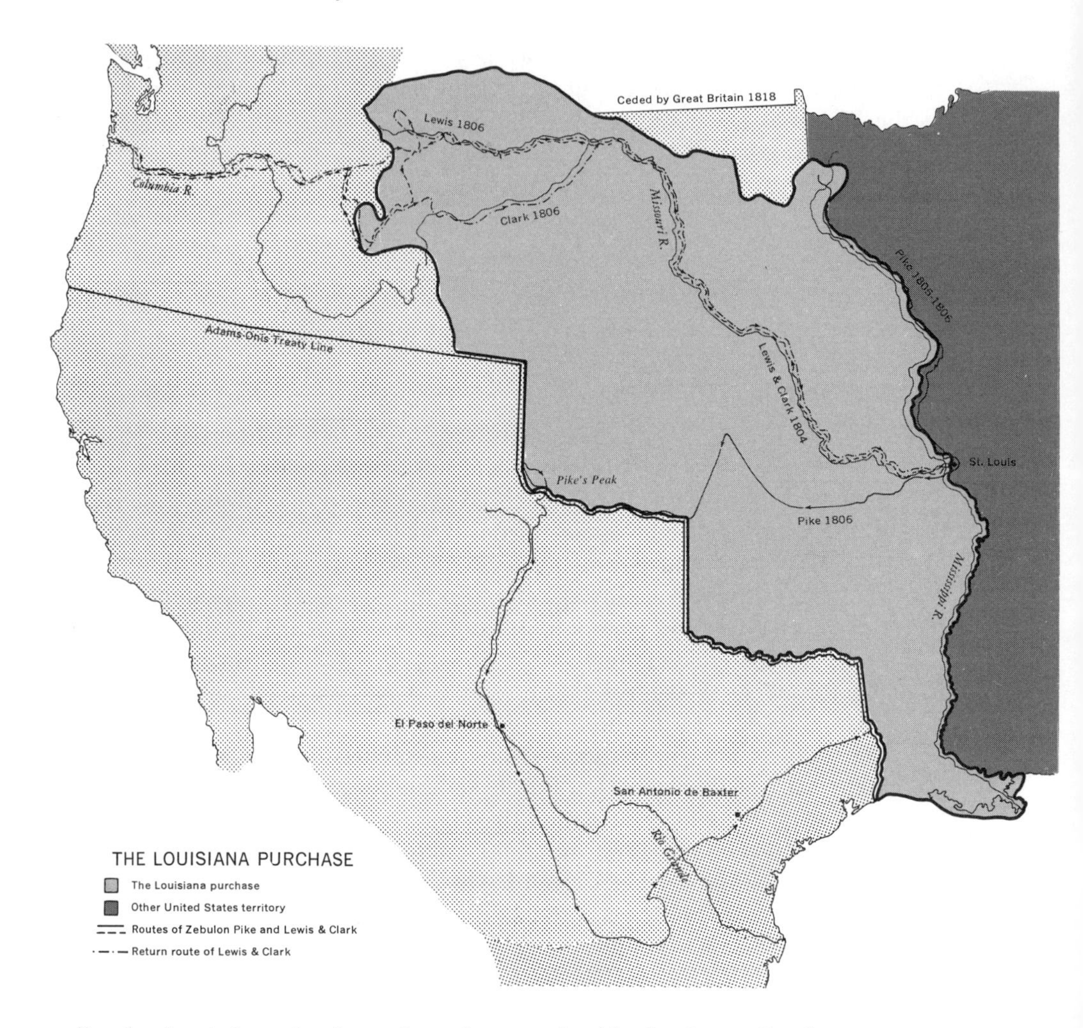

miles by boat, horseback, and on foot, and with the loss of only one man, Captain Lewis reached Washington accompanied by several chiefs of the Mandan tribe.

Although neither Lewis nor Clark had scientific training (Jefferson himself instructed Lewis, his onetime private secretary, in the art of taking longitude) they gathered a wealth of miscellaneous scientific information about the hitherto unknown western part of the North American continent. They discovered the Lewis woodpecker and the Clark nutcracker, the Rocky Mountain rat, mountain goat, antelope, new varieties of grouse, many new plants and birds, and they gave the first thorough description of the prairie dog, the coyote, and the western grizzly bear. Packages containing skins, skeletons of animals, and plants and Indian robes and pottery were sent to the President, and the explorers returned with two grizzly bears which were kept in cages on the President's lawn.

In 1805-1806, before the return of the Lewis and Clark expedition, Jefferson sent Zebulon Pike on two expeditions: one, to explore the upper Mississippi; the second, to locate the source of the Arkansas and Rio Grande Rivers. In the course of his explorations, Pike discovered the mountain in Colorado named Pike's Peak. In 1810, after traversing the region between the Missouri and the Rockies, Pike reported that much of the region was too arid for agriculture. To the end of his life, Jefferson believed that, because of these "deserts," the Pacific Coast would probably be an independent English-speaking republic and that a large part of this area would remain forever an Indian hunting-ground.

18.

THE ATTACK UPON THE FEDERAL JUDICIARY AND THE BURR CONSPIRACY

THE ATTACK UPON THE FEDERALIST STRONGHOLD

Fresh from their diplomatic triumph, President Jefferson and the Republican party moved to settle their long-standing score with the Federalist judiciary. In *Marbury* v. *Madison,* Chief Justice Marshall had asserted the principle of judicial review—equivalent, in the President's mind, to usurping supreme power in the government—but no Republican had accepted Marshall's decision as the final word. Jefferson maintained that every branch of the government—Executive and Legislative as well as judicial—had a right to interpret the Constitution. By claiming final and exclusive jurisdiction for the Supreme Court, Chief Justice Marshall became a marked man among all Republicans. After Alexander Hamilton's death in 1804, the Chief Justice loomed as the veritable "Colossus" of Federalism.

Before moving against the Supreme Court, however, the Republicans decided to use the impeachment process upon one of the occupants of the lower federal bench. The plan was to cut out the strays before tackling the strongest members of the herd. Not surprisingly, the Republicans selected Judge John Pickering of New Hampshire as the most vulnerable of the judges. Pickering was a notorious drunkard, and his sanity was open to grave doubt. But politics required that Pickering be judged sane, because an insane judge

---

"The Trial of Aaron Burr," painting by C. W. Jefferys from Historical Pictures Service, Chicago.

Half Dollar with 15 Stars, 1796.

could not be impeached for crimes and misdemeanors. His case was diagnosed by Republicans as acute Federalism aggravated by alcoholism; and, as Jefferson had frequently observed, the line between Federalism and insanity was extremely thin. Over the protests of the impotent Federalist minority, Pickering was impeached and removed from office. The Republicans had acted just in time: Pickering, obviously a very ill man, died the year after his impeachment.

Pickering, the weakest link in the chain of Federalist judges, had been chosen to establish the validity of the impeachment process as a means of purging the judiciary. Next in line for removal was Justice Chase of the United States Supreme Court. Chase, the most rabidly partisan member of a highly partisan Court bench, had treated juries to political harangues, denounced "the ignorant mobocracy," and was alleged to have denied a fair trial to Fries and several victims of the Sedition Act. For these offenses, the Republicans considered him guilty of "judicial treason against the constitution of the country and the majesty of the people." The crime could be made to fit Chief Justice Marshall and most of his colleagues on the bench.

Yet none of the improprieties alleged against Chase constituted a crime or misdemeanor. The Republicans were therefore obliged to define impeachment as a mere "inquest of office"—a scrutiny by the legislature of the conduct and opinions of members of the judiciary. Under this definition, a two-thirds majority of the Senate could remove any judge under the impeachment process simply because he had offended the party in power.

If there was a truly revolutionary element in Jeffersonian Republicanism it appeared in the attitude of the President and his party toward the judiciary and the doctrine of judicial review. Had the policies of the Republican party prevailed, the principle of the separation of powers as regards the judicial branch would have been invalidated and the federal judiciary made answerable for its opinions to the President and Congress. In 1798, when he was fighting the Alien and Sedition Acts, Jefferson had described impeachment as "the most formidable weapon for the purposes of dominant faction that ever was contrived. It would be the most effectual one of getting rid of any man whom they consider as dangerous to their views. . ." But it was Jefferson himself, rather than the Federalists, who tried to use the impeachment process for this purpose.

In this struggle between the Court, the President, and Congress, the Federalists upheld the cause of an independent judiciary. They pointed out that in English history, arbitrary power had always found its most resolute enemy in the judiciary. Impeachment, they insisted, required proof of a crime or misdemeanor—and political partisanship had not yet been declared an indictable offense. They denied that Congress possessed any inquisitorial power over the conduct of judges of the Supreme Court; to them, the character of a judge was sacred and immaculate. Instead of censuring the morals of judges, Federalists recommended that Congress scrutinize its own morals.

In January 1805, after the House of Representatives, by a purely partisan vote, had adopted articles of impeachment against Chase, he was brought for trial before the Senate. John Randolph, Jefferson's lieutenant in the House, served as the chief prosecutor while Vice-President Burr presided over the Senate with his customary *sangfroid*. Randolph declaimed against Chase with such vehemence that a Federalist spectator reported that "in the midst of his harangue, the poor fellow [Randolph] cried like a baby, with clear, sheer madness." Tears and invective were alike unavailing: the Republicans broke ranks and the prosecution failed to muster the two-thirds vote necessary to convict.

By a slender margin the independence of the judiciary was preserved. But neither Randolph nor President Jefferson was willing to accept the verdict of the Senate as final. Randolph referred to Chase as an "acquitted felon." The Republican leaders drew up a constitutional amendment that would have permitted the President to remove any federal judge upon the application of a majority of both Houses of Congress. At no time had Alexander Hamilton—in Jefferson's eyes the arch-enemy of the Constitution—proposed a measure more destructive of the principle of the separation of powers. But because the proposed amendment failed to win the support of a two-thirds majority in Congress, it was never presented to the States.

Even though Chase was acquitted, the members of the Supreme Court had been given a fright from which they did not soon recover. Indeed, at one point during Chase's trial, when it seemed probable that the Republicans would prevail, Chief Justice Marshall was prepared to renounce all claims of judicial review on the part of the Supreme Court in exchange for a promise of immunity to the judges. Not until after Chase's acquittal did Marshall fully recover his nerve. Yet the right asserted by the Court in *Marbury* v. *Madison* was not again exercised until the Dred Scott decision of 1857.

DISINTEGRATION OF THE FEDERALIST PARTY

As his first administration drew to a close, Jefferson could look back upon a record of success marred only by his failure to discipline the judiciary. Popular approval of his stewardship was reflected in the state and congressional election returns: by 1804, even in New England, Federalism had begun to crumble. The President seemed well on the way to realizing his ambition of eradicating the distinctions between Republicans and Federalists and of "consolidating the union into one homogeneous mass." The only kind of consolidation which Jefferson approved was a union of heart and mind in which the American people as a whole participated.

President Jefferson gave the Federalists no overriding issue upon which to mount popular opposition. As a political leader, he struck a posture of mildness and benignity that utterly disarmed his adversaries. Whereas the Federalists lectured the American people upon their shortcomings, Jefferson told them the "truths" they loved to hear: that, when properly informed, they were wise and good and just; that they needed only a minimal government; that they were the advance agents of a coming world order based upon the principles of the Enlightenment; and that there was no place for special privilege (except, of course, for slaveowners) in the open, competitive society of the United States. Jefferson's confidence in the American people reflected their own confidence in themselves; when he said that they were capable of self-government, the people could not have agreed more; and his buoyant faith in an ever-expanding future seemed to be confirmed by the rapid growth of the American population and economy.

In America, optimism, belief in progress, and confidence in the natural goodness of human nature engendered by the Enlightenment became largely the property of the Jeffersonians. The Federalists, particularly after the French Revolution had reinforced their conviction that human nature was essentially vicious and that the belief in progress—particularly democratic progress—was a dangerous illusion, had become increasingly critical of the more facile assumptions of the Enlightenment and the "glittering generalities" of the Declaration of Independence. As the Reverend Timothy Dwight observed, the "fundamental folly of visionary philosophers" in regarding man's nature as essentially altruistic had "deluged republican France in misery and ruin," and the fate of that unhappy country ought to stand as an awful warning to American democrats.

Federalism tended to be most solidly entrenched in long-established, stable areas such as Connecticut, where the deferential attitude to wealth, education, and family remained strong. Although Federalism continued to flourish near salt water, Republicanism, too, drew strength from that element; increasingly the merchants, lawyers, professional men, and artisans of the seaport cities began to turn to the Republican party. Particularly in states where regnant Federalists were challenged by aspiring Republicans or where the two parties were evenly matched, voter participation was high. Republicanism also flourished in certain mature, static, and conservative areas such as eastern Virginia. But Republicanism meant very different things to different parts of the country and to different groups within the community. In general, Jeffersonian ideas appealed most strongly to the less developed, rapidly growing, and dynamic sections of the country and to ambitious, aggressive individuals who rebelled against the elitism practiced by the Federalists in business (which meant monopoly by privileged individuals) as well as in society.

After 1800, partly as a result of the policies adopted by the Federalists when they held power and by the prosperity generated in the United States by the European war, the Federalists were compelled to make political headway against a strong current of economic well-being. As usual, prosperity worked in favor of the party in power. Against this pervading sense of security and confidence, the Federalist leaders, steadily becoming more remote from reality, could oppose only an apocalyptic vision of pillaging, burning, and massacre by American "Jacobins."

One by one, the Federalist leaders retired to their estates, there to muse upon the iniquity of the times and to deplore evils they were powerless to correct. The younger members of the party tried to emulate the Republicans' organization and electioneering techniques (they adopted state nominating conventions and in 1812 held the first national nominating convention), but they had no new ideas to offer. Federalists, young and old, harped upon the theme of sectionalism: their stock-in-trade was the desolation certain to befall commerce and manufacturing at the hands of Southern and Western democrats. Reversing their earlier doctrinal position, they now upheld the supremacy of Congress over the Executive, freedom of the press, economy in government, the right of petition, and the inviolability of the state judiciaries. As John Adams said in 1808: "Our two great parties have crossed over the valley, and taken possession of each other's mountain." But the Federalists never quite succeeded in reaching the summit at Monticello where Jefferson dwelt.

By 1804, many Federalists had come to agree with Jefferson's assessment of the election of 1800 as a true revolution. Dismissals from office, the repeal of the excise, the attack upon the judiciary, and, above all, the acquisition of Louisiana by purchase rather than by conquest, seemed to prove that the triumph of the Jeffersonian Republicans had opened the bag of the winds, none of which blew good for the Federalist party. The leaders of that party gravely debated whether Jefferson, Madison, or Gallatin would play the role of chief executioner in the coming American Reign of Terror. Timothy Pickering was inclined to put his money on Jefferson, whom he described as a "coward wretch, like a Parisian revolutionary monster," who, in spite of his pratings about the rights of man, would take "infernal pleasure in the utter destruction of his opponents . . . Virtue and worth are his enemies and therefore he would overwhelm them."

So dismal was the prospect that the Federalists compared their plight to that of the black slaves on the southern plantations. "We feel that we are Virginia slaves now," said a New Hampshire Federalist, "and that we are to be delivered over to Kentucky and the other Western States, when our Virginia masters are tired of us." But their indignation was mainly directed against the three-fifths rule that had made possible Jefferson's election in 1800. In Federalist circles, Jefferson was referred to, among other things, as a "Negro President."

Sickened by democracy and despairing of ever regaining control of the federal government by constitutional means—indeed, the Constitution itself by the operation of the three-fifths rule seemed to foreclose that hope—a few New England Federalists attempted to form an independent Northern Confederacy. Their idea was to separate the righteous from the wicked by a geographical line; vice and villainy, said Timothy Pickering, would be confined within their natural limits—the southern and western states—whereas goodness, virtue, and tranquillity would reign on the northern side of the line. Pickering believed that the South would let the chaste sisters go in peace, but if resistance were offered to their departure he was prepared to break out of durance forcibly.

Although few New Englanders ordinarily included New York within the confines of morality and godliness, in this instance they yielded to political necessity. The plot took the form of an attempt to elect Aaron Burr governor of New York with the aid of Federalist votes; the next step required Burr to put himself at the head of the secession movement. Burr, as usual, promised nothing, but he gave the Federalist conspirators reason to hope for everything if he were elected to the governorship.

Burr had long since abandoned hope of preferment within the Republican party. Despite his heavy political debt to Burr, President Jefferson had no thought of making the New Yorker his heir apparent. As early as 1801, Jefferson had written off the Vice-President as an ambitious and calculating manipulator whose Republicanism was only superficial. Smooth, polished, and urbane as Burr was, he did not inspire trust: Washington, Hamilton, John Adams, and many others would have concurred in Jefferson's opinion that Burr was "a crooked gun, or other perverted machine, whose aim or shot you could never be sure of."

The President, therefore, felt no compunction in depriving Burr of the control of the patronage in New York. In 1802, realizing that he had fallen from favor, Burr gave as a toast at a Washington's Birthday celebration attended by Federalists the ringing slogan: "To the union of all honest men." Since the Federalists assumed that they were the only honest men in politics, they supposed that Burr was offering to defect from the Republican party. But Burr said no more; not until 1804 did he again raise the Federalists' hopes that his political allegiance was available to the highest bidder.

To the chagrin of the Federalist plotters, Alexander Hamilton refused to join the effort to break up the Union. Hamilton did not believe that vice and virtue could be segregated geographically; even in New England, he pointed out, the Jeffersonian Republicans—representing vice—were already within the citadel of righteousness. The evil, as he now saw it, was within human nature itself; even a sound Federalist upbringing could not wholly eradicate it. As for Burr, he thought no more highly of him than in 1800: the Vice-President, he said, "can never be anything else than the bane of a good cause."

Nor did Hamilton overlook the fact that the people of New England were not ready to follow a Federalist junto into secession. Pickering did not dare to make his plans public because he knew that the people would not approve; so secret was the plot that the conspirators hesitated to converse among themselves about disunion. They railed against the "apathy," "blindness," and "complacency" even of the Federalists, many of whom, they admitted, had "much of the Democratic taint about them." Few businessmen were ready to sever themselves from their customers and debtors—a circumstance that prompted Pickering to lament that the "love of money will be our ruin."

The effort to create a Northern Confederacy collapsed when Burr suffered a crushing reverse in his bid for the governorship of New York. For his defeat, Burr blamed Hamilton who had warned his fellow-Federalists against Burr's duplicity and ambition. The Vice-President challenged Hamilton to a duel. In July, 1804, at Weehawken, New Jersey, a well-placed bullet mortally wounded Hamilton. But in killing Hamilton, Burr put an end to his own polit-

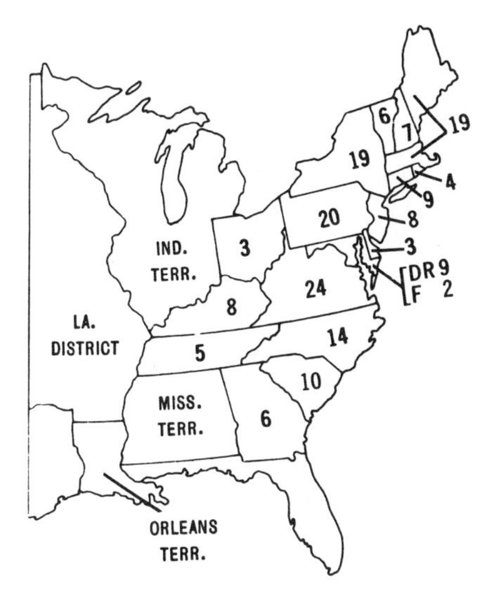

THE ELECTION OF 1804

	ELECTORAL VOTE BY STATE
REPUBLICAN Thomas Jefferson	162
FEDERALIST Charles C. Pinckney	14
	176

ical career. Already in bad odor with the Republicans, he forfeited all hope of favor from the Federalists by laying low the "Colossus of Federalism." Indeed, he could not even return to New Jersey, where an indictment for murder (dueling was illegal in that state) hung over his head, and he was disfranchised in New York. Like many another man down on his luck, Burr decided to go west along with the course of empire.

Chastened by their defeat in New York and left leaderless by the death of Hamilton, the Federalists did not even present a national ticket in the presidential election of 1804. As for President Jefferson, he neither stood nor ran for office—he simply sat. Most of the campaign was conducted around his dinner table, where, from the vantage point of a comfortable chair, the President held forth to congressmen and distinguished visitors. There was no need for the President to bestir himself: the electoral college gave him 162 votes compared with 14 votes for Charles C. Pinckney.

As a result of this election the sweep of Jeffersonian Democracy seemed irreversible. Of the 142 members of the House, only 27 were Federalists, not a sufficient number to demand a roll call. President Jefferson no longer asked them to dine at the President's house—treatment they resented, for partaking of the President's cuisine was one of the last consolations left them in Washington.

DIVISIONS IN THE REPUBLICAN PARTY

Although Jefferson's theoretical objections to "energetic" government remained as strong as ever, in practice he infused a degree of energy into the federal government it had not known since Hamilton. Like Hamilton, Jefferson assumed a directing role over Congress; the President frequently conferred with House and Senate leaders, to whom he indicated his wishes regarding legislation. In fact, in his relations with Congress, Jefferson proved to be one of the most effective leaders ever to occupy the presidency. It was an achievement hardly to be expected from a man who had bitterly condemned Hamilton for deploying "Executive influence" and manipulating votes in Congress and who had formulated a constitutional theory that made the legislature wholly independent of the Executive. As John Marshall had predicted in 1800, Jefferson embodied himself with Congress and combined in his person the presidency and the leadership of the Republican party. So well did he fill this role that a Federalist congressman said that if Jefferson "should recommend to us to repeal the Gospel of the Evangelist, a majority of Congress would do it."

To John Randolph of Roanoke it was apparent, as it was not to the Federalists, that the mantle of Alexander Hamilton, rather than that of Robespierre, had descended upon President Jefferson. Vaunting the purity of his own Republicanism, Randolph accused Jefferson of having apostatized from the true faith of strict construction, state rights, agrarianism, and minimal government. While Randolph conceded that Jefferson's first administration had been a republican "golden age," he found signs on every hand in the second term that Federalism had gained the ascendancy; the voice was Thomas Jefferson's but all the acts seemed to betray the stigmata of Federalism. In language reminiscent of Jefferson's own tirades against Hamilton, Randolph declared that the President's policies were leading the country into monarchy.

Although Randolph succeeded in recruiting what Jefferson called "a little band of schismaticks," he was far too eccentric and unstable to be an effective opposition leader. His irrationality, arrogance, and waspish temper destroyed whatever influence his brilliance as an orator and his position as chairman of the Ways and Means Committee might have given him. On one occasion, Randolph threw a glass of wine in the face of a fellow-congressman, broke the glass over his head, and tried to apply the coup de grace with the bottle. Josiah Quincy, a New England Federalist, attributed Randolph's temperament to his descent from Pocahontas: "he had," said Quincy, "the temper and spirit of his savage ancesters . . . His tomahawk was continually in his hand, and his scalping-knife ever hung at his side."

Randolph and his followers were called "Quids," but by no means all Quids acknowledged the shrill-voiced Virginian as their leader. A greater threat to the unity of the Republican party came from the factionalism that sprang up in Pennsylvania, New York, Virginia, and other states. In part, these divisions occurred because the Republicans had become so powerful that, having ceased to fear their Federalist rivals, they felt free to fall out over personal rivalries and disputes over the disposition of the federal patronage. Moreover, Jefferson had invited a struggle for the succession between Madison and Monroe by announcing early in his second term that he would not again be a candidate for the presidency. Nevertheless, by refusing to take sides in the quarrels that broke out among his followers, President Jefferson was able to maintain unity in the party and to retain his own position as its undisputed head.

THE BURR CONSPIRACY

Despite the purchase of Louisiana with its millions of square miles and unsurveyed riches, the United States was not a territorially satisfied power. Control of rivers flowing into the Gulf of Mexico was essential to the economic growth of the Southeast. This necessitated the acquisition by the United States of the Spanish province of West Florida, especially Mobile Bay. President Jefferson believed that, in buying Louisiana, the United States had also obtained title to West Florida and Texas—the boundaries of the French province of Louisiana. While East Florida admittedly had never been a part of Louisiana, Jefferson also claimed it as compensation for Spanish spoliations on American commerce.

The difficulty was that the Spaniards retained possession of these territories and showed no inclination to move out. Jefferson therefore concluded that the best hope of acquiring West Florida, the area first upon his list of priorities, was to cultivate good relations with Napoleon. After all, the unpredictable Corsican had deposited an empire in the lap of the United States: who could say that he could not change his mind again and compel Spain to surrender West Florida? So eager was the American President to propitiate the French Emperor that he offered to comply with Napoleon's demand that the United States prohibit the trade being carried on by armed American merchant ships with the black rebels in the western part of the island of Santo Domingo. American supplies continued to be brought to the rebels, however, and in 1804 Dessalines ascended the throne as Jean-Jacques the First, Emperor of Haiti. Haiti became the second country in the western hemisphere to achieve its independence, and, after 1820, the first black republic, but President Jefferson could claim none of the credit for that event.

In spite of these conciliatory gestures, Napoleon refused to adjust the territorial limits of Louisiana to accord with Jefferson's wishes. Napoleon let it be known that in his opinion the United States had not bought any territory on the east bank of the Mississippi and that American claims to Texas were wholly unfounded.

Nevertheless, Jefferson continued to act upon the assumption that the road to West Florida lay through Paris. In December 1805, having learned that Napoleon needed money, Jefferson asked Congress to appropriate several million dollars for an unspecified purpose. It was hardly a secret that this money was to be spent in Paris for the purchase of West Florida, with Napoleon acting as an honest broker between Spain and the United States. Although the money was duly appropriated, it had no other effect than widening a schism within the Republican party. John Randolph declared that he would never consent to such tortuous diplomatic methods. "I considered it a base prostration of the national character," Randolph told the House, "to excite one nation by money to bully another nation out of its property"—at which point, to emphasize his contempt, he threw his hat across the room. If the President wished to buy West Florida, Randolph advised him to deal directly with Spain.

Having placed all his hopes upon Napoleon, Jefferson had little to fall back upon when the Emperor refused to intervene on behalf of the United States. Napoleon had other plans for Spain: he already contemplated annexing it to his empire—in which event, he would find it to his advantage to preserve the territorial integrity of the Spanish empire. As a result, advocates of a forcible solution to the problem of West Florida and Texas made their voices heard: James Monroe, for example, demanded an armed attack upon these provinces. President Jefferson continued to rely upon diplomacy, but it was doubtful how long he could keep westerners themselves under control, particularly since Aaron Burr had seen an opportunity to fish in the troubled waters of the West.

Bankrupt politically as well as financially, Burr hoped to recoup his losses by carrying out the most grandiose scheme ever conceived by an American filibusterer. Upon graduating from Princeton, Burr had delivered an oration entitled "Building Castles in the Air." Thirty years later, a perennial romantic, he was still building. A lover of labyrinthian ways—he clothed even his commonplace acts with an air of mystery—Burr kept his real designs to himself while he tried to enlist support for what he variously described as an attempt to settle lands west of the Mississippi to which he held title, to break up the Union, hang Thomas Jefferson, seize Texas, conquer Mexico and ascend the throne of that country as Aaron I. To the British and Spanish ministers in Washington, for example, he told inconsistent stories that agreed only upon one point—that he needed money for his enterprise. Had these two ministers compared notes, it would have appeared to the Spanish minister that his government was being asked to contribute money to aid Burr in liquidating the Spanish empire in North America whereas the British minister was given to understand that Burr intended to detach the western states from the Union. Neither government gave Burr financial support: most of Burr's funds came from his son-in-law, a wealthy South Carolinian, and from Harman Blennerhasset, a rich and eccentric Irishman who had taken up residence on Blennerhasset's Island in the Ohio River.

Having dropped red herrings all over Washington, Burr went West, where he began to raise volunteers for what he said was an expedition to colonize a Spanish land-grant. But he told Henry Clay, Andrew Jackson, and others whose loyalty to the government was unquestionable that he intended to invade Texas with the approval and backing of President Jefferson himself. Everyone, in short, was told what they wanted to hear and what would be most likely to persuade them to contribute to the support of the expedition. This confusion was deliberately contrived by Burr: not knowing how the land lay, Burr had made several plans any one of which he could follow as circumstances dictated. A master of improvisation, he played the situation by ear and left the final decision to the arbitrament of events. Since he found a great deal more enthusiasm among westerners for attacking Texas than for severing the Union, it was upon this operation that Burr concentrated his attention.

Among those whom Burr took into his confidence was General James Wilkinson, the commander of the United States Army in the West and governor of Upper Louisiana. Wilkinson was assigned the task of crossing the Sabine River and drawing the Spaniards into a diversionary action while Burr and his men invaded the province of Texas and proclaimed it to be an independent republic. For this work, Wilkinson was promised $100,000 on future delivery. What Burr apparently did not know was that Wilkinson was also in Spanish pay. He proved to be an unreliable confederate: a man with as many employers as Wilkinson had was certain sooner or later to betray someone.

In the autumn of 1806, President Jefferson got wind of Burr's activities in the West. On the strength of the reports sent to Washington and his own long-standing distrust of Burr, the President concluded that the former Vice-President was trying simultaneously to destroy the Union and to lead an invasion of Texas and Mexico. Early in 1807, when he learned that Burr was on his way down the Ohio with a small flotilla, Jefferson ordered the state governors, federal marshals, and General Wilkinson to arrest Burr. In a message to Congress justifying this action, the President declared that there was no doubt that Burr was guilty of treason. At about this point, concluding that Burr was doomed, General Wilkinson decided to sell him out to the United States government. At the same time he took the precaution of informing the Spanish government of Burr's designs upon Texas.

Drifting down the Ohio with a party of about 100 men, Burr hardly seemed capable of shaking empires and severing the American Union. In New Orleans, General Wilkinson put out the report that Burr's "armada" of flatboats containing seven or eight thousand men was descending upon the city and that Burr's agents were swarming everywhere in the province. Accordingly, the general declared martial law and put suspects under military arrest. President Jefferson later defended this action on the ground that "self-preservation is paramount to all law." These alarms and excursions ended very tamely with Burr's arrest near Mobile by federal authorities and his removal to Virginia for trial.

Because he trusted General Wilkinson implicitly and because he very much wanted to see Burr convicted of treason, President Jefferson had moved too precipitately in quashing the expedition that had set out from Blennerhasset's Island. In April 1807, the President acknowledged that he did not have enough legal evidence to convict Burr of treason. Even so, the Chief Executive took personal charge of assembling the evidence against the former Vice-President and even instructed the government attorneys how to conduct the case.

Brought to trial in Richmond, Virginia, with Chief Justice John Marshall presiding, Burr, Blennerhasset, and several other defendants were indicted by the grand jury on a charge of treason. In August 1807, Burr's trial on this charge began. The weakness of the government's case quickly became manifest. Even the testimony of General Wilkinson, the prosecution's star witness, did not carry conviction; indeed, Wilkinson himself narrowly escaped being presented to the grand jury. Nor did Chief Justice Marshall neglect the opportunity to pay off his score against Jefferson: at the request of defense counsel,

Marshall issued a subpoena ordering the President to appear and give testimony to the court at Richmond. The President refused to comply with an order that would have clearly established the supremacy of the Judicial over the Executive branch of the government.

Chief Justice Marshall in effect put an end to the trial by charging the jury that the prosecution had not proved Burr's presence, upon the testimony of two or more witnesses, on Blennerhasset's Island while the expedition was gathering. The jury promptly returned a verdict of not guilty of the charge of treason. Burr was likewise acquitted on a technicality of the charge (a misdemeanor) of having attempted to raise men for the purpose of invading Spanish territory.

President Jefferson called the verdict at Richmond a miscarriage of justice and a defiance of public opinion which, in its wisdom, had already convicted Burr. In a message to Congress delivered in 1807, the President recommended changes in the law to preserve the government from "destruction by treason." But the President knew that as long as Marshall and his Federalist colleagues were on the bench to interpret the law, no statutory changes would suffice. He therefore also recommended to Congress that a constitutional amendment be proposed to the states enabling the President to remove federal judges at the request of both houses of Congress. The amendment was introduced into Congress but failed to pass. The Court continued to stand as a Federalist citadel in a Republican government.

The real traitor at Burr's trial was General Wilkinson. John Randolph offered to produce proof of Wilkinson's treasonable activities, but the general had a staunch champion in President Jefferson: if the general had seemed to connive with Burr, the President said, it was only to forewarn the government. The President's opinion was vindicated by a military court of inquiry which gave Wilkinson a clean bill of health. On the other hand, Jefferson refused to acquit the Federalists of aiding and abetting Burr's "treason"; had they seen a chance of Burr's success, he said, they would have joined the ex-Vice-President in establishing a monarchy just as readily as they would have joined "any other enemy, foreign or domestic, who could rid them of this hateful republic."

19.
THE *CHESAPEAKE* INCIDENT

Inevitably, the renewal of the European war in 1803, while restoring American prosperity, left the commerce of the republic exposed to the depredations of the belligerents. Despite the government's dedication to the freedom of the seas, it almost ostentatiously avoided making any preparations that would commit it to the use of force. Indeed, at the very time that the Jefferson administration was carrying war to the shores of Tripoli, the President had made clear that he had no intention of waging a naval war in the Atlantic in defense of American commerce.

Despite the luster conferred upon his administration by the Navy, Jefferson did not significantly change his attitude toward that service. He still believed that a strong Navy was likely to precipitate an unnecessary and unwanted war and that it was incompatible with a balanced budget. Even during the war with Tripoli, he had occupied himself in devising ways whereby the country could be relieved of the incubus of a Navy. In 1802 he suggested that a large covered drydock be constructed at Alexandria where the ships, then doing duty in the Mediterranean, might be stored in peacetime and their crews laid off.

Nevertheless, the President admitted that naval craft might play a useful role if they were confined to home defense and their operations limited to American territorial waters. For this purpose, he recommended in 1804 that Congress authorize the construction of a flotilla of gunboats—the only craft, he asserted, that could spare the country from "the ruinous folly of a Navy."

"Impressment of American Sailors Previous to the War of 1812," detail of an engraving from The Bettmann Archive.

Castorland Medal, 1796.

Gunboats had for the President the irresistible attraction of being cheap to construct, easy to man, and convenient to store when not in use. And, finally, unlike frigates and sloops, they would never start a war.

Despite the care and affection lavished by President Jefferson upon these unpromising midgets (John Randolph called them "contemptible insects"), they turned out badly. No American officer etched his name in glory by commanding a gunboat. But they, together with coastal batteries and other fortifications, did permit the Republican party to enjoy briefly the illusion that the defenses of the United States were being looked after. Upon the regular ships of the Navy, however, the effect of the gunboat policy was calamitous. After the sloops *Wasp* and *Frolic* were commissioned in 1806, no more large naval vessels went down the ways for six years. The lumber collected by the Adams administration to build ships of the line was cut up for gunboats. All told, the money expended upon gunboats would have built and equipped four frigates.

THE IMPRESSMENT QUESTION

While gunboats had the merit of sparing the country the risk of war by mischance, they afforded no protection to American ships and seamen on the high seas. After 1803, as the momentum of the war picked up, neutral shipping again became a pawn in the struggle between France and Great Britain. In a decision in the *Essex* case in 1805, British admiralty courts placed new restrictions upon American ships engaged in bringing to Europe cargoes from the French West Indies. In 1806, the British Ministry imposed a paper blockade upon the coast of much of northern Europe; American ships entered this area at their peril.

Above all, relations between the United States and Great Britain were strained by the impressment from American ships of seamen, many of whom claimed to be American citizens. While the British never asserted a right to impress an American seaman from an American merchant ship, nationality was often blurred by common language and appearance. Because naturalization papers could be illegally purchased for a few dollars in waterfront dives, officers in charge of boarding parties often took as Britons the likeliest looking men lined up for their inspection, regardless of their papers or their protests. Many hundreds of American mariners had reason to regret the absence of a language barrier. Speaking of impressment to the Duke of Leeds, Gouverneur Morris observed: "I believe, my Lord, this is the only Instance in which we are not treated as Aliens." To which the Duke responded jocularly that in this respect at least the United States was treated as the most favored nation.

British ship captains in search of deserters and contraband did not hesitate to board American vessels within the territorial waters of the United States.

In April 1806, a British ship, trying to put a cannon shot across the bow of an American ship, killed a seaman. President Jefferson ordered British warships out of American ports and demanded that the offending ship's captain be punished. The Americans got no satisfaction: the British captain was tried but acquitted.

By 1806, impressment had become the major cause of friction between the United States and Great Britain. In this dispute, both sides adopted fixed positions from which there was no real possibility of retreat. The British insisted that the exercise of impressment was essential to the nation's survival. And, in fact, attracted by the higher wages and better working conditions offered by the Americans, thousands of Britons jumped ship to take service under the Stars and Stripes. The resulting manpower drain weakened both the British merchant marine and the Royal Navy. Without the threat of impressment from American ships—and in the case of deserters from the British Navy the penalty was death—the desertion rate might have endangered Great Britain's maritime supremacy. For its part, the United States took the position that a ship flying the American flag was invested with all the attributes of sovereignty quite as much as was the soil of the United States. To Americans, impressment was a badge of servitude—the final and conclusive proof that Great Britain did not recognize the United States as a truly independent and sovereign nation.

Yet, as a sovereign and independent nation, the United States government never took steps to prevent the enlistment of English seamen in the American merchant marine. Indeed, without the aid of these trained seamen and of free blacks, the expansion of American shipping during the Napoleonic Wars would have been seriously curtailed. For there were never enough native-born white Americans willing to abandon their farms to take service aboard a merchantman. In insisting that every seaman aboard an American ship be presumed to be an American—that, in effect, the flag protected the crew as well as the cargo—the United States government was protecting a vital source of manpower for its own shipping.

Impressment proved to be an insurmountable obstacle to every effort to negotiate the settlement of other causes of Anglo-American conflict. In 1806, Jay's treaty having expired, President Jefferson sent William Pinkney as Envoy Extraordinary to London to aid James Monroe, the resident United States minister, in obtaining compensation for American ships seized by the British and to secure guarantees against future interference with American neutral rights on the high seas. Although instructed to sign no treaty that did not contain an explicit renunciation by the British government of the right of impressment, Pinkney and Monroe accepted a tacit agreement with the British government that seamen would not be impressed from American vessels on the high seas except under extraordinary circumstances and that "the greatest caution" would be observed. Otherwise, the treaty followed the lines laid down by Jay's treaty, except that it was less favorable to American trade with India. It exacted a promise from the United States not to undertake economic coercion against Great Britain for a period of ten years, and Great Britain reserved the right to withhold ratification unless the United States resisted Napoleon's decree placing the British Isles in a state of blockade.

So unacceptable were these terms to President Jefferson and Secretary of State Madison that they rejected the treaty without even the formality of submitting it to the Senate. The President based the case against the Monroe-Pinkney treaty almost wholly on the ground that it did not protect American seamen from impressment. As Madison said, if the treaty were ratified, the administration would be guilty of abandoning its moral and political duty to its citizens and to the sovereign rights of the United States. To secure those rights Jefferson preferred to trust to the course of future events. When the war ended in Europe, Jefferson hoped that Napoleon and Alexander of Russia would see to it that the treaty of peace enunciated the principle of the freedom of the seas.

Although Jefferson was not aware of it, he had rejected the best offer he or his successor would ever receive for settling the impressment issue. By holding out for an explicit and definitive renunciation by the British government he succeeded only in stiffening British resistance to any concessions whatever. Moreover, by the death of Charles James Fox, which occurred early in 1807, the United States lost its best friend in the British government; his successors, disciples of William Pitt the Younger, saw no need to propitiate the United States.

A BRITISH ACT OF WAR

Jefferson's and Madison's insistence upon giving primacy to the impressment controversy seemed fully vindicated in August 1807 when H.M.S. *Leopard,* acting under orders from Admiral Berkeley, commander of the British fleet in North American waters, stopped the U.S.S. *Chesapeake* and prepared to send a party aboard the American warship to recover British deserters. When Captain Barron, the commanding officer of the *Chesapeake,* refused to permit an inspection of his crew, the *Leopard* opened fire, killing three and wounding almost a score of American sailors. Taken by surprise, Captain Barron struck his colors and offered to surrender his ship. The British commander refused to accept the *Chesapeake* as a prize of war; instead, a boarding party removed four seamen whose American citizenship seemed in doubt.

Only one of the seamen impressed from the *Chesapeake* proved to be a British subject, and he was hanged at Halifax as a traitor. Two of the other seamen were American Negroes who had volunteered to serve in the British Navy. The fourth sailor, a white man, previously had been forcibly impressed into British service and had escaped to sign aboard the *Chesapeake.*

The British Navy had committed an act of war against the United States. No other construction could be put upon the event. Not since Lexington, President Jefferson declared, had he seen the American people gripped by such excitement and indignation. He later said that he held the issue of peace or war in the palm of his hand: "I had only to open it to let havoc loose."

And yet the President did not open the palm of his hand. Instead, he kept the "*Chesapeake* outrage" within the bounds of diplomacy. Instructions were sent to Monroe in London to demand a British disavowal, British warships were ordered out of American waters, and 100,000 militia were directed to hold themselves in readiness. But Jefferson did not summon Congress into special session, nor did he try to inflame public opinion against "British barbarity."

Largely responsible for the President's restraint was his conviction that the attack upon the *Chesapeake* had not been authorized by the British government and that the act of war would be promptly disavowed. As Jefferson was well aware, Great Britain had never claimed the right of boarding and removing members of the crew of a United States warship. Improbable as it seemed that Admiral Berkeley had acted without orders, it was still more improbable that he had acted with them.

For this reason, President Jefferson felt that he would be acting dishonestly toward the American people if he led them to believe that the British government had deliberately committed an act of war against the United States and that it would support Admiral Berkeley to the hilt. Therefore, while preparing for the worst, the President gave the British government an opportunity to retreat from the untenable position in which it had been placed. By so doing, the President saved the peace, for, without waiting for the American protest, the British government disavowed Admiral Berkeley's act and apologized to the United States.

But President Jefferson had no intention of letting the British off lightly. James Monroe was instructed to demand the punishment of Admiral Berkeley and to couple the *Chesapeake* incident with the impressment of seamen from American vessels. While the British government was willing to transfer Admiral Berkeley to another station, to give assurances that no American warships would be molested in the future, to compensate the families of the seamen killed by the *Leopard*'s fire, and to return the survivors to the United States, it refused even to discuss the impressment issue. In fact, in December 1807, British commanders were instructed to continue to search neutral ships and to impress British deserters.

As a result, the *Chesapeake* affair dragged on for years. The controversy afforded an opportunity for statesmen on both sides of the Atlantic to exercise their talents for vituperation and insult. In 1809, for example, James Madison, resentful of the British government's refusal to court-martial Admiral Berkeley, inserted in an American state paper the caustic observation that the punishment of the offending admiral "would best comport with what was due from his Britannic Majesty to his own honor"—a thrust that sent cries of outrage and anguish reverberating through the corridors of power at Whitehall.

While the statesmen wrangled, the surviving crewmen who had been impressed from the *Chesapeake* remained in prison. Not until 1811 were they restored with full honors to the deck of the ship from which they had been forcibly removed four years before.

20.
THE EMBARGO

THE END OF NEUTRAL RIGHTS

Caught between the millstones of the belligerents' war machines, neutral rights were ground exceedingly small. Neither France nor Great Britain would permit neutral trade to benefit its adversary, and each power sought to control in its own interest the shipping of the neutral powers. In November 1806, Napoleon issued from Berlin a decree declaring the British Isles to be in a state of blockade: henceforth every neutral vessel that touched at a British port became lawful prize. At the same time, Napoleon closed the European continent, insofar as it was under French control, to British merchandise. Thus was inaugurated the "Continental System," Napoleon's answer to British domination of the sea.

Great Britain responded by issuing two Orders in Council, both aimed at controlling neutral trade in the interests of the British war effort. In January, an Order in Council prohibited American and other neutral ships from engaging in trade between two European ports. A second Order issued on November 11, 1807, required all neutral ships carrying cargoes to French-controlled Europe to touch first at a British port, there to submit to an inspection and, in the case of colonial products, pay taxes, port duties, handling charges, and reexportation duties, and, finally, to buy a license which permitted them to proceed to their European destination.

In issuing these Orders in Council, the British government had no intention of destroying American commerce. Rather, it proposed to use the American merchant marine to carry British manufactured goods to the continent in defiance of the Continental System and, by making Great Britain the en-

---

"Mill Where Samuel Slater's First Spinning Frame Was Used, Pawtucket, R.I.," detail of a painting from The Smithsonian Institution.

Half Eagle, Five Dollar Gold Piece with 15 Stars, 1797.

trepôt of all neutral trade with the European continent, to enrich British merchants and the government itself. The British government intended to force the sale of goods, including colonial products, upon France and French-dominated Europe *via* England. Napoleon's Berlin decree announced that there should be no trade with England; the Order in Council of November 1807 asserted that France should have no trade except with England. Great Britain had to export or die; the Orders in Council were intended to make sure that the United States and other neutral carriers worked for Britain's survival.

Americans might have submitted to the Orders in Council without suffering serious financial loss; indeed, northern shipowners and merchants had long since discovered that their economic well-being was compatible with obedience to British regulations. Had the decision been left to the business community in the United States, the Orders in Council might have occasioned only a protest. But the merchants and shipowners were not making American policy: that was the province of the Republican leadership.

Napoleon exaggerated when he said after the issuance of the Berlin decree and the British Orders in Council that there were no more neutrals. But certainly there were no more neutral rights. France and Great Britain had made it plain that they would tolerate no neutral trade that did not redound to their own advantage. The British government justified the Orders in Council on the ground that the United States had acquiesced in the Berlin decree; Napoleon vindicated his decree on the ground that the United States had submitted to the Orders in Council.

THE ATTEMPT TO PRESERVE NEUTRAL RIGHTS

Unofficial reports of the Order in Council of November 11 reached Jefferson late in December 1807. His immediate—and, indeed his enduring—conviction was that Great Britain intended to lay claim to absolute dominion of the ocean and to prescribe the terms and conditions under which other nations might navigate upon it. If the Order in Council of November 11 were permitted to pass unchallenged, no ship could move upon the high seas without the permission of His Britannic Majesty; and obeisance and tribute were to be exacted of every sea-going neutral. The Order in Council struck the President as a Heaven-defying ordinance, a brazen attempt to countermand the law of nature by which the seas were made free to the ships of all nations.

Yet the President was not yet ready to go to war. Instead, he saw in the crisis a providential opportunity to put into effect his long-cherished plan of coercing Great Britain into showing a decent respect for the rights of neutrals by depriving the island kingdom of the economic and financial sustenance it drew from trade with the United States.

President Jefferson undertook this trial of strength supremely confident of victory over the belligerents. Simply by withdrawing from the sea and denying its resources to the warring powers, the United States, he felt sure, could compel them to yield every right claimed by the United States. Jefferson's calculations were based upon the assumption that Europe needed American supplies and markets more than the United States needed European supplies and markets. In this regard, he considered Great Britain to be especially vulnerable: the white workers in English factories and the black slaves in the British West Indies would be quickly reduced to starvation at the discretion of the Congress of the United States.

Accordingly, on December 18, 1807, President Jefferson sent a secret message to both houses of Congress recommending that all American merchant ships be confined to port. The United States would abandon the ocean to the "Great Leviathan"; the British might rule the sea but it would be empty of American ships and cargoes. Although foreign ships were permitted to enter United States ports, they could not carry away any cargo which was the growth or product of the United States. Congress promptly executed the President's recommendations even though no one could be sure whether the President intended it to be a temporary precaution to save American ships and seamen or a long-range policy intended to vindicate American rights at sea. But Congress was not left long in doubt on this score: by early January 1809, it had become clear that Jefferson was resolved to ascertain "by a fair experiment . . . the power of this great weapon, the embargo."

Jefferson's decision to impound all American ships seemed vindicated by Napoleon's as well as by Great Britain's acts. In November 1807, Napoleon issued the Milan decree, which subjected to confiscation all neutral ships carrying British merchandise and all ships that had put into a British port.

ENFORCEMENT OF THE EMBARGO

The embargo was adopted despite the opposition of the Federalist party. Rather than withdraw from the sea, the mercantile part of the community preferred to seek an accommodation with Great Britain. Not only did the embargo signalize the end of American prosperity, it seemed to the Federalists certain to produce a war with Great Britain and an alliance with France. Timothy Pickering suspected that the President intended to provoke Great Britain to war by means of the embargo: "he may then mount his war-horse, and, Britain hunted down and gasping, he may come in at the death, and have some merit with the world's master." Even the modest and obviously defensive military measures taken by the government appeared to Pickering as proof of Jefferson's ulterior aim of destroying Great Britain.

Like the war that Jefferson dreaded, the embargo necessitated a concentration of power in the federal government and a vast expansion of the authority of the Chief Executive. In fact, the enforcement of the embargo violated every principle and precept laid down by Jefferson as leader of the opposition to the Hamiltonian Federalists. But the President experienced no twinges of conscience in recommending measures which, had they been introduced by Federalists, he would have been the first to condemn as tyrannical.

No less than three separate enforcement acts, each progressively more severe, were enacted by Congress. Such a multitude of regulations were imposed upon American citizens that it was humorously said that a baby could not be born without clearance from the custom house. Every ship, including fishing and coastwise vessels, that cleared port was required to give bonds, ultimately increased to six times the value of the cargo. Attempts to violate the embargo were made punishable by the confiscation of the ship and cargo and a fine of four times the value. One half of the proceeds realized from the confiscation and fine were to go to the informer. No ship could be loaded without a revenue officer on hand to inspect the cargo and certify the manifest, and clearance papers were given only by the special permission of the President. Collectors of the United States customs were authorized to conduct searches without warrants or any other legal authorization. These officials could seize property if they suspected an intention to violate the embargo. Naval officers were instructed to stop and search vessels to determine if they carried cargo that might be sold to foreign buyers. American shipmasters learned that the "contemptible" gun boats, however useless against a foreign enemy, were formidable when deployed against American citizens who tried to evade the embargo.

By these enforcement acts, the President and Congress challenged Yankee ingenuity in evading unpopular laws—something the British government had long since learned to treat with respect. The embargo created a new species of criminal offense—smuggling goods out of the United States—but New Englanders proved equally adept going both ways.

Much of the smuggling took place along the Canadian border, particularly in the Lake Champlain-St. John's River area, where a thriving export-import trade was carried on. During the winter of 1808-1809, seven hundred sledges operated between Vermont and Montreal; Quebec cleared more shipping than the entire United States; and Halifax enjoyed an unprecedented boom. The British governor of Nova Scotia declared that the embargo was "well calculated to promote the true interests of His Majesty's American Colonies." From Canada and the St. Mary's River (the boundary between the United States and Spanish Florida), supplies reached the British West Indies, thereby easing the pinch that President Jefferson hoped to apply to the economy of those islands.

Resistance to the embargo merely whetted the President's determination to enforce it. "The tories of Boston openly threaten insurrection if their exportation of flour is stopped," Jefferson said in August 1808. "The next post will stop it." More precisely, the next post carried the President's orders to stop it; the trade itself went on surreptitiously. To those who objected that civil liberties were sacred, Jefferson answered that attempts to violate the embargo made war inevitable and that therefore its enforcement must take precedence over all other considerations. In effect, the President was saying that in order to prevent war, the people must submit to wartime restrictions upon their freedom. But in portraying the embargo as the only practical alternative to war, the President ruled out the possibility of discussing it upon its merits.

Among Republicans, it had always been axiomatic that a standing army would be used to establish despotism at home. But it remained for President Jefferson to demonstrate that the Army could be used by a Republican as well as by a Federalist administration to put teeth in the laws. The President called upon the Army to aid in preventing smuggling on Lake Champlain when it became apparent that the situation was beyond the control of the state militia. Detecting in Congress a certain reluctance to subordinate civil liberties to the enforcement of the embargo, Jefferson exhibited an unwonted imperiousness in his bearing toward the legislature: when he referred to enforcement measures pending before Congress, he used the word "must" for the first time. "Congress," he said, "must *realize* all means which may be necessary to attain its *end*." The sentiment was worthy of Alexander Hamilton; indeed, it had been expressed by Hamilton in his defense of the Bank of the United States.

Because the embargo sought to effect without time limit an absolute prohibition of commerce, the Federalists contended that it was a violation of the Constitution—for the power given Congress to regulate commerce could not be construed to authorize its annihilation. Even though federal judges upheld the constitutionality of the embargo, they acted with doubts and misgivings: Justice Joseph Story of the United States Supreme Court said that he considered the embargo "a measure which went to the utmost limit of constructive power under the Constitution. It stands upon the extreme verge of the Constitution." By Story's standard of measurement, Alexander Hamilton always had stayed well within constitutional bounds.

THE EFFECT OF THE EMBARGO

Even with illicit trade, the economy of the United States suffered acutely from the effects of the embargo. By imposing a self-blockade, the republic demonstrated its own vulnerability. Great Britain was the republic's main source of manufactured goods and the best customer for its cotton, tobacco, and flour. American prosperity had become largely dependent upon the British economy; by depriving the United States of its main overseas markets, the government was striking at the roots of the country's well-being. During 1808, exports fell from $108 million to $22,430,000, and the government's revenue shrank from $17 million to $7,773,000.

Insofar as it curtailed the supply of American foodstuffs to the British Army fighting in Spain and Portugal in 1808, the embargo set back the liberation movements in those countries struggling against the French army of occupation. But under Presidents Jefferson and Madison, the United States government never acknowledged that it was in any way concerned with freeing Europe from French control. Instead, these two presidents took the position that the effort to secure the freedom of the seas must go on regardless of its

AMERICAN FOREIGN TRADE, 1790-1815

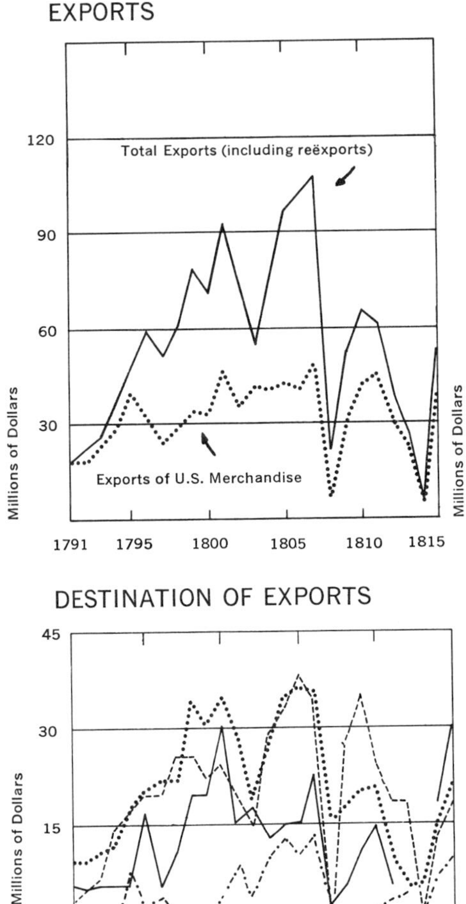

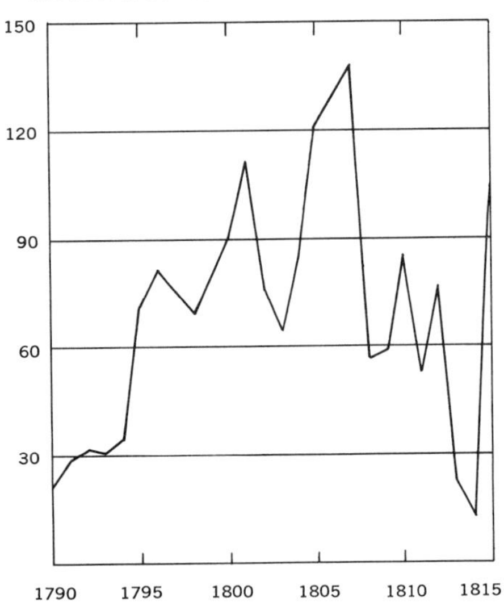

1791 1796 1801 1806 1811 1816

——— Great Britain
—·—·— France
– – – – Other European Nations
•••• •• Non-European Nations

Events in Europe had a direct effect on American foreign trade, most of which was with Western Europe. The Napoleonic wars increased the demand for American products and gave the United States a larger share of the carrying trade. The brief peace in Europe during 1802 caused a depression in the United States; however, the resumption of hostilities brought an even greater growth in American trade. Even the British Orders in Council and Napoleon's Continental System could not destroy it. *Source: Historical Statistics of the United States.*

consequences to the cause of freedom upon the European continent. While professing his warm friendship for the Spanish patriots President Jefferson made clear that he was primarily concerned with what happened to Spain's possessions in the western hemisphere rather than with events in the Iberian peninsula. His principal objective was to secure the Floridas; whatever happened upon the European continent that facilitated this acquisition was all to the good.

Most adversely affected were the southern planters. During 1808, the value of cotton exported from the United States dropped from $14,232,000 to $2,221,000, while exports of tobacco declined from $5,476,000 to $838,000. The price of tobacco reached the giveaway price of one cent per pound; wheat sold for less than half the price it had commanded in 1807. Moreover, the plight of the planters was compounded by the fact that, unlike northern businessmen, they were obliged to feed and clothe their slaves and pay the fixed charges inseparable from the maintenance of their large landed estates.

Even so, surprisingly little protest was heard from the southern planters. Almost to the end, they retained their confidence in the superior wisdom of a Virginia President and a Republican Congress and bore with exemplary patience the policy that put the farms and plantations of the United States in the forefront of the struggle for maritime rights.

Disastrous as were the effects of the embargo upon commerce and agriculture, it proved to be a boon to manufacturing. The high price or unavailability of British merchandise forced Americans to manufacture for themselves—usually in their own households. President Jefferson was delighted to see his countrywomen busy at looms and spindles in their own homes. Household manufactures had received so much impetus from the embargo, he said in 1809, that "let our intercourse with England be opened when it may, not one half the amount of what we have heretofore taken from her, will ever again be demanded."

In the North, particularly in New England, the embargo stimulated manufacturing not only in households but in factories. Paul Revere's firm which after the Revolution had turned to rolling copper into sheets—and so became the Revere Copper Company—flourished after the elimination of British competition. Prior to the embargo, the United States had fifteen cotton mills; by 1810, eighty-seven mills had been established, of which sixty-two were in operation. The efforts of a southern President to convert the American economy into an instrument for compelling belligerents to respect American rights aggravated the growing imbalance between an industrialized North and an agricultural, staple-producing South.

Politically, the Federalists were the principal beneficiaries of the embargo, for it rejuvenated their party just when it had seemed to be headed for oblivion. In the elections of 1808, Federalists gained strength in New England, New York, New Jersey, and Delaware. With some important exceptions, the mercantile interest which President Jefferson had seemed to be on the point of detaching from the Federalists and incorporating into the Republican party

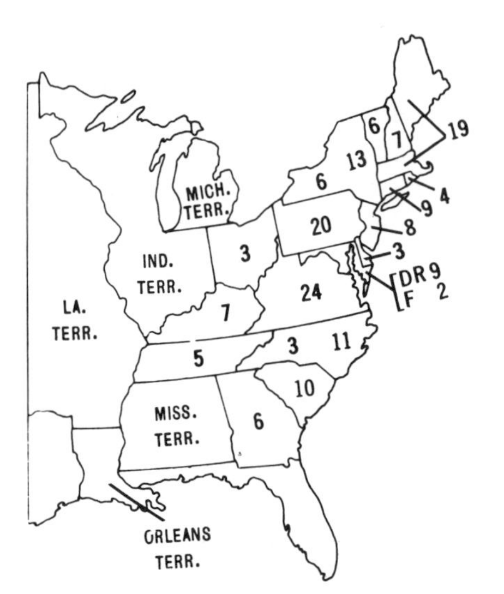

THE ELECTION OF 1808

	ELECTORAL VOTE BY STATE
REPUBLICAN James Madison	122
FEDERALIST Charles C. Pinckney	47
INDEPENDENT-REPUBLICAN George Clinton	6
NOT VOTED	1
	176

was now arrayed against him, but Jefferson always consoled himself with the reflection that war would have been even more divisive in its consequences.

Yet the embargo, unlike war, did not stir men's souls; it inspired no patriotic songs and gave rise to no heroic actions. It was unlikely that any American would ever tell his grandchildren what he did during the Great Embargo. Despite the President's efforts to invest the embargo with the aura of patriotism, it remained a mute, inglorious, and frustrating struggle. From the beginning, Secretary of the Treasury Gallatin had regarded the embargo with misgivings: he complained that it was ruinous to the Treasury and exposed the impotence of the government. In the summer of 1808, Gallatin predicted that, unless the embargo were abandoned, the Republican party would lose the presidential election of 1808. Party unity was cracking under the strain: northern Republicans found themselves confronted with the prospect of alienating their constituents by following the President.

Despite the rebirth of the Federalist party and factionalism within the Republican party, Madison received 122 electoral votes whereas Charles C. Pinckney, the Federalist candidate, polled 47. In the congressional elections, although the Federalists improved their position in the House, the Republicans retained a majority of 64 votes. It was a remarkable demonstration of how party unity could survive the bruising shocks of a measure as costly and unpopular as the embargo.

Inevitably, the embargo was primarily directed against Great Britain, the principal customer and supplier of the United States. France escaped relatively unscathed for the reason that she had so much less to lose by a trade stoppage. Napoleon even managed to turn the embargo to his own advantage: he seized and confiscated American ships that entered French ports and justified his acts by alleging that he was merely helping President Jefferson enforce the embargo.

Much to Jefferson's mortification, neither "the whale of the ocean" nor "the robber of the land" showed any signs of yielding to economic pressure from the United States. The spectacle of the United States torn by dissension and with the authority of the government openly flouted was not calculated to make either France or Great Britain rush to make terms with the republic. George Canning, the British Foreign Secretary, responded with a gibe to one of Jefferson's messages asking the British government to repeal the Orders in Council and thereby free commerce between the two countries: His Majesty's Government, said Canning, would gladly facilitate the removal of the embargo "as a measure of inconvenient restriction upon the American people."

In November 1808, Jefferson informed Congress that the embargo had failed to advance the cause of the freedom of the seas. At the same time, he asserted that the United States had proved to the world that it was capable of acting with firmness, moderation, and dignity. As was his custom, the President left the next step to "the wisdom of Congress," but, as was also his custom, he made sure that Congress did not want for wise guidance from the Executive.

In January 1809, Congress adopted an Enforcing Act that reflected the administration's view that there was nothing wrong with the embargo that stricter enforcement would not cure. This act marked the widest extension in American history of the federal government's control over commerce in time of peace. The law prohibited the loading of ships without permission from federal officials, authorized those officials to seize goods being conveyed by wagon in the direction of the Canadian border, and legalized anticipatory arrest by federal agents on grounds of suspicious behavior. In case resistance were offered, these agents were directed to call upon the Army, Navy, and militia for aid, and the President was authorized to charter thirty additional naval craft for the purpose of confining American vessels to port. The Navy, it appeared, could serve a useful purpose after all!

But the days of the embargo were numbered. The northern Republicans revolted against a measure that seemed to have no other effect than to weaken the United States. In February 1809, Congress enacted a bill that brought the embargo to an end the day before Jefferson relinquished the office of president to James Madison.

21. CONGRESSIONAL DIPLOMACY: THE NONINTERCOURSE ACT

The repeal of the embargo did not free American commerce of all restraints. The embargo was replaced by a nonintercourse act which, while it permitted American ships to put to sea, prohibited the entry of French and British warships and merchantmen into United States ports, forbade the importation of the merchandise of both countries, and ordered American ships not to touch at ports controlled by either belligerent. The way was left open, however, for France and Great Britain to restore themselves to the good graces of the United States government: the President was authorized to reopen trade with the nation or nations that ceased to violate American neutral rights.

Madison's administration opened with two diplomatic triumphs that stemmed in part from the embargo. In April 1809, the British government modified the Orders in Council by permitting American ships to trade directly with the Baltic countries and Germany and reducing the duties imposed upon the transit of goods through the British Isles to the European continent. And in April 1809, David Erskine, the British minister to the United States, signed a treaty at Washington by which the British government pledged itself to repeal the Orders in Council provided that the United States repealed nonintercourse against Great Britain while continuing it against France. Even though nothing was said in the Erskine agreement about impressment, President Madison jubilantly proclaimed that nonintercourse as applied to Great

---

"Arch Street Ferry, Philadelphia, Pa.," detail of an engraving by W. Birch from The Granger Collection.

Silver Dollar, 1799.

Britain would end on June 10, 1809. Celebrations took place all over the country and hundreds of American ships set sail for Great Britain.

For the moment, it appeared that the British ministry by its timely concessions had overreached Napoleon and had carried off the prize of American trade and good will. During a single week in June 1809 more American cotton was landed at Liverpool than had been received at that port during the entire year of 1808. While the two English-speaking nations had seemingly settled their differences or, as in the case of impressment, swept them under the rug, France was left out in the cold: as regards that power, nonintercourse remained in effect.

But the apparent agreement was short-lived. At the advice of George Canning, the Foreign Secretary, the British government repudiated Erskine's agreement and recalled Erskine himself on the ground that he had violated his instructions. True, the United States government had not agreed to recognize the validity of the Rule of 1756 and to permit the British Navy to capture American ships violating nonintercourse with France, two points upon which Canning had insisted—but Erskine had carried the main point: he had put the resources and shipping of the United States at the disposal of Great Britain while denying them to France.

Angry and crestfallen, President Madison was obliged in August 1809 to withdraw his proclamation and to declare nonintercourse again in force against both Great Britain and France. Although Madison complained bitterly about British duplicity, the fact is that in 1807 he and President Jefferson had consigned the Monroe-Pinckney treaty to the diplomatic wastebasket without so much as tendering it to the Senate. The score was now even, but henceforth each side assumed an increasingly unyielding and defiant posture and made no pretence of concealing its doubts of its adversary's good faith.

Hardly less insulting than the repudiation of the Erskine agreement, from the American point of view, was appointment of Francis "Copenhagen" Jackson as Erskine's successor in Washington. Jackson had won the sobriquet of "Copenhagen" because he had conducted the negotiations which ended in the seizure of the Danish fleet and the bombardment of the Danish capital in 1807. Instead of applying emollient to the abrasions left by George Canning, Jackson opened up fresh wounds. "I came prepared to treat with a regular government," Jackson informed the Ministry, "and have had to deal with a mob and mob-leaders." His recall was demanded by the United States government, and he returned to Great Britain where he regaled society with hair-raising tales about the uncouth savages living on the wrong side of the Atlantic.

The Nonimportation Act injured the United States far more than it did Great Britain or France. Congress and the Executive seemed remarkably fertile in expedients that recoiled upon the American economy. In the case of the Nonimportation Act, the law itself was an invitation to smuggling, with consequent loss to the government of revenue and higher prices to the consumer. Moreover, once American ships put to sea, their owners felt free to throw off the restraints imposed by Congress. American shipmasters might clear for the East Indies or South America and yet wind up in Liverpool with a cargo of sugar or cotton. On the other hand, American ships trying to reach French ports were likely to be haled into a British admiralty court. As regards the prohibition laid by the Nonintercourse Act upon trade with France, the British Navy was far more successful in enforcing this provision than was the United States government itself.

CONGRESSIONAL DIPLOMACY

In 1810, after nonimportation had abundantly demonstrated its inadequacies, Congress adopted Macon's Bill #2, named after the North Carolina Congressman. This piece of legislation did not accord with Nathaniel Macon's views, although he ultimately gave it his approval. Macon's Law #2 reopened trade with all countries for one year, but it served notice upon Great Britain and France that if either rescinded its regulations restraining American trade before March 3, 1811, and the other country did not follow suit within three months, nonimportation would go into effect against the noncomplying country.

Until the last days of Jefferson's administration, the foreign policy of the United States had been firmly controlled by the Chief Executive. Macon's Bill #2 represented congressional intervention in a sphere hitherto jealously guarded by previous presidents. Congress acted without benefit of executive leadership; although President Madison signed the bill, he made no effort to claim it as an administration-inspired measure.

In Macon's Act #2, the United States offered to bestow its favors upon either belligerent; it drew no invidious distinctions and expressed no partiality between France and Great Britain. The first nation that accepted the United States' terms was promised full access to the American market and the inestimable advantage of supplying its need of colonial and other products with the aid of the American merchant marine.

The immediate effect of Macon's Law #2 was to put American shipping at the disposal of Great Britain. In fact, during the Napoleonic Wars, any neutrality policy adopted by the United States was certain to work to the advantage of the dominant sea power. Macon's Act #2 legitimized United States trade with Great Britain, but it did not prevent the British Navy from interdicting American trade with France. Congress might declare the oceans free, but it was Great Britain that ruled that element. As a result, American shipmasters either danced to the tune of the British hornpipe or ended up in a British admiralty court.

Against British seapower, Napoleon could bring to bear an almost inexhaustible store of guile. And in Macon's Bill #2 the French Emperor saw an unexampled opportunity for the exercise of this peculiar talent. If he could convince the United States that he had revoked the Berlin and Milan decrees, he could secure a much-needed supply of colonial products, put the United States merchant marine on the side of France, and embroil the republic in a dispute with Great Britain over the Orders in Council that, hopefully, might produce war between the two English-speaking countries. Indeed, it was hard for Napoleon to see how he could lose if he played with his accustomed finesse the cards dealt him by the United States Congress.

Accordingly, in August 1810, Count Cadore, Napoleon's Foreign Minister, gave the American minister to France a letter written by the Emperor himself declaring that the Berlin and Milan decrees were revoked and would cease to have effect after November 1, 1810—provided that the British repealed the Orders in Council and the United States "caused their rights to be respected by the English." As any translation clerk in the State Department would have known, the so-called Cadore Note offered at the most a conditional repeal of the Berlin and Milan decrees.

In view of Napoleon's well-deserved reputation for dissimulation and deceit, President Madison would have been justified in treating the Cadore note skeptically and waiting for proof of the Emperor's sincerity. Instead, the American President took Napoleon at his word with an alacrity that might well have astonished Napoleon himself. Madison declared that the Cadore Note satisfied all the requirements stipulated by Macon's Bill #2. On November 2, 1810, without waiting to learn what positive action had been taken by the French government on November 1, the President issued a proclamation declaring that nonintercourse against France was suspended and warning Great Britain that if the Orders in Council were not repealed within three months, nonimportation would go into effect against that country. Congress ratified the President's action and on February 2, 1811, no action having been taken by the British government, Macon's Act #2 was permitted to take its course.

If President Madison acted precipitately in accepting the Cadore note as a genuine compliance with Macon's Bill #2, it was because he hoped thereby to compel the British to repeal the Orders in Council. By taking a calculated risk, he undertook to free American commerce from both the Napoleonic decrees and the Orders in Council.

Madison was playing for high stakes. If the British could be compelled to repeal the Orders in Council and Napoleon made good his promise to revoke his decrees, the freedom of the seas would become a reality. American trade with Europe would no longer be obliged to pass through Great Britain, and the continent itself would be open to American ships to go and come as they pleased. Free to supply all the belligerents in Europe, the United States would have achieved what Americans regarded as their Heaven-ordained right to furnish Europeans with the means of prosecuting their wars as long as they had strength to fight. The destiny of the United States, as it was then conceived, presupposed that the republic would rise upon the ruins of Europe.

Napoleon's self-created image as a friend of neutral maritime rights and an admirer of the United States varied sharply from his deeds. Greedy for booty, Napoleon invited American ships to enter French ports, then, when the net was full, he scooped them up with trumped-up charges of violating the laws of the empire. The ships were sequestered and the cargoes sold, the proceeds going to the French treasury. In order to keep the game going, Napoleon occasionally released a few ships from detention. But his true policy was contained in his advice to the King of Prussia: "Let the American ships enter your ports! Seize them afterward. You shall deliver the cargoes to me, and I will take them in part payment of the Prussian war debt." Altogether, from these confiscations and forced sales, Napoleon realized over $7 million in clear profit.

As a result of Napoleon's policy of replenishing his treasury at the expense of American shipowners, Russia became the only country on the European continent where American vessels could trade without fear of seizure. After 1809, with Great Britain's aid, Americans made Archangel an important market for British merchandise and colonial products.

Despite all evidence to the contrary, the official position of the United States government remained what it had been on November 2, 1810—that Napoleon had made a bona fide revocation of the Berlin and Milan decrees. To strengthen the illusion, Napoleon ordered his foreign minister to give Joel Barlow, the United States minister to France, a decree purporting to have been signed by the Emperor at St. Cloud on April 28, 1811, unconditionally rescinding the decrees. Although Barlow saw through the trick—indeed, the ink was hardly dry on the document—he avoided raising embarrassing questions. Nor did President Madison concern himself with such minutiae; instead, he cited the St. Cloud decree as conclusive evidence of Napoleon's probity and good will.

But the British government stubbornly remained incredulous, despite the "proof" submitted by President Madison, that Napoleon had actually revoked his decrees. As seen from London, Madison appeared to be either a dupe or, more probably, Napoleon's collaborator in the effort to destroy Great Britain.

Napoleon did confer some benefits upon the United States, but it was wholly by inadvertence and in his capacity as warmaker, not in that of his assumed role of defender of the freedom of the seas. In 1808, the Emperor placed his brother Joseph upon the throne of Spain. The war that engulfed the Iberian peninsula—involving the presence of a large British expeditionary force operating out of Portugal—gave the United States its long-awaited opportunity of seizing West Florida. In 1810, carefully timing his move, President Madison ordered the occupation of West Florida as far as the Pearl River, and in 1812, virtually the entire province, extending to the Perdido River, was incorporated in the territory of Mississippi. Thus did the United States vindicate its claim that it had bought West Florida in the Louisiana Purchase of 1803.

THE BATTLE OF TIPPECANOE

In spite of its involvement in the European war, Great Britain, unlike Spain, was in a position to impede the westward advance of the United States. Moreover, Great Britain possessed formidable allies in the Indians of the upper Mississippi valley who needed little coaxing to induce them to take the warpath against the Americans. As a result, the United States was obliged to fight an Indian war in the Northwest to clear the way for white settlement.

Ever since the United States had won its independence, it had been a settled conviction among westerners that their troubles with the Indians stemmed from the practice of the British government of supplying the Indians with arms and ammunition and inciting them to ravage the frontier settlements. Ultimate responsibility for every massacre that occurred on the northern border was consequently laid at the door of the British Ministry. In actuality, the British government, while it kept the Indians supplied with such "presents" as guns, ammunition, and blankets, did not unleash the redskins against American settlers. Although the government was eager to keep the allegiance of the Indians living on the American side of the border, it wished them to sharpen their knives in preparation for a war between the United States and Great Britain rather than to dissipate their strength in small border forays. But what most impressed the tribesmen was the concern for their welfare manifested by the Great White Father in London and the avidity for their tribal lands displayed by American frontiersmen.

Even so, the Northwest frontier might have remained comparatively quiet had it not been for the most remarkable twin brothers produced by any Indian tribe in recorded history. Tecumseh and The Prophet were Shawnees who, had they been fighting in any other cause than that of holding up the advance of white settlement, would have gone down in history as heroes of the struggle for freedom. Tecumseh was the orator and the warrior; The Prophet supplied the mysticism and the fervor that inspired the Shawnees to fight with reckless courage. Claiming to hold direct communication with the Great Spirit and to possess miraculous powers, The Prophet called upon all Indians to abjure the white man's firewater and firearms alike and to take up the ancestral weapons of the bow and arrows and tomahawks. Tecumseh organized the Indians in accord with his brother's vision: all Indians, he declared, were one people, all lands belonged to the tribes in common, and no lands could be sold without the consent of all.

In 1808, The Prophet took up headquarters at the Tippecanoe River, a northern branch of the Wabash. Here the faithful gathered to engage in fasting and other religious exercises, imploring the Great Spirit to bring sorrow and desolation upon the white man.

But William Henry Harrison, the governor of Indiana Territory, was no respecter of the injunctions of the Great Spirit, particularly when they stood in the way of the appropriation by the white man of the natives' lands. In a single transaction, he cleared the title to three million acres of tribal land at a price that made the Louisiana Purchase seem exorbitant. A better way of bringing on an Indian war could hardly have been devised, but when hostilities occurred it was the British government that was held responsible for "inciting" the natives.

In November 1811, Governor Harrison at the head of an army composed of militiamen and a few regulars moved against The Prophet at Tippecanoe. The Indians gave battle and, although Harrison lost two hundred men, he held his ground and, after burning an Indian town, returned to the Ohio. Contrary to The Prophet's injunctions, some braves used British-made guns rather than bows and arrows against the Americans, but their losses were heavy and the Indian confederacy was weakened on the eve of the war for which the British had been holding back their Indian allies. And, in the telling, the battle of Tippecanoe became an epic of heroism and consummate generalship. Out of this myth a future president of the United States was created.

The conclusion drawn by westerners from these events was that the Northwest would know no peace until the British were driven from Canada. Andrew Jackson exclaimed that "the blood of our murdered heroes must be revenged!" But, he warned his countrymen, it was not enough to kill Indians—the final pacification of the country required that the Britons, too, bite the dust.

22. THE COMING OF THE WAR

WAR HAWKS

The idea that only by war could American rights on the high seas and security in the West be achieved gained ground simultaneously in Congress, the administration, and the popular mind. Disenchantment with embargoes, nonimportation, nonintercourse, and all other measures short of war tended to enhance the attractions of war. Americans' stock of forbearance was beginning to be exhausted; even Thomas Jefferson, in retirement at Monticello, admitted that the policy of palliating and enduring no longer held out hope of redress of grievances. The peaceful diplomacy of Jefferson and Madison had tried the souls of many American patriots more than war itself.

Peace—the quasi-peace the United States had known since 1808—had its frustrations from which war promised quick relief. War would resolve all the doubts and dilemmas arising from a fruitless and interminable controversy over neutral rights. Unless the United States was prepared to submit to the Orders in Council—and Jefferson and Madison had asserted that submission would be slavery—there seemed nowhere to go but to war. "War," said John Randolph, "is the price to be paid for the consistency of gentlemen who think that they have gone too far to recede."

It was also the price British statesmen were compelled to pay for having

---

"Preparation for War to Defend Commerce," detail of an engraving by W. Birch from the Free Library of Philadelphia.

Half Cent, Draped Bust, 1800.

derided Americans' pretensions to be a great power. If Americans tamely submitted to this kind of treatment, it seemed entirely possible that they would lose their sense of national identity and pride; certainly they could hardly continue to regard themselves as the champions of a new order in international affairs based upon the Laws of Nature. It was for this reason that John Adams advocated war: "it is," he said, "necessary against England; necessary to convince France that we are something; and above all necessary to convince ourselves, that we are not-Nothing."

The congressional elections of 1810-1811 reflected this new commitment to militancy. While the Republicans, as usual, scored a sweeping victory, over sixty of the incumbent Republicans were replaced by new members, many of whom were impatient with the Jeffersonian-Madisonian policy of economic coercion. They conceived war, not economic reprisals, to be the natural continuation of diplomacy, particularly when it had become clear, as it had to them, that American rights and honor could be preserved in no other way.

As orators, parliamentarians, and leaders, these men—soon to be called "War Hawks"—were as talented as any who have sat in Congress. Chief among them were John C. Calhoun, Langdon Cheves, and William Lowndes of South Carolina, Richard Johnson and Henry Clay of Kentucky, Felix Grundy of Tennessee, and Peter B. Porter of New York. Clay, in particular, burst upon the stage of American politics as a young Lochinvar come out of the West; with him, the Romantic Age entered American politics. Handsome, eloquent, and suave, Clay fascinated women; it was his tragedy that he was born before women had the right to vote. Men, too, succumbed to his charm. And, as a duelist, he proved his courage repeatedly on the field of honor. Indeed, he injected into American politics the spirit and punctilio of the duelist: he was as quick to resent a slight upon his country's honor as upon his own. As the British minister observed, Clay and his friends had convinced themselves that war was "as necessary to America as a duel is to a young naval officer to prevent his being bullied and elbowed in society."

In 1810, sensing that the seat of power lay in the House of Representatives, Clay resigned his seat in the Senate to run for the House. He had no sooner presented his credentials to the House than he was elected Speaker. It was an election more far-reaching in its consequences than some presidential elections.

Until Clay took the rostrum, the Speaker of the House had been a useful but relatively unimportant figure. He presided over the House just as the Vice-President presided over the Senate; except for this duty neither of these gentlemen seemed to have much to do. In his dealings with Congress, Jefferson had raised the Speaker to the rank of chief lieutenant of the Executive, but it remained for Clay to reveal the full potentialities of the office. He made the Speaker a power in his own right: he appointed members of the committees, planned legislation, shepherded bills through Congress, and, on occasion, put the President himself in his place. Under his regime, the rules of order were rigidly enforced: congressmen were no longer permitted to put their feet on their desks, and John Randolph's favorite hound-dog was banished from the chamber.

As Speaker, Clay revealed that he was far more a natural leader of men than was President Madison. Clay had personal magnetism and he never doubted that he was right (when he later said that he would rather be right than be President, he was absolutely sure that he knew what the right was). Clay made decisions with a minimum of inner conflict: he had a simple, straightforward solution for everything. In his conviction that every problem could be solved, he expressed the unquenchable optimism of his countrymen.

Clay injected himself and the House of Representatives into the vacuum left by President Madison's uninspiring leadership. Jefferson said that Madison was "the greatest man in the world," but little of this greatness manifested itself during his presidency. From the beginning, factionalism had disrupted his administration. Except for Secretary of the Treasury Albert Gallatin, a holdover from the Jefferson administration, Madison's cabinet contained no first-rate men. But if the heads of departments lacked ability, their ambition was boundless. The Smiths of Maryland—Robert and Samuel—organized an opposition to Gallatin and imposed their will upon the President. To appease the Smith faction, Madison appointed Robert Smith Secretary of State, although his strongest qualification for the post was that his brother Samuel was the senior senator from Maryland and a large contributor to Republican campaign funds. Gallatin threatened to resign unless Smith was removed from the State Department, but Smith remained until he was succeeded in 1812 by James Monroe. Gallatin escaped from the shambles by going to Europe.

By November 1811, President Madison's faith in peaceful coercion as a means of bringing Great Britain to terms had begun to erode. The repeal of the Orders in Council seemed as far away as ever and, thanks to the war hawks, the impressment issue had been made the chief point of controversy between the two countries. Since 1809, President Madison had permitted impressment to slip into the background while he concentrated his efforts upon securing the repeal of the Orders in Council. Upon the right of impressment the British stood adamant, and President Madison seemed to have decided that it was not worth a war. The President admitted that the settlement of the Chesapeake affair had taken "one splinter out of our wounds." Moreover, incidents had become less frequent, and British officers, as a result of American protests, were instructed to take more care in distinguishing between American and British seamen. But the war hawks could not let the issue go by the board: obviously, it was a greater affront to American pride to suffer the forcible removal of seamen from American ships than the confiscation of ships and cargoes. For this reason, "Free Ships and Sailors' Rights" became the watchword of the war party.

The clamor for war began in earnest in November 1811. The war hawks emitted such strident cries that the woods seemed full of them. In actuality, however, they were outnumbered in Congress by the doves—Federalists and peace-loving Republicans. Some doves, confident of their numerical superiority, tried to minimize the importance of the war hawks: Josiah Quincy described them as unfledged politicians, fluttering and cackling on the floor of the House, the shell still on their head and their pin feathers unshed. But he soon learned the error of confusing hawks with chickens: once fairly out of the shell, they left no doubt that they were of a very different species.

Paradoxically, the shipowners and merchants—the people most directly affected by the Orders in Council—were least inclined to go to war over neutral rights. For by submitting to British maritime rules they could still make a respectable profit. And, with few exceptions, they strenuously opposed a war in which, they feared they would be the victims. Repeatedly, President Madison and the war hawks rebuked American businessmen for putting profit above national honor. It was the politicians who tended the sacred flame of patriotism and proclaimed the primacy of questions of right over all other considerations.

Even the most bellicose war hawks could hardly fail to see that the country was not united in support of war. Yet they believed that if the flag were flung forward, the American people would rally round. The important thing was to commit the country to hostilities—and then dissent, branded as treason, would vanish and the people would be united in their determination to bring Great Britain to its knees. President Madison expected that even New Englanders would dismiss all misgivings about the war when they saw the stars and stripes fluttering in the breeze: they were, he said, "determined republicans—on the day of trial they would stand by the government."

Even though westerners were far removed from the scene of the maritime struggle between Great Britain and the United States, their sense of national honor was as highly developed as that of Americans living on the seaboard. Moreover, their material interests were directly affected: the loss of British markets and the withdrawal of the British merchant marine from American trade tended to depress the price of the commodities westerners sold and increased the cost of the manufactured goods they bought. Finally, in the persistent attacks by the northwest Indians, they had a special reason for hating England.

Many Americans were also acutely aware of the depredations committed by France upon American shipping. In 1812, some congressmen declared themselves in favor of a simultaneous declaration of war against both France and Great Britain. Had war been directed against the nation most guilty of seizing and confiscating American ships and cargoes, the administration would have been hard pressed to decide against which of the European belligerents to begin hostilities. From 1804-1812, the British seized 917 American vessels, but more than 500 of these ships had been restored by the order of British Admiralty Courts. During the same period, the French and their allies had seized over 1000 ships, but comparatively few of these had been restored.

As Nathaniel Macon observed, "the Devil himself could not tell which government, England or France, is the most wicked."

The unanswerable argument for going to war with Great Britain rather than with France was put succinctly by Henry Clay: "The one we can strike, the other we cannot reach." The United States had already fought an undeclared war with France and found it yielded no material profit, and even the spiritual balm provided by victorious naval actions had not saved the Federalist party from defeat. War with Great Britain, on the other hand, gave the United States an opportunity of fighting upon ground of its own choosing and with excellent prospects of making important territorial acquisitions. Moreover, as regards one all-important American right, Great Britain was the prime aggressor: France impressed far fewer American seamen.

None of the slogans coined by Americans in 1812 mentioned Canada: officially, the United States government sought only to vindicate American rights. Yet Canada had not slipped over Americans' horizon. To westerners, in particular, the conquest and annexation of Canada promised to be the solution of the Indian problem and to provide room for expansion. Thomas Jefferson, among others, dreamed of the day when Great Britain would be wholly expelled from the North American continent, thereby insuring the triumph of republicanism. Finally, Canada had a special place in Americans' affections: although it had never been a member of the family, an honored place had always been reserved for it in that happy circle.

While the hope of acquiring Canada was not the paramount cause of the War of 1812—without the Orders in Council and impressment there would have been no conflict—it provided the theater upon which the war was expected to be fought and a possible indemnity for the losses in ships and cargoes Americans had sustained from the operation of the Orders in Council.

Of all the arguments in favor of the acquisition of Canada none was more persuasive than the ease with which it was expected to be accomplished. Thomas Jefferson predicted that the conquest of Canada as far as Quebec in 1812 would be "a mere matter of marching," and Andrew Jackson assured the Tennessee volunteers that the invasion would turn out to be "a military promenade." In short, it was to be a sporting war with a Grand Tour of Canada thrown in as an added attraction.

The conquest of Canada, easy though it promised to be, raised disturbing questions regarding sectional balance. Manifestly, the North stood to profit more than the South from the addition of this great expanse of territory, unless East Florida were brought into the Union as a counterpoise. The full implications of the sectional problem were not squarely faced in 1812. Usually the difficulty was evaded by saying that Canada, once within the grasp of the United States, would be retained for bargaining purposes at the peace table. By thus leaving the final disposition of Canada to the arbitrament of events, a clash between North and South was avoided. Yet it is clear that if either Canada or East Florida or both had fallen to the United States and their incorporation into the Union been decided upon, some sort of sectional arrangement would have been imperative.

THE DECLARATION OF WAR

President Madison's last hope was that the Prince of Wales, who became Regent in February 1812 (his father, George III, now hopelessly insane, was confined at Windsor Castle) would dismiss the Ministry and appoint men disposed to cultivate Anglo-American amity. Instead, in March 1812, the Prince Regent issued a proclamation asserting that Great Britain would enforce the Orders in Council until Napoleon had unequivocally revoked the Berlin and Milan decrees. On May 22, 1812, Madison received from Castlereagh, the British Foreign Secretary, a note reaffirming his government's decision to stand firm on every issue in dispute between the two countries. On that same day, a delegation of congressmen headed by Henry Clay assured the President of congressional support if he recommended a resort to hostilities. On June 1, despairing of ever making an impression upon the British government by economic coercion, President Madison delivered to Congress a special message recommending that it make the decision whether the United States should remain passive or meet force with force. For the first time since the settlement of the Chesapeake affair, President Madison put impressment at the top of American grievances—thereby making his bow to the war hawks.

Despite the war hawks' assertion that a vote against war was "a vote for England against America," Congress was not stampeded into declaring war. Because of a Federalist filibuster—one Federalist speaker after another held the floor, requiring the House to remain in session day and night—the declaration did not pass the House until June 18, 1812. The vote was 79 to 49; in the Senate, 19 votes were cast in favor, 13 were opposed.

While almost half the votes cast for war in the House of Representatives came from states south of Mason and Dixon's line, it was far from being a sectional war. Least of all it was war forced upon the country by the West: the western states disposed of only nine votes in the House. Pennsylvania, which voted 16 to 2 for war, contributed more votes in support of the President's policy than did the entire West. Six affirmative votes came from Massachusetts. In fact, without the votes cast by northern Republicans, the declaration could not have been carried.

Nor was it the work of the war hawks alone. The balance of power was in the hands of moderates, many of them long-term members of the House, who had voted for the embargo and nonintercourse acts, but who had been persuaded by British intransigence and President Madison's message of June 1, to write off the policy of economic coercion as a failure.

The war did not stem from any overwhelming public demand. Although many citizens were eager for war, the enthusiasm centered in Washington,

D.C., among Republican politicians. It was not, as Federalists said, "Mr. Madison's War": it was the Republican party's war. Party regularity, more than public opinion or sectionalism, produced the war: the conservative wing of the Republican party, led by the President, went over to the war hawks not because the hawks were all-powerful but because the administration's policy of peaceable economic coercion had seemingly collapsed. War with Great Britain became a test of party loyalty and, in some instances, overrode sectional considerations. Almost 90 percent of the Republican members of Congress present on June 18, 1812, voted for war. Six Republican members from Massachusetts voted "aye" when the roll was called. They served their party far better than they served their constituents, and most of them paid the penalty of being retired to private life.

Because some politicians put party above sectionalism and the wishes of their constituents, the vote in Congress did not faithfully mirror the public temper. But the Federalist minority exhibited even greater cohesion than did the Republicans: not a Federalist broke ranks to vote for war.

Rightly, the war was celebrated as a party triumph. When John C. Calhoun learned that the United States had declared war he reportedly threw his arms around the neck of Henry Clay and led his friends in a Shawnee war dance. A Baltimore mob wrecked the office of an antiwar newspaper and burned the house of a free Negro accused of harboring pro-British sentiments. Troops had to be called out to prevent the whites from burning a Negro church. In trying to restrain the mob, General Henry (Light-Horse) Lee, the father of General Robert E. Lee, suffered injuries that left him crippled for life.

As for President Madison, at the reception held to celebrate the declaration of war, he appeared pale and distraught. But the self-confidence of Clay, Calhoun, and other militants acted like a cordial upon the President's sagging morale, soothing his qualms and stiffening his backbone. The President soon demonstrated that he could be as inflexible as any war hawk.

To the Federalists, the United States had chosen to fight the wrong country: if the United States must go to war, they felt that it ought to be against France rather than Great Britain, which, despite its unfortunate habit of humiliating the United States, they persisted in regarding as a natural ally against French imperialism. They emptied their bumpers to the toast: "the world's best hope, Britain's fast-anchored isle," and, contrary to everything the administration said, they continued to believe that Great Britain was fighting the battles of the United States. Federalists never depreciated the power of the British Navy.

Although Madison, Clay, and Calhoun stoutly denied that the United States was in any sense an ally of France or guilty of abetting Napoleon's schemes of conquest, their protestations did not alter the fact that the United States entered the war in England's darkest hour. The Federalists objected to the war on the ground, among others, that the United States appeared to have struck Great Britain "in the mean hope of coming in at the death of the

Old Lion and sharing a scrap of the spoil." Certainly the American action was perfectly timed for Napoleon's purposes. A few days after the American declaration, Napoleon's armies began the invasion of Russia, the one European country Jefferson regarded as the true friend of the United States. No American war hawk ever said that it was to the interests of the United States to help Napoleon raise the imperial eagles in Moscow and London but the policy of the United States worked indirectly to that end. Indeed, the War of 1812 stands as one of the most notable of Napoleon's diplomatic achievements: at the time most critical for his own fortunes he had laid the specter of an Anglo-American alliance that had haunted French leaders since Jay's treaty.

23.

THE WAR OF 1812: BY LAND AND BY SEA

Ironically, almost at the very moment that President Madison abandoned the policy of economic coercion it was on the point of achieving momentous results. Madison gave up too soon: had he palliated and endured for another two months it is doubtful if all the war hawks in Washington could have averted peace.

As a result of the operations of the Continental System and the nonintercourse act, a succession of bad harvests, widespread unemployment, and the need of American supplies for the Peninsular War, Britons' devotion to the Orders in Council began to waver. Through the Whig party, British merchants and manufacturers brought pressure upon Parliament to repeal the Orders. In May 1812, an assassin removed the most formidable obstacle to repeal: Spencer Perceval, the British Prime Minister and one of the authors of the Orders in Council, was struck down in the House of Commons, the last British Prime Minister to be assassinated. His death signalized the almost simultaneous demise of the Orders in Council.

On June 23, 1812, the Orders in Council were revoked on condition that the United States repeal the nonintercourse act against Great Britain. The sailing ships carrying the news of the declaration of war and the revocation of the Orders in Council passed each other in mid-Atlantic.

Although he had agonized for many months over declaring war, President Madison rejected the British peace overture without hesitation. Had he done otherwise, he would have forfeited the support of the most vocal members

---

"Battle Between the *Constitution* and the *Guerriere,*" engraving from a painting by Alonzo Chappel from The Granger Collection.

Half Dime, Draped Bust Type, Heraldic Eagle Reverse, 1800.

of his party: the war hawks seemed to have swallowed the doves, for hardly a peep came from the dovecotes. The war hawks were not inclined to forgive a hardened sinner who repented on his death-bed—and in the summer of 1812, Great Britain seemed to them to be at its last gasp. Napoleon was moving across Russia while the Russian armies fell back. If Moscow fell could London be far behind?

In spurning peace at this moment of history, President Madison in effect repudiated the idea that the United States had a vital concern in the preservation of a balance of power in Europe. Instead, the doctrine of the two spheres was invoked to justify the United States in waging a private war with Great Britain while it abstained from any involvement in the affairs of Europe. The United States and Europe, it was said, had a totally different set of primary interests: the cardinal objective of the United States was to secure the freedom of the seas; what happened to freedom in Europe was Europe's concern, not the United States'. The American government expressed sympathy for the people of Europe in their struggle against Napoleon, but it continued to wage war against the enemy of the French Emperor. It was small consolation to freedom-loving Europeans that Americans said that they wished Napoleon only exactly as much success as would serve the United States' purposes, but no more. John Adams put the case succinctly when he said in 1814 that "if Europe submits to the maritime Despotism of England, the whole Globe is enslaved. Napoleon's Despotism could not extend beyond Europe."

From the point of view of the Madison administration, the repeal of the Orders in Council had not put an end to Great Britain's "maritime despotism." Upon the subject of impressment, the British government said not a word: apparently, this issue was not negotiable even though Great Britain was on its last legs. It was for this reason that President Madison decided that the war must go on: the United States would settle for nothing less than the total freedom of the seas.

On the record, therefore, the United States fought the war for sailors' rights. Impressment alone provided the ostensible justification for protracting hostilities. The acquisition of Canada was not mentioned—it was, indeed, the great unmentionable of the administration's war objectives. Nor did the British government say anything about the Indians whose depredations made the surrender of Canada seem to many westerners a *sine qua non* of peace with Great Britain.

To the last moment, the British government hoped that the suspension of the Orders in Council would bring the war to an end. Not until October 1812 was authority for general reprisals given to British ship captains. On November 27, a blockade was imposed upon the North American coast south of Rhode Island.

Yet President Madison did not close the door on all peace negotiations. In November 1812, having had some second thoughts on the matter—and the military position of the United States at this time was calculated to encourage second thoughts—President Madison offered to declare an armistice if the

British agreed to stop impressment. On this occasion, for the first and only time in the history of these protracted negotiations over impressment, the United States government promised to prevent the enlistment of foreign seamen in the American merchant marine. This time it was the British government's turn to refuse to discuss peace; encouraged by success, the British were now seeking a decisive victory over the United States.

THE ATTACK ON CANADA

Rushing unprepared into war was the quintessence of the Romantic spirit. In 1812, as Americans conceived it, war consisted largely in hurling themselves *en masse* upon the enemy. The conquest of Canada promised to be such a walkover that many Americans seem to have felt that if they paid too much attention to logistics and other mundane matters the war would cease even to be a sporting event.

The administration relied chiefly not upon military preparedness but upon the justice of the cause in which it had summoned the country to fight. Armored with a sense of righteousness and imbued with hatred of British "tyranny," scores of thousands of mettlesome militiamen were expected to spring to arms.

Despite the pervasive overconfidence in which Americans launched the war, Congress and the administration had not wholly neglected to strengthen the armed forces. Early in 1812, Congress authorized an increase of ten thousand men in the regular army. To encourage enlistments, a bounty of cash and one hundred acres of land was offered to volunteers, and in April 1812 whipping was abolished in the army. Even so, comparatively few men enlisted in the regular army—and thereby spared the government the embarrassment of turning men away because of the lack of clothing, guns, and equipment. There was even a shortage of fifes and drums with which to stir up the martial enthusiasm of prospective volunteers. As a result, at the outbreak of the war only about 7000 men were in uniform out of the 35,000 Congress had authorized.

The shortage extended even to the highest ranks of the army: most of those entitled by seniority to command troops in battle were veterans of the Revolutionary War who had seen little or no action for over thirty years. The generals of the American War of Independence did not fade away: they were resurrected to fight the battles of the War of 1812.

Unprepared militarily, the United States was disarmed financially by the Republicans. Aversion to war preparations of any kind seemed to stand roughly in proportion to the degree of belligerency felt toward Great Britain. In 1811, the charter of the Bank of the United States came up for renewal. The Directors offered the government a bonus of $1,250,000 for a new charter. Gallatin and Madison favored extending the life of the bank—Gallatin even wished to increase its capital from $10 to $30 million—but the institution had become unpopular in many quarters, particularly among the stockholders and directors of the state banks and the politicians responsive to pressures from these financial institutions. The state banks chafed under the restraints imposed by the Bank of the United States, and they promised borrowers easy credit once the controls were lifted. Among patriots, the Bank of the United States was regarded as a foreign-owned corporation. President Madison did not make a fight for the recharter of the Bank of the United States, with the result that in 1811 it was abolished by a vote of 65 to 64 in the House and 18 to 17 in the Senate. The government thereby abdicated whatever degree of financial control it exercised over the American economy; it was a triumph of states' rights and financial decentralization at a time when the financial resources of the country were about to be cruelly strained by war.

In July 1812 General William Hull bravely kicked off the invasion of Canada. A month later, he surrendered to General Isaac Brock, the British commander, under the threat of being massacred by the Indian allies of the British. A few months later, another American army that had crossed into Canada near Niagara was forced to surrender while a large body of New York militiamen watched from the American side of the river. In November 1812 General Dearborn moved out of his base camp at Plattsburg on Lake Champlain and marched off for Canada, but, after traveling a few miles, his men became mutinous and the army returned ignominiously to Plattsburg. But in the West things went even worse for the Americans: the British captured Forts Michilimackinac, Detroit, and Dearborn (the present site of Chicago) and gained undisputed control of the Great Lakes, the waterway to the West.

Nevertheless, bad as was the news from the fighting fronts, Madison won reelection to the presidency. But the margin was narrow: the electoral vote of Pennsylvania, had it gone the other way, would almost have brought victory to De Witt Clinton of New York, a rival Republican who enjoyed the support of the Federalists. North of the Potomac, the Federalist-Republican coalition carried every state except two. To add to the discomfiture of the Madisonian Republicans, the Federalists increased their strength in the House of Representatives.

Although the Madison administration continued to deny that the Anglo-American war had anything to do with the European war—one being a crusade to establish the rights of man on the high seas, the other a struggle between rival imperialisms—the course of the European conflict had a direct bearing upon events across the Atlantic. In consequence of the fact that the Grand Army perished in the snows of Russia, 1813 promised to be the year of decision for the United States in its war with Great Britain. The end of the war in Europe would release thousands of British troops for service in North America. Canada, therefore, had to be conquered lest, as in 1777, it be converted by the British into a base for an invasion of the United States.

In April General Dearborn opened the campaign of 1813 by crossing Lake Ontario. He got as far as York (now Toronto), where his troops burned

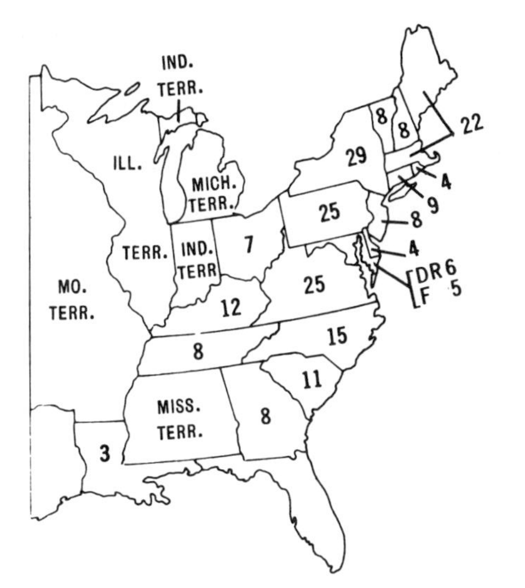

THE ELECTION OF 1812

	ELECTORAL VOTE BY STATE
REPUBLICAN James Madison	128
FUSION De Witt Clinton	89
NOT VOTED	1
	218

the governor's house and other public buildings. The raid had no military value, and Dearborn soon retreated south of the border. General James Wilkinson, grown grey in the service of Spain and the United States, struck at Canada only to suffer a humiliating defeat.

Unable to penetrate Canada, the best the United States could hope to do in 1813 was to cut British communications with the West by means of the Great Lakes. Because of the absence of roads, water transport provided the only practicable access to the Illinois country. Of the Great Lakes, Lake Erie occupied the most strategic position for both sides. In 1813, therefore, the British and Americans began to prepare for a naval struggle, the outcome of which promised to decide the fate of the region between the Mississippi and the Ohio Rivers.

Late in the summer of 1813, an American flotilla built of green timber and manned by crews consisting of "a motley set of blacks, soldiers, and boys," under the command of Oliver Hazard Perry, gave battle to an equally makeshift British fleet. After a hard fight, the Americans succeeded in capturing or disabling all the ships of His Majesty's squadron. As laconic as Caesar, Perry merely reported that "We have met the enemy, and they are ours." This terse announcement gave no hint of the courage displayed by Perry and his men. After all the crewmen of his ship, the *Lawrence,* had been killed or wounded, Perry himself, assisted by the purser and chaplain, fired the last operable gun before abandoning ship. Perry continued the fight from the *Niagara* until victory had been won.

It was a small battle, but its consequences were out of all proportion to the number of ships and men engaged. Cut off from supplies and manpower in Canada, the British and their Indian allies were unable to maintain their hold upon the Illinois country. Tecumseh's death, following closely upon Perry's victory on Lake Erie, completed the ruin of the Indian confederacy. Moreover, in October 1813, the Americans finally won an important battle on land when General Harrison, whose army was ferried across Lake Erie by Perry's ships, defeated General Proctor at the Battle of the Thames. As a result of these land and naval triumphs, the upper lakes passed temporarily under American control, and Detroit, the key to the West, fell to an American army.

Even though the British plan of securing the Illinois country for their Indian allies was dealt a severe reverse, the defenses of Canada remained intact. In December 1813, Niagara fell to the British and remained in their hands until the end of the war. In 1814, the British gained naval control of Lake Ontario. The promenade into Canada upon which Americans had embarked so lightheartedly in 1812 had ended in a rout; at the end of the year not an American remained in Canada except as a prisoner of war.

On the Pacific Coast, too, the war went against the United States. In 1812, the American Fur Company, organized by John Jacob Astor, a German immigrant to the United States, established a small trading post at Astoria near the mouth of the Columbia River. Here the Americans competed with the British Northwest Company for the furs of the Oregon country. But the next year, recognizing that they could not hold out against an expected British attack by sea, the settlers at Astoria sold out to the Northwest Company. The last vestige of American influence disappeared from the region "where rolls the Oregon."

The ill-success of the war merely intensified the Federalists' opposition to it; they viewed American defeats as a vindication of their prophecies, not as calls to action to save the country. They condemned the invasion of Canada as "cruel, wanton, senseless and wicked"—a war without hope either of plunder or glory unless, as Josiah Quincy of Massachusetts said, "it is the glory of the tiger which lifts its jaws, all foul and bloody from the bowels of his victim, and roars for his companion of the wood to come and witness his prowess and his spoil." In actuality, however, the American tiger had never appeared more like a paper cutout of that fearsome animal.

OPPOSITION TO THE WAR

After Napoleon's invasion of Russia, the opponents of the administration celebrated Russian victories over the French even though those victories hastened the day when the full power of the British Navy and Army would be turned against the United States. In June 1813, Robert G. Harper, a prominent Federalist congressman from South Carolina, in the presence of the Russian Minister, praised Russian valor and toasted "Alexander the Deliverer." "In the redemption of the world, by the arms of Russia," Harper declared, "all nations must rejoice!"

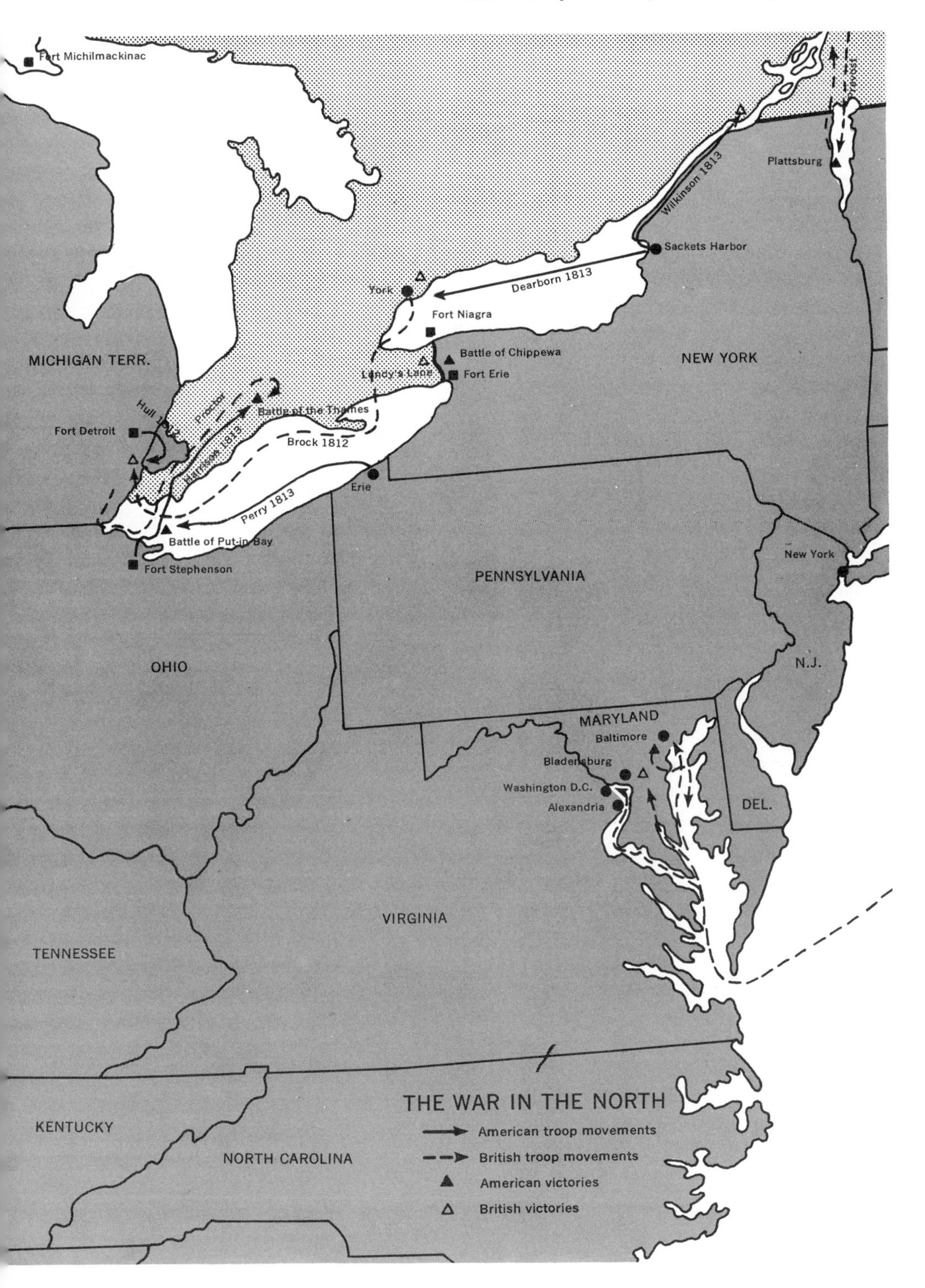
Fort Michilmackinac
MICHIGAN TERR.
Fort Detroit
Hull 1812
Proctor
Harrison 1813
Battle of the Thames
Brock 1812
Perry 1813
Battle of Put-in-Bay
Fort Stephenson
Erie
York
Fort Niagra
Dearborn 1813
Sackets Harbor
Wilkinson 1813
Prevost
Plattsburg
Battle of Chippewa
Lundy's Lane
Fort Erie
NEW YORK
PENNSYLVANIA
New York
N.J.
OHIO
MARYLAND
Baltimore
Bladensburg
Washington D.C.
Alexandria
DEL.
VIRGINIA
TENNESSEE
KENTUCKY
NORTH CAROLINA
THE WAR IN THE NORTH
American troop movements
British troop movements
American victories
British victories

Neither the Russians nor the Spanish patriots fighting for liberation from France had reason to bless the United States for waging war with Great Britain. The beef and flour necessary to sustain the British armies fighting in Portugal and Spain could no longer reach the Iberian peninsula in sufficient quantities; and the American ships that had helped make Archangel a great entrepôt of trade were now bottled up in port.

Some New England officials carried their opposition to a war they considered "not becoming a moral and religious people" to the length of sabotaging the war effort. Several governors refused to place detachments of their state militia under the command of United States Army officers; the Governor of Massachusetts did not even condescend to answer the President's requisition for artillery and men from the state militia; and in 1813, the Governor of New Hampshire called home the militia of his state serving under United States officers. As a result, the trained reserves of the New England states were jealously kept at home at a time when their fighting prowess might have proved decisive in Canada.

And yet not all New Englanders were antiwar Federalists. Fifteen regiments of volunteers were raised in the New England states, more than any other section of the Union. The entire South contributed only ten regiments. Moreover, thousands of New England seamen, made jobless by the British blockade, served on board privateers and the ships of the United States Navy.

For their part, the British did everything in their power to encourage New Englanders to regard the war as "Mr. Madison's War." British men-of-war abetted infractions by Americans of laws prohibiting trade with the enemy; ships resembling floating bazaars lay off the coast; and until 1814, New England was excluded from the effect of the British blockade of the American coast. Nor did British interfere with neutral ships trading with the United States; since these ships carried British goods, the American doctrine of free ships make free goods was scrupulously observed. On Lake Champlain the flag of Sweden gave protection to a blockade-runner.

The most strenuous opposition to the war came from the Federalist elite —the merchants, bankers, politicians, lawyers, and clergymen. These men held the purse-strings in New England, and they made sure that the financial resources of their section were not placed at the disposal of the government. New England, as a result of its relatively large manufacturing potential and its long exemption from the effects of the British blockade, had become the financial center of the United States—for American dollars, all roads seemed to lead to Boston, particularly after the banks in the rest of the country suspended specie payments in 1814. Thus, the refusal to aid in financing the war proved to be as severe a reverse to the Madison administration as any defeat suffered in battle.

Fortunately for his reputation as a financier, Albert Gallatin abandoned the Treasury in 1812 for the diplomatic service. Although he recommended increasing taxes to finance the war, his advice was not adopted until 1813 when Congress imposed higher internal duties. Loans were the government's principal resource but money could be secured only by paying a price that made the loans floated by the Federalists seem bargains by comparison. Of the $60 million in bonds offered for sale by the government during the war, only $8 million were sold at par; and only about $28 million in specie value was realized from the entire transaction. The South and West, where enthusiasm for the war was stronger than in New England, had little surplus cash, with the result that the burden fell almost wholly upon the middle states. In 1814, when the government tried to float a loan of $16 million, New Englanders subscribed less than $500,000; the government's credit was saved by two Republican businessmen, John Jacob Astor and Stephen Girard.

Bereft of all governmental controls, the American economy went into a war-induced inflationary spiral. Expenditures by the government in excess of revenue—from 1812-1815 the government spent $68,600,000 more than it took in—accounted for part of this general rise in prices, but of far greater significance was the issuance by state banks of large quantities of paper money. Since the Bank of the United States no longer served as a restraining influence upon the state banks (during the war, 158 new banks were chartered by the states), they printed bank notes without regard to their specie reserves; the only limit seemed to be the paper supply and the capacity of the printing presses to grind out money.

Economically, the war took its heaviest toll in the Virginia Tidewater area, already decaying as a result of generations of wasteful and destructive agriculture. With their tobacco perishing upon their hands and a large slave population to feed, the planters either abandoned their estates or went down to ruin with their land. Travelers found dismantled country houses, desolate and tumbledown churches, and careworn, disheartened people. Yet the planters supported the war as loyally as they had the embargo. No state of the Union was as ill served economically by the presidents it gave to the country as was Virginia.

NAVAL DUELS

However severely Americans' morale was shaken by the news from Canada, they could take heart from the victories won by the United States Navy. This was the exact opposite of what had been expected: the laurels of the war were to be gathered on land not on the sea. Even the war hawks, despite their cries of free trade and sailors' rights, shared Thomas Jefferson's aversion to blue water. Traditionally, Republicans had feared that a Navy would involve the United States in war; after June 1812, they feared that a Navy, hopelessly outclassed by the British, would force the country to make peace. Accordingly, while the Army was being strengthened, at least on paper, the Navy was kept on short rations: not until June 27, 1812, was $300,000 appropriated for repairing and fitting out the *Constitution, Chesapeake,* and *Adams* frigates. At the same time, three additional frigates were ordered to be completed over a three-year period. Surveyors reported that three frigates that had been laid up in drydock during the Republicans' economy drive were too rotten to be repaired. Old salts wept, but many Republicans welcomed the opportunity of saving money on a Navy which if it were foolhardy enough to tangle with the British Navy was certain to go down with all hands.

Certainly the odds seemed heavily stacked against the Americans. With 10 frigates, only 2 of which were ready to put to sea in June 1812, a few sloops, 2 brigs, and 170 gunboats, the United States Navy was opposed by a British force of 7 ships of the line, 23 frigates, and a large number of small craft. It was with this painfully obvious disparity of strength in mind that John Randolph asked rhetorically: "Shall this great mammoth of the American forest leave his native element and plunge into the water in a mad contest with the shark?"

Due in part to the sporting spirit learned by Britons on the playing fields of Eton and elsewhere, this discrepancy did not preclude a trial of strength and seamanship between single ships of the two navies. Rashly, as the event sometimes proved, the British consented to duels at sea in which a British frigate or sloop fought its counterpart from the American Navy without interference from other naval ships. Chivalry had not altogether vanished from the war at sea; the code of the duel was scrupulously observed, and many a brave lad trying to preserve the honor of his ship and his flag was sent to his sleep in the deep.

In some instances—notably in the engagement between the *Constitution* and the *Guerriere* and the *Java*—the American ship was larger and threw a heavier broadside than did its British adversary. Americans gave their frigates greater length, a wider beam, and packed more firepower aboard than the conventional frigates of the day; indeed, they more nearly resembled ships of the line.[1] Yet superior American gunnery, seamanship, and discipline also played a part. American commanders insisted on frequent target practice and offered a pound of tobacco to every gunner who hit the bull's-eye.

Despite their losses in these duels, the British came back for more—and sometimes with disastrous results for the Americans. In June 1813 Captain Broke of H.M.S. *Shannon* sent a challenge to Captain Lawrence of the *Chesapeake,* twice victorious in single-ship actions. Captain Broke meticulously observed all the punctilio that governed such affairs, and Lawrence accepted in the same spirit. The two ships kept the appointed rendezvous at sea; Captain Lawrence was mortally wounded; the *Chesapeake* was boarded by the victorious crew of the *Shannon;* the American colors were hauled down, and the Union Jack raised over the luckless American ship.

Single-ship duels, while they heightened the morale of Americans and compelled Britons seriously to qualify the opinion of a newspaper writer that the United States Navy consisted of "a piece of striped bunting flying at the masthead of a few fir-built frigates, manned by a handful of bastards and out-

---

[1]American frigates carried 44 guns compared with 38 guns aboard British frigates. During the war, the United States began the construction of ships of the line, each of which carried 74 guns.

laws," did not materially affect the outcome of the war at sea. After the first year of the war, the increasingly effective British blockade kept most of the ships of the United States Navy as well as privateers bottled up in port. A war for sailors' rights put most of them on the beach. Moreover, the Admiralty issued orders to British commanders to avoid single-ship engagements; henceforth they patrolled only in company. During 1814, only three single-ship actions occurred, all of them favorable to the Americans. The ships of the United States Navy that remained at sea carried the war to the British in every quarter of the globe. Captain Porter of the *Essex* rounded Cape Horn and for over a year pillaged British shipping and whaling ships in the South Pacific until the *Essex* was sunk off the coast of Chile. The last action of the war was fought in the East Indies on June 30, 1815, six months after the signing of the peace treaty.

Far more costly in terms of property loss to the British were the depredations committed by American privateers. During the period of the Articles of Confederation, Americans had tried to abolish privateering, but in 1812 they sent swarms of privateers to sea. During the first year of the war, these privateers captured over 500 British merchantmen; even the English Channel was not secure against their forays. All told, notwithstanding the reluctance of the Federalists to engage in privateering, the United States issued letters of marque and reprisal to 256 ships, and they took 1344 prizes. The British losses would have been even higher had not the Admiralty developed the convoy system to a high pitch of efficiency.

24.
A FAMOUS VICTORY

THE WAR IN THE NORTH

Fortunately for the United States, no sizable British reinforcements reached Canada in 1813. But in March 1814 the armies of the European allies made a triumphal entry into Paris, and on April 11, 1814, Napoleon abdicated. Great Britain could now turn its undivided military attention to the North American theater. Nearly thirteen thousand additional British troops, all seasoned veterans, were ordered to North America. Sir George Prevost was ordered to invade the United States from Niagara and Lake Champlain, and an attack was planned upon New Orleans. As a diversionary move, the British Navy was ordered to raid the cities on Chesapeake Bay. On May 3, 1814, the British blockade was extended to include the entire coast of the United States. No longer was New England a privileged sanctuary for blockade runners and an entrepôt for contraband merchandise.

An attempt to forestall the expected British attack from Canada came, as usual, to grief. In March 1814, striking out boldly for Canada, General Wilkinson at the head of four thousand men was repulsed by an outpost of two hundred men, largely French-Canadians. By June 1814, Canada was entirely cleared of American troops and the British were in possession of Fort Niagara, held naval superiority on Lake Ontario, and occupied Maine east of Penobscot. The Americans maintained their hold upon Detroit and naval control of Lake Erie. After two years of warfare, the Americans had suffered a net loss of territory in the North, and the British were in a strong position to begin a drive southward.

Until 1814, the war had taken the form of small forces of British regulars

---

"Defense of New Orleans, January 8, 1815," detail of an Oxford print, courtesy of the U.S. Army.

Large Cent, 1804.

and Canadian militiamen repelling incursions by American troops. On neither side did the civilian population respond enthusiastically to the politicians' cries for glory and heroic death. But with the entry of large numbers of British regulars into the conflict, the fighting assumed a ferocity on both sides that completely dispelled any idea that it was a comic-opera war filled with bombast and mock heroics. In July 1814, when the British, led by General Drummond, sallied from Fort Niagara to attack the American position at Fort Erie, they gained a new respect at Chippewa for the fighting qualities of American soldiers. Drilled by Generals Winfield Scott and Jacob Brown and fully baptized by fire, the Americans charged with bayonets and closed in hand-to-hand combat with the enemy. In the summer of 1814, Lundy's Lane was the scene of a particularly bloody engagement in which each side suffered over 850 casualties. The British had the advantage of numbers and position and the battle could be accounted a British victory, for the Americans left the battlefield and retired to Fort Erie. Nevertheless, Lundy's Lane proved to be one of the decisive battles of the war. It so weakened the British Army that it was unable to capture Fort Erie; and with that failure, the campaign on the Niagara frontier collapsed.

But an even greater danger threatened the Americans when Sir George Prevost at the head of thirteen thousand British troops and Indian auxiliaries marched down the shore of Lake Champlain along the historic invasion route followed by Burgoyne in 1777. Without encountering much resistance, he reached Plattsburg. But the British had learned on Lake Erie the importance of maintaining control of the waterways—hence Prevost took care not to get too far ahead of the small British flotilla on Lake Champlain. Outgunned and outmanned, the American flotilla under the command of 28-year-old Captain Thomas Macdonough, gave battle to the British squadron in Plattsburg Harbor. By wisely choosing his position, Macdonough, who had seen service in the Barbary war, forced the British to fight at a disadvantage. Both sides suffered heavy losses, but General Prevost did not choose to remain in a position that had become uncomfortably reminiscent of Burgoyne's campaign. He therefore ordered his army to return to Canada. This retreat left the British with no valid claims to American territory except part of Maine to serve as a bargaining counter at the peace table.

THE BURNING OF WASHINGTON

In 1813, Rear Admiral Sir George Cockburn sent a letter to Mrs. Madison informing her that he would shortly "make his bow" in her drawing room. This event—certainly a stunning climax to the Washington social season—President Madison was resolved at all costs to prevent. In preparation for Sir George's coming, the government ordered Fort Washington, guarding the Potomac twelve miles below the capital, to be repaired, the militia was called out, and the free blacks of the District set to work constructing earthworks. But the British baronet failed to keep his engagement with Mrs. Madison (his social calendar was filled with raiding parties upon the American coast), and Washington sank back into its accustomed lethargy.

Yet in August 1814, Sir George and his squadron made their long-deferred appearance in the Chesapeake. Captain Joshua Barney, in command of a small flotilla, tried to intercept the British fleet as it sailed up the estuary, but his ships were driven ashore. However, Barney and his men, about four hundred marines and sailors, were not eliminated as a fighting force. Without further opposition, a British army of close to four thousand seasoned veteran soldiers and one thousand marines landed near Washington where they were joined by one hundred runaway slaves. This British expeditionary force was commanded by General Robert Ross, a veteran of the Napoleonic wars. President Madison called upon the governors of Maryland and Virginia to order their militias into action, but they insisted upon retaining most of their men for home defense. As a result, the protection of the capital became the responsibility of the District militia, whose commander was General William Winder. Having conspicuously demonstrated his incapacity on the Canadian front, Winder was now in a position to rise to new heights of ineptitude.

With President Madison and several cabinet members on hand as spectators, the two armies made contact at Bladensburg, a small village near Washington, where the British army, fifteen hundred strong, found its way barred by about seven thousand militiamen entrenched behind earthworks. After a perfunctory resistance, the American militia broke and fled, carrying with them the President, cabinet members, and General Winder. Only Captain Barney and his Four Hundred stood their ground but they, too, were forced to abandon the field. Altogether, the engagement lasted only about half an hour, but the British suffered 256 casualties, mostly inflicted by Captain Barney's sailors and marines.

While the Americans were being routed at Bladensburg, Dolley Madison was working feverishly in the President's House to save the silver, dishes, cabinet papers, paintings, and other valuables. Deserted by the one hundred men who had been stationed to guard the President's House and without the wagons she had counted upon, she was aided by several Negro slaves, one of whom offered to lay a train of powder with which to blow up the enemy when they entered the premises. "To this proposition," Mrs. Madison later said, "I positively objected, without being able, however, to make him understand why all advantages in war may not be taken." Not until the British were two hours away did Mrs. Madison, momentarily expecting the arrival of the President, consent to leave—but she took with her Gilbert Stuart's portrait of George Washington. She rode through Georgetown accompanied by only one officer with a drawn sword.

Late that afternoon, the British marched unopposed into Washington. At the President's House, they found the table prepared for Mr. and Mrs. Madison. Admiral Cockburn took as souvenirs an old *chapeau de bras* of the President and a cushion from Mrs. Madison's chair. Then the British commanders, ostensibly in retaliation for the American burning of York (although they had already retaliated in kind by burning Buffalo in December 1813), ordered that the President's House and all other public buildings in Washington be put to the torch. The Library of Congress made a particularly brilliant display as it went up in flames. Only one building, the Patent Office, was spared —apparently because Dr. Thornton, the Superintendent of Patents, warned a British major that the destruction of the Patent Office would be a crime against civilization comparable to the burning of the library at Alexandria— "for which," said Dr. Thornton, "the Turks have been ever since condemned by all enlightened nations."[1] The office of the *National Intelligencer* was wrecked and its latest edition consigned to the flames.

During this night's and the next day's work, the British troops were under strict discipline: no private houses were burned and no citizens molested. Most of the looting that took place was done by Americans. Still, had not a rainstorm providentially occurred, most of the city might have been destroyed by fire.

Four days after the burning of Washington, a British squadron sailed up the Potomac past Fort Washington. The American commander blew up the fort when he sighted the British squadron. (He was later court-martialed for cowardice.) At Alexandria, the Americans themselves burned the naval yards, including a frigate under construction, thereby depriving the British tars of that satisfaction. The invaders returned to their ships in safety: neither at Alexandria nor Washington was a shot fired at them.

Baltimore was the next port-of-call on the British tour of the Chesapeake. But here they ran into stiffer resistance than they had any reason to expect from Americans. When Sir Peter Parker landed above Baltimore to create a diversion for the main attack, his men were driven back to their boats and Sir Peter himself was killed. Outside Baltimore itself, the Maryland militia, before they broke and fled, inflicted serious losses upon the British. Among the casualties was General Ross, killed by an American rifleman.

Still, Baltimore might have fallen had it not been for the failure of the British fleet to silence the batteries at Fort McHenry and to pass the obstructions placed by the Americans in the channel leading to the city. The battle for Fort McHenry inspired Francis Scott Key, a prisoner aboard a British ship, to write "The Star-Spangled Banner." Unaware that they had helped inadvertently to compose the American national anthem but aware that Baltimore was a very hard nut to crack, the British fleet and army withdrew.

The burning of the public buildings at Washington, even if justified as an act of reprisal, had the opposite effect of what the British intended. It tended to unite Americans in execrating "British barbarity." Everyone agreed that the British in Washington had behaved worse than had Napoleon in Moscow; and even the sparing of the Patent Office did not spare them unflattering com-

[1]Dr. Thornton's history was faulty—the much-maligned Turks had nothing to do with the burning of Alexandria, but their reputation as barbarians served the United States in good stead.

parisons with the Turks. The New England Federalists who had wished success to British arms in order to discomfit President Madison and his party, did not relish seeing British success carried to *that* length. The spectacle of the President of the United States fleeing for his life from British redcoats awakened the hitherto largely latent patriotism of the American people. Had the British returned to the Chesapeake a second time, they would have had a far warmer reception.

American patriotism was nourished by more than defeat and national humiliation. The heroic defense of Baltimore, although overshadowed by later events in New Orleans, together with Lundy's Lane and Plattsburg, restored Americans' pride in the fighting qualities of their soldiers. It was as though the spirit of the people experienced the same kind of transmutation that occurred in Washington, D.C. From the devastated city emerged the White House, so-called because it was found necessary to paint the building white to cover the effects of fire, smoke, and grime.

THE BATTLE OF NEW ORLEANS

In 1814, British strategy called for a simultaneous attack upon both the North and the South. The American republic, if the plans laid in London succeeded, would be caught in a vast pincers movement. A British army, put ashore in Louisiana, would quickly eliminate all organized opposition—like the Americans in Canada, the British in Louisiana expected to be welcomed by the French inhabitants—capture New Orleans and close the Mississippi to American shipping. The conquered territory was to be held permanently by Great Britain or used as a counter in the peace negotiations.

For this operation, the British planned to use the Spanish port of Pensacola as a base, Spain and Great Britain being allies in the European war. But Andrew Jackson upset the British plan of using the territory of Spain, with which the United States was not at war, as a privileged sanctuary for mounting an offensive against the United States. In March 1814 Jackson and his army of frontiersmen broke the power of the Creek Indians allied with Spain and armed and supplied by the British. And in November 1814 Jackson captured Pensacola. Not until the British fleet had departed the port did Jackson consent to restore Pensacola to the Spanish authorities.

Jackson's victories in East Florida did not prevent the British from launching an attack upon New Orleans. Late in December, a British fleet landed an expeditionary force of six thousand white and one thousand black Jamaican troops near the city. The army was under the command of Sir Edward Pakenham, the Duke of Wellington's son-in-law, who had served in Spain as Wellington's adjutant but who had never before commanded an army. New Orleans proved to be an unfortunate place for his first lesson, especially since his instructor was Andrew Jackson. At the beginning, however, the pupil seemed likely to give the master a few pointers in the art of war. Fearing an attack

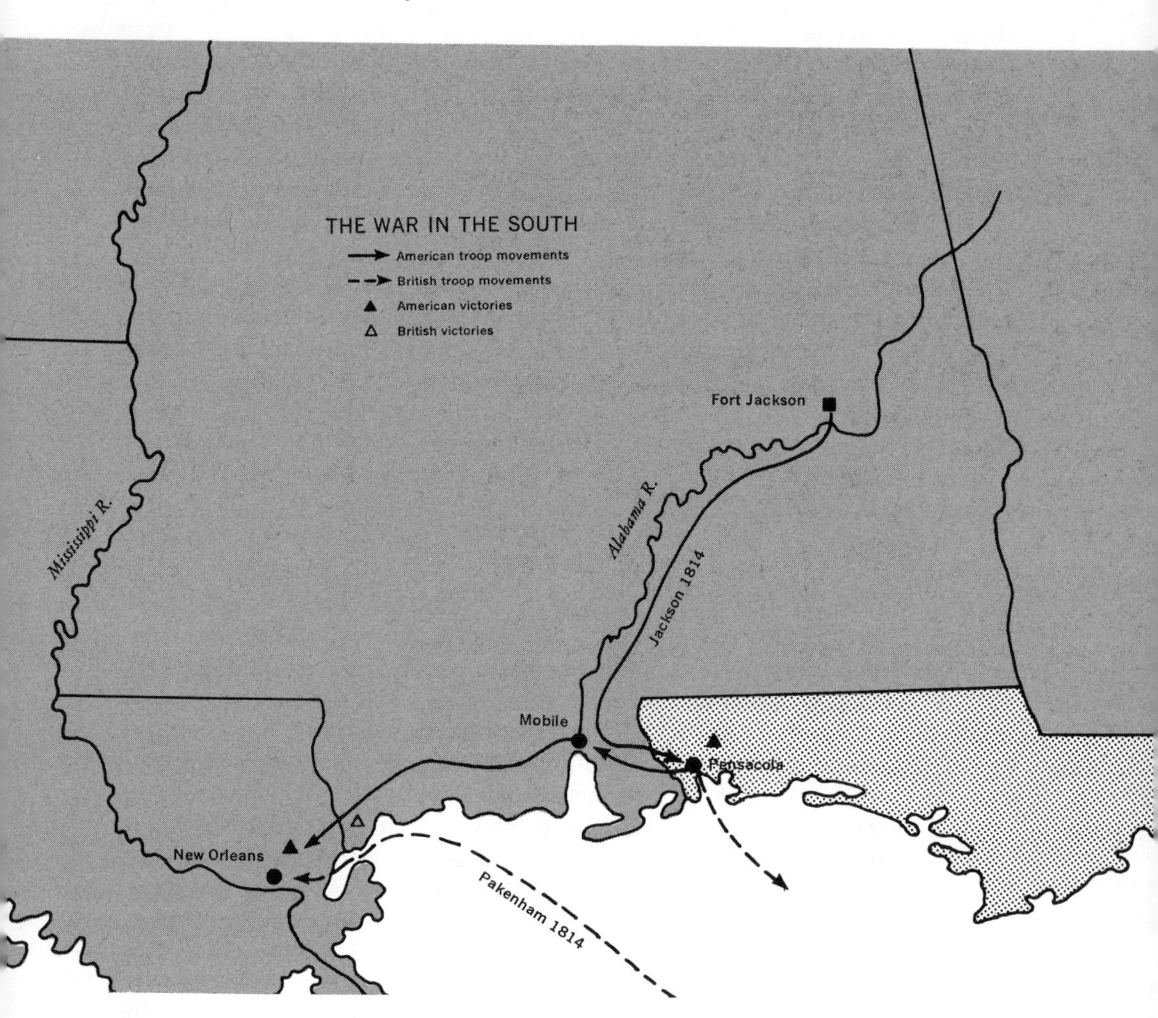

upon Mobile, Jackson had left most of his best troops to guard that city while he went on to New Orleans. As a result, Jackson was compelled to improvise an army in the face of the enemy. He recruited men from the waterfront population of New Orleans, including Lafitte and his pirates of Barataria, smugglers, sailors, and townspeople, together with a band of free Negroes, two regiments of regulars and several companies of militia, mostly Creoles. His total force numbered less than half that of the troops under Pakenham's command.

Jackson took a position behind a canal where he threw up mud breastworks reinforced by cotton bales and sugar barrels. On the right side of the river he positioned batteries manned by Kentuckians. At heavy cost, the British succeeded in capturing the batteries which, however, had been spiked by the Americans before they retreated. Having executed a successful flanking action, had the British turned their naval guns against Jackson's main position, he might have been driven from his position on the left bank of the river. Instead, after the artillery had failed to breach Jackson's line, Pakenham ordered a frontal attack by almost six thousand men against Jackson and his men. In close formation, bayonets gleaming, fifes and drums playing, and resplendent in their red uniforms, the British regulars marched across the open ground. They were met by a withering fire from American cannon and small arms. It was the American cannon, however, rather than rifle, that did the real execution in the massed ranks of British soldiers. Not even the veterans of the Napoleonic wars could stand up against such concentrated firepower; they broke ranks and retreated out of range of the American artillery.

In less than half an hour, 2600 British soldiers had been killed or wounded, among them 3 major generals and 8 colonels. Pakenham himself was killed. The Americans suffered only 13 men killed and 58 wounded.

American newspapers broke the news with such headlines as: Glorious News! Almost Incredible Victory! Unparalleled Victory! Rising Glory of the American Republic! The victory was declared to be the work of the virtuous, resourceful, and always courageous American farmer who, despite his lack of training and experience, had turned back the best the British had to offer. Jackson himself was portrayed as a simple farmer—a true Cincinatus, who, unlike the aristocratic Cincinnati whose only thought was to lord it over their countrymen, could not wait to get back to his plow.

It was a famous victory, but it had no bearing whatever upon the peace settlement. The battle was fought only because of the slowness of communications across the Atlantic. The treaty of peace had already been signed when Jackson and his men mowed down the British regulars.

The battle of New Orleans gave Americans the comforting illusion that they had won the war. A generation of English travelers in the United States was forced to listen to American boasting about New Orleans which, together with tobacco-chewing and spitting, was accounted one of the worst trials faced by visitors to the states.

THE HARTFORD CONVENTION

The ill success of the war redounded to the advantage of the Federalist party. In the elections of 1814, Federalists carried forty-three out of forty-five New England congressional districts. Apparently all the Federalists had to do was to allow the Republicans to encompass their own political ruin by protracting an increasingly unpopular and futile war. But to a small group of Federalist leaders, New England's plight did not admit of a political remedy; having long calculated the value of the Union, they had now come to the conclusion that it was worthless.

While the extension of the British blockade to New England in April 1814 injured New England commercially—the Yankees were now in the same boat with the rest of the country—the extremists' grievances were political rather than economic. Primarily they were in revolt against the shift in political power that had occurred since 1800. Certainly the rule of Madison and the war hawks was no less insupportable to many New Englanders than was the "rule of witches" to Thomas Jefferson in 1798-1799. The war brought to the surface all the discontents, jealousies, and animosities that had been rankling New Englanders for many years: the three-fifths rule; the succession of Virginia-born presidents; the Louisiana Purchase and the admission of Louisiana as a state; the "jealousy and hatred of commerce" manifested by the government in Washington; a war for free trade and sailors' rights that compelled Americans to abandon the sea and to forego all the profits derived from commerce. It seemed to Josiah Quincy of Boston that "the slave-holders' power bestrode the Union as the Old Man of the Sea did the shoulders of Sinbad the Sailor." To Quincy, Timothy Pickering, John Lowell, and others, the break-up of the Union was the only way to cast off the incubus of southern power.

The idea of a solemn convocation of delegates from the New England states for the purpose of issuing an ordinance of secession was originally advocated by Pickering and his fellow extremists. But by the summer of 1814 they had come to distrust such a convention for the sufficient reason that it seemed likely to fall under the control of moderates. As for the moderates themselves—chief among whom were George Cabot and Harrison Gray Otis —a convention appeared to be the surest means of heading off a secessionist plot. New England, they admitted, had grievances that must be redressed— but within the Union. The majority of people wanted an honorable peace with Great Britain, and it seemed necessary to prod the government into accelerating negotiations with the enemy. A convention therefore had the merit of being the constitutional and peaceable way of registering New England's objections to the war and of asserting its right of dissociating itself from the war.

When the convention assembled in Hartford on December 15, 1814—only Massachusetts, Connecticut, and Rhode Island were represented—it was clear that the fire-eaters were in a minority. Under the leadership of George Cabot and Harrison Gray Otis, an orator of such persuasive powers that it was said that "if it had pleased him, at the end of one of his speeches, to give a hurrah, and call on the people to follow him to burn the town, they would have done it," the convention adopted a series of resolutions intended to become amendments to the Constitution. These amendments would have abolished the three-fifths rule; confined officeholding to native-born citizens; limited the presidency to one term; and required a two-thirds vote in both houses of Congress to admit new states, to impose restrictions on commerce, or to declare war. The Hartford Address concluded by appealing to southerners to unite with northerners against the ambition and insatiable land-hunger of the West which promised to keep the United States perpetually embroiled in wars in which the older sections of the Union had no real concern.

Anticlimactic as was the Report, it did afford some measure of satisfaction to the radicals. If the Constitution were not revised and if it should appear that the causes of New England's ills were deep and permanent, a separation by equitable arrangement might have to be considered. In the meantime, however, the Report cautioned against precipitate action.

Early in January 1815 the Massachusetts legislature, after approving the proceedings of the convention, appointed three commissioners to go to Washington to press for the adoption of the recommended constitutional amendments. They reached Washington to be greeted by the news that peace had been made and a great victory had been won at New Orleans. The commissioners folded their tents and silently stole away to New England. But nothing could undo the damage the Federalist party inflicted upon itself at Hartford; in the hour of the republic's trial, the party leaders had thought not of how they might serve their country but of how they might convert the republic's distress into sectional advantage.

25.
THE PEACE OF CHRISTMAS EVE

THE TREATY OF GHENT

In the autumn of 1812, with Napoleon's Grand Army advancing upon Moscow, Czar Alexander I offered to mediate in the war between the United States and Great Britain. Fighting for the independence of his country, Alexander perceived a truth against which American Republicans resolutely shut their eyes: that the Anglo-American war, regardless of the Madison administration's intent, aided Napoleon's efforts to subjugate the European continent. In February 1813, President Madison accepted the Czar's offer and appointed Albert Gallatin as minister to St. Petersburg. But in making this move toward peace, President Madison did not yield an iota of the United States war aims: Gallatin was instructed to demand that the British renounce all claim of right to impressment: "if this encroachment of Great Britain is not provided against," said the President, "the United States has applied to arms in vain . . . Our flag must protect the crew or the United States cannot consider themselves an independent nation." But Gallatin had no chance to argue the American case: without closing the door on direct negotiations, the British government rejected the Czar's offer of mediation.

In the late spring of 1814, having received assurances from the British government that it was disposed to negotiate, President Madison appointed five members of a commission—the most important members of which were Henry Clay, John Quincy Adams, and Albert Gallatin—to conduct negotia-

---

"Signing the Treaty of Ghent, December 24, 1814," detail of a painting by A. Forester from The Bettmann Archive.

Half Dollar, 1805.

tions with their British counterparts at Ghent. When the British emissaries finally arrived at Ghent, it was clear that they came not to bargain but to deliver ultimata. As a *sine qua non,* they demanded the creation of an Indian state—an area comprising about one third of the territory of the United States which was to remain forever as a hunting ground for about twenty thousand Indians. They demanded a rectification of the United States-Canadian boundary that would have sliced off northern Maine, and the United States was told that it must renounce the right to fortify and maintain a naval force on the Great Lakes while Great Britain reserved its full rights; that the United States no longer had any rights in the Newfoundland fishery; and that New Orleans must be ceded to Great Britain. (The British peacemakers supposed that New Orleans was at this time securely in the hands of the British army.)

To the stunned American representatives, the British "peace offer" resembled the terms dictated by a victor to a vanquished nation. Henry Clay, an experienced gambler (on several occasions, John Quincy Adams, going down to breakfast, heard a card party breaking up in Clay's rooms), thought that the British were bluffing, but seeing no high cards in his own hand he did not venture to call.

Placed on the defensive from the beginning, the American commissioners made few demands of their own. In an accession of extravagant optimism, Secretary of State James Monroe instructed the peacemakers to demand the cession of Canada, but, after a perfunctory observance of the Secretary's directive, that subject was dropped from the agenda. In June 1814, neatly reversing himself on the issue over which the war had been fought, President Madison authorized the commissioners to omit any reference to impressment in the peace treaty "if found indispensably necessary to terminate the war." The way was thereby cleared for negotiations—provided that the British really wanted peace.

As Clay suspected, the British were putting forward demands which could be sustained only in the event of decisive victories in North America. Instead, news arrived of British defeats and retreats in the North. Nor did the Duke of Wellington give the Ministry any comfort: until naval command of the Great Lakes had been secured, he declined to assume command of the British forces in North America, and he bluntly told the cabinet that in the existing posture of affairs, it had no right to demand the cession of any territory from the United States. The Congress of Vienna, summoned to redraw the map of Europe after Napoleon's downfall, required the undivided attention of the British government. For these reasons, without waiting for the outcome of the expedition against New Orleans, the ministry dropped most of the demands with which it had opened the peace talks. With that change of front, the peace negotiations finally got under way.

In the bargaining that followed, the British agreed to restore the prewar boundaries of the United States and Canada even though this necessitated evacuating part of Maine. Other boundary questions were referred to four boundary commissions, and the conflicting claims of the United States and

Great Britain to the Oregon territory were left for later discussion. In effect, these agreements gave the United States time to consolidate its position upon the North American continent—and time was all the republic needed.

But in the give and take of these negotiations, the giving was not wholly done by one side. The American commissioners were unable to write into the treaty any of the objectives for which the United States had gone to war. No mention was made of impressment, freedom of the seas, blockades, or compensation for seizures under the Orders in Council. On the other hand, the Indian buffer state was watered down to a mere promise on the part of the United States to restore to Tecumseh's warriors their tribal lands. Since most of Tecumseh's warriors had gone to a happy hunting ground beyond the jurisdiction of the United States government, the problem of what to do with the Indians hardly seemed important enough to be included in the treaty of peace. In fact, the Indians were the only losers by the war. No longer assured of British protection, firearms, and supplies and decimated by the war itself, the aborigines were left to the mercy of the white Americans.

On Christmas Eve 1814, five months after the British and American commissioners had first sat down together, the treaty of peace was signed.

The glory of the War of 1812 was concentrated in a few battles and single-ship engagements; no trace appeared in the treaty of peace. Henry Clay, who signed it, said that it was "a damned bad treaty." It contained neither indemnity for the past nor security for the future. Because the treaty was silent upon the subjects of impressment or freedom of the seas, Thomas Jefferson considered it to be a mere truce in a struggle between the United States and Great Britain which, he said, might end in the "extermination of the one or the other party."

A NATIONAL SPIRIT

Yet, happily, this dire event did not occur. Although the British did not renounce the right to impressment, they never again found occasion for its use. After 1815, prejudice, resentment, and animosity did not disappear upon either side of the Atlantic but powerful countervailing forces began to make their influence felt. Americans believed that they had made good their independence by waging this second war with Great Britain, and many Britons accepted the result as marking a decisive change in the relations between the two countries. Eight years after the peace of Ghent, a British Foreign Secretary proposed a virtual alliance between his country and the United States for the defense of the western hemisphere. Blood did prove thicker than water, but it required the shedding of blood to make it so: over 2200 Americans died in battle during the War of 1812.

The ending of the war in Europe in 1815 left the American people free to turn their energies to the internal development of their country. For almost the first time since Independence they were liberated not only from the foreign entanglements but from the foreign sympathies that had divided and weakened the nation. Moreover, the causes of friction between the United States as a neutral and the European powers as belligerents which had inexorably drawn the United States into the affairs of Europe ceased to operate after 1815. As a result, the attitude toward Europe that President Washington had urged upon his countrymen in his Farewell Address became at last a reality.

But the most important effects of the second war of independence lay in the realm of the spirit. National feeling won an ascendancy that was not impaired until the great controversy over sectional power and slavery. In a war marked by defeat quite as much as by victory, Americans gained a new sense of self-confidence, self-sufficiency, and national purpose. The cardinal objective of the war hawks—"the reestablishment of the national character"—was achieved even beyond their expectations. A French observer, Edouard de Montulé, thought that Americans' boundless faith in themselves and their destiny helped explain the rapidity of the rise of the United States: the certainty that they were the greatest people in the world animated them to attain that exalted station. "The Romans too had this pride," observed de Montulé; "it made them and kept them for a long time the masters of the world."

26. THE UNITED STATES: 1783–1815 THE SOCIAL SCENE

RELIGION IN AMERICA

The Age of Reason, in which the American republic was born, was distinguished by its skeptical attitude toward revealed religion. Eighteenth-century intellectuals broke with orthodox Christianity and embraced Deism, a form of religion that emphasized reason rather than emotion, the goodness rather than the depravity of man, and found the essence of the Deity in benevolence, rationality, and good will toward men.

Most of the Founding Fathers, even when they were church members, were tinctured by the Deistic teachings that had infiltrated the churches. In their company, a religious bigot would have cut a singular and unsympathetic figure. Religious toleration came comparatively easy to them; almost the only things they found intolerable were intolerant fanaticism and religious "enthusiasm."

Even in the churches, intolerance and enthusiasm could not hold their ground against the pervasive rationality of the age. In many denominations, the Church Militant was in the process of being the Church Recumbent. Religion was growing increasingly secular in tone; sermons dealt with morality more than with old-fashioned theology. Clergymen tended to become mild-mannered, humane, and diffident toward their congregations: "if their con-

---

"Fourth of July in Center Square," detail of a painting by J. L. Krimmel, courtesy of The Pennsylvania Academy of the Fine Arts.

Half Cent, 1809.

duct were otherwise," said Rochefoucault-Liancourt, "their parishioners would change them just as readily as withdraw their employment from a shoemaker, should he make bad shoes."

In Virginia, Thomas Jefferson and James Madison, with the aid of Presbyterians, Baptists, and liberal Episcopalians, succeeded in 1785 in disestablishing the Church of England—a procedure that was followed in all the southern states and the four lower counties of New York where the church had been established during the colonial period. In Connecticut and Massachusetts the established Congregational churches survived the Revolution but with their privileges curtailed. Full freedom of conscience, however, prevailed only in New York, Virginia, Delaware, Kentucky, Georgia, and Louisiana; in all the other states, the exercise of such civil rights as voting and officeholding was denied non-Christians.

Alone among the important countries of the West, the United States did not have an official religion. In part, this circumstance was owing to the large number of denominations that existed in the United States, no one of which was able to gain sufficient ascendancy to impose its will upon the others. In 1815, a Philadelphian could take his choice of forty-two different denominations, each of which conducted services in the City of Brotherly Love. Not to belong to one of these churches argued a degree of finicalness as to almost warrant the suspicion of atheism. Nor was Roman Catholicism—the "Whore of Babylon" of the Puritans—excepted from this dispensation. Under the bishopric of the Reverend John Carroll, the Roman Catholic Church became an active force in American life. Yet, even though there were about 100,000 Roman Catholics in the United States, when the first Roman Catholic church was consecrated in Boston in 1803 there were so few Catholics present that the church was half-filled with Protestants.

President Washington, portrayed by Parson Weems as a paragon of piety and a pillar of orthodoxy, actually shared the secular, utilitarian, and tolerant attitude toward religion of most of the leaders of the American Revolution. As President, he issued only two proclamations calling upon the people to render thanks to the Almighty for their blessings. (He was inclined to attribute American prosperity to the effects of the European war.) In 1795, he urged that thanks be given to the "Great Ruler of Nations," and in the Farewell Address he declared that "reason and experience both forbid us to expect that national morality can prevail in the exclusion of religious principles" but he assigned no priority to any particular kind of religion. Nor did he believe that the "Great Ruler of Nations" was exclusively concerned with the welfare of Christian nations: indeed, addressing himself to the Barbary powers, the President pointed out that the United States was not in any sense founded upon the Christian religion. President Jefferson was even more chary of connecting the government with religion: he refused to recommend that his countrymen observe a day of fasting and prayer lest he seem to countenance the idea that the United States government claimed authority over religious exercises.

Orthodoxy was challenged even in its citadel, the American colleges. Some college students, emboldened by liberalism that had crept into those institutions, moved from Deism to agnosticism and even to atheism. During the 1790's, students at Yale addressed each other as Voltaire, Rousseau, D'Alembert, etc. A worried Harvard professor declared that "some of the more sprightly and free-thinking geniuses of America" seemed in danger of succumbing to atheism. At Princeton a group of undergraduates burned the Bible, and, in 1802, when Nassau Hall went up in flames, the President attributed the event to "the progress of vice and irreligion."

But it was soon apparent that the backsliding was not confined to the student body: even some of the professors showed an indulgence toward "error" that marked them, in the eyes of straight-laced conservatives, as the disciples of French freethinkers. In 1808, alarmed by the growing laxness and deviationism at Harvard, conservatives founded Andover Theological Institute to save orthodox Calvinism from liberals. But the monolithic doctrinal front of Congregationalism had long since been shattered by Deism, Arminianism, and Unitarianism. The defenders of the old ways and the old dogmas discovered that the enemy was in their midst.

Religion pitched in the key of sweet reasonableness did not satisfy the emotional hunger of the people. Within their range of experience, the idea of a Deity imbued with good will toward men seemed contrary to the facts of life. To them, Deism was a religion for dehydrated intellectuals and the arrived, not for those who sought God in ecstasy and felt in anticipation the flames of Hell fire. The Enlightenment had completely eliminated Hell and cast doubt upon the reality of Heaven; now, it was felt by many, these places had to be restored to the center of mens' consciousness and refurbished according to the specifications laid down by John Calvin.

These ingredients were provided not by American intellectuals—least of all by President Jefferson—but by revivalists. Beginning in Kentucky in 1800, revivalism began to sweep the American West. The gospel was carried by itinerant preachers, many of them unordained, who acted upon the belief that feeling—the more intense the better—was the key to salvation. At the large open-air camp meetings where the faithful assembled to seek the Lord, the preachers pounded the Bible and conducted themselves, as Abraham Lincoln later observed, as though they were fighting a swarm of bees. Upon their audiences, the effect of this hot gospeling was electrifying: men, women, and children shrieked, frothed, groveled, jerked, and prostrated themselves in the dust as the Spirit moved them.

The four-square gospel, as preached by the revivalists, restored the sense of immediacy of Heaven and Hell. But the Open Book from which they drew inspiration provided an Open Road to salvation: Heaven was portrayed not as an exclusive residence for Saints, as the early Puritans had imagined, but a crowded, bustling place in which all who had accepted Christ and repented of their sins were sure of accommodations. If man was totally depraved and wholly incapable of doing good, as the revivalists depicted him, his sinful nature could always be regenerated by coming to the Lord. Thus was American religion democratized even before the doctrine of equality and natural rights had fully democratized American politics.

Methodist and Baptist churches profited most from this outpouring of the spirit. Both churches were already active in the areas where the revival had its greatest impact: both were frontier churches equipped with lay preachers, circuit riders, and proselytizing zeal. American Methodism, ultimately the most numerous and powerful of the American Protestant denominations, was an offshoot of the Church of England that owed its success to the thoroughness with which it adapted itself to American conditions. In this work, the moving spirit was Francis Asbury, the first of the Methodist episcopate—a bishop with a stipend of $80 a year, who was constantly on the road seeking converts and who took the world for his parish.

Among the most important social effects of the labors of Asbury and other itinerant preachers was the impetus they gave to the establishment of order, morality, and self-discipline among frontiersmen. That westerners did not become the "white savages" that haunted the imagination of John Jay was owing in part to the countervailing civilizing forces embodied by the frontier churches.

THE AMERICAN WAY OF LIFE

If, as Thomas Jefferson said, farmers were the chosen people of God, the United States was indeed blessed in that particular. As yet, there was no exodus from the farms to the cities; rapid as was the growth of the cities, they failed to keep pace with the growth of the farming areas. As a result, the rural character of America tended to become more pronounced. In 1810, of seven million Americans only about 6 percent lived in towns of over 5000 inhabitants. New York City, with a population of 96,373, was the largest city in the United States, closely followed by Philadelphia with 92,247. The most rapid rate of growth was registered by Baltimore. Before the Revolution it had consisted of a few houses; by 1810 it contained 13,000 more inhabitants than Boston. Its prosperity was owing to its position as a center for the export of wheat and tobacco and to the dredging of the harbor in 1794 with large machines worked by oxen. As for Boston, lacking a navigable river connecting it with the West, it appeared doomed to suffer commercial stagnation.

Before the advent of rail transportation, navigable water was the first requirement for a city. In this age of water transport, roads rarely made a city, nor could an eastern seaport that lacked water communication with the West hope to partake fully in the general prosperity. Lancaster, Pennsylvania, was the only large inland town without any kind of navigation whatever: it owed its importance to its manufactures and to turnpikes which made it a distributing center.

In manufacturing, a definite regional pattern was beginning to emerge. In

New England, where water power, capital, and skilled labor were comparatively plentiful, cotton factories sprang up in the old maritime centers; by 1815, Pawtucket, Rhode Island, had thirteen cotton factories. Twenty-five textile factories employing nearly twelve hundred persons were in operation in Connecticut. Shoes were turned out by the thousands at Lynn, Massachusetts. Although Paterson, New Jersey, which enjoyed both water power and access to the sea, failed to become the great manufacturing center envisaged by Alexander Hamilton, a few cotton mills survived the depression that descended upon the place after 1795. Rifles were the specialty of Lancaster, Pennsylvania, and Harper's Ferry, Maryland. As early as 1817, citizens of Pittsburgh were complaining that smoke blackened the houses and gave the town a gloomy appearance, and in 1810 an English visitor to Richmond, Virginia, was oppressed by the cloud of smoke hanging over the city, reminiscent of an English coal mining town. On the Brandywine River in Delaware, Du Pont de Nemours established a powder works, a paper mill, and a cluster of textile factories.

New York City, with a large population of English, French, Dutch, Irish, Jews, Germans, and Negroes, preserved the cosmopolitan appearance it had possessed since its founding as New Amsterdam by the Dutch. Broadway was the favorite promenade of dandies and fashionable women, yet as late as 1804, a traveler encountered "two Indian young men, with each a bow and arrow in his hand, tripping nimbly along, like two wild animals yet unbroken to the yoke." Wall Street, already the headquarters of banks, insurance firms, and brokerage houses, was crowded with foot traffic and carriages; everyone, it was observed, seemed to be in a hurry. Already, by early afternoon, many businessmen were slightly under the influence of liquor—a condition described as "half and half." It was the climate and the pace of life, they said, that necessitated this frequent use of alcoholic refreshment.

The water supply in New York provided another compelling argument for resorting to bottled beverages. The Manhattan Company, organized in 1800, provided water pumped by a steam engine but it was so brackish that it was usually mixed with a little brandy to make it potable.[1] After the body of a young woman was found mysteriously drowned in the Manhattan Company's well, topers were given an even more plausible reason for not drinking the stuff.

Washington, the new capital of the United States, was a city of magnificent distances and vast open spaces. It was possible to ride for miles within the District of Columbia without seeing a single person; much of the terrain was as wild as Kentucky. Pennsylvania Avenue and Capitol Hill afforded excellent snipe shooting, but hunters were advised to keep a sharp watch for the cows that grazed along the city streets, most of which were designated only by a sign. Grass grew in the streets and everyone rejoiced because it was so much better than the mud or dust that usually plagued pedestrians. In June 1800,

---

[1]In his will, Benjamin Franklin bequeathed one thousand pounds to Boston and Philadelphia for the purpose of constructing aqueducts to bring water to the inhabitants of these cities.

Mrs. John Adams lost her way in the forest and marshes that surrounded the city. Yet she escaped a more serious hazard: those who undertook to explore the grounds of the President's House were warned that they might "perchance, fall into a pit, or stumble over a heap of rubbish." A story made the rounds that some visitors, after viewing the state buildings expressed a wish to see the city while they were standing in its very center.

Citizens with a fastidious sense of smell were well advised to stay off the streets of American cities. All refuse was thrown into the streets and pigs and hogs were entrusted with the work of garbage disposal. Sometimes they tripped up promenaders on Broadway, attacked little children, and contributed to the spread of cholera, but the use of these worthy animals as scavengers and as food outweighed their disadvantages. Pork was the poor man's meat, and most of the hogs that roamed the streets of the metropolis were owned by free Negroes.

Although the hogs kept the law officers busy, there was comparatively little crime to occupy their attention. New York had few robberies or murders, a circumstance that was attributed to police efficiency, full employment, and the pervasive influence of republican "virtue."

Of course, the evidences of republican morality were less apparent in the slums and waterfront dives of eastern cities, in the lusty, brawling life of the frontier communities, and in large areas of the South where the frontier spirit remained ascendant. The South presented the spectacle of a society consciously imitative, at its highest levels, of the English squirearchy, existing sometimes in intimate juxtaposition to a community not far removed in its manners and way of life from the wilderness stage. In part, the relative backwardness of a large segment of southern white society was due to disease induced by dietary deficiencies, but to contemporaries it seemed to confirm the theory that human beings degenerated as a result of a too indulgent climate and too easy conditions of life.

In the United States, progress was regarded not as a theory but as an incontestable fact. It was exemplified by the unparalleled rapidity with which Americans increased their numbers, conquered the wilderness, eliminated the aborigines, built cities, forged ahead with manufacturing, and filled the seas with their ships and, in the process, attained the highest standard of living in the world. In terms of physical growth and the production of wealth, the United States had achieved a success unparalleled in history. No country more effectively refuted the theory that man was born in a certain station from which he never rose. Americans unremittingly devoted their efforts to getting ahead in the world, and they were, in general, well rewarded. As Americans saw it, the United States was a self-made country consisting of self-made individuals. Everyone attributed his success, under Providence, to his own skill and hard work. The ease of making a living—a workman could support his family by working three days a week—did not create a leisured society. On the contrary, the hustle and preoccupation with moneymaking seemed to

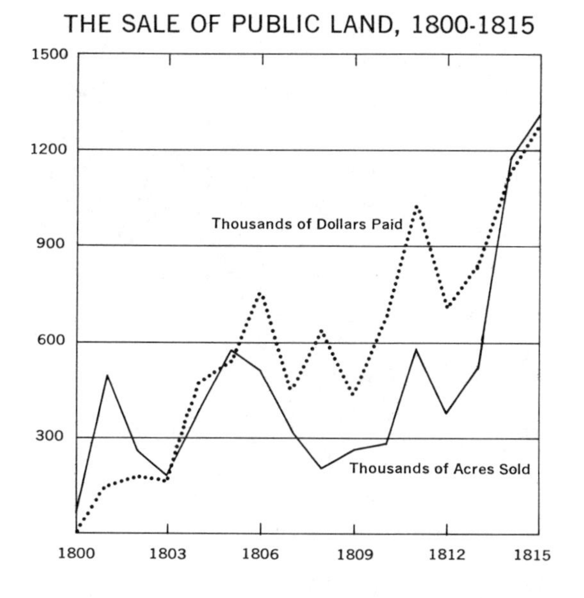

By 1795 Jay's treaty, Pinckney's Treaty, and the Treaty of Grenville had cleared the way for the rapid settlement of the Appalachian Plateau. Speculators' advertisements and new roads tempted thousands of people to leave the seaboard states because of overcrowding, poor soil, or encroaching plantations. *Source: Historical Statistics of the United States.*

increase in ratio to the affluence and opportunities for leisure of the American male.

Ohio, which before the Revolution had not contained a single white inhabitant, by the early 1800's was being converted into an annex of Connecticut, then the most thickly populated state in the Union. Every year, ten thousand or more Connecticut Yankees packed their families, household furniture, and farming utensils into a wagon, shouldered their axes, whistled Yankee Doodle and set off for the wilderness. To them, however, it was not the wilderness but the Promised Land.

Even Daniel Boone had difficulty in keeping ahead of the torrent of pioneers that poured into Kentucky and beyond. In 1775, he had settled on the site of Boonesboro, Kentucky, but 25 years later Kentucky had a population of about 200,000 and Boone was complaining of overcrowding and the scarcity of game. By 1815, Boone had reached the Missouri, but by this time it was clear that no matter how far west Boone traveled he never could be sure of enjoying the kind of solitude he sought. If he lived long enough, it was predicted, he would eventually reach the mouth of the Columbia "and there, perhaps, sit down, like another Alexander of Macedon and weep, because there are no more worlds to settle."

For many citizens of the republic, the American dream would seem to have been converted into a substantial reality. But an ambitious, ever-striving people could not find contentment in a country where so much remained to

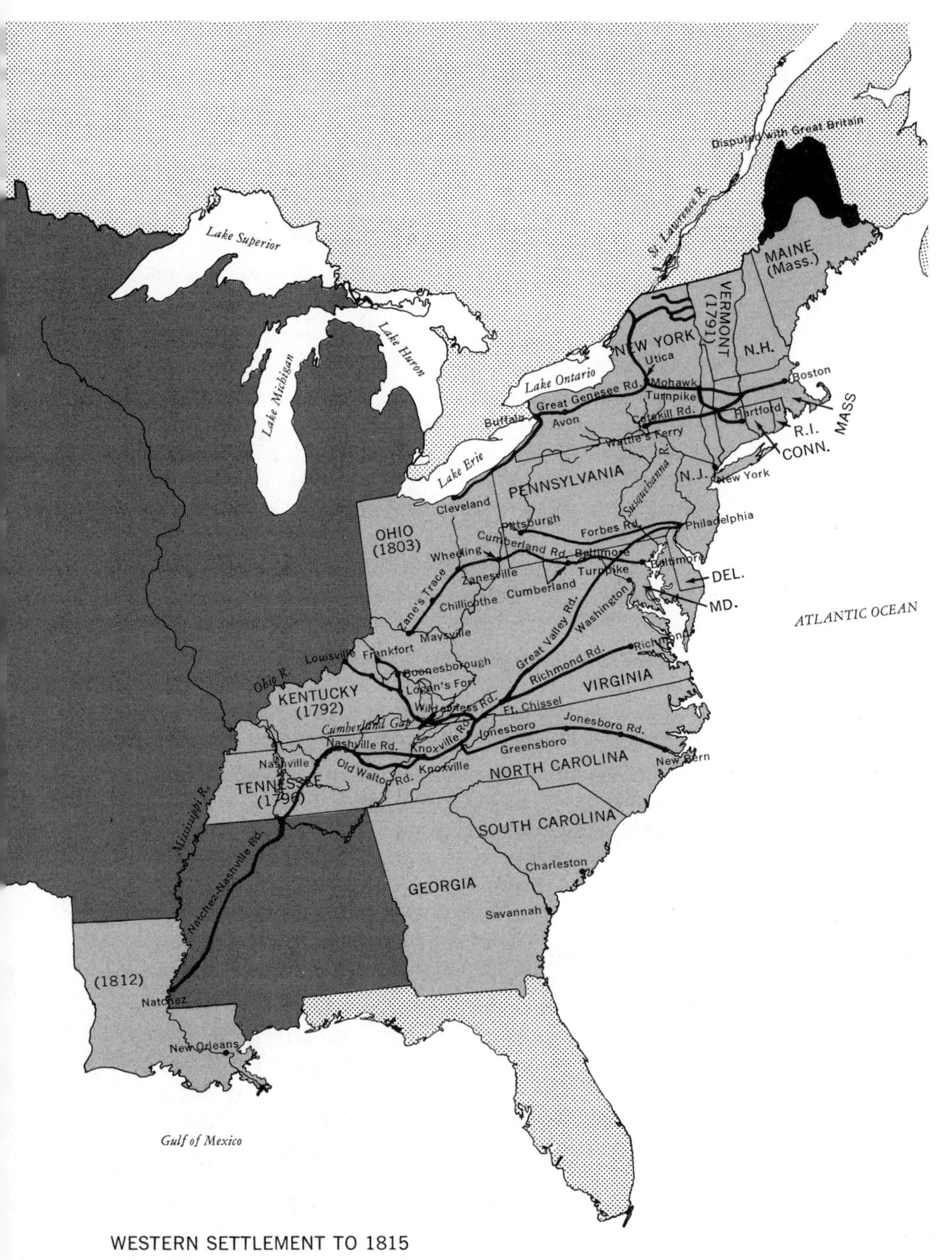
Disputed with Great Britain
Lake Superior
St. Lawrence R.
MAINE (Mass.)
VERMONT (1791)
N.H.
NEW YORK
Lake Huron
Lake Michigan
Lake Ontario
Utica
Mohawk
Turnpike
Boston
Great Genesee Rd.
Catskill Rd.
Hartford
MASS
R.I.
CONN.
Buffalo
Avon
Wattle's Ferry
Lake Erie
PENNSYLVANIA
N.J.
New York
Susquehanna R.
Cleveland
OHIO (1803)
Pittsburgh
Forbes Rd.
Philadelphia
Wheeling
Cumberland Rd.
Baltimore
Turnpike
Baltimore
DEL.
Zanesville
Zane's Trace
Chillicothe
Cumberland
Washington
MD.
ATLANTIC OCEAN
Great Valley Rd.
Maysville
Louisville
Frankfort
Richmond
Boonesborough
Richmond Rd.
Ohio R.
Logan's Fort
VIRGINIA
KENTUCKY (1792)
Wilderness Rd.
Ft. Chissel
Cumberland Gap
Jonesboro
Jonesboro Rd.
Nashville Rd.
Knoxville Rd.
Greensboro
Nashville
Old Walton Rd.
Knoxville
NORTH CAROLINA
New Bern
TENNESSEE (1796)
Mississippi R.
SOUTH CAROLINA
Natchez-Nashville Rd.
Charleston
GEORGIA
Savannah
(1812)
Natchez
New Orleans
Gulf of Mexico
WESTERN SETTLEMENT TO 1815
The United States in 1815
Territories of the United States
Areas disputed with foreign powers

be done and where the prospects opened up by individual enterprise seemed illimitable. Precisely because the future seemed to have so many good things in store, Americans tended to live in the future—like Thomas Jefferson, they "loved to dream." They were eager to hasten the future because it had never disappointed them.

The characteristics usually considered distinctively American—restlessness, optimism, rootlessness, preoccupation with moneymaking, willingness to "try anything once" and to take long chances—were the result of the interaction of the enterprising and adventurous kind of people who were drawn to the New World and a unique environment provided by a continent awaiting the vivifying touch of the pioneer, the farmer, and the businessman. In contrast to the relatively immobile European peasantry, Americans readily pulled up stakes and began life anew in some distant locality, usually to the west. It was observed that alone of all peoples, Americans had added rockers to their chairs because they could not sit still. The qualities essential to survival in raw frontier communities—resourcefulness, ingenuity, and hardihood—likewise left an imprint upon the American character. Not only frontiersmen exhibited these characteristics: Captain Basil Hall observed that American businessmen were "a people of shifts and expedients, always accommodating themselves to circumstances, never losing their confidence, but ever ready to try something else, after a failure in one thing." The American businessman had to learn how to land on his feet: bankruptcy, usually resulting from eagerness to get rich quickly, was a common occurrence. While little social stigma was attached to bankruptcy—it was considered an acceptable way of making a fresh start—it often led to imprisonment for debt. Some of the best-known businessmen of the day, including Robert Morris, spent long terms behind bars. It was not until the enactment of the Bankruptcy Act of 1800 and the easing by the states of the penalties attached to involuntary default that the spectre of imprisonment for debt was finally laid—only to be revived by the penalties for nonpayment of alimony.

Americans were a nation of speculators with a "rage for property." The building of the country was a vast speculation that, like most speculations in America, paid off. Farmers did not prosper merely or perhaps even principally by growing crops but by buying land cheap, developing it, and selling it at a higher price. Land was a commodity that was bought and sold with almost as much facility as the crops it produced. An American rarely allowed sentimentality to interfere with a good business deal. Talleyrand conceived a deep contempt for the American character because he encountered only one man in the United States who was not willing to sell anything he possessed for a price. This unique individual refused to part with his dog.

In the early republic, the principal object of speculation was not government securities or bank stock but land. The most gigantic speculation in American history was the Yazoo scandal. In 1795, by dint of bribing every member save one of the Georgia legislature, four land companies were able to gain possession for $500,000 of 35 million acres, the area comprising almost all of the present states of Alabama and Mississippi. The next year, a newly elected legislature rescinded the contracts on the ground that they have been procured by fraud, but in the meantime the Yazoo companies had begun to sell land to private purchasers. New England, in particular, was swept by a Yazoo craze; land sold in Boston at 12 cents an acre, and hundreds of buyers invested their savings in this dubious real estate.

In 1802, Georgia ceded the territory to the United States for $1,250,000, and in 1814 the holders of Yazoo land warrants were awarded $48 million by the United States government. Everyone profited from the fraud—the speculators, Georgia, and the United States; only the Indians who were forced to cede their lands to the government as part of the settlement came off badly. And in 1810, in the case of Fletcher *v.* Peck, the United States Supreme Court, Chief Justice Marshall presiding, held that the constitutional prohibition against the impairment of the obligation of contracts applied to the Yazoo deal: the state legislature could not invalidate a grant of land made by a previous legislature even though it were obtained by fraud. The doctrine of the sanctity of contracts could hardly have been carried much farther than the Supreme Court took it in this decision.

Nor did Americans overlook the possibilities of profit in urban real estate. Thanks in large measure to his speculations in Philadelphia real estate, Benjamin Franklin died a rich man. Fortunes were made and lost in land speculation in the District of Columbia. For these operations, the credit afforded by the banks was indispensable; without a steady flow of paper money and credit from these banks, the whole land boom would have collapsed.

Even in their eating habits, Americans did not forget the adage that time is money. Dinner, observed Captain Basil Hall, was "a mere business to be got over, not a rational pleasure to be enjoyed." In New York City, a British lady reported, fifty persons sat down to dinner and fifteen minutes later every one of them had left the room. The feat was accomplished by "lifting a spoon from the potatoes and diving straight into the pudding."

Although in the travel books written by British travelers the American figured as hardly more than a moneymaking animal, the emphasis put by Americans upon getting rich was largely because it seemed to be within almost everyone's grasp. Acquiring money came under the general heading of making the most of one's opportunities, and in America to neglect one's opportunities was accounted far more reprehensible than to abuse them. Moreover, concern for moneymaking was part of the greater business of opening up the country. Love of money was not less prevalent in Europe than in America. but there was far more opportunity in America to indulge "the passion for riches." Speaking of Americans' alleged preoccupation with material things, a French traveler remarked that he would "only ask those who have judged them thus, if they have carefully examined their own countries."

Since the way to wealth in the United States lay in taking chances, betting came naturally to Americans. For Virginians, in particular, the savor of the sport consisted in the wager. Bets were placed upon virtually every game and sport: faro, dice, billiards, horse-racing, and cockfighting. The proclivity of Virginians to ruin themselves by betting caused the legislators to enact a law in 1792 prohibiting wagers at horse-races or cockfights and making it legally impossible to lose more than $20 at cards within a period of twenty-four hours. Except for the clause canceling all debts above the statutory limit, the law was ignored. As a further protection for improvident gamesters, the law forbade the seizure of land or other immovable property for payment of debts. Although slaves and movable property were subject to distraint, the law could be easily evaded by feigned transfers of ownership.

While betting on the horses was frowned upon in New England, horse-racing was the closest approximation to a national sport Americans possessed. In 1803, for example, at the races held in Washington, President Jefferson, prominent clergymen, eight hundred people on horseback, and hundreds more in carriages attended the event. Large sums of money were wagered, and a congressman was reported to have lost $700. The most popular club in the capital was the Washington Jockey Club.

AMERICAN HUMANITARIANISM

One of the dominant themes of the eighteenth-century Enlightenment was humanitarianism; for the first time in the history of western civilization, the intellectual community began to identify itself with the interests of the poor and dispossessed and to concern itself with the amelioration of their lot in this world rather than in the next.

With the growth of cities, Americans became conscious for the first time of comparatively large pockets of poverty. Paradoxically, the more prosperous the majority of citizens became, the more evidences of destitution began to appear. In 1793-1794, the influx of several thousand refugees from the black uprising in Santo Domingo swelled the number of the needy, particularly in Philadelphia and Baltimore. The havoc wrought by the yellow fever epidemics in Philadelphia and New York in 1793 and 1798, aggravated the problem of caring for the destitute. While immigration from Europe declined as a result of the Wars of the French Revolution, many German and Irish redemptioners and indentured servants who arrived in the United States during this period were in dire need of help. In 1800, the Philadelphia Alms-House contained over a thousand inmates.

Since the federal government was debarred by Jefferson's and Madison's strict constructionism from aiding the impoverished—although in the case of the Santo Domingo refugees, part of the debt owed by the United States government to France was diverted to their relief—in general, the burden of caring for the poor fell upon local government and private philanthropy. In New England, the towns had long provided such relief, but troublemakers among the poor were "warned out" of town in order to save the taxpayers money and preserve religious orthodoxy. Every large American city had a tax-supported poorhouse, almshouse, orphanage, hospital, and dispensary. Yet it was primarily the humane and benevolent spirit of private citizens that made life bearable for the poor. Charitable and philanthropic organizations abounded in American cities: in New York City alone, over thirty benevolent societies, including the Tammany Society, were functioning in 1815. The Society for the Relief of Respectable, Aged, and Indigent Females provided employment for qualified applicants; another society aided distressed seamen; while a third concerned itself with preserving the morals of young girls. St. George's Society looked after distressed Englishmen in the United States; the Hibernian Society, St. Andrews', and Shamrock Society, together with German societies aided newcomers from Ireland, Scotland, and Germany. "In America," remarked the Swedish traveler, Baron Kinkowstrom, "everyone still remembers the time when he was poor and needed help. The heart of the American has not yet shut out the cry of the needy."

Thanks in part to the existence of a solicitude so pervasive that it seemed to delight in ferreting out objects for the exercise of charity, the streets of American cities bore a very different aspect from those of Great Britain and Europe. In America, the victims of poverty were so discreetly kept out of sight that it was easy to believe that there were no poor. For example, virtually no beggars importuned passers-by in the United States; Henry Fearon, an English traveler, saw only three beggars, one of whom accosted him in the House of Representatives.

The United States was peculiarly suited to serve as the proving ground for the ideas of the Enlightenment. In this new country, where everything seemed to be in a state of flux, there were far fewer barriers than in Europe to giving concrete form to the dreams of reformers. As regards changes in the criminal code and treatment of prisoners, for example, the United States clearly assumed leadership among the nations of the western world. The ideas came from Europe—in this instance from an Italian, Cesare Beccaria, whose "Essay on Crimes and Punishments" (1767) is a landmark in the history of penology. Beccaria advocated the abolition of the death penalty on the ground that it did not deter crime (at this time, with over two hundred capital offenses, Great Britain was the most crime-ridden country in Europe) and asserted that the principal purpose of imprisonment ought to be the rehabilitation rather than the punishment of criminals.

Although British reformers, notably William Eden and John Howard, and the enlightened despots on the European continent embraced Beccaria's ideas, it remained for the United States to give them their most thoroughgoing application. Reform of the criminal code began in Virginia as early as 1776. Hard labor was substituted for capital punishment except for treason and first-degree murder. Jefferson helped design the Richmond State Prison, where, for the first time in the United States, the inmates were segregated according to crime and sex. In 1812, the last public hanging took place on the Boston Common; a crowd estimated to number ten thousand witnessed the event. Five years later a young man was hanged in South Boston in the presence of twenty thousand spectators. In 1822 public hangings were finally discontinued in Massachusetts.

By far the most far-reaching trial of the ideas of Cesare Beccaria took place in Pennsylvania. In 1785-1787, Dr. Benjamin Rush, a Philadelphia physician and one of the founders of psychiatry (he diagnosed crime as a disease of the mind) published two pamphlets in which he popularized Beccaria's ideas together with a number of his own.

Rush advocated that all public punishment be abolished; that prisoners be set to work at productive labor; that they be given a low diet, clean rooms, and religious instruction; and that solitary confinement be substituted for corporal and capital punishment. Rush had the gratification, rare among reformers, of seeing his plans put into practice during his own lifetime. Working in favor of reform was the man-power shortage in the United States which rendered Americans receptive to schemes for the speedy rehabilitation of criminals. Likewise, the religious convictions of the Quakers ran counter to the infliction of the death penalty. In 1794, accordingly, Pennsylvania abolished the death penalty except for first-degree murder. At the same time, the Walnut Street prison in Philadelphia was becoming the scene of a unique experiment in penology: Lieutenant Francis Hall, a British traveler, pronounced it to be "a more interesting object to humanity than the most gorgeous palaces." Most of all, it resembled a factory: the prisoners worked for their livelihood at trades and in the prison garden, and the goods and vegetables they produced were sold in the Philadelphia market. But incorrigible prisoners and those convicted of serious crimes enjoyed none of the amenities of the place: they were kept in solitary confinement in a six-by-eight-foot cell for periods as long as twenty years. In order that they might feel the full force of the reproaches of their conscience and the bitterness of remorse, these prisoners were not permitted to speak with any other human being except visiting clergymen. This "wise, humane treatment," as Rush described it, was expected to produce a thorough reformation—unless, as sometimes happened, the culprit went insane before the rehabilitating process was complete.

Solitary confinement became one of the features of the American system of punishment and reform. The so-called Auburn Plan put in effect at Auburn, New York, required of the inmates complete silence and hard labor. Meals were taken by the prisoners alone in their cells. The New York prisons cost about one million dollars—a far larger sum than that expended upon education.

SCIENCE AND INVENTION

During the Enlightenment, it was widely believed that the study of science would bring in its train moral improvement, a deeper understanding and appreciation of Nature's laws, and an amelioration of the conditions of life. With few exceptions, the men of the eighteenth century attached high importance to utilitarianism. The greatest American scientist of the revolutionary period,

David Rittenhouse, won distinction in astronomy, mathematics, optics and physics, but he turned his discoveries to little practical purpose: no invention came from his laboratory. Benjamin Franklin, on the other hand, was more typical of the "philosophers" (the word was applied to intellectuals in general of the Enlightenment) in his predilection for applied science. Franklin supposed that an all-wise and benevolent Providence had decreed that the discovery of scientific truths would lead to inventions designed to "increase the Power of Man over Nature, and multiply the Conveniences and Pleasures of Life." For proof of this theorem, Franklin could cite his invention of the lightning rod, which proceeded from his study of electricity, and bifocal spectacles, which resulted from his research into optics. The career of Benjamin Thompson, Count Rumford, who began life as a New England farm boy, confirmed Franklin's view that scientific research, however pure, always eventuated in some useful invention. In the course of his investigations into the nature of heat, Rumford invented the thermos bottle and the "Rumford Stove."

In the field of medicine, except for the increased attention paid to sanitation, the era was marked by the discovery of few scientific "truths" or by new methods of effectively combating disease. During the yellow fever epidemic which ravaged Philadelphia in 1793, taking the lives of almost 4000 people, Dr. Benjamin Rush believed that he had hit upon a sovereign cure not only for yellow fever but for all disease. This "cure" consisted of massive bleeding and purging, often beyond the level of tolerance. Since Dr. Rush grossly overestimated the amount of blood in the human body, his patients were fortunate to recover from his ministrations. Rush's therapy, even though it was challenged by more competent physicians, unfortunately continued to enjoy considerable vogue down to the time of the Civil War.

The greatest scientific breakthrough of the period was the discovery in the late 1790's by Dr. Jenner, an English physician, of vaccination as a preventive of smallpox. Dr. Jenner's pamphlet, *An Enquiry into the Causes and Effects of the Variolae Vaccinae,* reached Dr. Benjamin Waterhouse of Boston in 1798. Dr. Waterhouse's experiments demonstrated the superiority of vaccination over the older method of inoculation. President Jefferson, who generally distrusted doctors and their alleged cures—he said that he never saw two or more of them together without looking up to see if there was not a buzzard aloft—promoted the introduction of vaccination no less enthusiastically than he did other innovations in science and technology.

Even though the average wage scale in the United States was 25–50 percent higher than in England and 50–75 percent higher than on the European continent, most skilled British and European immigrants preferred to become farmers than to pursue their trades. The Jeffersonian version of the good life seemed to have wholly captivated the American people: almost by definition, an American was a landowner who tilled his own soil.

While men fulfilled their dream of becoming landowners, women and children worked in the textile factories. In New England about 90 percent of the hands were young girls and boys; Captain Basil Hall remarked that "an urchin, before he is an inch bigger than a cotton bobbin, is turned to some use." A sail manufactory in Boston employed fourteen young girls, "the daughters of decayed families"; no child of bad character or dubious antecedents need apply. At David Humphrey's wool factory in Connecticut, most of the labor force consisted of boys from the New York almshouse and poor boys from neighboring villages. The carpet factory in Philadelphia that supplied the Senate chambers in Philadelphia gave employment to a number of poor women and children.

Some American factory owners tried conscientiously to apply in their mills the humanitarian ideals of the Enlightenment. It did not follow, said the *Gazette of the United States* in 1792, that "because the European artificer received but a mere pittance for his labor, the American manufacturers should be a meagre, pale, starveling crew of emaciated wretches." The American solution to the problems created by industrialism was to turn the factories into finishing schools for instruction in religion and good manners as well as for turning out salable merchandise. David Humphrey's youthful employees were obliged to attend evening classes and Sunday school. In the factories established at Lowell and Waltham, Massachusetts, by Francis Cabot Lowell and other Boston financiers, boarding houses were built by the company, provision was made for religious worship, and the workers, most of whom were "well-educated and virtuous females," were expected to spend their leisure in libraries and lecture halls. On the Brandywine, the Du Ponts created a model factory town in which the workers, most of whom were Swiss and French, lived in neat company houses, tended their gardens, and sang in the company choir.

In the United States, because of the scarcity and high price of labor and the magnitude of the tasks which challenged men's ingenuity, a high premium was placed upon inventions designed to reduce labor costs. In no country was labor-saving machinery more essential to industrial expansion than in the United States. Here there was still room for the gifted amateur. Thomas Jefferson, President of the American Philosophical Society from 1807-1815, invented a plow and numerous labor-saving devices which he installed at Monticello and in the President's House in Washington. Despite his fondness for household manufactures, Jefferson, as Secretary of State and as President, helped to introduce into the United States factory machinery that made household methods obsolete. Tom Paine invented an iron bridge of a single arch (he went to France in 1787 to build bridges, not to take part in the French Revolution), a smokeless candle, and a wheel turned by successive discharges of gunpowder. By 1820, as a result of Americans' inventive genius, the Patent Office in Washington contained over two thousand models, and officials were already beginning to complain of lack of space.

In the new republic the machine was welcomed as an ally, not as an enemy that displaced workers from their jobs. From the beginning of the industrial revolution, the United States was open to new ideas and new techniques, especially if they seemed likely to save man-hours. In 1814, for example,

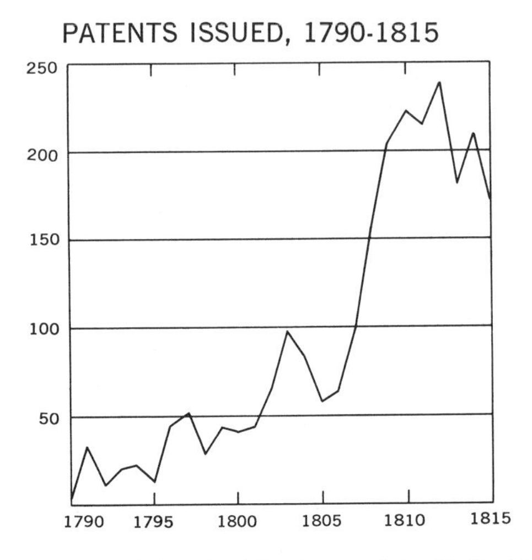

Congress enacted the first patent law on April 10, 1790, and patents were issued for fourteen years on demand of the applicant. No formal investigations for novelty or the other requirements of the law were made until 1836, when the United States Patent Office was created.

Source: Historical Statistics of the United States.

Francis Cabot Lowell and other New England capitalists formed the Boston Manufacturing Company. A power loom, designed by Lowell himself, was installed in the company's plant at Waltham, Massachusetts, where, for the first time in the United States, spinning and weaving were carried on at the same time in a single factory. As early as 1794, without benefit of electronics, Oliver Evans of Philadelphia succeeded in devising an automatic factory: a water-powered flour mill which, by the use of a system of conveyors for transporting bags of grain and flour and operating other machinery, made it unnecessary at any time during the milling process to touch the grain by hand. By 1818, machines were being used to cut rocks, cobble shoes, and fabricate nails. A few years later, coins were made in the Philadelphia mint by a machine powered by a steam engine.

Thus the American was already beginning to take his place upon the stage of history as the Man with the Machine. "The time is approaching," a Swedish traveler remarked in 1820, "when people will come here from the old continent to learn about inventions and perfected methods of production made by this nation."

Much as the United States needed labor-saving machinery the vast territorial expanse of the republic made an improvement of methods of transport and communications equally imperative. It was while on a journey in the West that the idea of a steamboat first occurred to John Fitch, a Connecticut Yankee clockmaker temporarily turned land speculator. Fitch exhibited his steamboat on the Delaware River on August 22, 1787; the trial run was observed by members of the Constitutional Convention who took the afternoon off for the occasion. James Ramsey of Maryland also patented a steamboat which won the approval of Benjamin Franklin and the American Philosophical Society. The two inventors and their respective backers competed for monopolies from the various states and even carried their rivalry to France, but neither succeeded in creating a reliable engine; the public remained indifferent, and their work was dismissed as hardly more than an ingenious toy.

Profiting from the ideas as well as the mistakes of the pioneer steamboat-builders, Robert Fulton, an artist who had taken up engineering, applied scientific principles to the problem and built a steamboat that outperformed sailing ships. Fulton enjoyed the financial backing of Robert R. Livingston, a wealthy New York banker, whose sister Fulton married. In 1807, the *Clermont,* Fulton's first American-built steamboat, made a successful run from New York to Albany. This voyage soon became a regular service. The steamboat traveled at a speed of five miles an hour and, when the wind was fair, sails were broken out to aid the twenty-horse-power engine.

Fulton and Livingston did not give the steamboat to the nation as a gift. Instead, they tried to make their fortunes by securing monopolies from the states. By 1819, they had been granted monopolies by several states, including New York, and even Russia gave the American entrepreneurs a monopoly of the use of its rivers for fifteen years. Thus the Volga boatmen, like the New York–Albany stage drivers, seemed destined to fall victim to technological advance. But the ambition of Fulton and Livingston to control the world's waterways overreached itself; competing steamboat builders championed free enterprise; and in 1824 the United States Supreme Court declared the steamboat monopoly in violation of the Constitution.

The steamboat was acclaimed as the crowning achievement of American inventive genius. Certainly it was the first American invention of world-wide importance that required a new technology and a sophisticated engineering. It was deemed especially fitting that a democratic country had brought applied science directly to the common man and in a way that affected his everyday life.

With the construction of roads, bridges, turnpikes, and canals, the improvement of navigable rivers, and the use of steamboats, important progress was made toward turning the republic into an economic unit. By 1817, there were 51,600 miles of passable road in the United States. On the turnpikes, stages traveled in good weather as much as eighty miles a day. In 1811, the Schuylkill River near Philadelphia was bridged by a single arch with a span of 340 feet built entirely of wood (Tom Paine's design of an iron bridge of 400 feet for the site was rejected). The highway that required the most advanced engineering was the road, 310 miles in length, from Philadelphia to Pittsburgh. This highway crossed the Allegheny Mountains and brought Philadelphia within five days of the rapidly growing metropolis on the Monongahela. Thanks to this and the other roads that radiated from Philadelphia, more than a thousand covered wagons were regularly engaged in transporting goods to and from the city, creating a serious traffic problem in Market Street. Canals connected the Schuylkill with the Delaware; a canal from the Cooper River to the Santee opened up a water route between Charleston and the West; and a canal through the Great Dismal Swamp diverted the trade of Albemarle Sound to Norfolk, Virginia. On the Susquehanna, flat-bottomed boats carried wheat and other commodities 300 miles from the interior; when these boats arrived at their destination they were broken up and sold as timber.

Of all the changes wrought by science during this period none were more important than those it brought to agriculture. Since the main business of Americans was sowing and reaping, any improvements in that field of endeavor were certain to affect directly thousands of citizens. Scientific agriculture, among the proponents of which were John Taylor of Carolina and Thomas Jefferson, led to the use of fertilizers, rotation of crops, the introduction of new and improved strains, and the improvement of plows and other equipment—all making for more intensive cultivation and the replenishment of worn-out soils. But, above all, science contributed an invention that changed the whole character of southern agriculture by giving that region a new and highly profitable cash crop.

In the early 1790's, the United States exported so little cotton that John Jay could agree in the treaty he concluded with Lord Grenville to a prohibition upon the export of cotton from the United States in American ships. But in 1794, even though Jay seemed unaware of it, the United States was on the verge of becoming the largest cotton-producing country in the world. One comparatively simple invention changed the course of history.

The problem was to separate the seeds from the lint in short-staple cotton which, although the South could produce in almost unlimited quantities, it could not prepare for market. In 1793, Eli Whitney, a New England farm boy who had grown up with tools and who had become a tutor in the family of General Nathanael Greene in Georgia, invented (or, more precisely, perfected) a cotton gin that did the trick. Whitney immediately took out a patent in the expectation that his gins would be leased to cotton planters who would pay a royalty in cotton based upon the amount of cotton ginned. But the first attempt at a patent monopoly in the United States failed: the machine was so simple that it could be built by any blacksmith. As a result, although Whitney brought many lawsuits to maintain his monopoly, infringements were too common to be controlled. Whitney learned to his cost that "an invention can be so valuable as to be worthless to the inventor." He had, he said, brought wealth to everyone except himself.

The invention of the cotton gin worked a revolution in southern agriculture. Cotton spread into the back country and superseded tobacco, rice, and indigo as the king of staples. The new monarch ruled with an absolutism possible only in a single-crop economy. At the same time, the dependence of the cotton-producing states upon Great Britain as an export market duplicated the state of affairs that had prevailed in the colonial period in the case of tobacco. King Cotton held his realm in fief to British textile manufacturers; and the British mill-owners themselves founded their industrial empires upon southern cotton. In 1790, a negligible quantity of southern cotton reached Great Britain; by 1812 the South accounted for over half the 63 million pounds imported by Great Britain; and in 1825 the South produced three-quarters of the 228 million pounds consumed by British factories. To this pass had come the planters' hopes of freeing the American economy from dependence upon Great Britain.

Eli Whitney made a far deeper impress upon the course of American history than did most of the political leaders of his own or succeeding generations. The cotton gin gave Negro slavery a new and seemingly unshakable hold upon the southern agricultural economy. The Cotton Kingdom that Whitney helped call into being was impelled to expand the plantation system and its concomitant, Negro slavery. Cotton and slavery became two of the ingredients that went into the making of the American Civil War.

But Whitney was far more than a one-shot inventor. During the undeclared war with France, Whitney contracted with the United States government to supply the Army with ten thousand muskets by 1801. To fulfill the terms of this contract within the specified time, Whitney used machines as tools in the manufacture of the locks of these weapons, a method that already had been proved successful by a French arms manufacturer. These machines produced parts so exactly similar that they were interchangeable.

Although Whitney failed to produce a true milling machine (the first such machine was used in 1818 by Robert Johnson in Middletown, Connecticut) and encountered so many delays in this new method of manufacturing that he did not complete his contract with the United States government until 1809, he was one of the pioneers in the method that ultimately led to mass production. Without this ability to produce large quantities of standardized goods, American manufacturers at a later time could not have taken advantage of the national market.

27.
THE FRANCHISE AND EQUALITY

THE RIGHT TO VOTE

In the changes it effected in the voting rights and habits of the American people, the Revolution exhibited its conservative, gradualist character. While the suffrage was expanded in six states—the remaining states either left untouched the qualifications for voting or, as in the case of Massachusetts, actually increased them—the change was generally accomplished within the traditional "stake in the country" concept, meaning that only freehold property owners were permitted to vote. The franchise, in short, was not regarded as an inalienable right but as a privilege accorded those who earned it by acquiring real estate.

Nevertheless, the conventional wisdom that confined suffrage to owners of freehold property did not pass unchallenged. During the War of Independence, Vermont established manhood suffrage. Other states either followed Vermont's example or extended the right to vote to owners of personal property or to taxpayers. In Pennsylvania, for example, the payment of a small county tax sufficed to enfranchise any male citizen over 21 years of age. Thus even the poll tax served to create manhood suffrage.

Property requirements for officeholding proved more resistant to change than did the requirements for voting. Even in states where virtual manhood suffrage prevailed, governors, and to a lesser degree legislators, were by law chosen only from the property-owning elite. The constitutions of seven states also exacted of officeholders an oath attesting to their belief in Christianity.

"The First Voyage of the Clermont, 1807," illustration by Stanley Arthurs first published in *Scribner's Magazine*.

Half Dollar, Capped Bust Type, 1812.

Virginians did not feel secure until the governor had sworn that he was orthodox upon the Trinity in Unity.

The democratization of the suffrage was not brought about by a single political party dedicated to the proposition that all men were entitled to the vote. In some states, notably South Carolina, the Jeffersonian Republicans opposed suffrage reform. In Maryland and Massachusetts the extension of the suffrage to taxpayers was effected by a coalition of Federalists and Republicans. As a rule, each party tended to champion democratic reform in the states where such reform would strengthen its position. Since the Republicans had most to gain from reform in the New England states where they were attempting to dislodge Federalist majorities, they undertook to broaden the base of popular support whereas Federalists tried to preserve the status quo insofar as it worked in their favor.

Nor was one section wholly responsible for this democratic advance. The constitutions of the newly created western states reflected the democratic changes taking place in the older parts of the Union. The overriding need of the western states was to attract settlers, and since most people were drawn to the West by the hope of escaping from the constraints and comparative lack of opportunity they had experienced at home, the architects of the new state constitutions tended to copy the most liberal provisions of the constitutions of the eastern states. The constitutions of Kentucky and Tennessee, for example, derived from the Pennsylvania Constitution of 1790. But it was a system of selective borrowing rather than of innovation. During the period 1791-1821, of the eight western states admitted to the Union, three required the payment of taxes for voting, while five granted adult manhood suffrage. None imposed property requirements of any kind for holding office. The process also worked in reverse: to keep their people at home, the eastern states were obliged to make concessions to nonpropertied voters.[1] But women remained outside the political pale: New Jersey alone permitted women to vote (provided they were unmarried) for a brief period around 1800.

In some of the eastern states themselves, the western counties acted as a democratic leaven upon the wealthier and more privileged society of the older section. Here the conflict was between a seaboard where power was strongly entrenched and an interior bent upon asserting its right to equality. The eastern section of these states usually ruled by virtue of an inequitable system of apportionment that discriminated against the west. Yet with population moving westward, it became increasingly difficult for the east to maintain its ascendancy. In response to the demands of westerners, state capitals were moved west, and the back country was reluctantly accorded a larger

[1]The federal government was also under pressure to liberalize the voting laws in the areas under its jurisdiction. In order to attract settlers, the federal government in 1811 abolished the fifty-acre freehold qualification for voting in the western territories and in 1819 it abandoned even the taxpaying requirement.

measure of representation in the state legislatures. In 1808, for example, a compromise was effected between the two sections in South Carolina whereby the west was able to secure a majority in the lower house while the east retained control of the upper house.

Even before 1820 the expansion of the electorate had proceeded to such lengths that some conservatives feared that the United States was rushing into democracy. George Cabot, the Massachusetts Federalist leader, declared that the United States was becoming more democratic than its institutions permitted; either democracy or the institutions must give way. Thomas Jefferson cautioned that the full rights of citizenship ought to be restricted to those who could read. But Daniel Webster dismissed these apprehensions: the United States, he declared, had nothing to fear from universal suffrage. He predicted that only in countries where great inequalities of property ownership created antagonistic classes would the enfranchised masses threaten property, liberty, and order.

EQUALITY IN AMERICA

Whether in the city or the country, one of the features of American life which most forcibly struck Europeans was the widespread insistence upon equality. Except for Negroes and the poorest white laborers and seamen, everyone was addressed as "Mister." Servants were referred to as "help": to call them servants to their face was to risk having them quit without notice. (The only people who rejoiced in the title of servant were politicians who wished to be known as "public servants.") In the United States, the word "servant" was used to describe a slave or an indentured servant, not a free man, however menial the task he performed. For this reason, the term "boss" was substituted for "master." In Royall Tyler's *The Contrast,* Jonathan, Colonel Manly's servant (the first stage Yankee to appear in the American theater) stoutly upholds the democratic canon:

Jessamy: "I say, Sir, I understand that Colonel Manly has the honour of having you for a servant."

Jonathan: "Servant! Sir, do you take me for a neger. I am Colonel Manly's waiter."

Jessamy: "A true Yankee distinction, egad, without a difference. Why, Sir, do you not perform all the offices of a servant? Do you not even blacken his boots?"

Jonathan: "Yes, I do grease them a bit sometimes; but I am a true blue son of liberty, for all that. Father said I should come as Colonel Manly's waiter to see the world, and all that; but no man shall master me; my father has as good a farm as the colonel. . . . We don't make any great matter of distinction in our state, between quality and other folks."

Even though affluent citizens had servants, they were seldom permitted to enjoy the illusion that they had solved the "servant problem." "We *desire,* we *direct,* we *request,* our domestics to fulfill their duties," remarked an American, "but even the spirit of domestics will not brook command." It was frequently noted that even day laborers advanced their opinions upon religious and political matters "with as much freedom as the gentleman or the scholar." An American workman or domestic servant expected to be treated with all the respect due a free, white citizen of the republic.

Under the impact of the American and French Revolutions, time-honored emblems of class distinction were obliterated by the new democratic egalitarianism. Elitism in dress, for example, did not long survive the introduction of long trousers for men—a fashion popularized by the French revolutionaries and adopted even by American conservatives. Although the term "silk-stocking district" was used to define the Federalist area in New York City, only a few relics of the Revolution such as Charles Carroll of Carrollton continued to wear gold buckles in their shoes and lace ruffles at their wrists and throat. British travelers who were offended by "the rude familiarity of the lower order" had difficulty in determining by dress alone just who belonged to that order. In New York City, every householder, regardless of wealth or class, was obliged to serve as a fireman at least to the extent of helping pull the engines to the fire. This service was accounted a civic duty; no able-bodied man could hire a substitute. Of New York retail merchants it was observed that instead of displaying the obsequiousness with which many London merchants approached their customers, they "stood with their hats on, or sit or lie along their counters, smoking segars and spitting in every direction."

While neither a patrician nor a plebeian order existed in the United States, there was an aristocracy composed of planters, merchants, physicians, clergymen, and lawyers. Because of the extreme litigiousness of Americans, lawyers abounded everywhere; it was said that there were more lawyers in the United States than beggars in Great Britain. More importantly, lawyers were replacing the clergy as the most influential body of men in America. But the American aristocracy, composed as it was of diverse elements, was always open to talent, and it could claim none of the prerogatives pertaining to a long-established aristocracy. Nor did upper-class Americans generally claim such distinctions; in public, they chose to be regarded simply as conspicuous representatives of a society most of the members of which were climbing the economic and social ladder.

Equality was not confined to the relations between social classes; in America, even children were beginning to assert their rights against parental authority. By European standards, American children were pert, impudent, and wholly lacking in respect for their elders. Intimidated by their own offspring, some parents adopted permissiveness as the course of least resistance. Frances Wright thought that this relative freedom from harshness at home and in the school produced "that mild friendliness of demeanour which distinguishes the American."

In the relations between the sexes, the freedom enjoyed by American women and the deference paid them by males gave a distinctive tone to American society. The cult of womanhood was already taking shape. Until proved otherwise, every female was accounted a lady. American girls and young women were permitted a latitude of freedom shocking to Europeans, but they conducted themselves with a decorum that occasioned even more astonishment to those same Europeans. This libertarianism extended even to the marriage bond: in most states, divorce was removed from the jurisdiction of the legislature and given to the courts, and grounds for divorce were extended to include cruelty, desertion, habitual drunkenness as well as adultery. In Connecticut, even mental cruelty was made actionable in divorce suits.

British travelers who recoiled from American males as "tobacco-spitting animals" usually had kind things to say about American women. They were, it was agreed, beautiful, kind, hospitable, and intelligent; but it would appear that their beauty quickly faded and that they lost their teeth at an early age. The badness of their teeth struck even British travelers. The subject was discussed in learned papers read before the American Philosophical Society, where the phenomenon was attributed to excessive consumption of hot drinks, cold drinks, sweets, apples, or salted meat.

During the first decade of the nineteenth century, the reigning belle of Washington society was Elizabeth Patterson of Maryland—described as "a sublimely beautiful girl"—who had married Jerome Bonaparte, brother of Napoleon. She affected an extreme decolleté: at a party in the capital none of the guests dared look at her except by stealth because "her neck, her bosom, part of her waist and her arms were uncover'd and the rest of her form visible." Wherever she went in Washington, her carriage was surrounded by mobs of urchins eager to look at "an almost naked woman." Several scandalized Washington hostesses informed Mrs. Bonaparte that unless she adopted a more proper attire she would not be invited to *their* parties. Cruelest of all, however, was Napoleon's order to his brother to put away this dreamboat and return to Europe to marry a mere princess.

If Americans were the freest people upon earth, they were also the most straight-laced. The moral tone of the republic particularly in sexual mores, was high; adultery was treated as an unforgivable sin, and prostitution, although it existed in the cities, was never mentioned. Indeed, ladies blushed at the mention of the word "leg." In New England, it was said that a man who valued his good name hardly dared to be absent from church. It was observed that "a certain puritanical air always sticks to these 'Boston Folks' even after they have turned rakes." At Peale's Museum in Philadelphia, the statue gallery was exhibited to ladies and gentlemen separately. Even the southern planters fell under the sway of the Presbyterian church—with the result that Charleston, South Carolina, once the gayest city in the United States, seemed more puritanical than Boston itself. The Puritan conscience, never confined to New England, appeared in the early nineteenth century to be merging with the republican vision of a morally perfected people.

If, as Tom Paine said, America inspired "great ideas," it also produced a strain of violence. Americans were not far removed, either in point of time or place, from the frontier where sudden death at the hands of an enemy was a constant threat. As a result, courage, strength, and quickness on the draw tended to be esteemed above all other qualities. Engaged in exterminating the aborigines, frontiersmen did not set high value upon human life, nor was magnanimity toward an enemy classed among the republican "virtues." The prevailing brutality was conspicuously seen in such sports as "gouging," a form of wrestling in which the objective was to squeeze the eye of an opponent out of its socket. Gouging was described by an English critic as "a diabolical practice which has never disgraced Europe, and for which other people have not even a name."

True, gouging was confined to the lower classes. In Virginia, gentlemen engaged in horse-racing and hunting to the hounds—sports to which no Englishmen would take exception. But in Virginia the hunt was conducted very differently than in England: the company entered the woods and beat up whatever game was available, from a stag to a rabbit, and set off in hot pursuit. The sport consisted in the chase and in killing an animal. Almost any animal would do.

When the fashion of dueling was introduced into the United States from Europe, Americans carried it to a point beyond anything known in the Old World. The idea of equality sometimes compelled a man to prove that he was as good as another by standing up to him in a test of personal courage. Challenges were issued upon slight provocation and injured honor was avenged upon the field with a well-placed pistol ball. Since Americans were generally good shots, the mortality rate was appallingly high.

Among congressmen and Army and Navy officers, the incidence of dueling was particularly frequent and bloody. A Kentucky representative declared that no one could claim to be a gentleman or command the respect of his constituents unless he had fought a duel and had at least wounded his adversary. John Randolph of Roanoke said that "he would shoot an impertinent fellow just as he would a mad dog." When he invited congressmen to dinner, the British minister always scrutinized the guest list carefully to avoid duels. Andrew Jackson killed his man in a duel and was himself badly wounded. The dispute was over a bet on a horse race. Jackson challenged Winfield Scott, but Scott declined on grounds of religious scruples and lived to become a major general in the United States Army. Commodore Oliver Hazard dueled with a captain in the Marine Corps, and Commodore Decatur fell before the fire of Commodore Barron. Indeed, the naval officers executed feats of mayhem upon each other that would have done credit to a foreign enemy of the United States.

The supreme paradox of American republicanism was that the freest white society in the world harbored a large and ever-increasing population of black slaves. The two extremes of freedom and servitude existed side by side within the same community; color was the sovereign determinant in a society dedicated to the realization of the ideals of the Declaration of Independence. Dr. Samuel Johnson's gibe still struck home: "How is it we hear the loudest yelps for liberty from drivers of negroes?" The census of 1810 revealed that of the 7,239,903 inhabitants of the United States, 1,191,364 were slaves. Every sixth American was in bondage. And, despite the Act of Congress of 1808 prohibiting the importation of Negroes from Africa, they continued to be smuggled into the country. The Fugitive Slave Law of 1793 put the United States government into the business of returning black fugitives to their masters.

Most alarming of all, by 1820 the great majority of southern whites refused to admit the existence of any conflict between American ideals and the institution of Negro slavery. It was only a step to glorifying slavery as an institution ordained by Heaven and sanctified by American republicanism.

Acute as was the problem of slavery, it was only part of the larger problem created by the presence of the black man in white America. For even when the Negro became free, he was not accorded full enjoyment of the rights of a freeman. Moreover, in attaining freedom, the Negro improved his status without achieving commensurate improvement in his social and economic position. One of the arguments advanced against emancipation was that the Negroes were worse off as freemen than as slaves. In rural New England and Pennsylvania and on the frontier where free Negroes were comparatively scarce, they were least discriminated against, but when they congregated in large numbers, as they did in the eastern cities, their color served as an emblem of inferiority. Usually the most uncompromising opposition to the free Negroes' claims to equality came from recently arrived immigrants from Ireland and Germany who competed for jobs as domestic servants, porters, and manual laborers. In the Philadelphia prison, white criminals insisted upon separate tables, and in the theaters of eastern cities a special gallery was reserved for blacks. Most churches segregated the races—doing on earth as, hopefully, would be done in Heaven. The blacks responded by forming "African" churches of their own.

So dire was the plight of the free Negro that, when the Society for Colonizing the Free People of Color in the United States was organized in 1816, it was hailed as a humanitarian enterprise. The Colonizing Society's objective was to remove free Negroes from the United States and to resettle them in Africa. Agents were sent to find a suitable site on the West Coast of Africa, and in 1819 Congress appropriated $100,000 toward defraying the cost of transporting free Negroes to their "ancestral homeland." Gradually Liberia came into existence, but the Colonization Society never succeeded in removing more than a fraction of even the annual increment of the black population. The Society read its doom in the census returns.

Despite the crushing disabilities imposed upon the blacks, they produced during this period several extraordinarily talented individuals: among them,

POPULATION IN THE UNITED STATES, 1790-1815

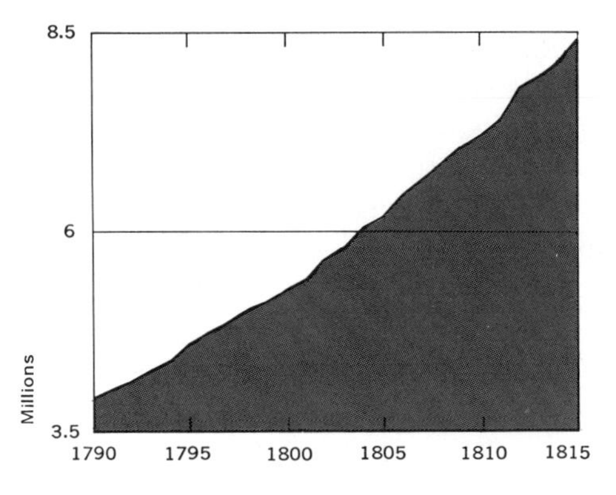

Source: Historical Statistics of the United States.

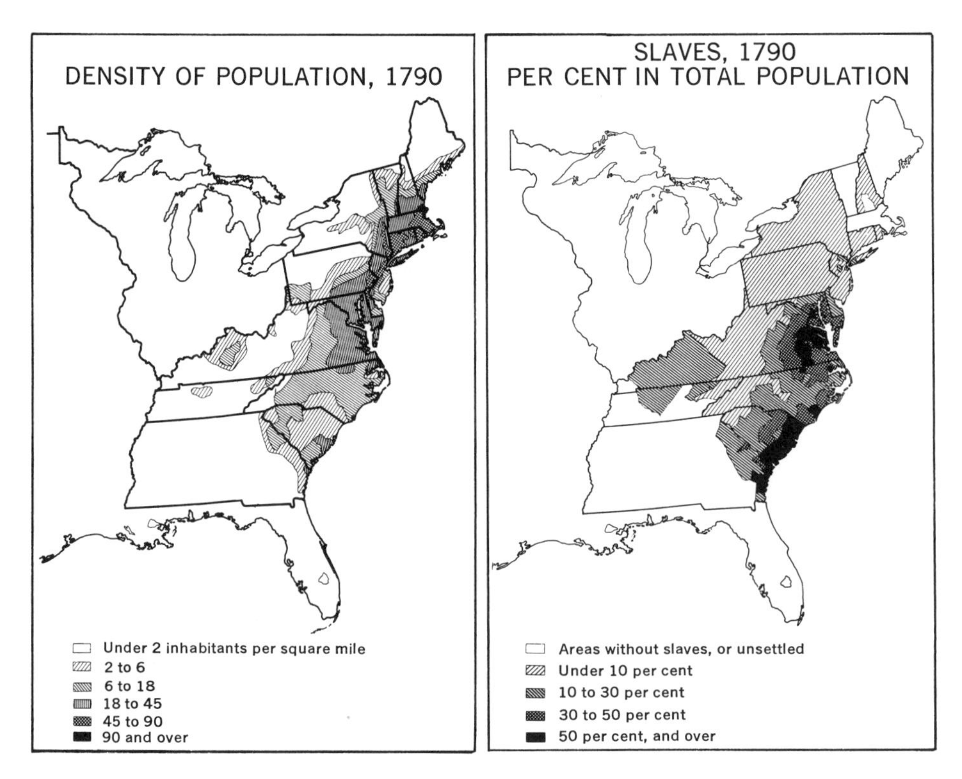

Source: Atlas of the Historical Geography of the United States.

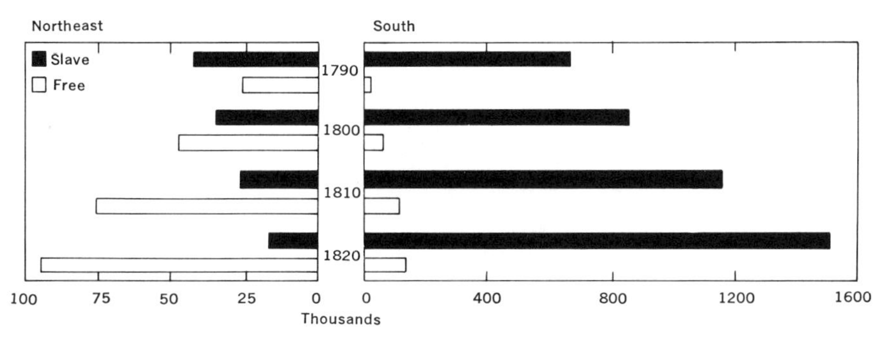

Source: Historical Statistics of the United States.

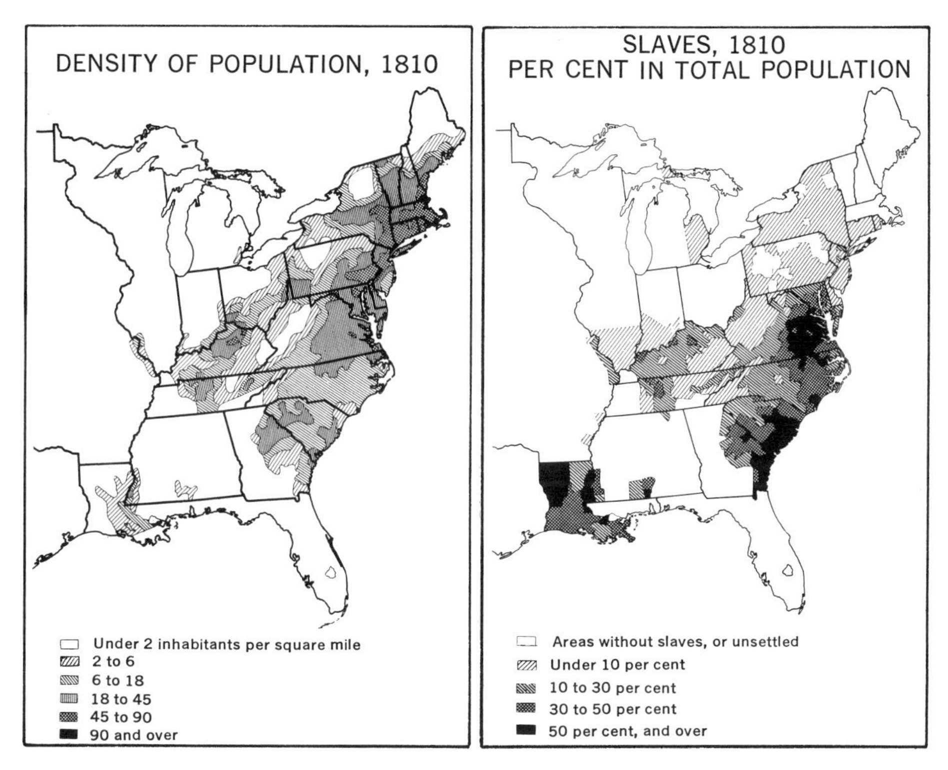

Source: Atlas of the Historical Geography of the United States.

28. AMERICAN NATIONALISM AND THE ARTS

AMERICAN EDUCATION

The national character that emerged from the War of 1812 was the consummation of a long effort by American patriots to inculcate "Americanism" by means of literature and the fine arts. Far from being a mere political revolution, the separation of the thirteen colonies from Great Britain was expected to usher in a renaissance of science and literature. Tom Paine rejoiced that Americans were not only politically free of Europe—even more important, in his opinion, their minds were free. As a result of the American Revolution and the alliance with France, he said, "our style and manner of thinking have undergone a revolution more extraordinary than the political revolution of the country. We see with other eyes; we hear with other ears; and think with other thoughts than those we formerly used. We can look back on our own prejudices, as if they had been the prejudices of other people. . . . We are really another people."

But Paine rejoiced too soon: ten years later, he was complaining of the subservience of the American mind to Great Britain. Independence, it was clear, was not the end but the beginning of the effort to Americanize the United States. A people who had endured 150 years of colonialism did not readily cast off their intellectual dependence upon the Old World.

In the work of equipping the American people with republican manners, morals and concepts, patriots assigned education a vital role. Schoolmasters, they thought, must take the rising generation in hand and develop to the full

---

"The Artist in His Museum," painting by Charles Willson Peale, courtesy of The Pennsylvania Academy of the Fine Arts.

Quarter Dollar, Capped Bust Type, 1815.

"the manly, noble and Sublime Qualities in human Nature." In this view, education became an instrument for carrying the American Revolution to its second stage—the creation of a broad consensus upon the fundamental principles of republicanism and the inculcation of a patriotism that embraced the United States as a whole.

Thus education was called upon to provide cement for the Union. Alexander Hamilton had proposed to attach the rich to the federal government by the ties of pecuniary self-interest, but Thomas Jefferson and his friends regarded education as a far more effective adhesive than stocks and bonds. Uniformity of thought became, therefore, of vital importance to the success of the republican experiment. Without denying the right of dissent, they sought by means of education to homogenize the American mind. Benjamin Rush, for example, thought that children ought to be turned into "republican machines" and Jefferson insisted upon a high degree of political orthodoxy at the University of Virginia. As Jefferson and Rush conceived it, the cardinal objective of education was to teach patriotism and republicanism. The free American was to be a thoroughly indoctrinated American.

If this method promised to create a more enduring union than did Hamilton's approach, there were formidable obstacles in the way of its successful implementation. During his frequent tours of the United States—the first was made in the early 1780's—Noah Webster found in every state and, indeed, in many towns, peculiarities in pronunciation which grated upon the sensibilities of people from other parts of the country. To his own ear, these "odious distinctions of provincial dialects" were particularly prevalent in Virginia where, he reported, a kind of Frenchified English was spoken, and in New England where the Yankee twang had expelled the more mellifluous sounds of the English language. Nor did he let the Middle States off lightly: there, he said, the language had been tinctured by outlandish German, Dutch and Scotch dialects.

By means of his *American Spelling Book,* the first edition of which appeared in 1783 and which, in numerous subsequent editions, sold nearly one hundred million copies, by his *Readers,* and by his *American Dictionary of the English Language,* Webster tried to establish uniform ways of pronouncing, spelling and defining words. Under the conviction that a national language was essential to the growth of a national spirit, he called for a truly American language responsive to the peculiar needs created by the distinctive environment and the republican institutions of the United States. His *Readers* introduced generations of American children to the great events of American history. "Every child in America," he said, "should be acquainted with his own country. . . . As soon as he opens his lips, he should lisp the praises of liberty and of those illustrious heroes and statesmen who have wrought a revolution in his favor."

As the Schoolmaster to America, Webster pointed a schoolmasterly finger at his countrymen for yielding to their penchant for imitating the manners, fashions, language, and vices of foreigners. When would Americans learn, he asked, that Europe was finished? To him, as to Thomas Jefferson, the evidences of its decay were everywhere apparent: its laws were perverted, its manners were licentious, its literature was declining, and its governments were corrupt and tyrannical. Nevertheless, he lamented, free Americans seemed to delight in aping this debased model across the Atlantic: "all our ladies, even those of the most scanty fortune," he said, "must dress like a dutchess in London; every shopkeeper must be as great a rake as an English lord." Webster urged his countrymen to look to a purer example—themselves. "An American," he declared, "ought not to ask what is the custom of London and Paris, but what is proper for us in our circumstances and what is becoming our dignity."

To make the people a safe repository of the power they had won by throwing off British rule, Jefferson believed that they must be educated. Although he supposed that men were equipped by the Creator with an innate moral sense, he thought that it must be supplemented by mass education at the elementary level, not in order to enable them to read the Bible or enjoy the beauties of literature, but in order that they could deal intelligently with the political problems which they were required to resolve. To him, the potentialities of education were illimitable: "enlighten the people generally," he predicted, "and tyranny and oppression of body and mind will vanish like evil spirits at the dawn of day."

While Jefferson severely restricted the functions of government in most areas of activity, he sought to expand its duties in the field of education. For Virginia he drew up a comprehensive plan of education from the elementary grades to the university: had his "Bill for the More General Diffusion of Knowledge" been adopted, Virginia would have taken a clear lead over all countries of the world in providing education for its citizens. The system he devised was highly competitive, but it had the saving grace of giving the children of the poor scholarship aid at the college level if they showed unusual talent or ability. He stipulated that these natural aristocrats—he called them "geniuses raked from the rubbish"—should dedicate themselves to public service.

Utilitarianism in education was not wholly directed toward making Americans more moral and patriotic citizens. On the ground that the principal task before the American people was to build up the country, some citizens argued that education ought to consist wholly of vocational subjects. Benjamin Rush deprecated the study of classical languages: "Can you resolve me," he asked, "by your Latin, the Question: If one bushel of corn costs four shillings, what cost fifty bushels?" Instead of studying Greek and Latin, young Americans were advised by Rush to give their attention to Indian languages. Although Jefferson could not bring himself to eliminate Latin and Greek altogether (he read the classical authors in the original and wished to preserve classical scholarship in the United States), he also favored the study of Indian languages and anthropology. Jefferson agreed with Rush that Americans preferred the useful to the ornamental—and, he added, rightly so. The curricula he devised for William and Mary College and the University of Virginia were heavily weighted on the side of science and "useful" subjects. He made no provision for a professor of theology at the University of Virginia.

Despite the efforts put forth by the schools to instruct Americans in the business of getting ahead in the world, it was not easy to convince the majority of citizens that they ought to pay taxes for the support of education. As Jefferson said, Americans were more disposed to build canals and highways than to lay out their money on schools. In this regard, the New England states, where, since colonial times, every town had been obliged by law to maintain a school and schoolmaster, were far ahead of other parts of the Union. Noah Webster observed that whereas the state constitutions were republican, the educational systems of the states outside New England were pure aristocracy.

Implicit in these educational plans was the idea of training an administrative elite. In 1787 Benjamin Rush advocated the establishment of a national university where students from all parts of the country could acquire a truly republican education consisting of such eminently useful subjects as history, government, agriculture, and economics. Rush envisaged this institution as a school of Americanism: from its classrooms would go forth the future teachers and administrators of the republic.

Although the Constitutional Convention of 1787 had rejected a motion that the new government be authorized to charter and endow a national university, President Washington, who keenly felt the "deficiency" of a college education, particularly in the presence of college graduates, recommended to Congress that such an institution of higher learning be financed by the federal government. As matters stood, the President said in his message to Congress, because of the lack of a national university, young Americans were tempted to go abroad where they ran the risk of "contracting principles unfriendly to Republican government." In 1795, Washington offered to give fifty shares in the Potomac Navigation Company and a tract of land in the District of Columbia toward an endowment for the national university. But Congress refused to act, and in 1796 it rejected a bill introduced by James Madison authorizing the federal government to receive donations for such an institution. Despite this rebuff, Washington devised by will fifty shares of Potomac Company stock to the federal government with the stipulation that it be used to set up a national university. Receipt of this gift was not acknowledged until 1905, when an embarrassed Secretary of the Treasury admitted that he did not know where the money had gone. The mystery was quickly cleared up: the President's supposedly munificent bequest had become long since worthless paper.

President Jefferson, to whom education was the soul of democracy, went far beyond the idea of a national university. In 1806, he recommended that Congress adopt poet Joel Barlow's plan of a national institute, modeled upon the National Institute of France, consisting of a national university, an observatory, a museum of national history, a conservatory of arts, a school of medicine, a school of mines, and a national library. But the bill introduced into Congress by Senator George Logan of Pennsylvania died in committee. For this untimely snuffing out of Barlow's vision President Jefferson was partly to blame. For Jefferson's constitutional scruples got the better of his zeal for education: from his legalistic perspective, the creation of a national university by the federal government required a constitutional amendment. He recommended such an amendment but because he failed to press for its passage it was never presented to the states. On the other hand, in 1803, the Military Academy at West Point was established to train young men in the arts of war without, apparently, doing any damage to the Constitution.

In his later years, Jefferson's heart was not really in the project of a national university. Increasingly he turned his eyes toward his first educational love—a state university in Virginia which would serve as the capstone of the educational system he had designed for his native state. Although a national university never materialized, Jefferson had the satisfaction of founding the University of Virginia, one of the three achievements of his career he believed most worthy of commemoration by posterity.

Among the most compelling arguments for a national university was that it would save young men from the corrupting effects of a British or European education. But after 1820, Thomas Jefferson advised southern parents to send their sons to a southern college to escape the contagion of "opinions and principles in discord with those of their own country." By their "country," Jefferson meant their native state; the focal center of contagion was no longer Europe but the northern states. In the case of his own grandson, Jefferson took no chances: the young man matriculated at South Carolina College, where only the orthodox doctrine of states' rights was taught.

During 1780-1815 almost forty colleges were founded in the United States. Many were denominational schools whose faculties attested to the dominant position still held by clergymen in American higher education. But even the denominational schools competed fiercely with each other for students and reached out beyond their own denominational bounds for bright young men capable of paying tuition. Some of the colleges founded during the colonial period—notably Harvard, Yale, and Columbia—became universities. In 1817, Harvard and the University of Pennsylvania established law schools. At Yale, President Timothy Dwight—sometimes called "Pope" Dwight because of his power in the Congregational Church—improved the faculty, abolished antiquated methods of maintaining discipline, and encouraged the teaching of science by establishing a medical school and bringing Benjamin Silliman, who subsequently became one of the country's most important scientists, to New Haven. But William and Mary College, after bringing forth John Marshall, James Monroe, and Thomas Jefferson, fell into decay. A contemporary described the young men at Williamsburg running riot "while the venerable professors are forced to look on, in the deep mortification of conscious impotence." Thomas Jefferson, whose last years were troubled by undergraduate disorders at the University of Virginia, lamented that the progress of education in the United States was threatened by the spirit of insubordination begot by "premature ideas of independence, too little repressed by parents." George III had said much the same thing about the American colonists.

REPUBLICAN LITERATURE

In the years immediately following the American Revolution, it was generally expected that republicanism would of its own accord generate a cultural explosion. In an oration delivered in 1778, Dr. David Ramsay of South Carolina asserted that since liberty and individual creative activity went hand in hand, republics offered the most favorable environment for the development of genius—from which he deduced that "the free governments of America will produce poets, orators, critics, and historians, equal to the most celebrated of the ancient commonwealths of Greece and Italy." The "long night" of British rule was over, he intoned, and Americans were now ready to take their rightful place among the sages, mentors, and benefactors of mankind.

To bring this flowering of arts and sciences to early fruition, Tom Paine urged in 1782 that the government foster their growth by financial outlays. "It is well worth remarking," he observed, "that Russia, who but a few years ago was scarcely known in Europe, owes a large share of her present greatness to the close attention she has paid, and the wise encouragement she has given, to every branch of science and learning." But Congress was not yet responsive to the necessity of catching up with Russia nor did the finances of the government admit of any expenditures for such frills as literature and the arts. The Continental Congress could not even afford to buy a modest library for the use of its members.

Yet even without a congressional appropriation, literature was expected to burgeon in the United States. Americans were confident that an Augustan age was about to dawn in the Western World if only because the events of the Revolution had provided American writers with enough raw material to enable them to carry literature to new heights.

In Americans' philosophy there was no place for the doctrine of art for art's sake. As they saw it, the function of literature was to extol the glories of the United States, spread the gospel of republicanism, and "inspire youth with a contempt of the unmanly vices of mankind, and a love of virtue, patriotism and religion." All literature, in short, must be directed toward helping the republic attain its lofty goals. A revolution in politics ought to be accompanied by a revolution in literature, and literature, in turn, ought to serve the purposes of the revolution. In the early republic, the literary impulse was compounded almost wholly of patriotism, utilitarianism, and, on the part of writers themselves, a desire for fame.

It was in this spirit that American men of letters addressed themselves to the task of crowning the revolution with a truly republican literature. Only an epic on the order of the *Aeneid,* it was felt, could do justice to the majesty of the American achievement and the grandeur of the American promise. An entire school of part-time men of letters, the so-called Hartford or Connecticut wits, all of whom were graduates of Yale College, vied with each other for the honor of composing this masterpiece. Their theme was the American Revolution and their heroes were the statesmen and soldiers who had presided over the birth of the republic.

These expectant laureates were John Trumbull, Timothy Dwight, David Humphreys, Joel Barlow, and Lemuel Hopkins. John Trumbull, the most popular American poet before Longfellow, did not attempt a patriotic epic; instead, he contented himself with a satiric exposé of education ("The Progress of Dulness") and a lampoon upon the Tories ("M'Fingal"). Like all the Wits, Trumbull was an infant prodigy: he passed the entrance requirements to Yale at the age of seven and his first poem was written at the age of four, although he waited until he was five until he ventured to publish. Timothy Dwight, equally distinguished for his precosity, wrote "The Conquest of Canaan," an epic poem as long as "Paradise Lost," before he was twenty. The poem was so frequently punctuated by thunder and lightning storms (there were at least forty disturbances of hurricane intensity) that John Trumbull remarked that it was not safe to read the poem without a lightning rod handy.

Joel Barlow spent eight years writing *The Vision of Columbus* (published in 1787) in which he predicted in metre that the United States would someday construct a canal across the Isthmus of Panama and eliminate the study of foreign languages in schools. In 1807, having scandalized his Connecticut neighbors by becoming an admirer of the French Revolution, Barlow rewrote the epic and published it under the title of the *Columbiad.* But he succeeded only in demonstrating that two mediocre epics do not add up to a great epic. Barlow recounted in verse the most important events in American history, from the discovery by Columbus to the Revolution, and, through the eyes of Hesper, the guardian genius of the western world, he surveyed the glory that lay in store for the United States. The book—the handsomest and most expensive ($20) volume published up to this time in the United States—sold fewer than five hundred copies. Despite the financial and literary ill success of the *Columbiad,* Barlow asserted that it represented at least a moral improvement over the *Iliad* and *Aeneid* inasmuch as instead of celebrating the destructive glories of war and conquest it commemorated peace and "rational liberty." But the reviewers, American as well as English, denied the *Columbiad* even this measure of merit. It was called a "huge and incongruous mass of political monstrosities" and a libel upon the memory of Columbus.

Fortunately for his literary fame, Barlow's reputation does not rest wholly upon his epics. In 1793, while campaigning for a seat in the French Convention (he had gone to France to sell land and had been swept into the French Revolution) Barlow wrote *The Hasty Pudding.* The inspiration that had proved deficient when he tried to write an epic, came to him when, like many other American tourists abroad, he thought of a home-cooked meal.

All the epics turned out by the Connecticut Wits were variations upon the theme that a new Golden Age was about to dawn in America, that American ideas would ultimately conquer the world and that it was the destiny of the United States to bring universal peace and freedom and to unite mankind in "one firm union." Americans, said David Humphreys, "embrace humanity's extended cause—. A world our empire, for a world our laws." John Trumbull predicted that in this great work of universal redemption, "fair Yalensia will lead the noble train."

In actuality, literature, when employed as an instrument for the indoctrination of American ideals, became hortatory, rhetorical, and chauvinistic. Aspiring to sublimity, the Connecticut Wits fell into banality. The first attempt by American men of letters to make the eagle scream elicited only faint pipings. No wonder that English critics could hardly wait to wring the neck of that offensive bird and thereby put an end to its vauntings of moral, intellectual, and artistic superiority. The great American epic stubbornly refused to be written. Despite the unremitting efforts of the Connecticut Wits, the Declaration of Independence remained the supreme literary monument of the American Revolution.

The nationalism that failed to inspire the Connecticut Wits to write great poetry brought them into the thick of the struggle over the ratification of the Federal Constitution. In the "Anarchiad," a collaborative effort written in the form of an ancient epic "on the Restoration of Chaos," the Wits portrayed the Shaysites and Antifederalists as abettors of the powers of Darkness whose only objective was to cheat their creditors with paper money and tender laws. Rhode Island figured in the poem as

> "A den of dragons, and a cave for bears;
> A nest of vipers, mix'd with adders foul."

It was no wonder that

> "The wiser race, the snares of law to shun,
> Like Lot from Sodom, from Rhode Island run."

In the concluding stanzas, Alexander Hamilton, the knight in shining armor, vanquished the forces of Chaos.

With the exception of Joel Barlow, all the Wits became pillars of the Federalist Establishment and inveterate enemies of the French Revolution. Timothy Dwight, later president of Yale (than which, in the opinion of the Wits, there was no higher office in the land) was a champion of orthodoxy who resolutely set his face against Deism and Unitarianism. Like a true Wit, Dwight took to verse to express his religious convictions. In the *Triumph of Infidelity* (1788) which he dedicated to Voltaire, Dwight recounted Satan's efforts to subvert Christ's Kingdom by means of his favorite instrument for such purposes, the Roman Catholic Church. In the end, Jonathan Edwards (who was, incidentally, Dwight's grandfather) triumphs over Satan, Deism, and Roman Catholicism, thereby saving New England for true religion.

Although the states and, later, the federal government, aided manufacturing and commerce, they left literature and the fine arts strictly to the writers and artists. In their hands, the work of Americanizing culture went forward briskly. Literary and artistic coteries flourished in all the large American cities. These cultural centers competed for preëminence; of New York and Philadelphia it was said that they were "forever disputing the palm of fashion, science, literature, and fine arts." Even before it laid claim to being the Athens of America, Boston prided itself upon its Athenaeum, a public library containing eighteen thousand volumes, and the Massachusetts Historical Society, chartered in 1794; Baltimore claimed to be the musical capital of the country, but Charleston with its St. Cecilia Society made that city a formidable rival. The American Philosophical Society, with headquarters in Philadelphia, was challenged in 1780 by the American Academy of Arts and Sciences, founded by New Englanders. Similarly, most of these cities boasted at least one magazine (usually short-lived) devoted to *belles lettres* such as *The American Museum, Columbian Magazine, American Magazine,* and the *American Review of History and Politics* (the first critical quarterly). Literature could not be wholly divorced from partisan politics: *The Port Folio,* the leading American review, edited from 1800 to 1808 by Joseph Dennie, was stridently Federalist in opinion. No less partisan was the *North American Review,* founded in 1815 by Massachusetts Federalists avowedly to "foster American genius and . . . instruct and guide the public taste."

The perennial theme of American writers was the superiority in all things of the United States over the monarchical, decadent, and "exhausted" Old World. Royall Tyler, an army officer in the War of Independence and the first successful American playwright, demonstrated in his play *The Contrast* (1787) the superiority of plain but honest American manners over the superficial polish acquired by travel in Europe. The foreign menace appears in the person of Dimple van Dumpling, "a flippant, pallid, polite beau who devotes the morning to his toilet, reads a few pages of Chesterfield's letters and then minces out, to put the infamous principles in practice upon every woman he meets." Yet this monster of affectations and vice, before he visited England, was a clean-living, clean-minded American boy. Although the heroine, and heiress, is at first dazzled by the specious manners of the Anglicized fop, she is won by Colonel Manly, the stalwart, outspoken, down-to-earth patriot.

No American play of this period equaled *The Contrast* in verve, characterization, and witty dialogue. For the most part, American dramatists tried to compensate for their literary shortcomings with the blare of "Yankee Doodle" and the waving of the American flag. William Dunlap, "the Father of the American Drama," produced a repertoire of box-office successes including *André* and *The Glory of Columbia—her Yeomanry.* Mrs. Ann Hamilton's play, *Tammany, or The Indian Chief,* was said to be "seasoned high with spices hot from Paris." But it was not a bedroom farce: the spicing consisted of Liberty, Equality, and Fraternity. Every international crisis brought forth a spate of patriotic plays such as *The New York Volunteer* or *Who's Afraid?* Who, indeed, could be afraid after seeing a rousing play that put Americans above all other nations in both peace and war?

A notable exception to these paeans of self-congratulation upon the superiority of American institutions was Hugh Henry Breckinridge's *Modern Chivalry,* the first part of which was published in 1792 and finally completed in 1815. Breckinridge, a contemporary of Philip Freneau at Princeton and coauthor with him of *The Rising Glory of America,* became a lawyer in eastern Pennsylvania. During the Whiskey Rebellion, while supporting the farmers' grievances, he carefully dissociated himself from all acts of violence. The follies, prejudice, and ignorance that he observed everywhere in the United States, and especially on the Pennsylvania frontier, provided him with a copious store of material for satire. *Modern Chivalry,* in form a picaresque novel of adventure, is essentially a criticism of what most of Breckinridge's fellow citizens were glorifying as "The American Way."

In this satire, Captain Farrago, an upright man who cherishes the republican institutions of the United States, is engaged in making a tour of the United States in company with his servant, Teague O'Regan. The people, disposed as always to adopt "what is new and ignoble," insist upon electing Teague, an ignorant and illiterate "bogtrotter," to Congress. When Captain Farrago attempts to point out Teague's lack of qualifications for the office, he draws upon himself the resentment of the people for interfering with the free exercise of their sovereign will. It is only after Captain Farrago warns Teague that by becoming a member of Congress he will be exposed to so much vilification in the newspapers that the name O'Regan would be no better than that of a sheep-stealer that Teague is finally persuaded to decline the proffered office. Whereupon the people, deprived of their first choice, elect an ignorant weaver to Congress.

But Breckinridge's satire was not directed merely at frontiersmen: the pervasive influence of ignorance and folly, he implied, had infected the ministry, law, the teaching profession, journalism, and even the American Philosophical Society. All careers are open to Teague because in America a total absence of qualifications is the highest recommendation. When he finds a dead owl he is immediately invited to become a member of the American Philosophical Society. Finally, being a handsome man with a plausible demeanor, he is taken up by the world of fashion—there is, in fact, "a kind of Teague-o-mania among the females"—and becomes Major O'Regan, a satirical thrust at Americans' fondness for military titles.

In its way, *Modern Chivalry* was a didactic novel. The antics of Teague and the even more reprehensible follies of the people were represented as fundamental defects of American democracy. Breckinridge's message was that the United States could not afford incompetence and ignorance either in its electorate or in its elected officials and that the uninhibited spirit of levelism destroyed excellence.

Certainly the task of creating a truly American literature was rendered more difficult by the predilection of the American reading public for English books and by the low price at which those books were sold. In the absence of an international copyright law, American publishers reprinted the works of English authors without paying royalties. As a result, pirated editions of British authors were sold in the United States for one-fourth of the overseas price. While American authors suffered from this practice, it did stimulate the paper, printing, and bookbinding industries in the United States.

Disregarding the disadvantageous competitive position of American authors, Charles Brockden Brown, a Philadelphia lawyer turned novelist, tried to live by his pen—the first creative writer in the United States to join what Adam Smith described as "that unprosperous race of men commonly called men of letters." Although he survived the ordeal—he lived in "a dismal room in a dismal street," wore threadbare clothes and down-at-heel shoes—he could not bear to inflict these hardships upon his family. In 1801, after a frenzied stint of writing in which he produced six novels in three years, he turned to magazine editing for a living. One after another of his magazines failed until, at the age of thirty-nine, Brown himself passed out of circulation.

As a disciple of William Godwin, a contemporary English philosophical anarchist, Brown was one of the most "advanced" thinkers of his day. He prided himself upon being a novelist of ideas: calling himself a "moral painter," he used the novel and essay to agitate for freer divorce laws, political rights for women, humanitarian reforms, the rule of reason, and the "truths" of Deism. His women characters are paragons of virtue and courage in adversity; they talk learnedly about philosophy, literature, and science. But he could not bring himself to eliminate the "vapors," those fainting fits and other evidences of extreme sensibility dear to writers of the Romantic school.

In his fondness for the "cult of horror," Brown derived from the Gothic novelists of the late eighteenth century; in his fascination with psychology and the macabre he foreshadowed Edgar Allan Poe. One of his heroines is given to self-analysis; when she hears a shriek in her closet at midnight she devotes five minutes to analyzing her emotions. In *Wieland,* Brown dealt with a case of religious melancholia aggravated by ventriloquism: by means of his skill as a ventriloquist, the enemy of the central character urges him to put his wife and children to death. *Edgar Huntley* (1799) is a detective novel —another link with Poe; while the scene of *Ormond* is Philadelphia during the yellow fever epidemic in 1793. *Ormond,* in fact, is a good example of Brown's consistent effort to domesticate the novel by giving it an American setting. He explicitly renounced Gothic castles, clanking chains, and the other paraphernalia used by Horace Walpole, Anne Radcliffe, and Matthew "Monk" Lewis. Instead, Brown said, "the incidents of Indian hostility, and the perils of the Western wilderness, are far more suitable; and for a native of America to overlook these would admit of no apology."

Poetry, too, drew its inspiration from distinctively American scenes and experiences. In 1784, in "The Dying Indian," Philip Freneau undertook to recreate in poetry the incidents of the American wilderness, and in 1817 William Cullen Bryant published *Thanatopsis,* a poem which, while influenced by Coleridge, Southey, and Wordsworth, celebrated the "noble" rivers, lakes, and mountains of the United States. It was said that "whoever saw Bryant, saw America."

Although Charles Brockden Brown failed to profit from it, the novel—except for the ubiquitous newspapers—became the most popular literary artform in the early republic. Thomas Jefferson expressed alarm lest his countrymen's passion for novel-reading vitiate their taste for more serious literature. "When this poison infects the mind," he observed, "it destroys its tone and revolts it against wholesome reading. . . . The result is a bloated imagination, sickly judgment, and disgust toward all the real businesses of life." Excessive indulgence in poetry, he warned, had the same debilitating effect. In 1815, when he tried to get Du Pont de Nemours's treatise on political economy published in the United States, Jefferson found that the printers were interested only in "novels and light reading."

Most of the early novels—in general the most popular proved to be the most ephemeral—borrowed their plot, characters, and dialogue from Samuel Richardson, the English master of the *genre.* In the Richardson manner, while these novelists dealt with seduction and male turpitude, they purported to paint a moral and to foster virtue. Authors assured their readers that the spice of the story was its moral "message." William Hill Brown's *The Power of Sympathy* (1789), the first moral novel written by an American, undertook to expose "the fatal consequences of seduction." The victim, less successful than Richardson's heroines in preserving her virtue, dies by taking poison. Brown varied Richardson's formula by injecting rape and incest into the story. Susanna Rowson, a New England schoolmarm, who published *Charlotte Temple* in 1791, and Hannah Foster, author of *The Coquette,* published in 1797, not only derived their plots from Richardson but imitated his technique of telling their stories in the form of letters. The scene of *The Coquette,* however, was Connecticut; even in the land of steady habits, it appeared, virtue was not safe from rakes and wastrels.

These novels, preoccupied as they were with morals and sex, were written for the women and adolescent girls who largely constituted the novel-reading public in the United States. Foreign travelers frequently observed that American males had no time for books: engrossed in business or farming, their intellectual fare was confined to newspapers and an occasional magazine. Pleasing the feminine taste had already become mandatory for a successful American novelist.

Jefferson had little cause to rejoice either in the content or form taken by American literature. With the exception of Philip Freneau and Charles Brockden Brown, the most eminent men of letters of the period were Federalists whose political partisanship plainly appeared in their works. William Cullen Bryant, later to be acclaimed the greatest poet of his generation, published in 1808 his poem *The Embargo* in which he enjoined President Jefferson to

> "Go, scan, Philosophist, thy Sally's charms,
> And sink supinely in her sable arms;
> But quit to abler hands the helm of state."

The Sally of the poem was one of Jefferson's slaves by whom he was alleged to have had several children. Since Bryant was at this time only 13 years old, obviously he was knowledgeable beyond his years upon a matter not usually considered fit for mention in a New England parlor or poem. But in Federalist circles, when the immoralities of President Jefferson were under discussion, the proprieties were cheerfully dispensed with.

Washington Irving, the first American professional writer to win a reputation abroad, began his literary career as an essayist. In January 1807, Irving and a group of friends began the publication in New York of *Salmagundi*—a magazine modeled upon the *Spectator* and the *Citizen of the World.* It satirized the foibles of the bon ton of *Gotham* (*Salmagundi* was the first to call New York by this name), the beaux, belles, and coxcombs; poked fun at the "whims, eccentricities and unseemly conceits" of the ladies of New York; reviewed plays and purveyed gossip. *Salmagundi* served as an apprenticeship for the publication in 1809 of Diedrich Knickerbocker's (Washington Irving's) *History of New York from the Beginning of the World to the End of the Dutch Dynasty,* a mock history, with political overtones, of the history of New Netherlands. Governor William Kieft of New Netherlands figures as a Dutch Thomas Jefferson: like Jefferson, Kieft has an eccentric taste in dress, encyclopedic learning, and a passion for ingenious but futile inventions. (Kieft invents "carts that went before the horse, Dutch ovens for roasting meat without fire and weather-cocks that turned against the wind.") During his term of office, Kieft tried so many political experiments that he ended by entangling the government in more knots "than half a dozen successors could have untied." Among these experiments was an embargo directed against the Yankees, but this "new and cheap method of fighting" recoiled disastrously upon its projectors. Contemporaries were expected to smile knowingly when they read that Kieft was a pacifist, an opponent of adequate national defense, an advocate of farcical military preparations (gunboats), and a lover of pompous manifestoes.

Having produced an impressive number of statesmen and military leaders, America imposed upon historians and biographers the duty of commemorating the virtues and achievements of these heroes. William Gordon, David Ramsay, and Mercy Otis Warren wrote histories of the American Revolution while the incidents they recounted were still fresh in the minds of their readers. Among biographers, William Wirt, the Virginia lawyer and politician, who had written *Letters of the British Spy,* a critical examination of American claims to political and literary primacy, also wrote a life of Patrick Henry;

William Dunlap was acclaimed as the American Vasari for his biographical sketches of American painters. Even Chief Justice John Marshall turned his hand to biography: his five-volume *Life of George Washington* appeared in 1804-1807. Although he had served with Washington during the War of Independence and knew him well, Marshall never succeeded in bringing Washington to life: his personality is submerged in the general history of the times.

The most prolific and widely read of the biographers of the revolutionary heroes was Mason "Parson" Weems. An itinerant book salesman and preacher, Weems peddled from door to door and tavern to tavern edifying tracts, many of which were written by himself, against drunkenness, gambling, dueling, adultery, and other vices, and extolling the joys of holy matrimony and large families. In his war upon vice, Weems enlisted the aid of sensationalism: his tract against *Cruelty to Husbands* was illustrated, at Weems' direction with an engraving of "a very beautiful woman distorted or convulsed with Diabolical passion in the act of murdering, with uplifted axe, her husband in sleep." *The Drunkard's Looking Glass* contained the case histories of fifty alcoholics, all of whom perished miserably, bringing disgrace upon themselves and their families.

Vice thus received its deserts, but Weems was primarily concerned in showing, through the lives of American sages and heroes, how virtue was rewarded. In his biography of Benjamin Franklin—which he described as "a savoury dish . . . cooked up for Juvenile palates," he outdid Poor Richard himself in extolling Industry, Sobriety, Frugality, and Honesty. His chef d'oeuvre, *A History of the Life and Death, Virtues and Exploits of General Washington* exhibited Washington as the exemplar of human perfectibility, "the Hero and the Demigod." Although Weems helped mightily to build up the image of Washington as a sanctimonious prig, he broke new biographical ground by recounting incidents (sometimes wholly imaginary) from the Hero's private life. The story of the little hatchet and the cherry tree and of Washington praying in the snow at Valley Forge were only part of Weems' contribution to the myth of the Father of His Country.

Having put forward claims of superiority in all things, Americans displayed extraordinary sensitivity to criticism by foreigners. What particularly rankled Americans were the travel books written by British visitors, who, subjected to the interminable bragging of the Yankees about the excellence of their constitution and invincibility in war, vented their resentment in what Americans called "effusions of splenetic hostility." "They begin with a sneer," exclaimed an outraged American, "and end with a calumny." To refute these canards, Americans took to the road and wrote travel books about their own country. Timothy Dwight published his *Travels in New England and New York*—taking five volumes to show how utterly groundless were the aspersions of British travelers. Dwight boasted that he had traveled two-thirds the distance round the globe without leaving New York and New England, and, fortified with statistics, he itemized the points in which the United States was superior to Europe: manners, education, religion, and "the noblest institutions man has seen, Since time his reign began." James K. Paulding, brother-in-law of Washington Irving, compared British travelers with Baron Munchausen. To expose the falsity of their accounts, Paulding wrote a "Sketch of Old England." Since he had not been in England the obvious inference was that many English travelers who wrote books about the United States had never visited the country. Robert Walsh, Jr., the author of "An Appeal from the judgment of Great Britain respecting the United States," used the reports of an investigating committee of the British House of Commons to show how industrialism was producing destitution, ugliness, misery, and crime in Great Britain.

In 1789, after five years of travel (he paid his expenses by preaching) the Reverend Jedidiah Morse, a New England clergyman, published his *American Geography,* in which he asserted the superiority of the United States, especially of New England, "over all other nations in point of climate, natural resources and the industriousness of the population." Ten years later, Joseph Scott published *A New and Universal Gazeteer or Modern Geographical Dictionary* in four volumes. Scott claimed to have corrected over five hundred errors in previous works dealing with the United States, beginning with the *Encyclopaedia Britannica* and ending with Jedidiah Morse, whom Scott described as a "monkish bigot" whose New England prejudices had led him to slander the character of the people of the southern states quite as much as had any British traveler.

Of far more importance than these compendiums was William Bartram's *Travels Through North and South Carolina, Georgia, East and West Florida* (1791). Bartram, an explorer and naturalist, epitomized the "man of feeling" of the late eighteenth century. To him, Nature was benevolent and pacific—qualities of which the entire animal kingdom partook. Even rattlesnakes, he asserted, were "magnanimous." The beauties of Nature moved him to write rhapsodies in prose, but his special affection was reserved for Indians. Having a first-hand knowledge of Indians (which Rousseau did not) Bartram exalted them to the status of "noble savages," simple, honorable men who lived wholly in accord with the dictates of Nature. For Bartram, Indian girls are always "nymphs" who frolic in "sylvan groves." Bartram and Philip Freneau were the only writers of this generation to influence English men of letters: Bartram's description of a battle between alligators left an imprint upon the poetry of Coleridge.

By 1795, an American encyclopedia was in print. Even though it consisted in large part of material extracted from the *Encyclopaedia Britannica,* Americans could henceforth pursue knowledge without being reminded on every page of their dependence upon Britannia. Yet literary vassalage was not easily overcome; certainly it was not achieved merely by writing a declaration of literary independence or by a pseudo-epic. What Emerson called "our day of independence, our long apprenticeship to the learning of other lands" was not ended as long as Great Britain remained the arbiter of taste and the source of literary fashions. Under the circumstances, the best that

Americans could do was to keep abreast of English literary developments. But this achievement fell far short of their expectations that the Revolution would usher in a new Augustan age of letters. In 1817, James K. Paulding said despondingly that "the Genius that has awakened in our country, is not the genius of America, but a mongrel, imitative creature, expatriated in his affections, and incapable of connecting the poetry of the country with the feelings, attachments and associations of the people for whom he affects to write." He despaired too soon: James Fenimore Cooper and the Deerslayer tales were about to effect a memorable conjunction between literature and the American experience.

PAINTING AND ARCHITECTURE

Having raised their expectations of national greatness in government, art, and science to the empyrean, Americans were bound to be disappointed by their actual achievement. Yet in painting and architecture they came surprisingly close to scaling the heights.

American painters, like men of letters, tried to make art serve the purpose of indoctrinating the people with patriotism, morality, and "republican virtue." Benjamin West, the most widely acclaimed American painter of the late eighteenth century—in Rome, where he studied, he was called the American Raphael—specialized in vast canvases depicting classical and religious scenes. His canvases were so huge that one of his pupils remarked that he was great only by the acre. The function of art, as West conceived it, was to inculcate patriotism and morality—therefore the grander the scale of the composition, the more effectively it conveyed its message. In 1792, after almost thirty years of residence in England where he enjoyed the patronage and friendship of George III, West was elected President of the Royal Academy. His fame far transcended his real merit, but he was a generous and kindly man who aided a large number of young Americans studying art in London. Indeed, the list of his pupils reads almost like the roster of the important American painters of the period 1783-1820.

In actuality, however, American painters won enduring fame with canvases designed not to make the beholder a more moral citizen but with portraits that revealed character. By their work in this field, Gilbert Stuart, John Singleton Copley, Thomas Sully, Charles Willson Peale, and S. F. B. Morse elevated the reputation of the United States in the artistic world. The demand for portraits by well-to-do Americans seemed insatiable: in 1810 ten portrait painters found employment in Philadelphia alone. Charles Willson Peale (several of whose six sons, Titian, Rubens, Franklin, Linnaeus, Raphael, and Rembrandt—Van Dyke died in infancy—became painters) made so many copies of his portraits of Washington that it was said that he was "peeling" the Father of his Country. Gilbert Stuart dashed off copies of his portrait of Washington for $100 apiece to pay his numerous creditors. In his painting

The Declaration of Independence, John Trumbull put on a single huge canvas portraits of many of the most eminent men of the revolutionary period. But President John Adams was unhappy with the portraits painted of him by John Singleton Copley and other artists. They had made him a monster, he exclaimed, fit only for exhibition as a clown. "The age of painting and sculpture has not yet arrived in this country," he declared, "and I hope it will not arrive very soon."

So numerous had American artists become that in 1805 Charles Willson Peale founded the Pennsylvania Academy of Fine Arts. This institution, the first of its kind in the United States, was closely followed by the New York Academy of Fine Arts, which was enriched by Napoleon with engravings and portfolios of landscapes. Because of this benefaction, Napoleon was elected an honorary member. In 1810, the Society of Artists of the United States was organized with a charter membership of one hundred. The purpose of this organization was to "promote the prosperity, glory and independence" of the United States by establishing schools, arranging for the public exhibition of the work of American artists, and commemorating the American Revolution. President Madison gave the society his benediction by accepting the title of Patron. In 1811, the society held its first public exhibition of the arts: five hundred engravings, designs, paintings, models, and drawings, half of which were the work of American artists, were displayed to "a vast concourse of visitors."

The proliferation of banks stimulated the arts as well as the economy. Banking helped to foster the concentration of wealth that in turn created patrons of the arts; but, even more directly, the need for engraved bank notes brought about a sudden burgeoning of the art of engraving. Every bank that issued notes required a distinctive emblematic design for denominations ranging from one to one thousand dollars and, in order to prevent counterfeiting, designs were changed frequently.

It was in architecture that Americans succeeded in emancipating themselves most decisively from contemporary European and British influences. Thomas Jefferson, the leader of this movement, found his inspiration in the architecture of the Roman Empire. His design for the Virginia State Capitol at Richmond was an enlarged version, with some necessary modifications, of the *Maison Carrée* at Nimes, France. Jefferson could imagine no higher praise than to say of this edifice that it was "worthy of being exhibited alongside the most celebrated remains of antiquity." The classical revival was the modernism of Jefferson's day; he had only contempt for medieval, Gothic, and Georgian architecture. William and Mary College he likened to a brick kiln. The new architecture followed the rules laid down by classical architects revived and expanded by Palladio, the Renaissance architect. It was Jefferson who established the national style in public building. Derived from the temple form, these impressive structures were intended to give stability, dignity, and permanence to the buildings that housed legislators and other public officials of the republic.

Jefferson was almost the last of the gifted amateurs who during the colonial period and the early republic had dominated the field of architecture. Professionals now took over from the amateurs—an event signalized in 1787 by the return to Boston of Charles Bulfinch from the Grand Tour. In his luggage, Bulfinch brought a large collection of architectural books and portfolios of drawings. Patronized by wealthy Boston merchants, Bulfinch built many mansions and designed, among other buildings, the Massachusetts State House on Beacon Hill and the Massachusetts State Prison at Charlestown. Bulfinch was responsible for the neoclassical façade that graced the public buildings and private houses of the Puritan metropolis; it was said that he found Boston a city of wood and left it a city of brick.

Architecturally, the University of Virginia, designed by Jefferson in his old age, had little influence upon the academic world. In the nineteenth century, American colleges and universities succumbed to the neo-Gothic style. Banks, on the other hand, exhibited the effects of the Greek revival. Of this style the most notable examples were the Bank of Pennsylvania (1799-1801) and the Bank of the United States (1819-1824), both the work of Benjamin Latrobe.

In both the Roman and the Greek revivals, the United States played an important part. Never has a country that prided itself upon its progressivism sought more eagerly to emulate the edifices of antiquity. The desire to return, to cling to the permanent, and to recapture the past even while embracing the present and seeking the future reveals the spirit of the nation which came into being during the years 1783-1815. It is indicative of the prevalence of this spirit that the Constitution of the United States is today the oldest written constitution in the world.

BIBLIOGRAPHY

1. PROSPECTS AND PROBLEMS OF A NEW REPUBLIC

Barnby, H. G. *The Prisoners of Algiers.* New York, 1966.

Brant, Irving. *James Madison: The Virginia Revolutionist.* Indianapolis, 1941.

Colles, Christopher. *A Survey of the Roads of the United States of America, 1789.* Cambridge, 1961.

Lopez, Claude-Anne. *Mon Cher Papa: Franklin and the Ladies of Paris.* New Haven, 1966.

McColley, Robert. *Slavery and Jeffersonian Virginia.* Urbana, Ill., 1965.

Main, Jackson Turner. *The Upper House in Revolutionary America.* Princeton, 1967.

Malone, Dumas. *Jefferson and the Rights of Man.* Boston, 1959.

Morison, Samuel Eliot. *The Maritime History of Massachusetts, 1783-1860.* Boston, 1921.

Nevins, Allan. *The American States During and After the Revolution.* New York, 1924.

Van Alstyne, R. W. *The Rising American Empire.* New York, 1960.

Zilversmit, Arthur. *The First Emancipation.* Chicago, 1967.

2. THE ECONOMIC CONSEQUENCES OF INDEPENDENCE

Nettels, Curtis P. *The Emergence of a National Economy, 1775-1815.* New York, 1962.

Taylor, George R. "American Economic Growth Before 1840," *Journal of Economic History,* XXIV (1964), pp. 427-444.

3. THE IMPOTENCE OF THE CONFEDERACY

Freeman, Douglas Southall. *George Washington,* Vols. V, VI. New York, 1954.

4. "A LITTLE REBELLION" AND ITS CONSEQUENCES

Howe, John R., Jr. *The Changing Political Thought of John Adams.* Princeton, 1966.

Starkey, Marion L. *A Little Rebellion.* New York, 1955.

5. THE CONSTITUTIONAL CONVENTION

Beard, Charles A. *An Economic Interpretation of the Constitution.* New York, 1931.

Brown, Robert E. *Charles Beard and the Constitution.* Princeton, 1956.

Brown, Stuart Gerry. *The First Republicans.* Syracuse, 1954.

Crosskey, William W. *Politics and the Constitution.* 2 vols. Chicago, 1953.

Farrand, Max. *The Framing of the Constitution of the United States.* New Haven, 1913.

McDonald, Forrest. *We the People.* Chicago, 1958.

Rossiter, Clinton. *Alexander Hamilton and the Constitution.* New York, 1964.

Schachner, Nathan. *The Founding Fathers.* New York, 1954.

Smith, Charles P. *James Wilson, Founding Father.* Chapel Hill, 1956.

Strayer, Joseph R., ed. *The Delegate from New York.* Princeton, 1939.

Wheare, K. C. *Federal Government.* New York, 1953.

____________________. *Modern Constitutions.* New York, 1951.

6. THE RATIFICATION OF THE CONSTITUTION

Borden, Morton. *The Antifederalist Papers.* Lansing, 1965.

Brant, Irving. *The Bill of Rights.* Indianapolis, 1965.

Brunhouse, Robert L. *The Counter-Revolution in Pennsylvania, 1776-1790.* Harrisburg, Pa., 1942.

Dietze, Gottfried. *The Federalist.* Baltimore, 1960.

Harding, Samuel B. *The Contest over the Ratification of the Federal Constitution in the State of Massachusetts.* New York, 1896.

Kenyon, Cecelia M. *The Antifederalists.* Indianapolis, 1966.

Mason, Alpheus. *The States Rights Debate: Antifederalism and the Constitution.* Englewood, N.J., 1964.

Rutland, Robert A. *Ordeal of the Constitution.* Norman, Okla., 1965.

____________________. *The Birth of the Bill of Rights.* Chapel Hill, 1955.

7. ORGANIZING THE NEW GOVERNMENT

Bassett, John S. *The Federalist System, 1789-1801*. New York, 1906.
Channing, Edward. *A History of the United States*. New York, 1905-1925.
Charles, Joseph. *The Origins of the American Party System*. Williamsburg, 1956.
Hart, James. *The American Presidency in Action*. New York, 1948.
Maclay, E. S., ed. *The Journal of William Maclay, 1789-1791*. New York, 1890.
White, Leonard D. *The Federalists*. New York, 1948.

8. THE HAMILTONIAN DISPENSATION

Bassett, John S. *The Federalist System*. New York, 1906.
Cooke, Jacob E., ed. *Alexander Hamilton: A Profile*. New York, 1967.
Hammond, Bray. *Banks and Politics in Early America*. Princeton, 1957.
Lipset, Seymour Martin. *The First New Nation*. New York, 1963.
Nichols, Roy E. *The Invention of the American Political Parties*. New York, 1967.
Roche, John P., ed. *Origins of American Political Thought*. New York, 1967.
Rogers, George C., Jr. *Evolution of a Federalist: William Loughton Smith*. Columbia, S.C., 1962.
White, Leonard D. *The Federalists*. New York, 1948.

9. JEFFERSON AND HAMILTON

Axelrad, Jacob. *Philip Freneau*. Austin, Tex., 1967.
Boorstin, Daniel J. *The Lost World of Thomas Jefferson*. New York, 1948.
Borden, Morton. *Parties and Politics in the Early Republic, 1789-1815*. New York, 1967.
Boyd, Julian. *Number 7*. Princeton, 1964.
Carroll, John A., and Mary W. Ashworth. *George Washington,* vol. VII. New York, 1957.
Chambers, William Nisbet. *Political Parties in a New Nation, 1776-1809*. New York, 1964.
Charles, Joseph. *The Origins of the American Party System*. Williamsburg, 1956.
Griswold, Rufus W. *The Republican Court*. New York, 1867.
Koch, Adrienne. *Jefferson and Madison*. New York, 1950.
———. *Madison's Advice to My Country*. Princeton, 1966.
Malone, Dumas. *Jefferson and the Ordeal of Liberty*. Boston, 1962.
Wharton, Anne Holligsworth. *Social Life in the Early Republic*. Philadelphia, 1902.
White, Morton and Lucia. *The Intellectual vs. The City*. Cambridge, 1962.

10. CITIZEN GENÊT AND THE FRENCH ALLIANCE

Hazen, Charles D. *Contemporary American Opinion of the French Revolution*. Baltimore, 1897.
Hyneman, Charles S. *The First American Neutrality*. Urbana, Ill., 1934.
Thomas, Charles M. *American Neutrality in 1793*. New York, 1931.
Tinkcom, Henry M. *The Republicans and Federalists in Pennsylvania, 1790-1801*. Harrisburg, Pa., 1950.
Turner, Frederick Jackson, ed. *Correspondence of the French Ministers to the United States, 1791-1797*. Report of the American Historical Association for 1903, 2 vols. Washington, 1904.

11. JOHN JAY SAVES THE PEACE

Baldwin, Leland D. *Whiskey Rebels: The Story of a Frontier Uprising*. Pittsburgh, 1939.
Bemis, Samuel F. *Jay's Treaty*. New York, 1924.
———. *Pinckney's Treaty*. New York, 1926.
Bernhard, Winfred E. A. *Fisher Ames*. Chapel Hill, 1965.
Graham, Gerald S. *Sea Power and British North America, 1783-1820*. Cambridge, Mass., 1941.
Perkins, Bradford. *The First Rapprochement: England and the United States, 1795-1805*. Philadelphia, 1955.

12. THE FAREWELL ADDRESS

Bemis, Samuel F. "Washington's Farewell Address," *American Historical Review,* XXXIX (1934).
Gilbert, Felix. *To the Farewell Address*. Princeton, 1961.
Lyon, E. W. "The Directory and the United States," *American Historical Review,* XLIII (1938).

13. THE UNDECLARED WAR WITH FRANCE

DeConde, Alexander. *The Quasi-War*. New York, 1966.
Kurtz, Stephen G. *The Presidency of John Adams*. Philadelphia, 1957.
Miller, John C. *Crisis in Freedom*. Boston, 1951.
Monroe, James. *Autobiography,* ed. Stuart Gerry Brown. Syracuse, 1959.
Smith, James Morton. *Freedom's Fetters*. Ithaca, N.Y., 1956.

14. THE VIRGINIA AND KENTUCKY RESOLUTIONS

Koch, Adrienne. *Jefferson and Madison.* New York, 1950.

Malone, Dumas. *Jefferson and the Ordeal of Liberty.* Boston, 1962.

Miller, John C. *Crisis in Freedom.* Boston, 1951.

Smelser, Marshall. "George Washington and the Alien and Sedition Acts," *American Historical Review,* LIX (1954).

Smith, James Morton. *Freedom's Fetters.* Ithaca, 1956.

15. THE ELECTION OF 1800

Adams, Henry. *Life of Albert Gallatin.* Philadelphia, 1879.

Bemis, Samuel F. *John Quincy Adams and the Foundations of American Foreign Policy.* New York, 1949.

Borden, Morton. *The Federalism of James A. Bayard.* New York, 1954.

Dauer, Manning J. *The Adams Federalists.* Baltimore, 1953.

Horton, James T. *James Kent: A Study in Conservatism.* New York, 1934.

Lerche, Charles O. "Jefferson and the Election of 1800," *William and Mary Quarterly,* Third Series (1948).

16. THE JEFFERSONIAN "REVOLUTION"

Cunningham, Noble E., Jr. *The Jeffersonian Republicans in Power.* Chapel Hill, 1963.

———. *The Jeffersonian Republicans.* Chapel Hill, 1957.

Goodman, Paul. *The Democratic-Republicans of Massachusetts.* Cambridge, 1964.

Konefsky, Samuel J. *John Marshall and Alexander Hamilton.* New York, 1964.

Levy, Leonard W. *Jefferson and Civil Liberties: The Darker Side.* Cambridge, 1963.

Malone, Dumas. *Thomas Jefferson as a Political Leader.* Berkeley, 1963.

Peterson, Merrill D., ed. *Thomas Jefferson: A Profile.* Princeton, 1968.

Prince, Carl E. *New Jersey's Jeffersonian Republicans.* Chapel Hill, 1967.

Walters, Raymond, Jr. *Albert Gallatin.* New York, 1957.

White, Leonard D. *The Jeffersonians.* New York, 1950.

Wiltse, Charles M. *The New Nation, 1800-1845.* New York, 1961.

17. FOREIGN AFFAIRS: THE BARBARY CORSAIRS AND THE LOUISIANA PURCHASE

Cole, Herbert. *Christophe: King of Haiti.* New York, 1967.

De Voto, Bernard, ed. *The Journals of Lewis and Clark.* Cambridge, 1953.

Lyon, E. W. *The Man Who Sold Louisiana: The Life of Francois Barbe-Marbois.* Baltimore, 1942.

18. THE ATTACK UPON THE FEDERAL JUDICIARY AND THE BURR CONSPIRACY

Abernethy, Thomas Perkins. *The Burr Conspiracy.* New York, 1954.

Adams, Henry. *Documents Relating to New England Federalism.* Boston, 1877.

Beirne, Francis F. *Shout Treason.* New York, 1959.

Jones, W. Melville. *John Marshall: A Reappraisal.* Ithaca, N.Y., 1956.

19. THE CHESAPEAKE INCIDENT

Adams, Henry. *History of the United States During the Administration of Thomas Jefferson.* New York, 1930.

Brant, Irving. *James Madison, Secretary of State.* Indianapolis, 1954.

Mahan, A. T. *The Influence of Sea Power upon the French Revolution and Empire.* 2 vols. Boston, 1892.

Sears, L. M. *Jefferson and the Embargo.* New York, 1927.

20. THE EMBARGO

Adams, Henry. *History of the United States During the Administration of Thomas Jefferson.* New York, 1930.

Daniels, G. W. "American Cotton Trade Under the Embargo," *American Historical Review,* XXI (1916).

Perkins, Bradford. *Prologue to War: England and the United States.* Berkeley, 1961.

Sears, L. M. *Jefferson and the Embargo.* New York, 1927.

Zimmerman, J. F. *Impressment of American Seamen.* New York, 1925.

21. CONGRESSIONAL DIPLOMACY

Crosby, Alfred W. *America, Russia, Hemp, and Napoleon.* Columbus, O., 1965.

Horsman, Reginald. *The Causes of the War of 1812.* New York, 1962.

Mayo, Bernard. *Henry Clay: Spokesman of the New West.* Boston, 1927.

Perkins, Bradford. *Prologue to War.* Berkeley, 1961.

Wiltse, Charles M. *John C. Calhoun: Nationalist, 1782-1828.* New York, 1944.

22. THE COMING OF THE WAR

Brant, Irving. *James Madison, the President.* Indianapolis, 1956.

Brown, Roger H. *The Republic in Peril.* New York, 1964.
Carr, Albert Z. *The Coming of the War.* New York, 1960.
Gray, Dennis. *Spencer Perceval.* Manchester, England, 1963.
Pratt, Julius W. *The Expansionists of 1812.* New York, 1825.
Updyke, Frank A. *The Diplomacy of the War of 1812.* Baltimore, 1915.
Watson, J. Steven. *The Reign of George III.* Oxford, 1960.

23. THE WAR OF 1812: BY LAND AND BY SEA

Adams, Henry. *History of the United States Under James Madison.* New York, 1930.
Brant, Irving. *James Madison: Commander in Chief, 1812-1836.* Indianapolis, 1961.
James, Marquis. *Andrew Jackson: The Border Captain.* Indianapolis, 1933.
Mahan, A. T. *Sea Power in Its Relation to the War of 1812.* 2 vols. Boston, 1905.
Roosevelt, Theodore. *The Naval War of 1812.* Boston, 1882.

24. A FAMOUS VICTORY

Dwight, Timothy. *The History of the Hartford Convention.* New York, 1833.
James, Marquis. *Andrew Jackson: The Border Captain.* Indianapolis, 1933.
Morison, Samuel Eliot. *Harrison Gray Otis.* 2 vols. Boston, 1913.

25. THE PEACE OF CHRISTMAS EVE

Bemis, Samuel F. *John Quincy Adams and the Foundations of American Foreign Policy.* New York, 1949.
Morison, Samuel Eliot. *Harrison Gray Otis.* 2 vols. Boston, 1913.
Perkins, Bradford. *Castlereagh and Adams, 1812-1813.* Berkeley, 1964.

26. THE UNITED STATES: 1783-1815, THE SOCIAL SCENE

Adams, Henry. *History of the United States During the Administration of Thomas Jefferson.* New York, 1930.
Bernard, John. *Retrospections of America: 1797-1811.* New York, 1887.
Brissot de Warville, J. P. *New Travels in America.* 2 vols. Boston, 1797.
Elkins, Stanley M. *Slavery.* Chicago, 1959.
McManus, Edgar J. *A History of Negro Slavery in New York.* Syracuse, 1966.
Melish, John. *Travels in the United States of America.* Philadelphia, 1812.
LaRouchefoucauld-Liancourt. *Travels Through the United States.* London, 1799.
Nevins, Allan, ed. *American Social History as Recorded by British Travelers.* New York, 1948.
Roberts, Kenneth and Anna M., eds. and trans. *Moureau de St. Mery's American Journal.* Boston, 1948.
Scott, Franklin, ed. *Baron Kickowstrom's America.* Evanston, Ill., 1952.
Tyack, David. "Forming the National Character: Paradox in the Educational Thought of the Revolutionary Generation," *Harvard Educational Review,* Vol. 36, 1966.
Wansey, Henry. *An Excursion in the United States.* Salisbury, England, 1798.
Williams, Eric. *Capitalism and Slavery.* New York, 1966.

27. THE FRANCHISE AND EQUALITY

Conant, James B. *Thomas Jefferson and the Development of Public Education.* Berkeley, 1963.
Nevins, Allan, and Jeannette Mirsky. *Eli Whitney.* New York, 1952.
Williamson, Chilton. *The American Suffrage from Property to Democracy, 1760-1860.* Princeton, 1964.

28. AMERICAN NATIONALISM AND THE ARTS

Carpenter, Charles. *History of American Schoolbooks.* Philadelphia, 1963.
Dangerfield, George. *The Awakening of American Nationalism, 1815-1828.* New York, 1965.
Flexner, James T. *Gilbert Stuart.* New York, 1955.
Harris, Neil. *The Artist in American Society: The Formative Years, 1790-1860.* New York, 1966.
Jones, Howard Mumford. *The Theory of American Literature.* Ithaca, N.Y., 1965.
Kohn, Hans. *American Nationalism.* New York, 1961.
Mendelowitz, Daniel M. *A History of American Art.* New York, 1960.
Miller, Perry. *The Life of the Mind in America.* New York, 1965.
Parrington, Vernon L. *The Connecticut Wits.* New York, 1926.
Runes, Dagobert D., ed. *The Selected Writings of Benjamin Rush.* New York, 1947.
Spiller, Robert E. *The Cycle of American Literature.* New York, 1956.
———. *The American Literary Revolution, 1783-1837.* New York, 1967.
Webster, Noah. *On Being an American,* ed. Homer D. Babbidge, Jr. New York, 1967.

INDEX

A

Adams, Abigail, 141, 142
Adams, John, 23-25, 136, 137, 139; attempts to reelect, 158, 159; "midnight judges" appointed by, 176n; peace with France, 145-147; slander against, 159, 160
Adet, Pierre, 133, 134, 136
Age of Reason, 267
Agnosticism, 269
Agrarian philosophy, 105-107
Agriculture, developments and improvements in, 284, 285; effect of embargo of 1807, 217; predominance of, 101, 103; revolution in, 284, 285
Algiers, treaty of United States with, 126
Alien Act of 1798, 141-144; opposition to, 149-151; resolutions in answer to, 152, 153
American, connotation of term, 6
American Age, 4
American Dictionary of the English Language, 300
American Fur Company, 245
American Philosophical Society, 185
American Spelling Book, 300
Amiens, Peace of, 181
Andover Theological Institute, 269
Antifederalists, 68, 73-76; debate over ratification of the Constitution, 81-84; status as states' rights party, 87
Antimonarchism, 110
Arch Street Ferry, *illus.* 220
Architecture, 315, 316
Army of the United States, and undeclared war with France, 144, 145
Art, 314-316
Articles of Confederation, 6, 7; impotence of, 31-46
Asbury, Francis, 270
Astor, John Jacob, 245
Atheism, 269
Auburn Plan, 279
Automatic factory system, 282

B

Baltimore, British attempt to capture, 254
Bank of the United States, abolishment of, 242; chartering of, 99; constitutionality of, 99, 100; incorporation of, 100; Jefferson's attack on, 171; scope of operations of, 100; *illus.* 166
Banking, and the arts, 315
Bankruptcy Act of 1800, 275
Baptist Church, 270
Barbary Corsairs, 11, 12, 126, 179, 180
Barlow, Joel, 305, 306
Bartram, William, 313
Battle of New Orleans. *See* New Orleans, battle of
Battle of Tippecanoe, 226, 227
Bavarian Illuminati, 143
Bayard, James, 163, 164
Beccaria, Cesare, 278, 279
Benevolent societies, 277, 278
Berlin decree, 211, 212; revocation of, 224
Betting in America, 276, 277
Bill of Rights, adoption and scope of, 90, 91
Bonaparte, Jerome, wife of, 291
Boone, Daniel, 273
Boston Manufacturing Company, 282
Bottling of beverages, 271
Bowditch, Nathaniel, 13n
Breckinridge, Hugh Henry, 308
Breckinridge, John, 151
British credit, 5, 6
British Northwest Company, 245
Brown, Charles Brockden, 309, 310
Burr, Aaron, 194; conspiracy of, 197-200; electioneering methods, 158; slaying of Alexander Hamilton, 194; tie vote in electoral college with Jefferson, 160, 161; treason, trial for, 199, 200; *illus.* 188
Buying spree, 5, 6

C

Cadore Note, 224
Calder v. *Bull,* 174
Calhoun, John C., 235
Calvin, John, 269
Canada, American affection for, 233; attack on, 241-245; British attack from, 251, 252, *map* 244; conquest of, 233; invasion of, 242-244
Central banks, American need for, 99; European establishment of, 99
Central government, need for establishment of, 53, 54
Characteristics of Americans, 275
Charitable organizations, 277, 278
Chase, Salmon P., 190, 191
Checks and balances, system of, abandonment of, 31; absence of, 7; Constitutional Convention provision for, 66

Chesapeake incident, 203-208
China, trade with, 13, 14
Chisholm v. *Georgia,* 174
Church of England, disestablishment of, 268
Cincinnati. *See* Society of the Cincinnati
Civil liberties, Jefferson's policies, 170
Civil War, seeds of, 285
Clark, William, 185-187
Class distinction, obliteration of, 290
Clay, Henry, 230, 231, 233-235, 262, 263
Clermont, 283, *illus.* 286
College education, need for, 302
College students, religion of, 269
Colleges, founding of, 303
Commerce. *See* Trade
Confederacy. *See* Articles of Confederation
Congregational churches, 268
Congress of the United States, First, 88; organization of new government by, 88-91; violence in, *illus.* 148
Connecticut Compromise, 61
Connecticut Wits, 305, 306
Conspiracy theory, 54
Constitution of the United States, drafting of, 65-69, *illus.* 56; Eleventh Amendment to, 174; provisions and principles embodied in, 65-69; ratification of, 71-85. *See also* Ratification of the Constitution
Constitutional Convention, 57-69; drafting of Constitution, 65-69; Great Compromise, 61-63; Large State Plan, 60; members of, 57, 58; New Jersey Plan, 60, 61; president, office of, 62, 63; proportional representation in House of Representatives, 61; results of, 65-69; slavery question, 63-65; state conventions, 72, 81-85; state equality in Senate, 61, 62; Virginia Plan, 58-60, 62
Constitutions of the states, revisions of, 87, 88
Continental Congress, 6-10; control of commerce sought by, 27, 28; economizing, efforts at, 22; weakness of, 19, 20, 44, 45, 52
Continental System, 211
Cooper, James Fenimore, 314
Copley, John Singleton, 315
Corsairs. *See* Barbary Corsairs
Cotton gin, 284, 285
Court system, 93
Credit, lifeblood of American economy, 32
Criminal code reform, 278
Cumberland Road, construction of, 172

D

Debtor class, absence of, 32
Debtor relief, state legislation for, 34, 35
Deism, 267, 269
Destiny of America, 2, 4
Dialects in language, 300
Direct democracy, 53
Directory. *See* France
Divorce, grounds for, 291
Doves, 232
Dred Scott decision, 191
Dueling, 292
Dunlap, William, 307
Dutch loan crisis, 45, 46
Dwight, Timothy, 305, 306, 312

E

Economic coercion, abandonment of policy of, 239; Jeffersonian-Madisonian policy of, 230
Economic consequences of independence, 14, 15, 19-29
Education, 299-303
Egalitarianism, 290
Election campaign of 1800, balloting by states in Congress, 163; electoral college tie between Burr and Jefferson, 160, 161; Federalist position and Republican position compared, 155-158; Hamilton's appeals, 162; Jefferson's election, 164, 167; Order of Saint Tammany, 158; *map* 161
Elections, congressional, (1788-1789), 87, 155; (1810-1811) commitment to militancy, 230
Elections, presidential, (1796), 136, 137, *map* 136; (1800), 155-164, *map* 161. *See also* Election campaign of 1800; (1804), *map* 195; (1808), *map* 218; (1812), *map* 243
Electoral college, means of electing president and vice-president, 63; tie between Burr and Jefferson, 160, 161
Ely, Samuel, 50
Embargo of 1807, 211-219; effect of, 215-219; end of, 219; enforcement of, 213-215; repeal of, 221; replacement by nonintercourse act, 221-227
Encyclopedia, publication of, 313
Enforcing Act of 1809, 219
Enlightenment, The, 192, 269, 278
Entail, abolishment of, 34, 36
Equality in America, 289-296
Erskine agreement, 221; repudiation of, 222
External enemy, need for, 27

F

Far East, trade with, 13
Father of the American Drama, 307
Federal government finances, *chart* 170

Federalism. *See* Federalists
Federalist, The, publication and views of, 78-80, 83
Federalist state of mind, 52-54
Federalists, 67, 76-78, 129; attack upon, 189-191; clash with Republicans, *illus.* 148; debate over ratification of the Constitution, 78-81; disintegration of party, 191-195; division of party on French war or peace, 149; election campaign of 1800, 156, 158; and embargo of 1807, 217, 218; foreign policy, 134; judiciary, control of, 174, 175; looked upon as monarchists, 173; loss of control by, 158, 160, 162, 174; majority in House of Representatives in 1800, 155; men of letters, 310; opposition to Louisiana purchase, 184; pledges in 1800 election campaign, 159; removal from government positions, 173, 174; split in party, 158; War of 1812, opposition to, 245-247; War of 1812, position on, 234, 235
Fenno, John, 108
Feudal system of land tenure, replacement with fee system, 36
Financing the government, 19-23
Fiscal policy, objectives of Alexander Hamilton, 93-95
Fitch, John, 282
Fletcher v. *Peck,* 276
Foreign debt, satisfaction of, 22, 23
Foreign policy, division over, 115-117, 134; farewell address of George Washington, 135; objectives of, 115
Foreign trade. *See* Trade
Fort McHenry, battle for, 254
France, alliance with, 117-121; depredations upon American shipping, 232; Directory of, 139, 140, 145, 146; effect of ratification of Jay's treaty, 133, 139; emergence as republic, 117; marauders on high seas, 140; and nonintercourse, 221, 224; peace with, 145-147; Russian victories over, 245; seizure of American vessels, 225; severing of diplomatic relations with, 141; undeclared war with, 139-147; war with Great Britain, 117; XYZ Affair, 139-141
Franchise, right of, 287-289
Franklin, Benjamin, 4, 280
French Revolution, neutrality of America in, 117-121; outbreak of, 103, 117
Freneau, Philip, 108, 109, 308
Fries, Peter, 147
Frontier posts, British retention of, 26
Fulton, Robert, 283
Funding of debt, compromise agreement, 97, 98; fight over, 96-98; national, 21, 95; state, 22
Fur trade, 245

G

Gallatin, Albert, 171, 231, 241, 246, 261
Gambling, 276, 277
Gardoqui, treaty negotiations with, 41-44
Gazette of the United States, 108
Genêt, Edmond (Citizen), 117-121; dismissal of, 121; *illus.* 114
Ghent, Treaty of. *See* Treaty of Ghent
Gouging, sport of, 292
Government by majority, 53
Great Britain, Chesapeake incident as act of war, 206-208; crisis in relations with, 124; economic boom, 25; firmness of position prior to War of 1812, 234; high seas violations, 123, 124; Indians' allegiance to, 40, 41; Jay's treaty with, 127-129, 133, 139; negotiations in War of 1812, 261-263; Orders in Council. *See* Orders in Council; refusal to trade with America, 24, 25; relations with, 23-29, 89, 90; repeal of nonintercourse against, 221; straining of relations with, 204-206; threat of war with, 123-126; trade with, 5, 6, 11, 129; unwitting strengthening of union by, 27-29; war with France, 117
Great Compromise, 61-63
Gunboat policy, 203, 204

H

Haiti, 197
Hamilton, Alexander, 78-80, 144, 145, 162, 300; controversy with Thomas Jefferson, 107-112; fiscal policy, 93-95; integration of northern and southern economies sought by, 101; Report on a National Bank, 98; Report on Manufactures, 101-103, 105; Report on Public Credit, 94, 96; slaying by Aaron Burr, 194; *illus.* 92
Hancock, John, 82
Harrison, William Henry, 226, 227
Hartford Convention, 257-259
Henry, Patrick, 57, 58
House of Representatives, Federalist majority in 1800, 155; proportional representation in, 61; Speaker's status in, 230, 231
Humanitarianism, 277-279

I

Impeachment process, Republicans' use of, 189-191
Impost, power to lay and collect, 20, 21
Impressment of American sailors, 204-206; controversy with Great Britain, 231; justification for War of 1812, 240; protracted negotiations over, 240, 241; *illus.* 202

Independent judiciary, advocation of, 190
Indians, allegiance to British, 40, 41; losses resulting from War of 1812, 263; massacres by, 125; ruin of confederacy of, 245; war in Northwest territory with, 226, 227
Industrial revolution, 101
Inventions, development of, 279-285
Irving, Washington, 311
Isolationism, and Washington's Farewell Address, 135

J

Jackson, Andrew, 233, 292; and War of 1812, 255-257
Jacobin, 136, 192
Jay, John, 41-44, 78, 79; appointment as minister to England, 124, 125; difficulties in Britain, 126, 127; treaty with Great Britain, 127-129, 133, 139, 205; *illus.* 122
Jay's treaty, 126-129; effect of ratification of, 133, 139; expiration of, 205
Jefferson, Thomas, 4, 5, 97, 98, 128, 129, 150-152, 300-303, 315, 316; agrarian philosophy of, 105-107; Bank of the United States, attack on, 171; consolidation of union sought by, 191; controversy with Alexander Hamilton, 107-112; dealings with Napoleon over Louisiana boundaries, 197, 198; description of person and character of, 168, 169; economizing by, 169; election as president in 1800, 164, 167; farmers' position, 171, 172; inaugural speech, 167, 168, 173, 179; judiciary, attack upon, 189-191; Louisiana purchase, 183; Mediterranean, second war in, 179, 180; monarchical pomp abolished by, 168; Navy, attitude concerning, 203, 204; policies of, 169-172; religious views, 268; removals of Federalists from government offices, 173, 174; Report on Commerce, 124; second term of, 195, 196; slander against, 159; tie vote in electoral college with Burr, 160, 161; unification of nation, attempts at, 172-174; views concerning Aaron Burr, 194; *illus.* 104
Jeffersonian "revolution," 167-177
Jenner, Edward, 280
Jensen, Merrill, 13n
Judicial review, principle of, 189, 190
Judiciary, 93; attack upon, 189-191; Federalist control of, 174, 175; independence of, 190;
Judiciary Act of 1789, 93; deficiencies in, 175
Judiciary Act of 1801, repeal of, 175, 176
Judiciary Act of 1802, constitutionality of, 176; provisions of, 176

K

Kentucky resolution, states' rights and, 151-153
Key, Francis Scott, 254

L

Labor-saving machinery, 281, 282
Lafitte, Jean, 256
Land boom, 156
Land ownership changes, 34, 36
Land speculation, 275, 276
Legislative omnipotence, 34
Lewis, Meriwether, 185-187
Lewis and Clark Expedition, 185-187
Libertarianism, 291
Literature, 304-314; function of, 304
Livingston, Robert R., 283
Logan Act, 146
Louisiana purchase, 181-185; adjustment of territorial limits of, 197; constitutional issue involved in, 184; Federalist opposition to, 184; *illus.* 178; *map* 186
Louisiana territory, explorations of, 185, 186
Louisiana Treaty, 183
Lowell, Francis Cabot, 282
Loyalists, confiscation of property of, 25

M

Macon, Nathaniel, 223, 233
Macon's Act #2, 223, 224
Madison, Dolly, evacuation of burning Washington, D.C., 253
Madison, James, 58-60, 78, 79, 96, 97, 105, 128, 129, 151-153, 231, 235; declaration of War of 1812, 239, 240; election of, 219; nonintercourse declared in force by, 222; occupation of West Florida ordered by, 225; patron of the arts, 315; protection of capital ordered by, 253; reelection of, 242
Majority rule in state governments, 34
Manufactures, embargo of 1807 as boon to, 217; promotion of, 102, 103; regional pattern in, 270, 271; report on, 101-103, 105
Manumission acts, 2
Marbury v. *Madison,* 176, 189, 191
Marshall, John, 140, 176, 177, 189, 191, 196, 276
Massachusetts, financial obligations of, 49, 50; ill effects of independence, 12, 13; rebellion in, 50-52; tax system adopted by, 49, 50
Medicine, developments in, 280
Mediterranean. *See* Barbary Corsairs

Mercantilism, retaliation against British policies of, 28, 29
Merchant marine, growth of, *chart* 157
Methodism, 270
Middle Passage, 65
"Midnight judges," 176n
Milan decree, 213; revocation of, 224
Militancy, period prior to War of 1812, 229-233
"Monarchal conspiracy," 108; Jefferson's views, 173
Monarchism, 108-110; counterrevolution against, 171; Jefferson's abolishment of, 168
Money-making trait of Americans, 276
Monroe, James, 181-183, 185, 205, 207, 262
Monroe-Pinkney treaty, 205, 222
Morris, Robert, 20, 21, 156

N

Napoleon, 181, 182, 184, 197, 198, 211-213, 223-225, 236, 240; abdication of, 251
National bank, report on, 98; views regarding creation of, 98-100
National capital, transfer of location of, 97, 98
National debt, 19-23; arguments for funding of, 95; compromise in funding of, 97, 98; fight over funding of, 96-98; funding of, 21, 95; prewar, prevention of collection of, 26; state assumption of, 22
National Gazette, 108, 109
National university, recommendation for, 302, 303
Nationalism, cultivation of sense of, 135; v. sectionalism, 101
Naturalization, Jefferson's policies, 170
Naturalization Act of 1798, 141-144; replacement of, 170
Navigation Acts, 10; adoption of, 88-90
Navy of the United States, Jefferson's attitude concerning, 203, 204; sea battles with France, 141, 144; undeclared war with France, 144; War of 1812 battles, 247-249; *illus.* 238
Negro, status of, 293
Nelson, Horatio, 124
Neutrality, attempt to preserve, 212, 213; end of rights of, 211, 212; European wars and America, 117-121
New England, British blockade extended to, 257, 258; opposition to War of 1812, 246, 247; revolt against shift in political power, 258-259
New government, organization of, 87-91
New Orleans, battle of, 255-257; *illus.* 250; *map* 256
New York Academy of Fine Arts, 315
New York City, description of, 271
New York Stock Exchange, *illus.* 18
New York Times v. *Sullivan,* 142n
Nonimportation Act, 222
Nonintercourse act, reinstatement of, 222; replaces embargo, 221; suspension against France, 224
Northwest Ordinance, 39
Northwest posts, British retention of, 26
Northwest territories, Indian massacres, 125; Indian war fought in, 226, 227; movement into, 38-40; organization of, 38-40; securing boundaries of, 40-44
Nouveaux riches, 33
Novels, writing of, 310

O

Ohio, growth of, 273; organization of territory of, 38-40; settlement of, 125
Ohio Company, The, 39, 40
Order of Saint Tammany, 158
Orders in Council, 211, 212; issuance of, 123, 124; modification of, 221; proclamation asserting enforcement of, 234; revocation of, 239, 240; wavering of devotion to, 239
Ordinance of 1785, 39
Ordinance of 1787, 39

P

Paine, Tom, 292, 299, 304
Painting, 314, 315
Paper money, demand for, 32; Rhode Island policies concerning, 35, 36; state issuance of, 33
Parent-child relationships, 290
Paris, Treaty of, 1; ratification of, 9; territorial provisions of, 2; violations of, 25-27
Patents, 281, *chart* 282
Peace of Amiens, 181
Peale, Charles Willson, 314, 315
Pennamite Yankee War, 10
Pennsylvania Academy of Fine Arts, founding of, 315
Perry, Oliver Hazard, 243, 244
Philanthropic organizations, 277, 278
Pickering, John, 189, 190
Pickering, Timothy, 146, 193
Pike, Zebulon, 187
Pinckney, Charles C., 130, 139, 140, 159, 160
Pinkney, William, 205
Pirates. *See* Barbary Corsairs
Poetry, 309, 310
Political parties, rise of, 134
Population, 270, *chart* 294-295
Postwar period, depression during, 31; eco-

nomic and financial difficulties, 14, 15, 19-29; relations with Great Britain, 23-29
Potomac Company, organization of, 42, 43
Poverty, evidences of, 277
President of the United States, inauguration of first, 88, *illus.* 86; office of, establishment of, 62, 63
Prevost, George, 251-253
Prewar debts, prevention of collection of, 26
Primogeniture, abolishment of, 34, 36
Progress in America, 272
Prophet, The, 226, 227
Public land, sale of, *chart* 273
Punishment and reform, system of, 279
Putnam, General Rufus, *illus.* 30

Q

Quasi-war, United States period prior to 1812, 229; with France, 139-147
Quids, 196

R

Randolph, Edmund, 58-60
Randolph, John, 191, 196, 197, 199, 200, 292
Ratification of the Constitution, Antifederalist views on, 73-76, 81-84; appeal to the people for, 72, 73; debate over, 78-85; Federalist views on, 76-81; majority rule, 72; nonsigners' position, 71; state conventions, 72, 81-85; unanimity in, impression of, 71, 72; *illus.* 70
Refuse, disposition of, 272
Religion in America, 267-270; diversity of denominations, 268
Religious freedom, Constitutional provisions, 69
Report on a National Bank, 98
Report on Commerce, 124
Report on Manufactures, 101-103, 105
Report on Public Credit, 94; opposition to adoption of, 96
Republic, beginnings of, 1-6; problems and prospects of, 1-16
Republicanism, 109, 110. *See also* Republicans
Republicans, 109, 110, 129; caucus in 1800 election campaign, 158; clash with Federalists, *illus.* 148; divisions in the party, 195-197; election campaign of 1800, 155, 156; foreign policy, 134; impeachment process, use of, 189, 190; policies of Jefferson as president, 169-172; War of 1812, position on, 235
Requisition system, 8, 9; dependence upon, 21
Revere Copper Company, 217
Revivalism, 269
Rhode Island, unrestricted paper money issuance by, 35, 36
Richardson, Samuel, 310
Rittenhouse, David, 280
Roman Catholic Church, 268
Rural areas, growth of, 270
Rush, Benjamin, 279, 280, 300-302
Russia, offer to mediate in War of 1812, 261; trade with, 225; victories over France, 245

S

San Ildefonso, Convention of, 181, 185
San Lorenzo, Treaty of, 129, 130
Sanctity of contracts, doctrine of, 276
Santo Domingo, 181, 182, 197, 277
Satirical literature, 308
Scientific developments, 279-285; agricultural needs, 284, 285
Scioto Associates, 39, 40
Sectionalism, v. Nationalism, 101; period before War of 1812, 234, 235
Sedition Act of 1798, 141-144; opposition to, 149-151; resolutions in answer to, 152, 153
Senate, state equality in, 61
Separation of powers, absence of provision for, 7; principle of, 190
Servant, status as, 289, 290
Sex relationships, 291
Sexual mores, 291
Shays, Daniel, insurrection of, 50-52
Shays' Rebellion, 49-52, *illus.* 48
"Silk stocking district," 290
Slater, Samuel, *illus.* 210
Slavery, 2; acuteness of problem of, 293; Antifederalist view of, 75; Constitutional Convention, question at, 63-65; cotton gin, impact of, 285; increasing population of, 292, 293; Middle Passage, ordeal of, 65
Social classes, 289, 290
Social mores, 291
Society for Colonizing the Free People of Color, 293
Society of Artists of the United States, 315
Society of the Cincinnati, 36, 37, 76, 129; equivalent of, 158
Solitary confinement for crimes, 279
Spain, American threat to territory of, 41-43; territories in possession of, 197, 198; treaty negotiations with, 41-44; treaty with, 129, 130
Spanish America, proposed American intervention in, 145
Spanish Intendant at New Orleans, 181
Spoils system, beginning of, 158
Sports activities, 292
Standardized goods, production of, 285

Star-Spangled Banner, writing of, 254
State debts, funding of, 22
State legislatures, debtor relief and, 31-36; strength of, 31, 32; unilateral action to combat depression, 33
State sovereignty, 6-10
States' rights, defense of, 151-153; Kentucky resolution, 151-153; Virginia resolution, 151-153
Stay laws, 33
Steamboat, development of, 283; monopoly unconstitutional, 283; patenting of, 283
Stuart, Gilbert, 314
Suffrage, requirements for, 287-289
Supreme Court of the United States, attack on, 189-191; disappointment in activity of, 174; impeachment of justices, 189-191; unconstitutionality of Congressional laws, 176, 177
Symmes Associates, 39, 40

T

Talleyrand, 140, 145, 275
Tammany. *See* Order of Saint Tammany
Tariff of 1789, 88, 89
Tecumseh, 226; death of, 245
Teeth, loss of, 291
Tender acts, 33; Massachusetts, 50
Terror, reign of, 149, 150
Thermidorian Terror, 150
Tippecanoe, Battle of, 226, 227
Tobacco trade, 14, 15
Tonnage Act of 1789, 88
Tonnage duties, states' levy of, 28, 29
Tontine Coffee House, *illus.* 18
Town meeting, New England, *illus.* 132
Trade, embargo of 1807, effect of, 215-219; new worlds sought out, 13; predominance of, 101, 103; report on, 124; (1790-1815), *chart* 216; with China, 13, 14; with Far East, 13; with France, 10, 11; with Great Britain, 5, 6, 11, 129; with Russia, 225
Transportation, developments in, 283
Treason, Aaron Burr's trial, 199, 200
Treaty of Commerce of 1778, 117
Treaty of Ghent, 261-263, *illus.* 260
Treaty of San Lorenzo, 129, 130
Trevett v. *Weeden,* 35
Tripoli. *See* Barbary Corsairs
Trumbull, John, 305, 315
Two-party system, 159
Two spheres, doctrine of, 240

U

Undeclared War with France, 139-147
Uniformity of thought, 300
Union, strengthening of, 27, 44-46, 54
United States (1783), *map* 3
Universal suffrage, 289
University of Virginia, 316

V

Vaccination prevention of smallpox, 280
Vermont, admission as state, 10
Violence, in America, 292
Virginia, land ownership law changes, 34, 36; territorial claims ceded by, 38
Virginia resolutions, states' rights and, 151-153
Virginia Tidewater area, War of 1812 and, 247
Vote, right to, 287-289

W

War Hawks, 230-233, 240, 258; achievement of objective of, 264; declaration of War of 1812 and, 234; opposition to position of, 232
War of 1812, Baltimore, defense of, 254, 255; blockade imposed on North America, 240; British attack from Canada, 251, 252, *map* 244; burning of Washington, D.C., 252-255; Canada as theater of, 233; declaration of, 234-236, 239, 240; demands of British, 262; Federalist position on, 234, 235; Fort McHenry, battle for, 254; ill success of, 245; illusion of winning of, 257; increase in taxation for, 246, 247; inflationary spiral resulting from, 247; invasion of Canada, 242-244; Lundy's Lane, battle of, 252; manpower shortage, 241; national character emerging from, 299; national spirit rising after, 263, 264; naval duels, 247-249, *illus.* 238; negotiation with British, 261-263; New Orleans, battle of, 255-257, *illus.* 250, *map* 256; in north, *map* 244; opposition to, 245-247; Republicans' position on, 235; Russia's offer to mediate, 261; sectionalism prior to, 234, 235; shortage of equipment, etc., 241; in south, *map* 256; Treaty of Ghent, 261-263, *illus.* 260; *illus.* 138, 228, 238, 250
War of Independence, 1; public debt incurred during, 19
Washington, D.C., burning in War of 1812, 252-255; description of, 271
Washington, George, 58; farewell address of, 134, 135; financial troubles of, 15, 16; inauguration as president, 88; isolationism advocated by, 135; religious views, 268; second term of, 111, 112; signing of Constitution, 80; *illus.* xii, 86, 114
Waterhouse, Benjamin, 280
Way of life, 270-276

Wayne, General "Mad Anthony," 125
Webster, Noah, 300, 301
Weems, Mason "Parson," 312
West, Benjamin, 314
West, The. *See* Northwest territories
West Florida, attempt to acquire, 197, 198; occupation ordered by President Madison, 225
West Point Academy, establishment of, 169
Western farmers, rebellion of, 125, 126
Western settlement, *map* 274
Westward movement, 38-40
Whiskey rebellion, 125, 126, 134
Whiskey tax, repeal of, 172
Whitney, Eli, 284, 285
Wilkinson, James, 198-200
Women, status of, 291

X

XYZ Affair, 139-141, 147

Y

Yazoo land deal, 276
Yellow fever epidemics, 277, 280

2 3 4 5 6 7 8 9 10 11 12 13 14 15 16 17 18 19 20 21 22 23 24 25 78 77 76 75 74 73 72 71 70